Vol. X.

anon gf Co

Euidsfadno de fassobf

Caufidno   Cyffin Thomson

Homo wieth C er dernwtf̄re

K. Edwd. V. Kino but Ten weeks.
Grants in ye reignes of Edward V. & Rich. III.

39. B. 18.   10
─────────────────   ──
433.   11

Guestenbury, Cychester in the
Stewarde . . . . the
day of

No pardon for Thomas Hyot

British Library Harleian Manuscript 433, f.1

BRITISH LIBRARY
HARLEIAN MANUSCRIPT
433

edited by

ROSEMARY HORROX AND P.W. HAMMOND

VOLUME ONE

Register of Grants for
the Reigns of Edward V and
Richard III

RICHARD III SOCIETY

ISBN 0 904893 04 9

Printed in Great Britain by
Redwood Burn Limited, Trowbridge & Esher

Produced by
Alan Sutton Publishing Limited, Gloucester
for
The Richard III Society, 65 Howard Road,
Upminster, Essex, RM14 2UE

FOREWORD

The bulky manuscript volume in the British Library known as Harleian MS. 433 is unique in more ways than one. Its special importance for the study of Richard III's reign has been recognized since quite soon after its acquisition by the British Museum in 1753, along with the rest of the astonishing library of Edward Harley, Earl of Oxford. With the growing appreciation of the importance of record material for historical research, which is a feature of nineteenth-century scholarship, awareness of its value was enhanced. Extracts from the MS. were printed as long ago as 1844 by Caroline Halsted in her two-volume *Richard III*, and it provided J.A. Nichols with his *Grants of Edward V* (1854). That admirable scholar, James Gairdner, printed some of the diplomatic documents contained in the MS. in his *Letters and Papers . . . of the Reigns of Richard III and Henry VII* (1861-3), and made considerable use of it for his biography of Richard III (1898). For some time thereafter historians were content to rely on these previously printed extracts, until we come to the next substantial biography of King Richard by Paul Murray Kendall, first published in 1955. Whatever one's judgement on Kendall's style and approach to his subject, he has received less than a full acknowledgement for his extensive and careful use of Harleian 433; his footnotes contain literally scores of references to the original MS. Meanwhile, the MS. had been used for purposes of specialist inquiries, not exclusively or even primarily concerned with Richard III, notably by Miss C. Otway-Ruthven in her study of the evolution of the position of king's secretary and of the signet office during the fifteenth century, and in Dr. B.P. Wolffe's thorough and invaluable studies, published between 1956 and 1971, into English royal finances and the management of the royal estates during the fifteenth century. Only more recently has the crucial value of this MS. been appreciated for the very important topic of Richard's exercise of his royal patronage, the monarch's most important weapon in winning or retaining the loyalty of the politically conscious classes of his realm. Much of the study devoted to this theme, by Dr. Horrox and others, has yet to appear in print. Thus, although the MS. has been quite extensively used by scholars for various purposes, the overwhelming bulk of Harleian 433 has remained unprinted.

The uniqueness of Harleian 433 in another and wider context only now becomes apparent with the publication of this edition. Dr. Horrox's analysis of its structure and composition, and her examination as to how and why its contents came to be combined into a single volume, for the first time makes clear the nature and purpose of its compilation, which has often been the subject of scholarly misunderstanding. It is, Dr. Horrox observes, 'the most complete collection of medieval signet material to survive', and provides invaluable evidence of the range and volume of signet activity in the later fifteenth century. It was not, as she explains, an innovation. Similar registers existed in the reign of Edward IV, but only good fortune has preserved this example for posterity. The signet was a highly personal manifestation of the exercise of the sovereign's will. In the Yorkist period it was employed more frequently and with growing independent authority, as, for example, in the much disputed but perfectly valid grant under the signet of the other half of the Hereford estates to Duke Henry of Buckingham in 1483. This strongly reinforces what we already know about the immense dependence of Yorkist (and, indeed, early Tudor) government on the personal activity of the king.

Given the great historical importance of Harleian MS. 433 (only most summarily noticed in this Foreword), it is perhaps surprising that it has never been published in full before; but less surprising considering its sheer bulk. This will be only the first of four volumes needed to provide a complete text, together with an index. Not only members of the Richard III Society, but also historians in general and a wider public too, must, therefore, be grateful to the Society for its initiative in undertaking and financing its production. The Society has been fortunate in securing learned and perceptive editors in Dr. Horrox and Mr. Hammond. In publishing this edition, the Richard III Society may well claim to justify one of its declared major aims: 'to promote research into the life and times of Richard III, and to secure a re-assessment of the material relating to this period, and of the role in English history of this monarch'. The implications for Richard's reputation of the publication of this major source must be left to the judgement of its readers. It is safe to say that such judgements — as in all matters connected with Richard III — will not be unanimous.

Charles Ross

ACKNOWLEDGEMENTS

Many people to whom thanks are due have been involved in this first complete edition of British Library Harleian Manuscript 433. First and foremost comes Mrs. V.B. Lamb, lately Honorary Archivist at the College of Arms, who spent four arduous years making the first complete transcript ever of the English portions of the manuscript and compiling name and place indexes to it (available in the British Library Manuscripts Students Room). Without her work this edition would never have appeared, and all possible praise is due to her initiative. Miss E.M. McInnes, lately Archivist at St. Thomas' Hospital, initially transcribed and translated most of the Latin portions, overseen by the late Miss Ida Darlington, Head Archivist at the Greater London Record Office. Miss Roberta Routledge of Research Associates transcribed and translated the remaining Latin passages.

All of these transcriptions, both Latin and English, were checked before publication by Dr. Horrox, who also wrote the Introduction, compiled the Indexes in Volume Four, and checked the proofs. The work was co-ordinated and the manuscript prepared for the press by P.W. Hammond.

Others who have helped in the production of this work are Miss Anne Sutton and Mrs. Carolyn Hammond.

The Publishers wish to thank Professor Charles Ross for help and encouragement at critical times, and the British Library for permission to publish the manuscript and to reproduce the illustrations.

CONTENTS

viii

EDITORIAL PROCEDURE

In transcription suspension marks have always been extended, even where they are apparently used indiscriminately by the writer. Thus, for instance, the barred *-ll* has been rendered *-lle* wherever it occurs. Terminal flourishes on *-c*, *-d*, *-f*, *-k*, *-r* and *-t* however have been taken to represent an omitted *-e* only where they are used with sufficient discrimination by the writer to suggest that an abbreviation was intended. The only exceptions to this are English Christian names, which have been kept in their simplest English form throughout: Johñ has accordingly been rendered as John rather than as Johne or Johannes. Thorn and yogh have been rendered as *th* and *y* or *g* respectively.

Heavily abbreviated proper names have been silently extended even where the writer has not used an abbreviation sign: thus *duc of Bukingham* for *duc of Buk*, or *king Edward* for *king E*. County names have been treated similarly, being extended to the usual form, Latin or English, used in that passage. Upper and lower case *u* and *v*, which are indistinguishable in manuscript, have been given their modern values in the printed text; so have upper case *I* and *J*, although the use of lower case *j* for terminal *i* has been retained. In Latin passages the abbreviated and contracted words have been extended, using the endings indicated in the manuscript. Errors in endings have not been corrected, the translations allow for any mistakes. Errors in the English passages, e.g. repeated words, are indicated by [sic], none have been silently corrected. All Latin passages have been translated, but not those in French. The solitary Spanish passage (folio 236) is followed by a contemporary translation.

The punctuation and capital letters follow the manuscript, *ff* used initially has been rendered as *F* throughout. In the case of *D*, *M* and *W*, where it is often difficult to decide whether a capital was intended by the writer, modern usage has been followed in doubtful cases. Capitalisation of the translations follows modern usage.

All editorial additions and notes, e.g. folio numbers and translations, are in square brackets, deletions are in round brackets. Marginal notes are in italics at the beginning of the passage to which they refer, marginal crosses are indicated by [*cross*]. A space in the manuscript is represented by a uniform space of 6 ems. Paragraph marks, which are of frequent occurrence, have been omitted, and interlineations are silently placed where they belong. Passages and sections bracketed together in a more or less complex manner are arranged as nearly as possible to the original, and in general the layout of this edition is intended to be as near as practicable to that of the original manuscript.

INTRODUCTION

'A Book in folio . . . being a Register of the Grants &c. passing the Privy Seal, Royal Signet or sign manual during the Reigns of K. Edward V. & K. Richard III. with some other entries, made upon other occasions, or in other Reigns.'[1] This was how Humfrey Wanley, librarian of Robert Harley, described manuscript 433 in the Harleian collection. Wanley was evidently much impressed by the manuscript for he went on to list 2378 of its entries, the most detailed treatment afforded to any of the manuscripts in his catalogue. It is appropriate that Wanley's description should head this introduction since his list of the manuscript's contents explains the speed with which the importance of Harleian MS 433 was recognised after Harley's library was acquired by the British Museum in 1753. Within fifteen years Horace Walpole, at the prompting of his friend Thomas Gray, had published two of the letters from the manuscript in his *Historic Doubts*.[2] There is however no evidence that Walpole had read the manuscript himself or indeed that he was capable of doing so.[3]

Walpole's *Historic Doubts* and the replies which it provoked were the last studies of the reign to rely primarily on rational argument unsupported by original sources. The nineteenth century brought a growing awareness of the value of contemporary material and subsequent historians of Richard III made much fuller use of Harley 433.[4] The importance of the manuscript was acknowledged in two major editions of extracts from it. Nichols printed the sections relating to the reign of Edward V, and Gairdner included part of the diplomatic material in his *Letters and Papers*.[5] Gairdner also used Harley 433 more thoroughly than any previous historian in his *Richard the Third*.[6]

For Gairdner and his contemporaries the great value of Harley 433 was the light which it shed on the events of 1483-5. Speaking primarily of the lists of Richard III's grants contained in the manuscript Gairdner commented, 'Of no other king have we so minute a record'.[7] It is only in the twentieth century that the importance of the manuscript for the study of the wider issues of late medieval administration has become apparent. It is one of the best sources for the study of the signet office before the sixteenth century.[8] More recently the financial entries have been used to provide details of Yorkist chamber finance.[9]

It will be clear already that the range of material included in Harley 433 is very wide.[10] Early commentators tended to assume that the volume must therefore represent the work of a number of government departments gathered together in the hands of the chancellor:

> The volume appears to have been a docket book kept by Russell, bishop of Lincoln, of all the letters and documents that passed through his hands in his official capacity as Chancellor during the reigns of Edward V. and Richard III. It may be considered

as divided into two sections. The larger consists of copies or minutes of formal documents, such as the grants and warrants which passed the Great Seal, the Privy Seal, or the king's Signet; the other is a letter book. . . .[11]

The scope of the manuscript is, however, more limited and more coherent than this, as Dr Otway-Ruthven realised.[12] The bulk of the volume is made up of abstracts of material which passed the signet, the king's personal seal, in the reigns of Edward V and Richard III. For both reigns these abstracts were divided into two chronological lists, which contemporaries called registers.[13] Richard III's registers both have contemporary titles. The first is headed 'Grants made by king Richard from June 28 in the first year of his reign to. . .'.[14] No seal is mentioned in the title but it can only be a list of signet grants. A comparison with the patent rolls shows immediately that it is not a register of grants made under the great seal. Indeed, many of the grants were outside the competence of the chancellor. The register includes all the grants made upon the duchy of Lancaster, for instance, which were issued under the duchy's own great seal. Nor is it a register of grants which passed the privy seal. Many of the duchy of Lancaster grants listed bypassed the privy seal office and were warranted by signet letter rather than by privy seal writ.[15] The second register poses no such problems. It is explicitly headed 'Certain things that pass by the king's signet' and contains other signet material, mainly letters and commissions relating to the royal revenues.[16]

The existence of parallel registers covering the same period and often related subjects does much to explain the confusion of earlier commentators about the manuscript's origins and purpose. The distinction between the two Richard III registers is relatively clear cut. It is very rare indeed for the same document to be noted in both.[17] In several cases however different aspects of the same transaction are noted in each. In December 1483, for example, Nicholas Rigby was ordered to seize the castle of Bodiam on the king's behalf, and his signet commission was noted in the second register. In the following year he was made constable of the castle, and this entry is to be found in the register of grants. Similarly, Thomas Fouleshirst's appointment as constable of Chester is listed among the grants but a warrant ordering the payment of his wages appears in the other register.[18]

In the case of Edward V's signet material this distinction is blurred. The material is again divided into two registers, one of which includes all the king's signet grants. But in some details the scheme has evidently been upset. A letter to the sheriffs ordering them to ensure that suitable candidates take up knighthood is noted in the middle of the register of grants.[19] It is perhaps not surprising that, without the analogy of Richard III's double register, Nichols failed to realise that he was dealing with two distinct registers and ascribed the odd arrangement of his material to 'the convenience of the clerks'.[20]

Bound in with these registers is a variety of material which can best be described as reference material for the clerks of the signet, or for the king himself. Much of this provides a framework of reference for the making of grants. There are lists of office holders at the death of Edward IV, on some of which subsequent vacancies have been indicated. There is also a list of the fees due to officers on the royal estates and a glossary of legal terms occurring in royal letters, both necessary tools in the drafting of royal grants.

Much of the volume, therefore, relates in some way to the exercise of royal patronage. There are in addition two other important categories of material: a group of diplomatic letters, and various financial records and accounts. Diplomatic negotiations were an area of activity associated with the signet throughout the century and a number of the letters in Harley 433 were specifically given under the signet. This section also includes letters received by the king, for which there is a precedent among signet material of the fourteenth century.[21] The financial material takes two forms. The second register, which is explicitly signet material, includes numerous references to chamber finance, including the issue of letters of acquitance for royal receivers and warrants for payments of various types. The volume also includes a number of separate financial entries, covering such subjects as commissions for loans, household assignments and the administration of the crown lands. Most of these are in the form of memoranda, with no mention of an originating department, but they are all subjects which came within the sphere of chamber finance and this, as the second register shows, was closely identified with the use of the signet.

Harley 433 thus includes examples of all the major uses of the signet in this period: in authorising grants and issuing royal letters, and in chamber finance. Not all the entries in the volume can be positively linked with the signet office: the list of oaths, in particular, would not have been out of place in any government department. There is however nothing in the manuscript which can be identified as an intrusion from another government office. The conclusion must be that Harley 433 represents papers from the signet office of Edward V and Richard III, not only the department's registers but memoranda and general reference material.

This conclusion is supported by internal evidence.[22] The volume is remarkably uniform in appearance, suggesting that its contents were produced in a single department over a limited period of time. The volume was the work of a large number of hands but these recur throughout the various sections. The list of corrodies in the king's gift and the list of fees for office on the royal lands which follows it are almost certainly in the same hand as the page of signet warrants of the duke of Gloucester (ff.323, 335 *et seq*). The same clerk was perhaps also responsible for entering Edward V's grant to Thomas Fouleshirst (f.11). The distinctive hand of the letter requesting loans for the king (f.275b) can also be seen in the opening section of a licence to a Hull merchant (f.184b) and probably also in the letter concerning Thomas Lynom at the end of the volume.[23] As a final example, and a particularly useful one since it links the undated list of oaths with the rest of the manuscript, the oaths were copied out by the clerk responsible for noting the instructions given to Bernard de la Forssa, the king's ambassador to Spain (ff.244b, 301 *et seq*).

The range of paper used in the volume is limited. Most of it is of the same type, although slight variations in the watermark suggest that more than one batch of paper was in use. Other watermarks do occur, but only within Richard III's registers.[24] There is therefore no evidence that any of the material was intruded at a later date or from another source. However, neither the paper nor the handwriting can date the production of the volume precisely. It is theoretically possible that the volume is an early Tudor copy, compiled from the originals at some date before about 1520. There are, however, strong arguments in favour of dating the volume to the reign of Richard III. Some of the manuscript is visibly not a fair copy, notably the scribbled list of horses at grass (f.4). Many of the deletions and alterations elsewhere in the manuscript could be ascribed to careless copying of whatever date, but some look like attempts to bring the document up to date within Richard III's reign itself. The lists of gentry in each county, for instance, have been altered to take account of deaths before the early months of 1485.[25] The list of fees and wages granted by Edward IV includes marginal indications of grants which lapsed at the beginning of Richard III's reign, whether by death, forfeiture or replacement by another grant.[26] The irregular compilation of the registers also suggests that they are the original registers rather than a later copy. In places each entry is in a different hand while elsewhere several pages were entered up at one sitting.[27]

The handwriting suggests that if the volume is indeed a copy it must have been made within a generation of the original, and it is difficult to imagine the circumstances in which such a copy could have become necessary. Parts of the volume certainly remained in use under the Tudors, including the list of fees due to royal officials, but other sections would have had no place in a Tudor compilation. It is unlikely that a Tudor copyist would have included the full text of Richard III's proclamation against his rival.[28] It is hard to see, also, what use Henry VII would have made of the list of signet grants. Unlike Richard III who, at least initially, honoured most of his brother's grants, Henry VII began the reign with a wholesale resumption of his predecessor's grants.[29] Any dispute which subsequently arose over Richard's grants would in any case have been referred to the patent rolls, which preserved the text of the grant in full, rather than to the brief and occasionally inaccurate entries in the signet register.[30]

The form as well as the content of the volume argues against its being a later copy. The volume includes a number of blank pages which are explicable if the volume is made up of a number of original documents bound together, but less so if it is some form of precedent book or book of record compiled from the original documents at a later date. In this case one would also have expected the fragmentary entries in the final third of the volume to be omitted.

The most convincing explanation of Harley 433, therefore, is that it is made up of various documents from the signet archives which were collected and bound together at some point after the end of the reign. The most substantial documents so preserved are the four registers discussed above but the final third of the manuscript is made up of other signet material. The arrangement of these constituent parts within the volume, particularly the order of the individual memoranda which are collected at the end of the volume, is likely to have been more or less arbitrary. However, on the whole there are no indications that the manuscripts had become seriously disordered before or during binding, apart from some instances at the beginning and again towards the end of the volume, notably the inclusion of various incomplete and undated documents on ff.296-8. None of the major entries breaks off unexpectedly or shows signs of lost or misplaced folios. Even the placing of the Edward V material is less clumsy than appears at first sight. The register of grants for this reign stands immediately before the list of Richard III's grants, which is logical. The second register of Edward V was probably also intended to stand before the comparable register for Richard III's reign. However the final folio of the signature which ends Edward V's register was used to note lord Dynham's letter to the chancellor concerning affairs in France and this seems to have led whoever ordered the documents to place the whole register in front of the diplomatic correspondence on the assumption that the Dynham letter belonged with the other diplomatic letters.[31]

Although the manuscript contains no obvious lacunae, it does not follow that the volume represents the complete signet archive of the two reigns. There is no internal evidence of how many categories of material were omitted from the volume altogether and subsequently lost. For this, one is dependent on the few contemporary references to signet records and on the survival of original signet material and references to signet warranty in the records of other bodies. These sources normally refer only to letters and warrants which passed the signet. Any number of memoranda could have disappeared without trace, although some specific losses may be suspected. Harley 433 includes a note of the number of letters sent out to request loans for the king but there is no record of the names of those who lent money although such a list must have been compiled in order to facilitate repayment.

Fifteenth century references to the signet archive imply that the signet office, in common with other departments, kept a copy of each document which passed the signet together with the royal authorisation for its issue.[32] Such authorisations are not preserved among the material in Harley 433 although their existence is sometimes mentioned.[33] More important, the collection does not include all the letters and warrants known to have passed the signet during the reign of Richard III. A high proportion of the signet warrants which survive among the chancery records receive no mention in Harley 433.[34] The records of other bodies present a similar picture. A number of the signet letters preserved in the York records have no corresponding entry in Harley 433, nor has Richard's letter to Henry Vernon which survives among the Rutland papers.[35]

However, the registers preserved in Harley 433 are not merely a random or careless selection from the total signet output. Comparison with grants made under the great seal and the duchy of Lancaster seal suggests that the register of grants provides a full and reliable list of grants which passed the signet in the course of the reign. The entries in the second register, too, consist of abstracts on a common theme. They are almost all concerned with the administration of the crown lands and with other sources of royal revenue. A few of the entries do not fit into these categories, including the first five in the register, but this is not surprising among so much material. What is more, none of the omitted letters which can now be traced is concerned with the royal revenues, suggesting that within its terms of reference the second register is complete.

It has to be accepted that a whole category of signet letters has been lost. The form taken by this material can only be surmised. Dr Otway-Ruthven believed that the signet office did not usually enrol the documents which it issued in full, an argument which she based mainly on the brief entries in the Harley 433 registers themselves.[36] If this was so the missing material was presumably in the form of a third register similar to the two which survive. However, there is reason to doubt that all signet records were in the form of brief abstracts. Harley 433 itself contains a number of signet letters which fall into the missing category and which are not entered in either register. The most substantial group are the diplomatic letters but there are also individual examples scattered throughout the miscellaneous material which makes up the final third of the volume, including a letter to the chapter of Salisbury and another to the chancellor concerning the reformation of morality.[37] All are given in full and there are no grounds for assuming that they were isolated departures from the norm. The individual examples, at least, appear to be bound up in Harley 433 more or less by accident. For example, the letter to the chancellor occupies the back of the final page of a section devoted to arbitrations of local disputes. This element of accident and the diversity of their contents makes it probable that these letters are representative of a much larger collection of enrolled letters which is now lost.

This raises the problem of the relationship of such enrolled material to the registers preserved in Harley 433. Were all the letters and warrants which passed the signet enrolled in full and certain categories then abstracted for ease of reference, or did the registers provide the only record of the documents noted within them? The evidence is slight and unfortunately inconclusive. The registers in Harley 433 were evidently compiled at some point after the documents had been drawn up in the signet office. Most of the documents entered in Richard III's second register are dated. Their order, although roughly chronological, is not exactly so. On f.148, for instance, the entries are dated February 6, February 5, January 27 and February 5. This seems to rule out the possibility that the clerk who issued each document made an immediate note of its content in the register. But it does not follow that the register was abstracted subsequently from copies enrolled in full in the signet archives. The register could have been compiled from the originals before they were despatched but after they were drawn up, implying a delay of about a week before the original left the signet office.

Another explanation is put forward by Dr Otway-Ruthven, who suggests that the registers were not compiled from the signet letters themselves but from the royal authorisations for such letters, so that Harley 433 is a record of the instructions issued to the clerks of the signet.[38] This view gains some support from the register of Richard III's grants. Many of the entries in this register speak of 'your' castle or town, strongly suggesting that the details had been copied from a petition rather than from the signet warrant authorising the grant.[39] The comparable register for the reign of Edward V does indeed include complete petitions.[40] In such cases the king had presumably passed the petition, suitably endorsed, to the signet office where the appropriate warrant was then issued. This is directly analogous to examples preserved among the chancery records of petitions endorsed with the sign manual acting as sufficient warrant for letters patent.[41] The fact that the clerks who compiled the register took their details direct from the petition itself suggests that the signet office did not keep full copies of the signet warrants in such cases, although they retained the signed bills.[1a]

This procedure can, however, only have been used for letters and warrants originating as signed bills. It does not explain what happened to letters produced by the king himself. In such cases a variant of the same method may have been used, with the secretary producing a draft which the clerks then copied and despatched, retaining the draft in the signet office. Against this it should be noted that the signet letters in Harley 433 do not look like rough drafts. Most have a full dating clause, with the place and date of issue, which seems to suggest that they were copied from the full version rather than acting as a draft for it. If this is the case, the signet archive consisted of two main types of document: signed bills and full copies of any material which did not originate as a signed bill. The two surviving registers include material from both sources. The second register, in particular, includes references to letters which cannot have originated as signed bills.[43] It is, however, unclear whether in such cases the register entry is the signet archive's only version of the letter or whether the register entry was abstracted from a full copy of the letter which then remained in the archive. In the absence of complete signet records it is impossible to give a positive answer but it is more likely that the register entries were taken from full copies of the letters preserved elsewhere in the signet archive. This would mean that, as far as the registers were concerned, the treatment of signet letters was analogous to that of signed bills. That is, the signet office retained all its signed bills and copies of all the letters which it sent out which did not originate in a signed bill, and the registers were abstracted from both. There may have been a third register into which letters not abstracted in the two surviving registers were abstracted, so that all the signet business was recorded in two places, but this seems unlikely. It would be difficult to abstract diplomatic or political letters successfully and it is probable that the full copies retained by the signet office were allowed to stand as their sole record. Most of these letters have now been lost but it is possible that ff.263-72, a single signature which contains a chronological sequence of signet letters noted in full, represents part of the missing collection of letters.

The signet office procedure outlined here can be no more than inference. It does, however, explain the relationship of Harley 433 to the rest of the signet archive. The categories of record known to be lost, signed bills and enrolled letters, together made up the bulk of the signet records. Harley 433 is a subsidiary collection of reference material: abstracts of the main archive arranged by subject, memoranda and explicit reference works such as the lists of office holders. This collection is heavily biassed towards patronage and financial matters but it would be unsafe to argue from this that it represents some form of chamber finance archive. There is no suggestion elsewhere that chamber finance, although evidently of considerable importance, had secured the departmental status which this would imply. If it had, it would hardly have vanished so thoroughly during the early years of Henry VII's reign. The scope of the collection is also considerably wider than this. Not only does it include diplomatic correspondence and presentations to benefices, for example, but a number of entries in the list of grants are of warrants to the Exchequer and thus explicitly outside the sphere of chamber finance. This variety of material makes it probable that the collection was drawn from the signet office as a whole, although it does demonstrate the amount of work which the operation of chamber finance generated within the signet office.

Although Harley 433 represents only part of the signet archive for the reign of Richard III it is still the most complete collection of medieval signet material to survive. The destruction of the signet archive in the Banqueting House fire of 1619 means that for earlier reigns signet activity must be reconstructed almost entirely from signet letters and warrants surviving among the records of their recipients. Many of the records of the main recipient of signet warrants, the keeper of the privy seal, were destroyed in the same fire.[44] The destruction of these two archives raises problems for the study of Richard III's signet also, particularly in the field of signet office procedure, but the survival of the registers in Harley 433 offers invaluable evidence of the range and volume of signet activity. Nothing comparable to these registers has survived from an earlier period.

It is unlikely, however, that the registers in Harley 433 were an administrative innovation. The division of signet material into registers can be seen in the Edward V sections of the volume, which were compiled under the influence, if not the supervision, of Edward IV's secretary, Oliver King. King was removed from office and imprisoned in the middle of June 1483, which is after the date of the Edward V material included in Harley 433.[45] His authority may have been eclipsed before this. The inclusion of some of Gloucester's own signet letters in Harley 433, apparently entered in the same hand as part of the Edward V material, suggests some overlap between the secretariats of protector and king. This may have meant that in practice Oliver King's functions as secretary were being taken over by Richard's own secretary, John Kendale. However, Edward IV's signet clerks remained in office and much of the routine work no doubt continued to devolve on them.[46] Under these conditions it is likely that signet office procedure followed lines which had already been established.

The register devoted to financial matters was probably introduced in the reign of Edward IV. Edward's development of a system of chamber finance meant that for the first time the signet was used extensively in the administration of the royal revenues. Before his reign a separate register for such matters would hardly have been necessary. There is however no evidence to show whether he also initiated the register of grants or whether this was already in existence and served as a precedent for the second register. Edward IV was certainly aware of the possibilities for financial and political control offered by a careful use of patronage, and a readily accessible list of grants would have been of obvious use.[47] But the advantages of such a list might have been recognised earlier. A council ordinance of the early 1440s considered that one of the functions of the signet archive was to ensure that 'no thinge be writene contrary to that that passeth before', a principle of particular relevance to the making of grants.[48]

The survival of Harley 433 casts considerable doubt on Professor Chrimes' argument that the signet was still subordinate to the privy seal in most matters as late as the reign of Edward IV and was used mainly for diplomatic correspondence.[49] As far as royal grants were concerned the privy seal was already well on the way to becoming a merely formal stage between the signet and the great seal. A comparison of Harley 433 and the patent rolls show that almost all Richard III's grants were initially warranted by the signet. This, however, is not made clear by the chancery records themselves. The grants also passed the privy seal as an intermediate stage and are accordingly noted as warranted by privy seal in the patent rolls, which include no grants specifically warranted by the signet.

In some cases letters patent warranted by the king himself represent signet transactions. In 1448, when Thomas Danyell was made constable of Rising, the king sent a signet letter to the chancellor, notifying him of the appointment and requesting letters patent to be made out. The letter enclosed the original petition and a draft of the letters patent in Latin. The letters patent were accordingly issued and warranted by the king.[50] A similar procedure can be seen in Richard III's reign, slightly simplified. In September 1483 the king sent a signet warrant to his chancellor to make out letters patent to John Savage, granting him an annuity of 40 marks for life. The warrant was noted in the register of grants and the signet office probably retained the petition as their warrant. The grant was delayed by Buckingham's rebellion but the letters patent were finally issued in the following February, warranted by the king.[51]

The Savage grant is, however, unusual. By the reign of Richard III, if not earlier, it had become much more common to send the petition itself to the chancellor, endorsed with the sign manual and without any covering warrant.[52] The grant of an annuity to William Morland is a typical example. Morland, a chancery clerk, petitioned the king for an annuity of £20 until he was promoted to a benefice worth £40 *per annum*. His petition, endorsed by the king and with the figures amended to £10 and £20 respectively, reached the chancellor on 26 April, 1484, and letters patent were duly issued for the revised amount.[53] Many of these signed bills, although evidently not all, survive among the chancery records.[54] Letters issued in response to such bills were warranted in the patent rolls as by the king. However, the issue of letters patent in this way not only bypassed the privy seal, it bypassed the signet office too. Whereas an endorsed petition would normally be passed to the signet office for the details to be noted and a warrant issued, it was here being sent directly to the chancellor. Such grants do not therefore appear in Harley 433 and presumably had no place elsewhere in the signet archives.[55]

There is no shared characteristic among the grants treated in this way. Morland, as a chancery clerk himself, was well placed to take a signed bill direct to the chancellor, as was John Clerk, whose confirmation as chafewax was warranted by signed bill.[56] But this is not true of all recipients. A number, such as Robert Copley, a Scot who was made denizen, were insignificant figures, indistinguishable from the recipients of similar grants whose grants made the full journey from signet office to privy seal to chancery.[57] In other cases a single grant, out of a number made to the recipient in the course of the reign, would be warranted by signed bill while the remainder were processed in the normal way.[58] The conclusion seems to be that, while the usual procedure was for a signed bill to go to the signet office and thence to the privy seal, the king was prepared to hand it straight to the chancellor if he happened to be in attendance.[59]

The warranty of letters patent 'by the king' does not necessarily mean, therefore, that the signet had been used to bypass the privy seal. Indeed the contrary is normally true since in such cases the signet itself was rarely used, the bills being warranted by sign manual. The diminishing importance of the privy seal is better demonstrated by the usual procedure for processing grants. By this date the signet had come to be an invariable stage between the king and his keeper of the privy seal, instead of being employed primarily when the keeper was out of court.[60]

In the financial sphere also the signet was steadily gaining ground at the expense of the privy seal. In theory the privy seal's pre-eminence here was ensured by the Exchequer's unwillingness to accept any warranty other than that of privy seal.[61] In practice it was under attack from two directions. Under the Yorkist kings it was becoming increasingly common for warrants to the Exchequer to be authorised by signet or sign manual. Twenty-two of the fifty-seven warrants for issues surviving from the first year of Richard III did not pass the privy seal.[62] There is no visible distinction in the subject matter of the two types of warrant and here again the determining factor may have been no more than the king's convenience. At the same time the growth of chamber finance was taking a whole area of activity away from the Exchequer and thus away from the privy seal in favour of the signet.

This is reflected in the political eclipse of the keeper of the privy seal and the rise of the secretary, a process which culminated under the Tudors. Dr Otway-Ruthven argues that although the late fifteenth-century secretary had grown in importance he was still subordinate to the keeper of the privy seal; the keeper-ship was the preserve of established figures, while the secretaryship was a mere step towards promotion. She points out that although many keepers of the privy seal were bishops, secretaries attained a bishopric, if at all, only after they had ceased to be secretary.[63] This political relationship between the two posts does not seem, however, to be borne out by their holders under Richard III.

John Gunthorpe, the keeper of the privy seal, does not emerge from the records as a particularly imposing figure under Richard III. During the reign of Edward IV he had been for a time chaplain and secretary to the queen. In June 1471 he was made clerk of the parliament, an office he held for the rest of the reign, and by 1478 he was dean of the king's household.[64] He was an obvious candidate to succeed John Russell as keeper when Russell was made chancellor under Edward V. This was at a time when Gloucester, as protector, was anxious to win the support of his brother's men by retaining them in office.[65] Perhaps in Gunthorpe's case he subsequently regretted the decision for although Gunthorpe remained in office throughout Richard's reign he received few signs of royal favour beyond a gift of swans in Somerset.[66] This is in marked contrast to John Kendale, the secretary, who received an impressive array of royal grants. Ecclesiastical office, the traditional source of reward for royal clerks, was closed to Kendale as a layman and his reward had to be drawn from other sources. He accumulated other government offices: controller of the mint, keeper of the exchange within Calais and keeper of the rolls of common bench. He was also given a variety of local offices and a sizeable land grant.[67]

Such grants must have brought his income close to that of Gunthorpe, in spite of the fact that the secretary received no fee for his office whereas the keeper received twenty shillings a day.[68]

Socially the keepership carried more standing than the secretaryship, particularly when associated with high office in the church: Gunthorpe, although never made a bishop, was dean of Wells.[69] Most fifteenth-century secretaries came from relatively humble backgrounds although Kendale was apparently a member of the lesser Gloucestershire gentry.[70] The closeness of the secretary to the king, however, meant that the balance of political power was shifting in the secretary's favour. In Kendale's case this may well have been helped by his close association with Richard before his accession.[71] In the latter part of his reign Richard showed himself more willing to trust men in his service before 1483 than men with a background of service to his brother, particularly when, as with Gunthorpe, service to Edward IV had also involved links with the Woodvilles.[72]

The increase in the signet's importance not only enhanced the standing of the secretary, it must have necessitated considerable growth in the signet office. Apart from the secretary himself the formal complement of the office in the fifteenth century was about seven: four senior clerks and a group of apprentices.[73] Few of Richard III's clerks can be identified with certainty. One was William Herbert, who was appointed secretary to Richard's son but probably returned to the signet office after the prince's death.[74] Another was probably Richard Skipton.[75] Various other names occur as signatures to the warrants for issues sent from the king himself rather than via the privy seal office, but here a difficulty arises. A number of the signatures are of known chancery officials. Several of the warrants are signed 'Broun', probably the John Brown who had formerly been clerk of the little bag in chancery.[76] Brown may have transferred to the signet office but other warrants are signed by men still in the chancery, including Thomas Barowe, Richard Ive and Henry Sharpe; keeper of the rolls, clerk of the crown and protonotary respectively.[77] There are also warrants signed 'Curteis' presumably the William Curtis of the Chancery, but few of the other names can be identified.[78] The implication is that such warrants were prepared by anyone available.

If all the unidentified names in the warrants are taken as signet clerks it brings the known signet establishment to nine, excluding Kendale. Even this seems very low given the amount of work passing the signet by this date. It is probable that the signet clerks were augmented by a number of non-established clerks who were responsible for the routine jobs of enrolling and abstracting signet material while the more senior clerks drew up the warrants and letters. Certainly Harley 433 was the work of more than nine people. Unfortunately the entries in the volume are not signed although a few entries are followed by monograms. The most common apparently represents Th, which cannot be identified with any known signet clerk, and some are little more than flourishes, although none as elaborate as the flourishes which follow the signatures in the warrants for issues.

Harley 433 is not a precedent book or book of remembrance in the terms defined by Hubert Hall. Most of the types of document which he considered typical of such books: charters, statutes, *placita,* private deeds, correspondence, chronicles, treatises, topographies and genealogies, have no place in Harley 433.[79] The volume consists of the daily records of the signet office rather than a collection of precedents and as such ceased to be of much relevance after the death of Richard III.[80] The major exception seems to have been the list of fees for royal officials. This was certainly in use under Henry VII, as a note at the end makes clear, and possibly even later as the scale of fees for office changed only slowly.[81] As a result the volume came to be regarded as a book of remembrance, a concept with which the sixteenth century, like the fifteenth, was thoroughly familiar.[82] This explains why material from the reign of Henry VIII was copied into the manuscript. The entries, a description of the reception of the papal legate and a list of a French embassy and its English counterparts, have nothing in common with the rest of the volume but do represent the type of information considered appropriate for entry in a book of remembrance.[83]

This misconception probably accounts for the survival of the volume. The manuscript was purchased by Robert Harley from John Strype, the rector of Leyton (Essex). It had reputedly formed part of the collection of William Cecil, lord Burghley, some of which Strype had acquired from Sir William Hicks, a grandson of Burghley's secretary.[84] Burghley had a particular interest in collections of historical material which may well have led him to add the volume to his own collection.[85] In this context it is interesting to note that Harley 431, also purchased from Strype, is another medieval collection: John Prophete's *Registrum Epistolarum.* Prophete was secretary and then keeper of the privy seal to Henry IV and although the provenance of Harley 431 cannot be traced beyond Strype it seems likely that it had followed a similar descent to Harley 433, and for similar reasons.[86]

The importance of Harley 433, however, lies mainly in the abstracts of documents issued daily under the signet, which would have had no place in a true book of remembrance. None of the earlier formularies embodying signet material can offer so detailed a picture of signet activity. Collections such as Prophete's *Registrum* were by their very nature highly selective compilations. Most, moreover, date from periods when the signet was still a relatively minor part of the government process.[87] The survival of Harley 433 provides a uniquely detailed account of the signet at a crucial period in its development, when its growing importance at the expense of the privy seal foreshadowed the pre-eminence which it was to enjoy under the Tudors.

THE CONTENTS

Edward V Entries

The Edward V material in Harley 433 is in two groups: ff.3, 6-19b and ff.221-232. It was printed, together with the signet letters of the duke of Gloucester (f.323), as *Grants Etc of King Edward the Fifth* by J.G. Nichols, who attempted to rearrange the entries in chronological order, not with complete success as he himself admitted.[88] The two sections were evidently planned as two separate registers. The early entries in both are arranged in chronological order, with a heading for each day's business, and the dates in the two sections overlap. The sections correspond roughly to the two registers of Richard III. The first includes Edward V's grants, together with some entries which in Richard's reign would have gone into the second register, such as the letter to the inhabitants of Tilney announcing the appointment of a steward and letters to the royal auditors in Wales concerning the wages of the duke of Buckingham.[89] The second section, like Richard's second register, is largely made up of material concerning the royal lands and their issues but also includes some unrelated material such as diplomatic correspondence and letters referring to the military preparations against the Woodvilles.[90]

In both sections the entries are given in more detail than in the comparable registers for Richard III's reign, with some documents enrolled in full. This led Nichols to believe that some of the entries represented letters patent. It was not, however, unusual for signet warrants to include a draft of the letters required, and there is no reason to suppose that the registers include anything other than signet material. The full entries were cases where the clerk had enrolled the entire text of the letters authorised by signet warrant, just as some petitions were enrolled in full.[91] This explains the apparent inclusion of privy seal material, such as the indenture between Edward V and Northumberland concerning Berwick, which was almost certainly taken from the warrant sent to the keeper of the privy seal rather than being a true privy seal enrolment.[92] A similar ambiguity occurs in the Richard III registers with entries such as 'N hath a privy seal to the treasurer'.

The two registers, as far as it can be checked, include most of the signet output of the reign. There is an apparent break in the first register. The early entries were made chronologically, with daily date headings. May 14-16 and 19-22 occupy ff.6-11.[93] The order then breaks down for the rest of the register, as the job of abstracting the documents fell behind their issue. There is also, however, a single Edward V entry on f.3, headed May 5. It is possible that similar entries once existed for May 6-13 but there is no evidence for this. The Edward V entry occupies only the top of f.3, the rest is filled by a letter from Richard III's son as prince of Wales, and the dorse is blank. If this were a stray survival from a longer run of entries one would expect Edward V material to occupy both sides of the page. There is, moreover, no trace in the patent rolls of a group of grants corresponding to this gap. The only entries in the patent rolls which are otherwise unaccounted for date from later in the reign when the register is apparently intact: the appointment of Hastings as master of the mint and John Kendale's appointment as keeper of the rolls of common bench.[94] Both are noted as warranted by privy seal and must have originated with the king. Their omission from the register may have been accidental or the warrant to the keeper of the privy seal may have been warranted by the sign manual alone.

It is probable that the entry on f.3, letters of presentation for John Geffrey, was planned as the beginning of a third register devoted to ecclesiastical appointments. No other presentations were made under the signet and the rest of the page remained empty until it was used to note a letter early in the next reign. There are signs that a similar register was planned under Richard III although it was not consistently maintained. A list of benefices granted between January 1485 and the end of the reign is preserved on f.20, but most presentations were simply noted in the register of grants.

The Edward V entries in Harley 433 are confined to the period May 5 — June 11, that is, from the king's arrival in London to shortly before the arrest of Hastings at the Tower. The earliest grant is that to Geffrey which was made at St Albans but probably enrolled shortly after the king's arrival in London, when he had the resources of his father's signet office at his disposal. Signet activity did not, however, get thoroughly under way for a further four days, with the first entries in the second register dating from May 9 and in the register of grants from May 14. It then seems to have remained at a fairly steady level until the first week in June, when it began to slacken off, ceasing altogether after the crisis of June 13.[95] This abrupt end to signet activity may be the result of the imprisonment of Oliver King, the king's secretary, but it must also reflect the political uncertainty of the time. The arrest of Hastings and the removal of the duke of York from sanctuary made it clear to contemporaries that Richard had designs on the crown and the second Stallworth letter paints a vivid picture of the situation in London: 'I hold you happy that ye ar oute of the prese, for with huse is myche trobull, and every manne dowtes other'.[96]

The cessation of signet activity was paralleled elsewhere. The last letters to pass the great seal were the routine appointments of the chief baron of the Exchequer and two serjeants at law on June 14 and 15.[97] This was not only because royal initiative had ceased. There were a number of grants in the pipe line which had been warranted by the signet but now failed to pass the great seal. Most of these were subsequently issued early in Richard III's reign after new signet warrants had been prepared. A slowing down of government processes at a time of crisis was not unusual. Richard's own reign shows a similar hiatus during Buckingham's rebellion. The completeness of the shut down after June 13, however, strongly suggests that men were tacitly waiting for Richard's accession before resuming government business.

As Nichols realised, the entries for this reign reflect the policies and decisions of the duke of Gloucester rather than of the young king himself.[98] A number of the signet letters explicitly embody Gloucester's advice, but even where this is not stated there can be little doubt that the protector was responsible for issuing the letters. The relative importance of king and protector is suggested by three of the latter's own signet letters preserved in Harley 433 (f.323). Two authorised the recipients to seize forfeited Woodville land and the third was a grant of office. They were evidently intended to have the force of a royal signet warrant but, although all three include the clause 'on the king our soverayn lordes behalve', they were essentially the protector's private warrants. Obedience was enjoined on pain of forfeiting Gloucester's favour and one was specifically made during the duke's pleasure.

Gloucester undoubtedly used his power as protector to consolidate his own position. The recipients of grants in this period include a number of his own followers, notably the duke of Buckingham whose massive grants dominate the first register. But Richard was not attempting to surround the young king with his own men. The immediate circle around Edward V after his arrival in London was apparently composed of former servants of his father. The two men stated in Harley 433 to have been in Edward V's household, Walter Hungerford and John Norreys, had both been servants of Edward IV.[99] Gloucester's relative weakness in the south made it essential for him to retain the support of his brother's followers if he was to widen the basis of his power. He accordingly allowed most of his brother's grants to stand and filled the few vacancies which did occur with men from Edward IV's service as well as with members of his own northern affinity.[100]

The only group to suffer seriously by Richard's assumption of the protectorship were the Woodvilles and their immediate circle, Gloucester's main rivals for power after the death of Edward IV. Gloucester was understandably anxious to limit their power and, although the council overruled his claim that Rivers and his associates had been guilty of treason, he immediately treated their possessions as forfeit.[101] Both registers provide examples of the redistribution of their royal grants. Robert Bell, a former member of Edward IV's household, was given the manor of Woodham Martin which Rivers had been granted by Edward IV. Lord Lovell took over Rivers' office of chief butler. Richard Williams replaced Rivers and Rivers' son in law Robert Poyntz as constable of St Briavels, although Thomas Baynam, a local man, shared the office in both grants. Alfred Cornburgh received Thomas Vaghan's office of controller of the coinage of tin. There were also minor changes at a lower level.[102] At the same time Richard took steps to seize their family lands. Lovell was ordered to enter Thorpe Waterfield, one of the manors which had belonged to the duchess of Exeter and which had been settled by parliament on Dorset's infant son.[103] William Malyverer and Thomas Wortley seized the manors of More End and Mote.[104]

This policy met with no opposition. Most of Edward IV's servants were prepared to cooperate in the attack on the Woodvilles. Even bishop Russell of Lincoln, who was rumoured to have accepted the chancellorship unwillingly, was prepared to make pointed and unfriendly allusions to Earl Rivers in his draft speech for the opening of Edward V's parliament.[105] The clearest demonstration, however, is provided by Richard's countermeasures against Edward Woodville, whose fleet was threatening the south coast. Richard's first step was to give the key castles of Carisbrooke and Portchester, held by Robert Poyntz and Edward Woodville himself, to two local members of Edward IV's household, William Berkeley and William Uvedale respectively. The next day, May 10, Thomas Fulford and John Halwell were ordered to sea against Woodville, then reported to be standing off the Downs. On May 14 Richard authorised further action and again looked to former members of his brother's household. Berkeley and Uvedale, together with Roger Kelsale, one of Edward's yeomen of the crown, were ordered to victual a fleet under Edward Brampton, John Welles and Thomas Grey.[106]

The episode suggests that Gloucester could call upon the support of a large part of his brother's establishment and that he could accordingly exert authority in areas outside the scope of his own affinity. Part, at least, of this support was however due to him as protector of Edward V rather than in his own right, and it was jeopardised by his usurpation in June 1483. Although many of Edward IV's servants remained loyal to Richard III others made common ground with the Woodvilles. Of the eight men involved in the measures against Edward Woodville no fewer than six, Berkeley, Uvedale, Kelsale, Fulford, Halwell and Welles supported the Woodvilles five months later in their rebellion against Richard III.[107] Edward V's grants in Harley 433 paint the same picture. Alongside grants to men like John Sapcotes and Thomas Fowler, former servants of Edward IV who transferred their loyalty to Richard III, there are grants to Walter Hungerford and William Clifford, who subsequently rebelled.[108]

The Register of Richard III's Grants

The register occupies ff.22-105 of the volume, and includes abstracts of the grants which passed the signet in the course of the reign. It was intended to provide a more accessible list of grants than the signed bills and enrolled letters which made up the bulk of the signet archive, and information was kept to a minimum. Most entries are little more than statements that N has received X for a given period. Very few give any indication of the date of the warrant or of its recipient, although in most cases this would have been the keeper of the privy seal. An approximate date of issue can usually be reached by a comparison with other stages in the processing of the grant. In addition, it became more common in the course of the reign for the clerks to note each new month in the margin, presumably for their own ease of reference since the register was becoming a substantial document. The changes of month were apparently noted accurately: in one case a clerk has taken the trouble to squeeze in an additional entry at the end of one month after the next month's entries had been commenced.[109] The analogy of the second register, however, suggests that within each month the order of the entries may have varied within a few days.

The register provides a particularly clear picture of the range of Richard III's patronage. Virtually all the king's known grants passed the signet, the major exceptions being the signed bills which went straight to the chancellor or to his counterpart in the duchy of Lancaster, and the grants initiated by other officers of state. The chief butler, for instance, appointed his own deputies and their letters patent were warranted by his bill. The chancellor had the right to make certain routine confirmations and to present to minor benefices in the king's gift.[110] Such patronage was in any case not strictly 'royal' patronage and its omission from Harley 433 does not seriously distort the picture of the king's patronage. The signed bills are a more serious omission but the numbers involved are small.

The majority of grants noted in this register can be found elsewhere. Most are enrolled in the patent rolls or in the rolls of the duchy of Lancaster, a few in the French rolls. Some survive among the exchequer series of warrants for issues, such as the Christmas grant of £100 to the grooms and pages of the chamber.[111] It is, however, much easier to trace the development of Richard's patronage through the register than by attempting to collate the final versions of the grants. Although the order in the register may vary by a few days from the order in which the grants were initially authorised, this variation could grow to months by the time the final stages of the grant were reached. The entries on f.28b, for instance, are all grants which passed the signet in September 1483. The group of duchy of Lancaster offices given to Thomas Molyneux were authorised at York on 17 September and his letters patent bear the same date.[112] The grant to William Shoter passed the great seal on 25 September. Other grants made at the same time, however, became caught up in the administrative delays which accompanied Buckingham's rebellion. The grant to Sir John Savage passed the great seal in the following February, and the grant of the Langley wardship did not pass the great seal until March 1485.[113]

The register does, however, include notes of some grants which have not survived elsewhere. Often this was because the grant was in the form of a warrant sent directly to a local receiver or auditor rather than to the exchequer. The grant of a reward of £20 to Leonard Thornburgh (f.31), for instance, to be paid by the auditors of the Richmond lands, is only recorded in Harley 433. This does not, however, explain all the grants which appear only in the register. Several are indistinguishable from grants which were subsequently embodied in letters patent. In a few cases a grant may have been blocked after it had passed the signet. The grant of office to Walter Hungerford (f.27b), for instance, was probably cancelled before it reached the great seal because of his implication in Buckingham's rebellion.[114] In most cases, however, there is no reason to suppose that the grant was not meant to be effective. The fee of 50 marks granted to Richard Middleton as an esquire of the body never passed the great seal. Middleton was a close associate of Richard; had his grant been thought likely to be invalid it would certainly have been emended.[115]

The acceptability of a signet warrant as the official version of a grant may have been a corollary of the growth of chamber finance. The main practical purpose of a written grant was to authorise the payment of the wages or annuity granted. Letters patent issued some time after the recipient had taken up office would thus include a clause backdating the payment of wages or, in some cases, the king would grant a lump sum to cover the period between the recipient's taking up of office and the date of his grant. This also explains why so few appointments to household office were made the subject of a written grant. The main exceptions are the offices, notably the posts of yeoman of the crown and serjeant at arms, which carried a fixed fee payable from an outside source. Offices paid on a daily basis from the general household assignments are hardly ever embodied in a written grant.[116] As soon as receivers and auditors became accustomed to the idea of accepting a signet warrant as their authority for payment much of the need for letters under the great seal was removed, although most recipients of patronage continued to secure letters patent.

The exercise of royal patronage is a central issue in the reign of Richard III, accounting for much of the hostility which he aroused. At the outset of his reign Richard continued the policy which he had adopted as protector. Most of his brother's men remained in office and the limited amount of patronage available was given not only to Richard's own followers but to former supporters of Edward IV.[117] This policy was overturned by the rebellions of autumn 1483, involving men from most of the southern counties. The forfeitures which followed placed a massive amount of patronage at the king's disposal. Richard's response can be seen clearly in the register. Grants made in the first four months of 1484, after parliament had attainted the rebels, occupy over a third of the whole register, roughly ff.32-64. The main beneficiaries were members of the king's own affinity. The involvement of several of Edward's household men in the rebellions had shaken Richard's policy of conciliation. Rather than using the patronage at his disposal to build up a new affinity among the gentry of southern England he chose to 'plant' trusted members of his northern affinity in the areas most badly affected by the rebellions.[118] The resulting influx of northerners into the southern counties was enormously unpopular.[119]

Had the rebellions of 1483 been followed by a period of secure rule, Richard's reliance on his own affinity would probably have slackened and the basis of his power have begun to widen again. This, however, was not the case. From the summer of 1484 the king was faced by a series of minor risings, as well as by the threat of invasion from abroad. As a result he was driven to rely upon a narrowing circle of associates. The closing pages of the register demonstrate very clearly that major grants, at least, were almost all going to men who had already benefited from royal patronage. In other words, the grants were not securing new support for the king but strengthening the influence of his existing affinity. The result became apparent at Bosworth, when Richard III faced Tudor with much the same group of men who had brought him to power two years earlier.[120]

Richard III's Second Register

The register occupies ff.107-219, virtually the whole of volume II of the present edition. The final folio of volume II, f.220, although following on chronologically from the register, was probably not intended to form part of it. It is occupied by commissions of array and an incomplete proclamation against Tudor and separated from the register itself by the blank dorse of f.219. The register ends in the final week of June, 1485 when Richard was in the Midlands awaiting Tudor's invasion. The fact that the end of f.219 and f.219b are blank indicates that the register genuinely stopped at that point, rather than that subsequent folios have been lost.

The register entries are mainly concerned with the royal revenues, and they cast considerable light on the operation of chamber finance under Richard III.[121] Many of the entries are straightforward warrants for payment, including assignments for household expenses. There are also a number of receipts for money paid into the chamber. The register is also concerned with the administration of the crown lands, which generated most of the income handled by the chamber. It therefore includes some details of grants made from the royal estates and also more peripheral aspects of their administration, such as the letter to the bailiff of Ware who was to ensure that the inhabitants practised archery instead of playing unlawful games.[122]

The administration of land forfeited after the rebellions of 1483 also comes within the scope of the register. The initial signet commissions to seize forfeited land and levy the revenues on the king's behalf are noted, as are subsequent charges on the estates including the payment of debts owed by the rebels. The register provides the names of several rebels who are not mentioned in the 1484 act of attainder but whose lands and chattels were none the less forfeit, such as James Bonython in Cornwall and Robert and John Redeness in Holderness. [123] This concern with the possessions of the rebels probably explains the inclusion of items relating to the rebels but not of immediate relevance to the royal finances, for example the letter on behalf of Sir Thomas Delamare explaining that the king has pardoned him and his friends are therefore free to provide him with food without incurring the royal displeasure. [124] The inclusion of this and of other items related only tenuously to the main subject matter of the register perhaps indicates that the selection of material was left to the discretion of the signet clerks.

The register is also an important supplement to the register of grants. In several cases it includes warrants authorising payments for grants noted in the first register. The register of grants, for instance, includes the grant of an annuity of 40 marks to Sir John Ferrers from the lordship of Warwick, which passed the great seal in March 1484. In January the following year Ferrers was given a warrant to John Agard, the receiver of Warwick, authorising the payment of the annuity. [125] Many of the warrants noted in the second register, however, do not match grants recorded elsewhere. Grants made solely by signet warrant in this way also occur in the register of grants and the decision to enter them in one register or the other must have been more or less arbitrary. Each warrant was at once a royal grant and a charge on the royal revenues. On the whole the second element appears to have been regarded as dominant and the majority of such warrants were entered in the second register.

Other grants noted in the second register take the form of letters to local officials notifying them of grants within their area. As in the case of warrants for issues some of these letters parallel grants recorded elsewhere while others do not. In February 1485 the officers of the lordships of Skipton and Carlton in Craven were ordered to assist John Vavasour, who had been appointed receiver during the king's pleasure at 10 marks *per annum*. [126] There is no other record of Vavasour's appointment and the signet letter, which incorporates all the information normally found in a grant, may have been his sole authority. As receiver Vavasour was responsible for paying his own wages, which removed much of the need for a more formal grant. The same consideration explains why so few of the receivers named in Harley 433 are known to have been appointed by a written grant.

The survival of the second register confirms the impression that the late fifteenth century attitude to grants was much less formal than is often supposed. While many grants went through the full process of issue under signet, privy seal and great seal others were issued only under the signet and a considerable number do not seem to have been formally issued at all but are recorded only in the form of letters or warrants to third parties. This rather casual treatment of grants is confirmed by the occasions on which a grant was made, and operative,

long before it passed even the signet. The patent rolls contain several examples
of grants made by word of mouth some time before they were embodied in a
formal grant.[127] The second register contributes other examples. Sir William
Houghton received the grant of steward of Chadsey, master of the forest of
Hay and parker of Petherton in March 1485. The grant was in force, however,
at least as early as the previous January, when the local officials were ordered
to aid him.[128] Sometimes the delay was even more marked. Ralph Bigot was
acting as Richard's master of the ordnance in March 1484 but a grant of the
office did not pass the signet until the very end of the reign, and never passed
the great seal.[129]

In the light of this it is not difficult to accept that some grants may have
escaped record altogether, particularly when no payment was involved or when
it could be made at source by the recipient. Land grants fall into the first
category and of the list of Richard's land grants preserved as ff.282-9 no fewer
than 20% are otherwise unrecorded. Taking this list of land grants, discussed in
more detail below, and the two registers together it is unlikely that a significant
proportion of Richard's patronage has been lost. The survival of Harley 433
does demonstrate, however, how much of Richard's patronage is not recorded
in the traditional sources for royal patronage, letters patent and exchequer
warrants. The same is probably true of Edward IV's reign also, as the signet
gained in acceptance.

Other Financial Material
There are various financial entries in Harley 433 apart from the contents of the
second register. They fall into three main groups: entries relating to chamber
finance and the household; accounts and valuations; and details of the king's
attempts to raise loans.

The first group has been discussed, and largely printed, by Dr Wolffe.[130] The
household material includes details of the assignments made for the king's
main household and also the regulations and financial provisions for the
household set up at Sandal under Richard's nephew, the earl of Lincoln, in July
1484.[131] The new household was intended to replace that of the prince of
Wales, who had died that spring, as the centre of royal authority in the north.
At the same time that authority was given a more institutionalised form with
the setting up of the council of the north, again headed by Lincoln.[132] The two
northern households apparently shared the same personnel. John Dawney,
treasurer of the Sandal household, had also been the prince's treasurer and is
often referred to simply as the treasurer in the north parts.[133]

The volume also contains two important documents concerning the administration of the crown lands which summarize the aims and principles of
chamber finance. One is a general document, with the contemporary heading
'A remembrance made, as well for the hasty levy of the king's revenues
growing out of all his possessions and hereditaments, as for the profitable
estate and governance of the same possessions.'[134] As the title suggests, it sets
out the principles upon which the king could secure the best financial return
from his land. The second document translates these principles into a set of

instructions for the administration of a single honour, that of Tutbury, where Marmaduke Constable of Flamborough, one of Richard's knights of the body, was steward.[135]

Both documents were counsels of perfection. The royal lands were not only the source of much of the crown's income, they also provided much of its patronage in the form of office and annuities. Taken to extremes the two elements were incompatible. Over generous patronage seriously impoverished the crown but patronage could not be abandoned altogether since it offered the main method of exerting political control in the provinces. A medieval king had to balance the two. The *Remembrance* was vitiated by the assumption that patronage should be subordinated to the crown's financial benefit. Its suggestion that stewardships should be the preserve of men learned in the law rather then of uneducated knights and squires would have removed one of the most desirable forms of local patronage from the reach of its traditional beneficiaries. In this the memorandum was seriously out of step with contemporary opinion.[136] So was the instruction to Constable to replace any incompetent deputies of local office holders, which struck at the cherished right of office holders to appoint their own deputies.[137] In practice the king could not afford to insist on such recommendations and although the growing importance of chamber finance brought a reorganisation of central government procedures it had little impact on local patronage.

The volume does not include many valuations or accounts. The most extensive is the valuation of the lands of the archbishopric of York, drawn up in the last year of Edward IV's reign (ff.324-7b). The crown no doubt had similar valuations for all bishoprics but there seems no obvious reason for the inclusion of this one in Harley 433. The last vacancy had been at the death of George Neville in 1474 and there was no immediate prospect of another. The valuation is followed by the account of the receiver of the forfeited Staffordshire lands of the duke of Buckingham (ff.328-329). The account is undated but must refer to the financial year before Richard acquired the land since he subsequently regranted some of the offices mentioned in the account. The parker of Stafford and the bailiff of Stafford Green, for instance, are named as Humphrey Whitegreve and Reynold Hassall, whereas the offices were granted to Thomas Belle and Robert Wortley respectively in March 1484.[138]

The commissions to raise loans (ff.275b-277b) date from late February 1485. By this date Richard was evidently in some financial difficulty. The Croyland chronicler, the main source for the king's financial problems, regarded the king's difficulties unsympathetically. His assumptions, however, are coloured by his conviction that Edward IV had left a large treasure which Richard must have squandered in the early months of his reign.[139] It is likely that the chronicler was taking an unduly rosy view of Edward's finances. At the time of Edward's death England had been at war with Scotland for three years and the end of the French pension was not only a financial blow in itself but the prelude to expenditure on the war with France. The situation was aggravated by the Woodvilles' seizure of the royal treasure after Edward's death, at least some of which must have been permanently lost to Richard.[140] This, taken in conjunction with the heavy expenses of the reign, makes Richard's difficulties more explicable.[141]

The loans which Richard attempted to raise should be distinguished from the benevolences which had created so much ill feeling under Edward IV and which Richard had condemned in parliament in the previous year. The main difference was that repayment of the loan was guaranteed, in this case by June 1486.[142] Legally, Richard was completely within his rights. The Croyland chronicler is wrong in insisting that the loans were benevolences under another name and that Richard was thus breaking his own word.[143] But his violent attack on the king's attempts to raise money shows how much ill-will was created by the loans.

The commissioners were almost all household men, a number of whom combined chamber office with the post of royal receiver, such as Nicholas Spicer and John Greenhill, who were jointly responsible for Gloucestershire and Herefordshire.[144] Wherever possible Richard III used men native to the counties concerned, partly for their local knowledge but probably also as a concession to local feeling. The commissioners do not, however, seem to have been particularly successful. Gairdner estimated the return as £20,000 but the exchequer records for this half year show an income of only £4,500 from loans.[145] It is possible that the commissioners managed to raise more but paid all or part of the money directly into the chamber. However the material in Harley 433, although it gives no indication of who lent money, does imply that the commissioners met with opposition. The commissioners for each area were provided with a selection of unaddressed letters for various amounts, which they had to place as well as they could, and in addition with a few letters in which the recipient was also named. Three weeks after these original instructions, the collectors in a number of counties were supplied with much fuller lists of men to be asked for specified sums, which suggests that attempts to bargain with potential lenders had not proved successful.

The List of Land Grants

The list occupies a single signature (ff.282-9b) and is the work of one hand. The contemporary title states that it is a list of the manors, lordships, lands and tenements granted to various people and their heirs male by king Richard III. In other words, it is a list of land grants which were intended to be permanent alienations. It is also a list of new grants only. It does not include confirmations of grants made by Edward IV even when, as in the case of Nicholas Baker, they involved new letters patent.[146] Nor does the list include the restoration of land to pardoned rebels, such as John Fogge and Walter Hungerford.[147]

The list, however, is not complete, even within its stated limitations. Forty eight grants of land are known to have been omitted, of which at least a third were made to the recipient and his heirs male and thus came within the scope of the list. These omissions include a number of major grants, notably the extensive land in Wales and the Marches granted to William Stanley.[148] On the other hand, the list includes several grants, such as the eight on f.287, which were made for the lifetime of the recipient only, or during the king's pleasure. It also includes some examples where only the farm of the manor, not the manor itself, had been granted. The apparent grant of Oswaldkirk to John

Pikering falls into this category, although the list gives no indication that it was not an outright grant. [149]

The source of the list is unclear. It was clearly not compiled at any stage in the processing of the grants. It includes a large number of grants not recorded elsewhere, as well as omitting grants known to have been made under the signet or great seal. Where the same grant appears in both the list and the patent rolls the versions sometimes differ, which again suggests that the list was not compiled from signet or chancery records. The land grant to lord Ferrers, for instance, appears elsewhere in Harley 433 and in his letters patent as a grant of the manor of Cheshunt (Hertfordshire) with appurtenances in Cheshunt and Waltham. According to the Harley 433 list, however, he held the reversion of the manor of Maidcroft, not mentioned elsewhere, and the manor of Waltham near Cheshunt. [150] Moreover, the list is not in chronological order, which one would expect had it been copied from the signet or chancery records.

The list is probably related to the schedule of reserved rents which survives in the Public Record Office. [151] The aims and layout of the two documents differ, although the list of grants in each is very similar. The Harley 433 list is arranged more or less at random, but the land held by each recipient is listed in full. The schedule of reserved rents is arranged by shrievalty, although this is misleading since for each recipient only a single manor is named, even when the recipient held other manors elsewhere in the country. The purpose of the schedule, as the title suggests, is to provide details of the money due to the king from the land, and the name of the manor attached to each sum is little more than a reference to the full grant. Thus the reserved rent of £8 6s. 8d. is attached to the manor of Wickham, granted to Robert Carre, whereas it derived from a much larger grant made to Carre, including two other manors and associated land. [152] The schedule omits completely most land grants to which a reserved rent was not attached.

The exact relationship of the two lists is not entirely clear. There are some marked similarities. They share details of a number of grants not recorded elsewhere. Both describe John Talbot as 'of Scarborough' although neither usually goes into details of this sort. The lists, however, are not exactly parallel, even allowing for their stated omissions, and there is one major difference. The schedule records the manors of Glutton and Farnham (Somerset) as granted to Percival Thirlwall while the Harley 433 list assigns them to Thomas Markenfield. [153] It seems likely that both lists were drawn from a series of inquisition returns, now lost, although not from exactly the same returns or at the same time. [154] This would explain a number of the puzzling features of the Harley 433 list, notably the random order of entries and also the fact that a number of the names are incorrect or only partially remembered, a strange slip if the list had been compiled from royal grants. It does, however, make dating the list more difficult. The only guide is that the last grant to be included was apparently one to the duke of Norfolk made in late February 1485. [155]

The list of land grants, particularly when the omitted grants are added in, is striking evidence of the lavishness of Richard's patronage. The grants did not, however, seriously deplete the crown's income since virtually all of them were made from land forfeited by the rebels of 1483. The main exceptions are the grants which Richard made of land which he or Clarence had held under Edward IV, and much of this was land which had been initially forfeited by Lancastrian opponents of Edward IV. An important part of the duke of Norfolk's endowment was made up of land held by the duke of Gloucester in the previous reign, much of it former de Vere land. [156] Northumberland was given the Brian lands, which Clarence had held until his death in 1478. [157] There were also minor beneficiaries. Plympton, granted to Thomas Malyverer, had been held by Clarence as part of the earldom of Devon. Robert Percy received land in Cambridgeshire which had been held by Gloucester. [158]

In spite of his grants Richard III almost certainly enjoyed a greater landed endowment than his brother. His accession brought the remaining share of the Neville lands to the crown and these were kept more or less intact, apart from the grant of Aldborough and Catterick to Sir John Conyers. [159] Richard also retained part of the Mowbray estates, in spite of recognising John Howard and William Berkeley as the heirs of the last Mowbray duke. William Berkeley was persuaded to part with his share of the inheritance in return for a life annuity. [160] John Howard received his share, augmented by further grants of land in East Anglia and elsewhere. As further Mowbray land was released by the deaths of the dowager duchesses it apparently passed to the crown. Certainly when the dowager duchess Katherine died Richard immediately appointed an auditor for her lands. [161] Richard also retained a considerable amount of the forfeited land in his own hands, including virtually all the Stafford lands apart from the lordship of Holderness. [162] Furthermore Richard, unlike his predecessors, was careful to retain a financial interest in the land which he granted away. Most of the permanent alienations were charged with a rent of one shilling in the mark, giving the crown an annual return of one thirteenth the nominal value of the land. This was even levied on grants to his closest associates, including Norfolk who paid £100 for his land. [163]

Lists of Office Holders and Fees

The lists in Harley 433 fall into two groups. First, occupying ff.310-323b, is a group of lists in the same hand giving the fees and wages granted by Edward IV and in force at his death. Distinct from these is an undated list of offices with their fees (ff.336-9b) in the same hand as the list of corrodies which preceeds it and probably produced at the same time.

There are three main lists in the first category: fees and wages granted from the crown lands by Edward IV; duchy of Lancaster officers, but not annuitants, in the last year of Edward's reign; and offices on 'foreign' lands, that is, lands in the crown's possession which were not part of the royal desmesne. The third list includes the former Clarence estates, both land which he held by royal grant, such as the earldom of Devon, and his wife's inheritance which the crown held during the minority of the earl of Warwick. It also includes the land and offices formerly held by Anthony Woodville, Earl Rivers. All these lists were drawn up early in the reign of Richard III to provide the new king with a readily accessible list of his brother's patronage and in particular to show which grants were available for redistribution. Grants which had lapsed since Edward's death are indicated by marginal signs. Such notes only refer to the very beginning of the reign; offices forfeited by the rebels of autumn 1483, for instance, are not marked. In the Kent list (ff.312b-313) the offices of George Brown and the Hautes, who were under suspicion from the period of the usurpation, are marked but the fees of Thomas Borghchier, Thomas Seintleger and William Clifford, all lost in the aftermath of the rebellions, are not.

The emphasis throughout is on the recipients of the grants. There are very few offices for which a holder is not named and these are mostly offices within the central government with which the king would be fully conversant. This emphasis is sometimes at the expense of order. The list of grants made from the crown land is nominally arranged by county but all an individual's grants are entered at his first mention, regardless of their location. Thus under Norwich Edward Hardgill's fee of £9 2s. 6d., payable from the town's fee farm, is followed by other offices of his which were in fact in Oxfordshire and the New Forest and were payable there, details which the list does not make clear.[164] The argument behind this arrangement was probably that if Hardgill lost one office he would lose them all and that it was therefore more useful to have them grouped together.

The sources of the Edward IV lists vary. The Devonshire list was explicitly drawn from the ministers' accounts for the last year of the reign, and so probably were the earldom of Warwick and duchy of Lancaster lists. They are characterised by the arrangement of offices within each lordship in an approximate order of status and by their apparent completeness. Where minor offices have been omitted it was probably because they were in the gift of one of the office holders rather than of the king himself. The list of fees payable on the royal demesne cannot, however, have been compiled in the same way since the entries are not grouped entirely according to the source of payment. Stephen Fryon, for instance, received an anuity of £20 made up of £10 from the fee farms of York and Northampton. The list enters the full £20 under York, with no indication that York was not, in fact, responsible for it all.[165] It is more likely that the details of fees and wages were drawn from a list of royal grants, possibly a register of signet grants similar to Richard's own. This must have been a considerable undertaking, particularly since the lists were probably compiled at short notice. The document certainly shows some signs of haste. On f.312, for example, the clerk has written Gloucester for Colchester as the source of John Shutte's fee as yeoman of the crown, although the grant is listed correctly under Essex. There are also numerous omissions. In the Northamptonshire section (f.313b) the grants to the Hastings brothers and the corresponding payments are far from complete and a related office, the rangership of Cliff, Brigstoke and Rockingham, held by John Pylton, is omitted altogether.[166] So is William Porter's fee of the crown, payable on the farm of Northampton.[167]

Even taken together, the Edward IV lists do not provide a complete account of his patronage. Some important sources of patronage are omitted altogether, notably the duchy of York. Various categories of grant are omitted explicitly. No land grants are included, nor are charitable benefactions. Moreover, the list of fees charged on the demesne lands is the only one to include annuities. The other lists confine themselves to offices and their fees, although the duchy of Lancaster in particular was an important source of annuities.

The undated list differs in a number of ways from the lists considered above. The heading, 'Officers with their Salaries pertaining to the King's house, Lordships and Castles', is a much later addition and not a particularly helpful description. The list, as a list of officers, is markedly incomplete and badly arranged. Some lordships are omitted entirely, others are included with only a partial list of their officers, such as the Queensborough list which notes only the minor officials.[168] The undated list, unlike the others, is concerned primarily with the fees attached to each office rather than with the office holders, who are hardly ever named. It is arranged by the source of the fee rather than by the location of the grant. Thus there is no section for the offices in the Tower of London. The keeper of the wardrobe there is listed under Hertfordshire, because his fees were paid from the county revenues, while the keeper of the armoury is listed under Kent for the same reason. The list also distinguishes between the Windsor offices which were paid from the lordship itself and the office of Bagshot baillif in the forest of Windsor which was paid from the revenues of the county of Oxford.[169] This emphasis on the source of the fees makes it probable that the list was compiled from exchequer records rather than from a list of grants.

The list is a copy of one compiled under Henry VI. William Standard, listed as porter at Windsor, was appointed in 1418 and confirmed in 1422. Richard Ludlow, Bagshot baillif, held the office alone from 1437, although he had shared it earlier with John Hargreave.[170] Such lists could remain in use for several generations. A similar exchequer list, compiled in 1377, was still being cited as authority for fees granted by Richard III.[171] The fees noted in the Henry VI list are on the whole the same as those in the Edward IV lists. There are, however, a few striking differences. The Henry VI list gives a fee of £20 for the combined offices of constable and porter of Tickhill, compared with £9 14s. 0d. in 1482/3. The receiver of the same lordship received £25 from Henry VI against £5 from his successor.[172] These figures may represent a genuine change in the fees paid to the officials but it is more likely that the compiler of the Henry VI list has noted the total payment made to the constable and receiver, including an element for something other than their wages, such as the wages of their subordinates or the costs of their office. If this is the case it probably represents an error rather than common policy since the Tickhill fees are considerably higher than comparable fees elsewhere in the Henry VI list.

The Gentry Lists

The lists occupy ff.330-2b and provide the names of the upper gentry resident in about half the English counties. From internal evidence they seem to have been revised up to the early months of 1485, but there is no heading or other indication of their purpose.[173] The men named under each county do not correspond exactly to the personnel of any of Richard III's commissions. On the other hand, almost all the men in each list did serve on commissions of some sort in the course of the reign. In some cases all the men listed were JPs, as in the Huntingdon list. In the long Suffolk list, by contrast, thirteen of the twenty seven men named were JPs and a further eleven were commissioners of array. The lists apparently represent a pool of local gentry upon which the king could draw for commissions or other administrative functions. Inclusion thus presupposes a certain degree of loyalty to the crown. The only 1483 rebels to be noted are the two Gaynesfords under Surrey and by this date they seem to have been making their way back into favour.[174]

The lists, unlike most commissions, are confined to men resident in the county concerned. This does not necessarily mean that all the men were natives. The Hertfordshire list includes three men from northern families, all of whom had a landed interest in the county. Richard Scrope was a younger brother of lord Scrope of Bolton and the family, although primarily northern in its interests, had held Sawbridgeworth (Hertfordshire) for most of the century.[175] Edward Goldesburgh had acquired interests in the county by his marriage to Joan Walys, the widow of Ralph Grey the younger.[176] Nicholas Leventhorpe was a member of the West Riding family, of which the main branch had moved south under the Lancastrians, possibly as a result of a connection with the Scropes, from whom they held land in Sawbridgeworth. Nicholas held extensive royal office in the north but in 1476 he married the widow of lord de la Ware, the head of one of the leading Hertfordshire families.[177] The lists also differ from commissions in entering each name under one county only, although this must have entailed some arbitrary decisions. Thomas Wortley is deleted under Derby but entered under Stafford and Thomas Cokesay is removed from the Gloucestershire list in favour of the Warwickshire list, although he served on commissions for both.

Gentry lists in some form must have been a standard reference work in medieval government. The selection of commissioners presupposes a fairly detailed knowledge of the local gentry, as do the financial expedients of late medieval kings. Richard's commissioners for loans were not left entirely to their own devices: the crown was able to supply them with the names of the local gentry and the amount they were thought able to lend. Henry VII, when checking on the men eligible for knighthood who had not yet taken up the honour, was able to call on an extremely detailed list of lords, knights and gentlemen.[178] A surviving Yorkist list of the Hertfordshire gentry may also have had a financial origin.[179] The Harley 433 gentry lists, by contrast, are political or administrative compilations. They are accordingly more selective than the examples cited above. The Hertfordshire list in Harley 433 provides nine names, compared with seventy eight in the Yorkist list and twenty one in the Henry VII list. All, however, testify to the importance for a fifteenth-century king of a detailed knowledge of the gentry.

THE MANUSCRIPT

Harleian MS 433 is a collection of material from the signet archives of the reigns of Edward V and Richard III. It is made up of a number of distinct elements: four separate registers of abstracts and a quantity of individual memoranda and letters. Although the volume is strictly speaking a compilation it was nonetheless the work of a single department over a limited period of time and the overall impression it gives is one of considerable uniformity. Apart from their subject matter there is little distinction between the various elements of the volume. They are all written on similar paper and the same hands recur throughout the manuscript. The only major variation in paper type occurs not between sections but within the two registers from Richard III's reign, which are partially written on smaller sheets of paper. These are watermarked with variants of the gothic P whereas the more common paper type bears a non-representational watermark, reproduced in volume IV.

The present binding is modern, but the page order dates back at least to the eighteenth century, when Wanley compiled his calendar, and probably much earlier. There is evidence that the two Richard III registers, at least, were in their present relationship by the reign of Henry VII or VIII. The register of grants is followed by a blank page (f.106) on the dorse of which are various jottings including a copy of the first entry of the register of financial matters. The same hand has then noted the opening of a grant made by Henry VII or his son. Moreover if, as was argued above, the volume survived because parts of it remained in use under the Tudors it seems probable that it was already bound by that date or the extraneous sections, in Tudor eyes, would have been separated from the parts still in use. The picture which emerges is of an unbound collection of signet abstracts and memoranda left in the signet office at Richard III's death, which were gathered together and bound soon after that, probably as a matter of signet office routine. An early, routine binding would help to explain the absence of a formal title page. The first folio of the volume is little more than a collection of scribbles and jottings on the blank side of a page of miscellaneous memoranda (see frontispiece to volume I).

The volume is a substantial one, measuring 8½" × 12" and including 340 folios. Most of the pages are now single sheets and there is no indication how many of these were originally grouped in signatures. Thirteen signatures do, however, still survive, and their position is noted in the summary of contents which follows. Most occur within the registers and accordingly shed little light on the compilation of the manuscript. One, however, does link the end of Edward V's second register with some early signet material of Richard III. Another demonstrates that the ordinances for the household in the north were entered immediately after the diplomatic correspondence. These taken together form a chronological sequence and the signature may represent part of the collection of signet letters enrolled in full, the existence of which was suggested above. [180]

Summary of contents

All entries are *temp*. Richard III unless otherwise stated.

NOTES TO THE INTRODUCTION

1. *A Catalogue of the Harleian Manuscripts in the British Museum* (4 volumes, 1802-12) I p.256. My thanks are due to Professor C. Ross and Dr. G. Harriss for reading this Introduction in draft.

2. *Historic Doubts on the Life and Reign of King Richard the Third* in *The Works of Horatio Walpole, Earl of Orford* (6 volumes, 1798-1818) II pp.132, 174-5. The letters are to the duchess of York and the bishop of Lincoln: British Library, Harleian MS 433 ff.2b, 340b. References to this manuscript are henceforth cited by folio number only.

3. In March 1768 Walpole was lent a copy of an illustrated roll of the lords of Warwick and wrote to Gray: 'Mr Astle is to come to me tomorrow to explain the writing': *Horace Walpole's Correspondence* ed. W.S. Lewis (39 volumes, Oxford 1937-74) XIV p.178.

4. A.R. Myers 'Richard III and Historical Tradition', *History* 53 (1968) pp.194-8.

5. *Grants Etc from the Crown during the Reign of Edward the Fifth* ed. J.G. Nichols, Camden Society 60 (1854); *Letters and Papers Illustrative of the Reigns of Richard III and Henry VII* ed. J. Gairdner, Rolls Series (2 volumes, 1861-3). Gairdner calendared, but did not print in full, the diplomatic letters which had already been printed elsewhere: *ibid* I pp. lxv-lxix.

6. J. Gairdner *History of the Life and Reign of Richard the Third* (revised edition, Cambridge 1898).

7. *Ibid* p.145.

8. J. Otway-Ruthven *The King's Secretary and the Signet Office in the XV Century* (Cambridge 1939) pp.2, 117-8.

9. B.P. Wolffe *The Crown Lands 1461-1536* (1970) pp.59-65

10. The main categories of material included in the volume are discussed in detail in the second part of the Introduction. A summary of contents is printed at the end of the Introduction.

11. *Letters and Papers* I p. xiv; and compare *Grants Etc from the Crown* p.vi.

12. *The King's Secretary* pp.117-8. The most detailed discussion of the manuscript is, however, provided by Dr Wolffe *loc cit*.

13. f.23, Buckingham's grant of the justiciarships ends with the words *ut antea in Regestro* (as earlier in the register) which must refer to Edward V's register of grants.

14. f.22.

15. Public Record Office, Duchy of Lancaster, DL 42/20, enrolments of material passing the duchy great seal *temp*. Richard III.

16. f.107.

17. An exception is a signet warrant directed to the keeper of the privy seal, ordering him to make out letters to the treasurer authorising the payment of £14 11s. 5d. to John Belle. The warrant is entered in both registers: ff.34b, 138b. The privy seal warrant also survives: PRO Warrants for Issues, E 404/78/2/24.

18. Rigby: ff.71b, 132. Fouleshirst: ff.84, 187b.

19. f.9

20. *Grants Etc from the Crown* p.xxvii.
21. *The King's Secretary* pp.122-3.
22. I am most grateful to Professor T.J. Brown and Dr H.V. Baron for discussing the manuscript with me. In fairness to them both I should add that the conclusions which follow are my own.
23. The Lynom letter (f.340b) is followed by a note that Thomas Drury was paid 6s. in 9 Henry VII for searching the records for a copy. This, however, almost certainly refers to the fragment of a concord made in the reign of Edward II which follows. For this page, see the frontispiece to volume III.
24. For this point see the section on the manuscript at the end of this Introduction.
25. Sir John Wode, who died in August 1484, has been deleted, but Richard Scrope, who died in June 1485, has not: f.331-331b; J.S. Roskell 'Sir John Wood of Molesey' *Surrey Archaeological Collections* 56 (1959) pp.27-8; *Testamenta Eboracensia* III Surtees Society 45 (1864) p.299.
26. For example, on f.313 grants to George Brown and to William and Edmund Hawte, all implicated in the 1483 rebellions, have crosses beside them. On f.313b John Howard's fee as one of Edward IV's carvers, superseded when Richard made him duke of Norfolk, has a cross in the margin, as have two grants to lord Hastings who was executed in June 1483.
27. In places one script spans a change of month, as on f.60b where *Aprile* is entered in the margin but the entries continue without a break.
28. ff.273b-274.
29. *Rotuli Parliamentorum* VI pp.336-9.
30. It is not always made clear, for instance, that a grant is an *inspeximus*, on f.37 the grants to Swift and Roo are both confirmations: PRO DL 42/20 ff.13, 14v-15.
31. The dorse of Dynham's letter is blank, suggesting that it was not the first in the series of diplomatic letters but was placed with them later.
32. *The King's Secretary* pp.114-7.
33. A number of entries in the register of grants conclude with a variant of *prout plenius patet in billa* (as appears more fully in the bill), for instance ff.22, 27. In one case the entry is more specific and refers to a signed bill: f.22 (licence to de Nigrono).
34. PRO Signet warrants *temp.* Richard III C 81/1392. Of the twenty six warrants in this collection, fifteen do not appear in Harley 433.
35. *York Civic Records* I ed A. Raine, Yorkshire Archaeological Society 98 (1938) pp. 109, 115-6; *Historical Manuscripts Commission, Rutland* I (1888) pp.7-8.
36. *The King's Secretary* p.116.
37. ff.273, 281b.
38. *The King's Secretary* pp.116-7.
39. For instance in the grant to John Stokes on f.27b, where it has been allowed to stand, and in the grant to Thomas Tunstall (f.30) where it has been deleted.
40. ff.15b, 16b-17.

41. PRO Signed bills C81/1530-1 contains a number of such petitions. In one case, Northumberland's petition for the office of great chamberlain, the secretary has added a request that the signed bill be taken as sufficient warrant: C 81/1530/4.

42. *The King's Secretary* p.116.

43. For example, the king's letters to the towns of Southampton (f.115b) and Gloucester (f.127b).

44. *The King's Secretary* p.115

45. The last dated entry for Edward V's reign is June 11 (f.231). King was in the Tower by June 21: *The Stonor Letters and Papers 1290-1483* ed C.L. Kingsford, Camden Society third series 19-20 (1919) II p.161.

46. *The King's Secretary* pp.158-9. William Herbert certainly remained in the signet office after the death of Edward IV: PRO C 81/1392/1. So probably did Richard Decons, although references to him in Richard's reign are in other contexts: ff.195b, 199.

47. *Historia Croylandensis Continuatio* in *Rerum Anglicarum Scriptorum Veterum* I ed W. Fulman (Oxford 1684) p.564.

48. *The King's Secretary* p.115.

49. S.B. Chrimes *An Introduction to the Administrative History of Mediaeval England* (Oxford, 2nd ed 1959) p.259.

50. H.C. Maxwell-Lyte *Historical Notes on the Use of the Great Seal in England* (1926) pp.123-4; *Calendar of Patent Rolls 1446-52* p.203.

51. f.28b; PRO C 81/1392/5; *CPR 1476-85* p.413.

52. The signet warrants include only two orders to make out grants under the great seal: PRO C 81/1392/2, 5. The signed bills contain forty-eight petitions for grants, including pardons: C 81/1530-1.

53. PRO C 81/1531/36; E 404/78/3/2; *CPR 1476-85* p.449.

54. The appointment of John Elrington as constable of Windsor in October 1483 is warranted 'by the king' but no signed bill survives: *CPR 1476-85* p.367.

55. The duchy of Lancaster records shows that an occasional signed bill was noted in Harley 433. The appointment of Thomas Metcalfe as chancellor of the county palatine and duchy, warranted by signed bill, does appear in Harley 433 (f.5b) although subsequent grants warranted by signed bill do not: PRO DL 42/20 f.3.

56. PRO C 81/1530/36.

57. *Ibid*/18.

58. Viscount Lovell and William Catesby, for instance, were made constable of Rockingham in a grant authorised by signed bill, although their numerous other grants went through the usual channels: *ibid* /28.

59. A.L. Brown 'The Authorization of Letters under the Great Seal' *Bulletin of the Institute of Historical Research* 37 (1964) pp.145-7 for the king's willingness to bypass the privy seal on occasion.

60. *Ibid* p.137.

61. *The King's Secretary* p.54.

62. PRO E 404/78/2.

63. *The King's Secretary* pp.75, 87.

64. A.B. Emden *A Biographical Register of the University of Cambridge to 1500* (Cambridge 1963) pp.275-7; C.L. Scofield *The Life and Reign of Edward IV* (2 volumes, 1923) II p.205.

65. R.E. Horrox *The Extent and Use of Crown Patronage under Richard III* unpublished Cambridge PhD thesis (1977) pp.29-31, 43-5.

66. f.217b.

67. *CPR 1476-85* pp.367, 418, 454, 463, 506, 539, 540; ff.101, 289.

68. *The King's Secretary* pp.84-5; *CPR 1476-85* p.460.

69. *Historical Manuscripts Commission: Wells* II (1914) pp.692-3.

70. *The King's Secretary* p.81. In 1485 Kendale was seised of the manors of Pedington, Avonscourt and Wick in the parish of Berkeley (Gloucestershire): *Inquisitions post mortem* Henry VII volume III no 654; and compare f.309b. It is usually assumed, for example by P.M. Kendall *Richard the Third* (1955) p.488, that Kendale was killed at Bosworth, but the inquisition states only that he had been attainted, not that he was dead. He survived to marry Elizabeth, the widow of the Richard Charlton who died on Richard's side at Bosworth: *CPR 1485-94* p.439; *Inq.p.m.* Henry VII volume I no. 51, volume III nos. 732, 917. Kendale should not be confused with his three namesakes: Richard III's yeoman of the crown; Edward IV's controller of the works; and a brother of the order of St. John, one of Richard's councillors.

71. Kendale was in Gloucester's service, as clerk if not secretary, by December 1474: C.H. Hunter Blair 'Two Letters Patent from Hutton John near Penrith, Cumberland' *Archaeologia Aeliana* 39 (1961), although Hunter Blair mistranscribes his name as Randale. He was secretary by 1482: *Household Books of John duke of Norfolk and Thomas earl of Surrey 1481-1490* ed J. Payne Collier, Roxburghe Club (1844) p.161; see also *Stonor Letters and Papers* II p.82.

72. Horrox *op.cit.* pp.221-4.

73. *The King's Secretary* pp.112-3.

74. *Ibid* p.158; PRO C81/1392/1, 5; ff.34, 100b. The secretary should not be confused with his two namesakes, one 'of Raglan' and the other an esquire of the body: f.30.

75. *CPR 1476-85* p.541 where he is described as 'king's clerk'; PRO C 81/1531/68, expediting a signet letter; A.B. Emden *A Biographical Register of the University of Oxford to 1500* (3 volumes, Oxford 1957-9) III p.1708. It is not clear whether the royal clerk can be identified with a namesake who was clerk of the lead mines in the Neville lordship of Middleham in 1465: G.M. Coles *The Lordship of Middleham, especially in Yorkist and early Tudor times* unpublished Liverpool MA thesis (1961) p.177.

76. In January 1484 Brown was paid arrears as late clerk of the little bag: PRO E 404/78/2/29.

77. *CPR 1476-85* pp.410, 412, 438.

78. *Calendar of Close Rolls 1476-85* nos. 295, 314.

79. *The Red Book of the Exchequer* ed Hubert Hall, Rolls Series (3 volumes 1886-96) I p.iv.

80. A few entries are in the form of precedents, such as the entry *pro prebendo* on f.79b, but these, scattered at random throughout the volume, must have been all but useless for reference purposes. The only group of precedents is the list of religious precedents on f.21b.

81. f.339; the note refers to money received from John Heron, Henry VII's treasurer of the chamber. This page is reproduced in volume IV.

82. *Red Book* I p.ii.

83. ff.293-5.

84. C.E. Wright *Fontes Harleiani* (1972) p.321; Wanley's introduction to the calendar of the manuscript seems to imply some doubt on the connection with Burghley: *Catalogue of the Harleian Manuscripts* I p.256.

85. B.W. Beckingsale *Burghley, Tudor Statesman 1520-1598* (1967) pp.250-2; Burghley may have come across the volume during his time as secretary.

86. A.L. Brown *The Early History of the Clerkship of the Council* (Glasgow 1969) p.27; *The King's Secretary* pp.163-4.

87. *Ibid* pp. 118-23.

88. *Loc cit* p.xxvii.

89. ff.11-12, 17b, 18b.

90. f.221-221b.

91. *Grants Etc from the Crown* p.vi; *The King's Secretary* p.117.

92. ff.228b-229b.

93. The gap was due to the vigil and feast of Pentecost, which fell on May 17-18 that year.

94. *CPR 1476-85* pp.348, 349.

95. The cessation of signet activity gives some support to the traditional view that Hastings was executed on June 13, and not, as Mrs Hanham has argued, on June 20. For the dispute over the dating of his execution see: A. Hanham 'Richard III, Lord Hastings and the Historians' *English Historical Review* 87 (1972); B.P. Wolffe 'When and Why did Hastings lose his Head?' *EHR* 89 (1974); Hanham 'Hastings Redivivus' *EHR* 90 (1975); Wolffe 'Hastings Reinterred' *EHR* 91 (1976); J.A.F. Thomson 'Richard III and lord Hastings' *BIHR* 48 (1975); Anne F. Sutton and P.W. Hammond 'The Problems of Dating and the Dangers of Re-dating: the Acts of Court of the Mercers Company of London 1453-1527' *Journal of Society of Archivists* 6(1978).

96. *Stonor Letters and Papers* II p.161.

97. *CPR 1476-85* p.351.

98. *Grants Etc from the Crown* p.vi.

99. ff.16b, 225b; 'An Extract relating to the Burial of K. Edward IV' *Archaeologia* I (1770) p.350; *CPR 1467-77* p.548.

100. Horrox *op cit* pp.29-30.

101. Dominic Mancini *The Usurpation of Richard III* ed C.A.J. Armstrong (2nd ed, Oxford 1969) pp.84-5; compare J.S. Roskell 'The Office and Dignity of Protector of England' *EHR* 68 (1953) p.227.

102. ff.10b, 14b, 223, 226; for other examples see ff.13b, 14b, 17, 221.

103. f.323; *Rot Parl* VI pp.242-3.

104. f.221.
105. *Stonor Letters and Papers* II p.161; *Grants Etc from the Crown* pp.xl-xli.
106. f.221.
107. *Rot Parl* VI pp. 245-6; Fulford was attainted by lord Scrope at Exeter but was back in favour by autumn 1484 when he was made sheriff of Devon: R. Holinshed *Chronicles of England, Scotland and Ireland* (6 volumes, 1807-8) III p.421; *Calendar of Fine Rolls 1471-85* no. 860.
108. ff.8b, 16b, 18, 19.
109. f.86.
110. Brown 'Authorization of Letters' p.115.
111. f.30b; PRO E 404/78/2/18.
112. PRO DL 42/20. f.9-9b.
113. *CPR 1476-85* pp.413, 461, 541.
114. *Rot Parl* VI p.246.
115. f.29; Middleton was in Gloucester's household by 1480: *Test Ebor* III pp.209-10.
116. This distinction is partly recognised by the Black Book of Edward IV's household which states that serjeants at arms, unlike most household men, were appointed by letters patent and received fees from county issues: A.R. Myers *The Household of Edward IV* (Manchester 1959) p.131.
117. This phase occupies approximately ff.22-29 of the register.
118. Horrox *op cit* chapter 5.
119. A.J. Pollard 'The tyranny of Richard III' *Journal of Medieval History* 3 (1977) pp.157-62.
120. The ballad of *Bosworth ffeilde* apparently includes a contemporary list of those who fought at Bosworth: *Bishop Percy's Folio Manuscript* ed J.W. Hales and F.J. Furnivall (3 volumes, 1868) III pp. 233 *et seq*.
121. For the relevance of this register to chamber finance see Wolffe *op cit* pp.60-1.
122. f.215.
123. ff.123, 149b; for the identification of the Redeness family with Holderness see M.G.A. Vale *Piety, Charity and Literacy among the Yorkshire Gentry 1370-1480*, Borthwick Papers 50 (1976) p.26. Holderness was a Stafford lordship.
124. f.209b.
125. ff.42, 199b; *CPR 1476-85* p.390.
126. f.204b.
127. *CPR 1476-85* pp.367, 368, 372, 375, 381.
128. *Ibid* p.528; ff.99, 201b.
129. *CPR 1476-85* p.387; f.105.
130. Wolffe *op cit* pp.60-6, Document 14.
131. ff.269-70, 290-2b; Wolffe Document 14 (30, 33).
132. ff.264b-5; R. Reid *The King's Council in the North* (1921) pp.59-61.
133. ff.182b, 183, 184, 212b.
134. ff.271-2; Wolffe Document 14 (32).
135. ff.270-1; Wolffe Document 14 (31).

136. Compare, for instance, Caxton's *Order of Chivalry*, dedicated to Richard III, which states that local office should go to knights, because they are worthy to have authority over others: *The Book of the Ordre of Chyvalry* ed Alfred T.P. Byles, Early English Text Society, original series 168(1926) p.29; M. Kekewich 'Edward IV, William Caxton, and Literary Patronage in Yorkist England' *Modern Languages Review* 66 (1971) p.487.

137. *Plumpton Correspondence* ed Thomas Stapleton, Camden Society old series 4 (1839) pp.32-3.

138. f.55b; Hassall was subsequently restored by Henry VII: *Rot Parl* VI p.380.

139. Croyland pp.567, 571-2.

140. Scofield *Edward IV* II p.333; C. Ross *Edward IV* (1974) p.386; Mancini pp.78-9.

141. A. Steel *Receipt of the Exchequer 1377-1485* (Cambridge 1954) pp.317-20.

142. G.L. Harriss 'Aids, Loans and Benevolences' *Historical Journal* 6 (1963).

143. Croyland pp.571-2.

144. Spicer, an esquire of the body and gentlemen usher of the chamber, held numerous receiverships in Wales and the south west; Greenhill was a yeoman usher.

145. Gairdner *Richard the Third* p.198; Steel *op cit* p.319.

146. *CPR 1476-85* p.507.

147. ff.95, 98.

148. *CPR 1476-85* p.516.

149. *Ibid* p.372; f.287.

150. ff.73, 168, 285; *CPR 1476-85* p.513.

151. PRO Special Collections, SC 11/827, schedule of reserved rents. The schedule was drawn up under the privy seal in May 1485 for the information of the Exchequer.

152. *Ibid;* f.287b.

153. f.282. Neither grant appears in the patent rolls. The Harley 433 list apparently reflects the situation of March 1484 when Thirlwall received Bastendon (Berkshire) and Markenfield Glutton. In February 1485, however, Thirlwall was described as the holder of Farmham and Glutton as well as of Bastendon ff.45, 16lb, 208v.

154. Neither list can be related to the surviving inquisitions into the lands of attainted persons, which do not provide adequate details of the grants subsequently made of the land: PRO Chancery Inquisitions, C 145/330.

155. ff.97b, 288b.

156. *CPR 1467-77* pp.297, 466-7, 560; *ibid 1476-85* p.359.

157. ff.124b-125; B.P. Wolffe *The Royal Desmesne in English History* (1971) p.193.

158. *CPR 1476-85* pp.434, 531.

159. *Ibid* p.450.

160. f.272-272b; although this arrangement was not finalised until October 1484 the crown was using the Mowbray lands as a source of patronage

from the outset of the reign: *CPR 1476-85* pp.376, 414, 422, 438, 445, 511, 542-3; J. Smyth *Lives of the Berkeleys* ed J. Maclean (3 volumes, Gloucester 1883-5) II pp.126-7.

161. f.117b. This page forms the frontispiece to Volume II.
162. f.31.
163. PRO SC 11/827.
164. f.311b; *CPR 1461-7* p.24; *ibid 1467-77* p.90.
165. *Ibid 1476-85* p.221; f.311b.
166. *CPR 1467-77* p.599; *ibid 1476-85* pp.139-40.
167. *Ibid 1461-7* p.293
168. f.339.
169. ff.336, 337.
170. *CPR 1422-9* p.43; *ibid 1434-41* pp.49, 124.
171. *Ibid 1476-85* p.36, a grant to Roland Thornburgh of the keeping of the gate of Carlisle.
172. ff.318, 338.
173. For the dating of this list see note 25 above.
174. f.331b; A. Conway 'The Maidstone Sector of Buckingham's Rebellion' *Archaeologia Cantiana* 37 (1925) pp.116-8.
175. *Victoria County History of Hertfordshire* (4 volumes, 1902-14) III p.337; *Test Ebor* III p.299.
176. *VCH Hertfordshire* II p.197; IV p.82.
177. *Ibid* 111 pp.102, 337, 340; R. Clutterbuck *The History and Antiquities of the County of Hertford* (3 volumes, 1815-27) III pp.206-7; *CCR 1476-85* no. 75.
178. BL Harleian MS 6166 pp.95-123.
179. BL Harleian MS 1546.
180. The entries relating to the household in the north are not dated, although the household is said to have been set up in July 1484. The context, however, suggests that the entries were not made until Michaelmas that year: ff.264b-265, 269-70.
181. *VCH Middlesex* (5 volumes, 1911-76) V p.329. This is one of the few private deeds included in the manuscript and its presence in the signet archive is perhaps explained by the fact that Richard Sturgeon, the donor of the land conveyed to St Bartholomew, had been a royal clerk.

TEXT

[f1b]   parcelles of plate Received of henry horne at Gilford
Furst at gilford a crosse gilt with a fote and marye and John of the same
Item a Chales of silvere & gilt
Item a paxbrede of silvere & gild
Item ij Candilstykkis for the Awtere of silvere & parcelle gilt
Item a halywater stob with the spryngelle of silvere

        the xx day of Februarij Anno primo Ricardi iij^{cij}
(Memorandum that there (is) was put in my Maistere Casket iij obligacions of
Marchauntes of Londone bounden to the king & to John Sapcottes/that is to
say one of martyn harlewes of xix li paiable at Candilmesse last past A nothere
of John Skynneres of (xij li) xlij li paiable at the said Feste of Candilmesse

Anothere of Nicholas Penwaren of xxvij li paiable at the said fest

Item a obligacione of Richard Turges of the summe of xl li / xx li thereof paiable
at the Fest of pasche & xx li at Michilmas next cumyng Datum xxj° die
Februarij Anno primo Ricardi iij^{cij}

Item (an ob) two obligacions of the lady Dacres bounden to John K one of the
summe of CC marc paiable at Witsonday next comyng A nothere of the summe
of CC marc paiable at Alhalowmas next comyng Datum sexto die Februaij
Anno primo)

For the Stone
Take a lb of Ripe Cherys and stampe theim stones and alle and put the same
into the mylke of a Cowe being of oon color as ye doo ale to make a posset and
drinke it during the Chery season twyse or thries & that yere ye shal suffre no
peyne

[f2] Ricardus &c. Omnibus &c. salutem. Cum celsitudine magnificencieque
principum & regum officium existat proprium/magnificencias liberalitatesque
facere honoribusque decorare / Eosque fideli animo eis serviunt vel servire
cupiunt presertim in diebus & festis solempnibus quibis similia facere consue-
verunt / Igitur quia vos nobilis vir Gaufridus de Sasiola Legatus et enbaxiator
serenissime Domine Regine Ispaniarum Consanguinee nostre Carissime Con-
siliariusque servitatis sue ad nos in legacionem destinatus / interfuistis solempni

festo creacionique dilectissimi primogeniti nostri principis Edwardi / Et impenditis vos in servicium dicte serenissime domine Regine & nostrum / amatisque inter nos bonam pacem & consideracionem fidelique animo viribus eam procuratis ob contemplacionem dicte serenissime domine Regine consanguinee nostre carissime & ob honorem tanti festi & propter amorem & affeccionem quam in vos gerimus et quia scimus vos esse de nobili genere creamus & facimus vos militem decoramusque honorem militari per imposicionem (colleri) collari aurei quod vobis imponimus in collo vestro & per trinam percussionem regulis nostri gladij super humeros vestros cum verbis decentibus & per alia insignia nostra prout nobis moris est in similibus conficiendis. Volumus quod vos dicto honere militari & insignijs nostris uti tam in regno nostro quam extra ubique Regionum & terrarum tamquam dono Regio ad honorem decoremque vobis dato. In Cuius rei testimonium mandamus vobis dari has nostras presentes litteras sub nostro privato Sigillo que acta fuerunt in Civitate Eboracum in (ab) aula Regia presentibus dominis spiritualibus et temporalibus Regie Curie in actu creacionis dicti serenissimi principis Edwardi die nativitatis beate virginis Marie que fuit octava die mensis Septembris Anno domini 1483 & Regni nostri Anno primo /

[Richard etc. to all etc. greeting. Since it is the office of princes and kings, befitting their rank and magnificence, to show munificence and liberality and to adorn with honours those who serve them faithfully or desire to serve them, especially on days and solemn festivals on which it has been the custom to do the like, therefore, since you, the nobleman Geoffrey de Sasiola, emissary and ambassador of the most serene lady, our very dear kinswoman, the Queen of Spain, and counsellor in her service, were sent to us as ambassador and were present at the solemn feast and creation of our dearly beloved firstborn son Edward as Prince, and since you devote yourself to the service of the said most serene lady the queen and to ours, and faithfully desire and work for good peace and consideration between us, out of regard for the said most serene lady the queen our very dear kinswoman and in honour of so great a feast and on account of the love and affection we bear you and because we know you to be of noble birth, we create and make you a knight and decorate you with the honour of knighthood by the bestowal of the golden collar which we set on your neck and by the threefold stroke of the blade of our sword on your shoulders with fitting words and by the other insignia we are accustomed to use in such ceremonies. We desire you to use the said knighthood and our insignia both within our realm and in any regions and lands outside it as a royal gift given to you for honour and glory. In witness whereof we command that these our letters patent under our privy seal be given to you, which were drawn up in the city of York in the royal palace in the presence of the lords spiritual and temporal of the king's court on the occasion of the creation of the said serene Prince Edward on the nativity of the blessed Virgin Mary, the eighth day of the month of September in the year of the Lord 1483 and the first year of our reign.]

/ Fidelitas /

I shalbe feithfulle and true / and feithe & trouthe shalle bere to you my soverayne lord / and to youre heires kinges of England of lyff and of lymme / and of erthly worshippe forto lyve and dye ayenst alle people / and diligently I (shalle attende) shalbe attendaunt unto youre nedes and besinesse aftere my witte and power / And truly I shalle knowlage & doo the services due of the temporaltes of myne abbey of C / The whiche I clayme to hold of you soverayne lord / and the whiche ye yeve and yelde me / and to you and to youre commaundement in that / that apperteynethe & bilongethe to me for my said temporaltes I shalbee obeissaunt as god me help and his seintes

I A become true and feithfulle liegeman unto my soverain lord Richard iij^{de} by the grace of god king of England etc and to his heires kinges of England & to him and theim my feithe and trouthe shal bere during my lif naturalle and with him and in his cause and quarelle at alle tymes shal take his parte and be redy to leve and dy ayenst alle erthly creatures and utterly endevor me to the Resistence (of) and subpressing of his ennemyes Rebelles and traytors if I shal any knowe to the uttermost of my power and no thing courte that in any wise may be hurting to his noble & royal persone so god me helpe and thise holy evaungeliers

[f2b] Madam I recommaunde me to you as hertely as is to me possible Beseching you in my most humble (wise) and effectuouse wise of youre daly blissing to my Synguler comfort & defence in my nede And madam I hertely beseche you that I may often here from you to my Comfort / And suche Newes as bene here (here) my servaunt Thomas Bryane this berere shalle shew you / to whome please it you to yeve credence unto / And madam I beseche you to be good & graciouse lady to my lord my Chambreleyn to be youre officer in Wilshire in suche as Colingbourne had / I trust he shalle therein do you good service And that it please you that by this berere I may understande youre pleasure in this behalve / And I pray god sende you thaccomplishement of youre noble desires Written at Pountfreit the iij^{de} day of Juyne with the hande of
Youre most humble Son
Ricardus Rex

[f3] Quinto die Maij Anno primo Regis Edwardi quinti
Rex etc Custodi sigilli nostri Comitatus nostri Marchie salutem vobis mandamus quod sub dicto sigillo nostro in vestra Custodia nunc existente litteras patentes fieri faciatis in forma sequente / Rex etc Reverendo in Christo patri Thome divina providentia Herefordie Episcopo salutem Ad ecclesiam parochialem de Pembrigge vestre diocesis per mortem ultimi incumbentis eiusdem vacantem & ad nostram presentationem pleno iure spectantem dilectum nobis in Christo Johannem Geffrey Capellanum vobis presentamus Rogantes quatinus eundem Johannem ad ecclesiam predictam admittere ipsumque Rectorem in eadem Canonice instituere Ceteraque peragere que vestro in hac parte incumbunt officio pastorali velitis cum favore In cuius etc Teste meipso etc Et hee littere nostre vobis erunt sufficiens warrantum Datum nostro sub signeto apud villam Sancti Albani   die Maij Anno regni nostri primo

4

[On the fifth day of May in the first year of King Edward V
The king etc to the keeper of our seal of the earldom of March; greeting. We order you that you have letters patent made under our said seal, now in your custody, in the following form: The king etc to the reverend father in Christ Thomas, by divine providence Bishop of Hereford; greeting. We present to you, to the parish church of Pembrigge in your diocese, being vacant through the death of the last incumbent, and being in our gift by full right, our beloved in Christ John Geffrey, chaplain, asking that you will, with favour, admit the same John to the aforesaid church, and canonically install him as rector in the same and do the other things which are incumbent on your pastoral office in this regard. In which etc. In witness by me myself etc. And these our letters will be sufficient warrant to you. Given under our signet at the town of St Albans on the　　　　　day of May in the first year of our reign.]

Edward prince of Wales Duc of Cornwaille and Erle of Chestre Furstbegotten son of the right high & mighti prince Richard the iij^{de} by the grace of god King of England & of Fraunce and lord of Irland. To alle the knightes squiers gentils officers fermoures tenauntes & Reseantes within oure principalite in North Wales thise oure lettres forto see or here greting / Forsomuche as we at the commaundement of oure said moost drad lord and Fadere / and by thadvise of the lords of his Counselle / have ordeigned & assigned oure righte trusty & (welbeloved) righte entierly beloved Cousyne the duc of Buckkingham and suche othere Commissioners as by his discrescione shalbe deputed and ap-pointed forto take & Receive alle maner youre attendaunces Reconisances or tallages now unto us due and accustumed amonges you and the dayes of payment of the same Recognysances or tallages to appointe and prefix you and alle othere thinges to doo & execute in oure name aftere the custume of oure principalite of Wales and the cuntre there of olde tyme had & used / We therefore wolle and charge you alle & every of you that unto oure said Cousyne and Comissioners soo by him appoynted at a certaine day and place by theim unto you to be prefixed ye duely make before them youre said attendaunce & Recoignisaunces / over that doyng & payng youre tallages to us due and paiable in that behalve and alle othere thinges according to the said olde usages without failling as ye entende to advoid my said lordes displeasure and oures Yeven etc at York the xvjth day of Septembre the first yere of my said lordes Reigne

A like lettre for the principalite of Suth Wales

[f3b blank]

[f4] The names of horses being at grisse in havering parc
First liard whiche came from (Fichingham) Excetre trotting At Haveryng
liard Clervax of Croft. ambling there
The Whit whiche was Sir Rauf Hastinges. Ambling there

Baiard Babingtone. Ambling there
liard Strangwisshe ambling At Nottingham Greke
Baiard Rither. Ambling (th) Averyng
Liard Cultone. trotting there
The litille Whit of Knaresburghe ambling (h) at Nottingham/Norfolk
Thehoby whiche Maister potiere rode on in the west (grisse) contre. Ambling
Master peter Baxter
(The gray Gelding of Savelles trotting)
My ladys gray gelding Ambling at haveryng
liard Carlile trotting
liard Norffolk ambling at haveryng
(The whit gelding of the vicars of ledes Ambling here at Nottingham Gevene
to Jamys dale)
[above bracketted to] Summa xiiij

The names of horses being at grisse in holdernesse
liard Mountfort Ambling there
powisshe Tomlynsone here at Nottingham   [above bracketted to] Summa ij
Item a horse a Thorpe with Sir Jamys Danby there
Item a horse with Master Langton whiche was Sir John Constables Ambling at
Nottingham, for the sommer
Item a hoby with John Smythe at (C) Kippes. Ambling at Nottingham
Item a mere and fole at Helmesley with henry pulley

The names of the horses being at Hardmet at Nottingham
Lyard Danby Ambling
liard hoton Ambling at Nottingham
(The gret gray that come frome Gervaux Ambling) Trotting Moungomery
(Baiard Culton Trotting)
Morel of Cristalle Trotting at Nottingham
(the some hors)
Blak Morelle the beris the moule trotting at Nottingham
The Whit of Gervaux ambling for my Lady at haveryng
The Walssh (hoby) nag for my lady ambling at haveryng
Jak at Berswelle
liard Bradshare ambling at Nottingham
the litille Blak gelding of (henry) Savelles ambling at Nottingham Wak'
the gret Bay Gelding of Gervaux trotting haveryng
Baiard Verncy trotting at Barswelle Montford
the Blak of holdernes Trotting at haveryng
(The hoby of Griffithe Ambling)   Curteis
[above group bracketted to] Summa xvj
the hoby of Kildare at Nottingham Flint
lyard Say at Haveryng
Beyard lanthony at Nottingham Sir degery
Beyard Chambreleyne at Nottingham
liard Bowes at Nottingham Thomas Bane
The dover hoby at Nottingham John Wright
(liard hartre lyngtone)   Warmyngtone

6

[f4b blank]

[f5]   The rewardes of Shireffes in diverse Counties

Kent	C li
Surrey & Sussex	xl li
Essex & Hertford	Ciiij^{xx}xviij li
Bedford & Buckingham	lxx li
Northampton	C li
Warrwick and Leicestre	Clx li
Notingham & Derby	C li
York	CCCxl li
Norffolk & Suffolk	Clx li
Stafford	C li
Oxonford & Berkeshire	iiij^{xx}jx li
Cantebrige & Huntingdon	lxvj li xiij s iiij d
Rotelland	xiij li vj s viij d
Salopia	C li

[In later hand, possibly seventeenth century] Lincoln not to be accountable in
the Exchequer but by Apprisement by his Oath or by the oath of his Deputy

[f5b blank]

[f6]   Xiij die Maij Anno primo Regis Edwardi v^{ti}
To John Latymer squier the Corodie or Sustentacione in thabbey of Cerne in
the Counte of Dorset as one William Ede decessed (and) had & the kinges grace
to directe his lettres to the seid Abbot willing him to graunt the same to the seid
John for terme of his liff in like forme as the seid William it had etc

Willelmo Catesby armigero officium Cancellarij Comitatus Marchie habendum
cum custodia sigilli Comitatus predicti per se (vel per sufficientem deputatum
suum) ad terminum vite sue cum huiusmodi vadijs & feodis prout magister
Ricardus Martyn' nuper Cancellarius Comitatus predicti in eodem habuit
percipiendis de exitibus Comitatus illius per manus Receptoris eiusdem pro
tempore existentis ad terminos Sancti Michaelis & Pasche equaliter ac cum
omnibus alijs proficuis &c. Dantes & concedentes eidem Willelmo plenam
auctoritatem & potestatem faciendi exequendi exercendi & componendi omnia
que ad officium illud pertinent facienda & exercitenda. Mandantes insuper
omnibus & singulis quorum interest quod eidem Willelmo in execucione officij
predicti intendentes sint & obedientes prout decet. Eo quod expressa mencio
&c. In cuius &c.

[To William Catesby, esquire, the office of chancellor of the earldom of
March, to hold with the custody of the seal of the aforesaid earldom in his
own person for the term of his life with such wages and fees as Master

Richard Martyn late chancellor of the said earldom had in the same post, to be received from the issues of that earldom by the hands of the receiver of the same for the time being at the terms of Michaelmas and Easter by equal portions and with all other profits etc., giving and granting to the same William full authority and power to do, undertake, exercise and perform all relating to that office that is to be done and performed, and moreover commanding all and singular concerned to be attentive and obedient to the same William in the execution of the aforesaid office as is fitting. That express mention etc. In witness whereof etc.]

To William Tunstalle thoffice of waterbailliff within the port & Towne of Wynchelse for terme of his liff by him or his sufficient depute with wages & Fees thereto due & accustumed and with alle other profites etc

Johanni Haward militi domino Haward officium Capitalis Senescalli ducatus Lancastrie in partibus australibus citra Trentham habendum per se vel per sufficientem deputatum suum a xxj die Aprilis ultimo preterito pro termino vite sue percipiendo annuatim in eodem officio omnia & omnimoda vadia feoda regarda & proficua dicto officio annexa debita spectancia sive pertinencia ad terminos soluccionis eorundem consuetos de exitibus proficuis redditibus firmis & revencionibus ducatus predicti per manus generalis Receptoris eiusdem pro tempore existentis Necnon percipiendo in eodem officio vj s. viij. per diem quolibet die singulis temporibus quando predictus Johannes seu deputatus suus equitaverit pro negocijs dicti ducatus seu presens & occupatus fuerit in consilio eiusdem ducatus apud Westmonasterium seu alibi de exitibus proficuis &c. predictis per manus dicti Receptoris generalis ducatus predicti pro tempore existentis durante vita eiusdem Johannis Dantes & concedentes eidem Johanni per presentes plenam potestatem & auctoritatem ad faciendum & exercendum totum id quod ad officium pertinet supradictum Necnon ad tenendum curias letas visus francplegij ac turnos infra ducatum predictum in partibus predictis. Damus insuper universis & singulis ministris ac officiarijs & alijs quorum interest in hac parte tenore presencium firmiter in mandatis quod eidem Johanni & eius deputato officium predictum debite exercentibus intendentes sint &c. Eo quod expressa mencio &c. In cuius &c.

[To John Haward, knight, Lord Haward, the office of chief steward of the duchy of Lancaster in the south parts this side of Trent to hold in his own person or by a sufficient deputy from the 21st day of April last past for the term of his life receiving annually in that office all and every kind of wages fees, rewards and profits attached, owed, belonging or pertaining to the said office at the terms customary for payment of the same out of the issues, profits, rents, farms, and revenues of the aforesaid duchy by the hand of the receiver general of the same for the time being. Receiving in addition in that office 6/8d per day each time the aforesaid John or his deputy rides abroad on the business of the said duchy or is present and engaged in the council of the said duchy at Westminster or elsewhere to be paid from the issues, profits etc. aforesaid by the hand of the said receiver general of the aforesaid duchy for the time being during the life of the same John. Giving and granting to the

8

same John by these presents full power and authority to perform and execute
all that pertains to the aforesaid office and also to hold court leets, views of
frankpledge and tourns within the aforesaid duchy in the aforesaid parts.
Moreover we give to all and singular ministers, officers and others concerned
in this by the tenor of these presents a firm command to obey John and his
deputy in the due exercise of the aforesaid office etc. That express mention
etc. In witness whereof etc.]

Willelmo Chauntre Clerico decanatum libere Capelle Regie hospicij Regis ex
dimissione Johannis Gunthorp' Clerici nuper decani libre Capelle predicte
habendum eidem Willelmo ad terminum vite sue cum suis Juribus & pertinencijs quibuscunque. In cuius &c. Teste &c.

[To William Chauntre, clerk, the deanery of the free chapel royal of the
king's household by the surrender of John Gunthorp, clerk, late dean of the
aforesaid free chapel. To hold by the same William for the term of his life
with all its rights and appurtenances whatever. In witness whereof etc.
Witness etc.]

[f6b]   xv° Die Maij.
Henrico dux Bukingham officium Constabularij omnium Castrorum nostrorum ac officium Senescalli omnium Castrorum Dominiorum Maneriorum
terrarum & tenementorum nostrorum in Comitatibus Salop' Hereford' Somerset' Dorset' & Wilteshire. Habendum & exercendum scilicet illa officia predictorum officiorum que modo vacant & ad presens ad donacionem nostram
spectant a die date presencium litterarum nostrarum & omnia dicta alia officia
modo plena & non vacancia immedietate postquam ex quacunque causa vacaverint prefato Duci per se vel per sufficientem deputatum suum aut sufficientes
deputatos suos capiendo & percipiendo in officijs illis & eorum quolibet vadiis
feodis Regardis & commoditatibus officijs illis & eorum cuilibet debitis &
consuetis per Manus Receptoris ballivi Firmarij seu aliorum occupatorum Castrorum Dominiorum Maneriorum terrarum & tenementorum predictorum &
cuiuslibet inde parcelle pro tempore existentium. Eo quod expressa mencio de
vero valore Annuo aut aliquo alio valore seu certitudine premissorum aut
eorum alicuius seu de alijs donis vel concessionibus per nos prefato duci ante
hec tempora factis in presentibus minime facta existit aut aliquo Statuto actu
ordinacione seu Restriccione incontrarium facta edita seu ordinata aut aliqua
alia Re causa vel materia quacunque non obstante. Et insuper volumus & per
presentes concedimus eidem Duci quod ipse habeat omnia premissa sibi ut
predicitur concessa absque compoto seu aliquo alio inde nobis Reddendo ac
absque fine seu feodo faciendo seu solvendo ac si presens concessio nostra in
aliquo premissorum invalidus seu minus sufficiens existit quod extunc Cancellarius Regni nostri Anglie qui pro tempore fuerit habeat plenam potestatem
& auctoritatem per presentes ad faciendum eidem duci tales alias litteras
patentes sub magno sigillo nostro quales in hac parte erunt sufficientes &
oportune. In cuius Rei &c. Teste &c.

[To Henry, Duke of Buckingham, the office of constable of all our castles and the office of steward of all our castles, lordships, manors, lands and tenements in the counties of Shropshire, Hereford, Somerset, Dorset, and Wiltshire. To hold and exercise those offices of the aforesaid offices which are now vacant and at present in our gift from the day of the giving of these our present letters and all the other said offices now filled and not vacant immediately after they become vacant for any reason, by the aforesaid duke in his own person or by a sufficient deputy or deputies, taking and receiving in those offices and in any of them the wages, fees, rewards and emoluments due and accustomed in those offices and any of them by the hand of the receiver, bailiff, farmer or other occupiers of the castles, lordships, manors, lands and tenements aforesaid and of any part thereof for the time being. Notwithstanding that express mention of the true annual value or any other value or specification of the aforesaid or any of them or of other gifts or grants made by us to the aforesaid duke previously is not made in these presents, and notwithstanding any other statute, act, order or restraint made, issued or ordered or any other thing, cause or matter to the contrary. And moreover we desire and by these presents grant to the same duke that he hold all the premises as granted above said without making any account or anything else to us for it and without making or paying fine or fee. And if our present grant is invalid or insufficient in any of the foregoing, then the chancellor of our realm of England for the time being shall have full power and authority by these presents to make for the same duke such other letters patent under our great seal as shall be sufficient and necessary in this respect. In witness whereof etc. Witness etc.]

Rex &c. Omnibus ad quos &c. salutem. Sciatis quod nos fidelitatem strenuitatem & circumspeccionem predilecti Consanguinej nostri Henrici Ducis Bukingham considerantes pro securitate persone nostre & Regni nostri Anglie ac conservacione pacis nostre Necnon tranquillitate Subditorum nostrorum in Comitatibus Salop' Hereford' Somerset' Dorset' & Wilteshire habenda & continuanda dedimus & concessimus & per presentes damus & concedimus eidem Consanguineo nostro supervisionem omnium subditorum nostrorum qui nunc sunt & qui imposterum erunt in Comitatibus illis ac potestatem & auctoritatem ad eos defensibiliter arraiatos iuxta discrecionem ipsius ducis nomine nostro pro negocijs nostris convocandos coadunandos ac ipsos sic coadunatos & arraiatos nomine nostro pro securitate seu defencione nostra Regni nostri vel parcium illarum aut conservacione pacis nostre vel alijs negocijs nostris ad quemcunque locum vel quecunque loca infra idem Regnum nostrum ducendos seu mittendos de tempore in tempus infra idem Regnum nostrum iuxta discrecionem ipsius ducis. Et ulterius precipimus omnibus & singulis vicecomitibus Coronatoribus ballivis & alijs ministris predictis ac cuilibet ligeorum & subditorum nostrorum in Comitatibus predictis qui nunc sunt & qui imposterum erunt quod idem duci in ea parte in execucione huius concessionis & mandati nostri intendentes sint obedientes & auxiliantes periculo incumbente. In cuius &c. Teste &c.

[The king etc. to all to whom etc. greeting. Know that we, considering the faithfulness, energy and circumspection of our wellbeloved kinsman, Henry,

10

Duke of Buckingham, for the security of our person and our realm of England and the preservation of our peace and also to have and maintain the tranquillity of our subjects in the counties of Shropshire, Hereford, Somerset Dorset and Wiltshire, have given and granted and by these presents do give and grant to the same our kinsman the supervision of all our subjects who now are and in future shall be in those counties and power and authority to summon them and muster them defensively arrayed at the discretion of the same duke in our name for our business, and when they have been thus mustered and arrayed in our name for the safety or defence of our realm or those parts or to preserve our peace or for other business of ours, to lead or send them to any place or places within our same realm from time to time within our same kingdom at the discretion of the same duke. And further we charge all and singular sheriffs, coroners, bailiffs and other ministers aforesaid and any of our lieges and subjects in the aforesaid counties now or in the future to attend obey and aid the duke in this respect in the execution of this our grant and command under peril. In witness whereof etc. Witness etc.]

[f7] Rex &c. Sciatis quod de gracia nostra speciali & pro acceptabilibus obsequijs que carissimus noster Willelmus Comes Arundell' nobis (at) ante hec tempora impendit indiesque impendere not [sic] desistit fecimus constituimus & ordinavimus prefatum Comitem Magistrum deductus nostri omnium forestarum nostrarum ac omnium & singulorum Chacearum & parcorum nostrorum citra Trentham / Habendum & occupandum dictum officium per se vel per sufficientem deputatum suum seu deputatos suos (ff) sufficientes durante vita sua cum vadijs feodis proficuis & commoditatibus eidem officio pertinentibus seu quovismodo spectantibus eo quod expressa mencio de vero valore annuo vel alio valore quocunque officij & ceterorum premissorum aut de alijs donis & concessionibus per nos prefato Comiti ante hec tempora factis in presentibus facta non existit iuxta formam statutorum inde editorum non obstante. In cuius &c. Teste &c.

[The king etc. Know that of our especial grace and for the acceptable services which our very dear William, Earl of Arundel, has done us before this time and has never ceased to do, we have made, appointed and ordained the aforesaid earl master of our game in all our forests and all and every one of our chases and parks on this side of Trent, to have and to hold the said office in his own person, by a sufficient deputy, or by sufficient deputies during his life with the wages, fees, profits and emoluments appertaining to the same office or in any way belonging to it. Notwithstanding that express mention of the true annual value or any other value of the office and other things aforesaid or other grants and concessions made by us to the aforesaid earl previously is not made in these presents according to the form of the statutes relating thereto. In witness whereof etc. Witness etc.]

Henrico duci Bukingham dominus Rex prefecit Capitalem Justiciarium & Camerarium suum in Suthtwallia & Northtwallia ad terminum vite sue dedit & concessit dansque eidem durante vita sua potestatem & auctoritatem faciendi &c. in Northwallia & Suthtwallia omnia & singula que ad officia predicta pertinent adeo plene &c. prout aliquis Justiciarius vel Camerarius &c. Constituit eciam eundem ducem Constabularium Castri & Comitatus de Kermerden' in Comitatu Kermerden' Castri & Comititus de Cardigan &c. Castri de Aburstwyth' in Comitatu Cardigan' Castri de Denevay in Southwallia & Castri & ville de Tynbyth' in Comitatu Pembroch' Castri & dominij nostri de Kilgarran in Suthtwallia Castri & ville de Llanstephan' in Southtwallia dominij de (Wyn) Wallewynscastell' in Comitatu Pembroch' & Castri & dominij de Westhaverford in Southtwallia ac officia Constabularij omnium eorundem Castrorum &c. dedit & concessit. Constituit eciam eundem ducem Constabularium Senescallum & Receptorem Castri dominij & manerij de Usk Castri & dominij de Carlion' Castri dominij & manerij de Dynos Castri ac medietatis dominij & manerij de Ewyas Lacy Castri dominij & manerij de Belth' Castri dominij & manerij de Clifford, Castri dominij & Manerij de Ragenor, Castri dominij & manerij de Melenneth, Castri dominij & manerij de Mountgomery, Castri dominij & manerij de Dynbigh, Castri dominij & manerij de Elbell' Castri dominij & manerij de Nerbergh' ac Castri dominij & manerij de Wigmore in marchijs Wallie Castri dominij & manerij de Holt in marchijs Wallie dominij & manerij de Bromefeld in eisdem marchijs ac officia Constabularij Senescalli & Receptoris omnium eorundem Castrorum dominiorum & maneriorum & eorum cuiuslibet eidem duci dedit & concessit. Constituit eciam eundem ducem Senescallum & receptorem dominij & manerij de Norton' dominiorum & maneriorum de Knyghton' Raidon Overthrenyam Comotoydon Glasbury Winfreton' Charbury Terethis Haleseter Cadwyn Newton Kyrie in marchijs Wallie Staunton Lacy iuxta Ludlowe Beaudeley Nortclobury Clobury Barnys & Mortymer Clobury Hugeley Arnewode Cheilemershe Clewton' Pembrigge Grisleyn' Hinton' Orneton' Nethwode Wolfreylowe Marmeshill' Lacy in Wallia & marchia Wallie ac officia Senescalli & Receptoris omnium eorundem dominiorum & maneriorum ac omnium aliorum terrarum & tenementorum & hereditamentorum quorumcunque in Northwallia Suthwallia & marchijs predictis eidem dedit & concessit. Constituit eciam eundem ducem Constabularium Senescallum Thesaurarium & Receptorem Castri Comitatus dominij & manerij de Pembroch in Suthtwallia ac officia Constabularij Senescalli Thesaurarij & Receptoris Castri Comitatus dominij & manerij illorum eidem dedit & concessit ac Constituit eundem ducem Constabularium & Capitaneum Castrorum & villarum de Abrustwyth in Comitatu Cardigan' in Suthtwallia de Carnarvan' in Comitatu Carnarvan' de Conwey in eodem Comitatu de Beaumaries in Comitatu Anglesey de Harlegh in Comitatu Merioneth ac officia Constabularij & Capitanei omnium aliorum Castrorum in Northtwallia Suthwallia seu in marchijs predictis eidem dedit & concessit. Dedit ulterius eidem duci potestatem [f7b] constituendi &c. soldarios in omnibus Castris supradictis pro salva Custodia eorundem iuxta discrecionem eiusdem ducis. Dedit eciam eidem duci officium magistri sive Custodis Forestae de Snowdon' in Comitatu Carnarvan' & omnium aliarum Forestarum & chacearum in Suthtwallia Northtwallia & marchijs Wallie ac magistrum deductus ferarum eorundem Habendum omnia supradicta officia & alia premissa scilicet illa officia eorundem que nunc vacant a die data presencium litterarum patentium & omnia dicta alia officia immediate postquam ex aliqua causa vacaverint prefato duci per se vel per sufficientes deputatos suos pro quibus respondere voluerit ad terminum vite sue cum vadijs &c. eisdem officijs debitis & consuetis Capiendum & percipiendum de nobis & heredibus nostris in & pro predictis officijs Justiciarij & Camerarij Suthtwallie & Northtwallie talia vadia & feoda qualia Willelmus Herbert nuper Comes Pembrochie aut Johannes nuper Comes Wigornie seu aliquis alius nuper habuit & percepit ad Festa Sancti Michaelis & Pasche equis porcionibus per manus Camerarij Suthtwallie & Northtwallie pro tempore existentis ac in manibus ipsius ducis dum Camerarius Suthtwallie & Northwallie exstiterit retinendis. Capiendum eciam & annuatim percipiendum in & pro predictis alijs officijs & eorum quolibet ac pro tot soldarijs & sagittarijs in Castris predictis pro salva garda eorundem separaliter imponendis & moraturis talia vadia feoda Regarda & denariorum summas annuatim durante vita ipsius ducis qualia aliquis alius officia predicta habens sive exersens habuit & percepit ad festa predicta per manus Camerarij Suthtwallie & Northtwallie & Receptoris premissorum pro tempore existentium &c. dedit insuper prefato duci quod ipse habeat potestatem & auctoritatem faciendi constituendi & ordinandi de tempore in tempus quamdiu Carissimus avunculus noster Ricardus Dux Gloucestrie seu aliquis alius protector regni nostri Anglie durante nostra iuvenile etate exstiterit Vicecomites & Escaetores in Comitatibus Carmarden' Cardigan & Pembroch' ac in dominio de Haverford in Suthtwallia necnon in Comitatibus Carnarvan' Angles' & Merionneth' in Northtwallia ac faciendi omnes & omnimodos Ballivos parcarios & servientes in Northwallia & Suthtwallia ac attornatos tam in quibuscunque Curijs ibidem quam alibi in Northtwallia & Suthtwallia necnon buttellarios & Custumarios in portubus de Milford & Tennbye in predicto Comitatu Pembrochie & dicto dominio de Haverford' ac eciam omnes alios officiarios servientes & ministros quoscunque in Suthtwallia Northtwallia & marchijs Wallie prout dominus Rex faceret si presens concessio facta non fuisset ac omnia & omnimoda officia nunc vacancia aut nunc plena & imposterum vacatura in Sutht wallia Northwallia & marchijs Wallie eidem duci superius non concessa que ad donacionem Regis pertinent scilicet donandi & concedendi iuxta discrecionem ipsius ducis quibuscunque personis pro quibus respondere voluerit habendum eis durante tempore illo seu ad minora tempora ad libitum ipsius ducis. Et quod ille vel illi officiarij habeant potestatem occupandi (en) huius modi officia & percipiendi de domino Rege & heredibus suis feoda & vadia officijs illis debita eisdem modo & (modo &) forma prout de iure haberent seu habere possent si concessiones ille per litteras Regias facte fuissent per manus Camerarij Suthtwallie & Northtwallie pro tempore existentis. Et voluit & concessit eidem duci quod huiusmodi persone per ipsum sic in officijs posite eadem officia habeant per discrecionem ipsius ducis eodem tempore durante &c. quod habeant talia vadia qualia officijs illis tunc fuerunt debita per manus Camerarij pro tempore existentis. Et precepit & mandavit universis Vicecomitibus Coronatoribus Escaetoribus prepositis ballivis Forestarijs Ringillis & alijs officiarijs & ministris in Northtwallia Suthtwallia & marchijs Wallie qui nunc sunt & qui imposterum erunt quod eidem duci durante vita sua [f8] in debito exercio & execucione premissorum intendentes sint &c. Et pro maiori securitate persone Regis Regnique sui Anglie conservacione pacis & tranquillitate subditorum suorum in Suthtwallia Northwallia & marchijs Wallie predictis habenda & contynuanda Concessit prefato duci durante tempore illo gubernacionem & supervisionem omnium subditorum suorum qui nunc sunt & qui per imposterum erunt in Suthtwallia Northwallia & marchijs Wallie predictis & per idem tempus potestatem ad eos defensibiliter arraiatos iuxta discrecionem ipsius ducis nomine Regis pro negocijs suis coadunandi etc ad quemcunque locum seu loca infra idem Regnum per tempus illud ducendi seu mittendi de tempore in tempus iuxta discrecionem ipsius ducis. Et ulterius precepit omnibus & singulis Vice-comitibus Coronatoribus &c. quod eidem duci in execucione huius concession-is & mandati intendentes sint &c. periculo incumbente. Eo quod expressa mencio de vero valore annuo premissorum seu de alijs donis per Regem prefato duci ante hec tempora factis in presentibus minime facta existit aut aliquo statuto &c. seu aliqua causa Re &c. non obstante. Et insuper vult & concedit prefato duci quod ipse habeat omnia premissa absque compoto seu aliquo alio inde Regi reddendo nisi ratione (premissorum) predictorum offic-iorum Camerarij & Receptoris ac absque fine seu feodo fiendo seu solvendo ac si presens concessio in aliquo premissorum invalida seu minus sufficiens existat quod tunc Cancellarius Regni Anglie qui pro tempore fuerit habeat potestatem & auctoritatem per presentes ad faciendum eidem duci tales alias litteras Regis patentes sub magno sigillo suo quales in hac parte erunt sufficientes & oportune. In cuius &c.

[The lord king has appointed Henry, Duke of Buckingham, his chief justice and chamberlain in South Wales and North Wales for the term of his life and has given and granted to the same during his life power and authority to do &c. in North and South Wales all and singular which relate to the aforesaid offices as fully &c. as any justice or chamberlain &c. He has also appointed the same duke constable of the castle and county of Carmarthen in the county of Carmarthen, of the castle and county of Cardigan &c., of the castle of Aberystwyth in the county of Cardigan, of the castle of Denevay in South Wales and the castle and town of Tenby in the county of Pembroke, of our castle and lordship of Kilgarran in South Wales, of the castle and town of Llanstephan in South Wales, of the lordship of Wallewyns Castle in the county of Pembroke, of the castle and lordship of Haverford West in South Wales and has given and granted him the offices of constable of all the same castles etc. He has also appointed the same duke constable, steward and receiver of the castle, lordship and manor of Usk, the castle and lordship of Caerleon, the castle, lordship and manor of Dynes, the castle and half the lordship and manor of Ewyas Lacy, the castle, lordship and manor of Builth, the castle, lordship and manor of Clifford, the castle, lordship and manor of Ragenor, the castle, lordship and manor of Machynlleth, the castle, lordship and manor of Montgomery, the castle, lordship and manor of Denbigh, the castle, lordship and manor of Elbell, the castle, lordship and manor of Nerbergh and the castle, lordship, and manor of Wigmore in the Welsh Marches, the castle, lordship and manor of Holt in the Welsh Marches, the lordship and manor of Bromefeld in the same Marches, and he has given and granted to the same duke the offices of constable, steward and receiver of all the same castles, lordships and manors and any of them. He has also appointed the same duke steward and receiver of the lordship and manor of Norton and the lordships and manors of Knyghton, Raidon, Overthrenyam, Comotoydon, Glasbury, Winfreton, Charbury, Terethis, Halseter, Tadwyn, Newton Kyrie in the Welsh Marches, Staunton Lacy next Ludlowe, Beaud-eley, North Clobury, Clobury Barnys & Mortymer Clobury, Hugeley, Arnewode, Cheilemershe, Clewton, Pembridge, Grisleyn, Hinton, Orneton, Nethwode, Wolfreylowe, Marmeshill Lacy in Wales and the Welsh Marches and has given and granted to him the offices of steward and receiver of all the

same lordships and manors and all other lands and tenements and hereditaments whatever in North Wales, South Wales and the Marches aforesaid.
He has also appointed the same duke constable, steward, treasurer and
receiver of the castle, county, lordship and manor of Pembroke in South
Wales, and has given and granted hin the offices of constable, steward,
treasurer and receiver of that castle, county, lordship and manor and he has
appointed the same duke constable and captain of the castles and towns of
Aberystwyth in the county of Cardigan in South Wales, of Carnarvon in the
county of Carnarvon, of Conway in the same county, of Beaumaris in the
county of Anglesey, of Harlech in the county of Merioneth and has given and
granted him the offices of constable and captain of all other castles in North
Wales, South Wales or in the Marches aforesaid. Furthermore he has given
the same duke power of setting soldiers in all the castles aforesaid for the safe
custody of the same, at the discretion of the same duke. He has also given to
the same duke the office of master or keeper of the forest of Snowdon in the
county of Carnarvon and of all other forests and chases in South Wales,
North Wales and the Marches of Wales and master of the hunt of wild beasts
in the same, to hold all the abovementioned offices and other things aforesaid, that is, those offices which are now vacant from the day of the giving of
the present letters patent and all the other said offices immediately after
they have become vacant for any reason, in his own person or by his
sufficient deputies for whom he is willing to answer for the term of his life
with the wages etc. owed and customary to the same offices. To take and
receive from us and our heirs in and for the aforesaid offices of justice and
chamberlain of South Wales and North Wales such wages and fees as
William Herbert late Earl of Pembroke or John late Earl of Worcester or any
other lately had and received at the feasts of Michaelmas and Easter in equal
portions by the hand of the chamberlain of South Wales and North Wales for
the time being and to be retained in the hands of the same duke while
chamberlain of South Wales and North Wales. Also taking and receiving
annually in and for the aforesaid other offices and each one of them and for
putting and retaining so many soldiers and archers in the aforesaid castles for
the safeguarding of the same separately such wages, fees, rewards, and sums
of money annually during the life of the same duke as any other having or
exercising the aforesaid offices had and received at the feasts aforesaid by the
hand of the chamberlain of South Wales and North Wales and the receiver of
the foregoing for the time being etc. Moreover he has given to the aforesaid
duke the power and authority as long as our very dear uncle Richard, Duke of
Gloucester, or any other, is protector of our realm of England during our
minority, to make, create and appoint from time to time sheriffs and escheators in the counties of Carmarthen, Cardigan, and Pembroke and in the
lordship of Haverford in South Wales and also in the counties of Carnarvon,
Anglesey, and Merioneth in North Wales and to make all and every kind of
bailiffs, parkers and servants in North Wales and South Wales and attorneys
in whatsoever courts there and also elsewhere in North Wales and South
Wales as also butlers and customers in the ports of Milford and Tenby in the
aforesaid county of Pembroke and the said lordship of Haverford and also all
other officers, servants and ministers whatever in South Wales, North Wales,
and the Welsh Marches as the lord king would do if the present grant had not
been made, and all and every kind of office now vacant or now filled and later

to be vacant in South Wales, North Wales and the Welsh Marches not granted above to the same duke which are in the gift of the king, namely to give and grant at the discretion of the same duke to whatever persons he is willing to answer for to hold during that time or for shorter periods at the will of the same duke. And that officer or those officers are to have the power of occupying such offices and receiving from the lord king and his heirs the fees and wages due to those offices in the same manner and form as they would have of right or ought to have if those grants were made by royal letters by the hand of the chamberlain of South Wales and North Wales for the time being. And he has willed and granted to the same duke that persons of this kind thus placed by him in offices should hold the same offices at the discretion of the same duke during that time etc. and have such wages as were then due to those offices by the hands of the chamberlain for the time being. And he has ordered and commanded all sheriffs, coroners, escheators, reeves, bailiffs, foresters, rhingylls, and other officers and ministers in North Wales, South Wales, and the Marches of Wales now in office and afterwards to be appointed to be obedient to the same duke during his life in the due exercise and performance of the foregoing. And for the greater security of the person of the king and his realm of England, the conservation of peace and the tranquillity of his subjects in South Wales, North Wales and the Welsh Marches aforesaid to be had and continued, he has granted to the aforesaid duke during that time the rule and supervision of all his subjects who now are and in future will be in South Wales, North Wales and the Welsh Marches aforesaid and during the same time he has granted him the power of mustering them in defensive array at the discretion of the same duke in the name of the king for his business etc. to take or send them to any place or places within the same kingdom from time to time at the discretion of the same duke. And further he has commanded all and singular the sheriffs, coroners &c. to obey the same duke in the execution of this grant and mandate under peril. Notwithstanding that express mention of the true annual value of the foregoing or of other gifts made by the king to the aforesaid duke before this time has not been made in these presents and any statute &c. or other cause, matter &c. notwithstanding. And moreover he wills and grants to the aforesaid duke that he hold all the foregoing without account or rendering anything else to the king, except by reason of the aforesaid offices of chamberlain and receiver and without fine or fee being paid or rendered and if the present grant is invalid in any of the foregoing or insufficient, then the chancellor of the realm of England for the time being shall have the power and authority by these presents to make for the same duke such other letters patent of the king under the great seal as shall be sufficient and appropriate in this respect. In witness whereof &c.]

xvjª Maij.

Rex Omnibus &c. Sciatis quod de gracia nostra speciali Concessimus Johanni Wode Militi officium Thesaurarij Scaccarij nostri habendum & occupandum dictum officium quam diu nobis placuerit. In cuius &c.

[The king to all etc. Know that of our special grace we have granted to John Wode, knight, the office of treasurer of our exchequer, to hold and occupy the said office at our pleasure. In witness whereof etc.]

To Charles Belfeld Thoffice of the Bailliefwik of Salfordshire in the Counte of Lancastre to have by him or his sufficient depute during his liff with wages & fees accustumed etc. as Jamys Hille late yoman of Corone or any other afore him had etc.

Rex. Reverendissimo in Christo patri Thome eadem gratia Cardinali Archiepiscopo Cantuariensi salutem. Quibusdam arduis & urgentibus negocijs nos ad statum Regni nostri Anglie ac honorem & utilitatem ecclesie Anglicane intime concernentibus vobis in fide & dilecione quibus nobis tenemini rogando mandamus quatinus premissis debito intuitu attentis & ponderatis universos & singulos Episcopos vestre provincie ac decanos & priores ecclesiarum Cathedralium Abbes & priores ac alios electivos exemptos & non exemptos necnon Archidiaconos Capitula Conventus & Collegia totumque clerum cuiuslibet diocesis eiusdem provincie ad comparendum coram vobis in ecclesia sancti Pauli London vel alibi prout melius expedire videritis cum omni celeritate accomoda modo debito convocari facias ad tractandum consenciendum & concludendum super premissis & alijs que sibi clarius exponentur tunc ibidem ex parte nostra. Et hoc sicut nos & statum Regni nostri predicti ac honorem & utilitatem ecclesie predicte diligitis nullatenus omittatis. Teste &c.

[The king to the most reverend father in Christ Thomas, by the same grace Cardinal Archbishop of Canterbury, greeting. Having carefully considered and weighed certain difficult and urgent matters closely concerning us and the state of our realm of England and the honour and benefit of the English church, we command you in the faith and love in which you are held by us that you should cause to be summoned all and singular the bishops of your province and deans and priors of cathedral churches, abbots and priors and others elected exempt and non-exempt, and archdeacons, chapters, convents and colleges and all the clergy of any diocese of the same province to appear before you in St. Paul's church, London or elsewhere as shall seem more expedient, with all convenient speed and in due manner to treat, agree and conclude on the foregoing and other matters which will be expressed more clearly then and there on our part. And do not anywise fail in this as you love us and the state of our realm aforesaid and the honour and benefit of the aforesaid church. Witness etc.]

To John Lambert of Tikhille squier thoffice of feodarie of Thonor of Tikhille within the Countees of York & Nottingham parcelle of the duchie of Lancastre by him or his sufficient depute for terme of his liff as John Hunter or any other had etc.

[f 8b] Rex &c. constituit Henricum Ducem Bukingham Constabularium Senescallum & Receptorem Castri Manerij & ville de Monmouthe in Suthwallia ac omnium aliorum Castrorum dominiorum Maneriorum villarum terrarum &

tenementorum suorum que sunt parcelle ducatus sui Lancastrie in Suthwallia. Constituit insuper prefatum ducem Custodem sive Capitalem Forestarium foreste & Chacee sue de Hodenak' ac omnium aliarum forestarum & Chacearum suarum parcellarum ducatus predicti in Suthwallia / habendum eidem duci ad terminum vite sue per se vel per sufficientem deputatum suum aut sufficientes deputatos suos unacum vadijs feodis Regardis proficuis & commoditatibus &c. debitis & consuetis per manus Receptoris &c. Concessit eciam eidem duci potestatem & auctoritatem de tempore in tempus faciendi & constituendi omnes & omnimodos Senescallos Eschaetores ballivos itinerantes forestarios parcarios prepositos Ringildos ballivos & omnes officiarios & ministros in predictis Castris Dominijs Manerijs Villis Forestis chaceis & eorum quolibet necessarios & consuetos Et quod huiusmodi officiarij sive ministri sic per ipsum Ducem constituendi habeant & percipiant vadia feoda Regarda proficua & commoditates officiorum illorum & eorum cuilibet debita & consueta / Et similiter concessit eidem duci quod ipse habeat potestatem & auctoritatem de tempore in tempus iuxta discrecionem suam amovendi exonerandi & expellandi omnes & singulos Senescallos vicecomites ballivos itinerantes prepositos Ringildos ballivos & omnes alios officiarios & ministros suos in supradictis Castris Dominijs Manerijs terris tenementis & ceteris premissis qui pro tempore fuerint & alios officiarios locis eorum ordinandi faciendi & constituendi ac huiusmodi officia eis concedendi & omnes huiusmodi personas in possessionem & exercicium officiorum illorum ponendi & constituendi ad habendum & exercendum officia illa prout discrecioni & advisamento ipsius ducis fore videbitur conveniens & oportunum capiendo in officijs illis & eorum quolibet talia vadia feoda Regarda & proficua huiusmodi officij seu eorum alicui ab antiquo debita & consueta. Eo quod expressa mencio de vero valore Annuo aut aliquo alio valore seu certitudine premissorum aut eorum alicuius seu de alijs donis vel concessis per nos prefato duci ante hec tempora factis in presentibus minime facta existit aut aliquo statuto actu ordinacione provisione seu Restriccione in contrarium facta edita sive ordinata aut aliqua alia Re causa vel materia quacunque non obstante. In cuius rei &c. Teste &c.

[The king etc. has appointed Henry, Duke of Buckingham, constable, steward and receiver of the castle, manor and town of Monmouth in South Wales and all his other castles lordships manors towns lands and tenements which are part of his duchy of Lancaster in South Wales. Moreover he has appointed the above said duke keeper or chief forester of the forest and chase of Hodenak and of all other forests and chases parcel of the aforesaid duchy in South Wales. To hold to the same duke for the term of his life in person or by a sufficient deputy or deputies with the wages fees rewards profits and benefits etc. owed and customary by the hands of the receiver etc. He has also granted to the same duke power and authority from time to time to make and appoint all and all kinds of stewards escheators bailiffs errant foresters parkers reeves rhingylls bailiffs and all officers and ministers necessary and customary in the aforesaid castles lordships manors towns forests chases and anywhere else. And such officers or ministers thus appointed by the same duke shall have and receive the due and customary wages fees rewards profits and benefits of those offices and any of them. And he has likewise granted to the same duke that he has power and authority from time to time at his discretion to remove discharge and expel all and singular the stewards sheriffs bailiffs errant reeves rhingylls bailiffs and all his other officers and ministers in the aforesaid castles lordships manors lands tenements and other foregoing for the time being, and to ordain, make and appoint other officers in their place and to grant these offices to them and to set and appoint all such persons in the possession and exercise of those offices, to hold and exercise those ofices as it shall seem to be convenient and appropriate at the discretion and judgment of the same duke, receiving in those offices and any of them such wages fees rewards and profits of such offices or any of them owing and customary from of old. That express mention of the true annual value or any other value or the wages of the foregoing or any of them or of other gifts or grants made by us to the aforesaid duke before this time is not made in these presents and notwithstanding any statute act ordinance provision or restraint to the contrary made issued or ordained or any other thing cause or matter whatever. In witness whereof etc. Witness etc.]

xix^a Maij.

Rex &c. constituit Johannem Sapcote Armigerum Receptorem generalem Ducatus nostri Cornubie unacum portagio monete eidem Receptori pertinente habendum pe se vel per sufficientem deputatum suum quam diu dictus Rex placuerit cum omnibus alijs proficuis commoditatibus & emolumentis eidem (officio) Receptori cum portagio predicto debitis & consuetis percipiendo pro exercione dicti officij feoda & vadia & omnia alia proficua ab antiquo debita & consueta Et pro portagio predicto videlicet de quolibet Centum libris cariatis & per warrantum solutis viginti solidos de exitibus & proficuis & Revencionibus eiusdem ducatus provenientibus per manus suas proprias ad terminos Pasche & sancti Michaelis equis porcionibus &c.

[The king etc. has appointed John Sapcote, esquire, receiver general of our duchy of Cornwall with portage belonging to the same receiver to hold in person or by a sufficient deputy as long as it shall please the said king with all other profits benefits and emoluments owing and customary to the same receiver with portage aforesaid, receiving for the exercise of the said office fees and wages and all other profits owing and customary from of old. And for the aforesaid portage viz. for every hundred pounds carried and paid by warrant twenty shillings from the issues and profits and revenues arising from the same duchy by his own hands at the terms of Easter and Michaelmas by equal portions etc.]

Thome Brian officium ballivi de Sandegate & Hammes ac Receptorem dominiorum de de [sic] Sandgate & Hammes predictis habendum officium illud per se vel sufficientem deputatum suum pro termino vite sue (de) cum vadia pro illo officio de exitibus proficuis Revencionibus & commoditatibus domini-orum predictorum & eorum cuiuslibet unacum omnibus alijs proficuis com-moditatibus & Regardis &c.

[To Thomas Brian the office of bailiff of Sandegate and Hammes and receiver of the lordships of Sandegate and Hammes aforesaid; to hold that office in person or by his sufficient deputy for term of his life with wages for that office from the issues, profits, revenues and benefits of the aforesaid lordships and any of them, together with all other profits, benefits and rewards etc.]

[f9] Thomas Brian in ferme for xij yeres the lordships of Balingham and Milmanbroke with thappurtenaunces within the marches of Caleys yelding for the same yerely suche somme of money as Robert Ratcliff did etc.

xx die Maij

Robert Legh thoffice of keping of the Gaole within the Towne of Notingham during his lyff with wages and fees thereto due & accustumed & with alle other profites commodites & advailes to the same in any wise appertenyng or belonging etc.

Rex vicecomiti Middlesex salutem. Precipimus tibi quod per totam ballivam tuam tam infra libertates quam extra ubi expedire videris publice proclamari facias quod omnes illi qui quadraginta libratas terre vel Redditus per Annum in manibus suis vel ad eorum usum in manibus feoffatorum habent & eas per tres Annos habuerunt & milites non sunt penes presenciam nostram ordinem militarem suscepturi citra   diem Junij proximo futuro ad ultimum sub periculo incumbenti accedant Et de nominibus eorum qui quadraginta libratas terre vel Redditus in balliva tua habent diligenter inquiras et nos de nominibus illis in Cancellaria nostra ante dictam   diem Junij constare facias / Et hoc nullatenus omittas Remittens nobis hoc breve. Teste &c. Fiant consimilia brevia directa vicecomitibus in Comitatibus subscriptis modo & forma predicta videlicet in Comitatibus

Kanc'	Somerset	Hereford'	Essex'	Lincoln'	Northumbr'	Vicecomitibus London'
Surr'	Dors'	Wygorn'	Hertf'	Norht'	Westmorl'	
Sussex'	Devon'	Glouc'	Canterbr'	Rotel'	Cumbr'	
Sutht'	Cornub'	Oxon'	Hunt'	Notingham	Lanc'	
Wiltes	Staff'	Berk'	Norff'	Derb'	Warr'	
	Salop'	Bed'	Suff'	Ebor'	Leyc'	
		Buk'				

[The king to the sheriff of Middlesex greeting. We command you to make public proclamation throughout your whole bailiwick both within the liberties and without wherever it seems expedient that all those who have £40 a year in land or in rents in their hands or to their use in the hands of feoffees and have had them for three years and are not knights, should come to receive the order of knighthood in our presence before the   day of June next at the latest under peril. And you are to make diligent enquiry of the names of those who have £40 in land or rents in your bailiwick and inform us of those names in our chancery before the said   day of June. And in no wise neglect these matters, returning this writ to us. Witness etc.

Let similar writs be directed to the sheriffs of the counties written below in manner and form aforesaid viz. in the counties of

20

Kent	Somerset	Hereford	Essex	Lincoln-shire	Northum-berland	Sheriffs of London
Surrey	Dorset	Worcester-shire	Hertford-shire	Northamp-tonshire	Westmor-land	
Sussex	Devon	Gloucester-shire	Cambridge-shire	Rutland	Cumberland	
Southamp-ton	Cornwall	Oxfordshire	Hunting-donshire	Notting-hamshire	Lancashire	
Wiltshire	Stafford-shire	Berkshire	Norfolk	Derbyshire	Warwick-shire	
	Shropshire	Bedford-shire	Suffolk	Yorkshire	Leicester-shire	
		Bucking-hamshire				

Rex omnibus ad quos &c. salutem. Sciatis nos consideracione boni & laudabilis servicij per dilectum nobis Johannem Dynham militem multipliciter nobis impensi & imposterum impendendi dedimus & concessimus eidem Johanni Officium Senescalsie Ducatus nostri Cornubie habendum occupandum & exercendum dictum officium per se vel per deputatum suum sufficientem pro termino vite ipsius Johannis / percipiendum inde & pro dicto officio exercendo feoda & vadia eidem ab antiquo debita & consueta de (ex) exitibus proficuis (unacum omnibus alijs proficuis & commoditatibus eidem officio ab antiquo quoquo modo pertinentibus sive spectantibus prout aliquis alius) & Revencionibus ducatus predicti provenientis per manus Receptoris generalis eiusdem ducatus pro tempore existentis ad terminos Pasche & sancti Michaelis Archangeli equis porcionibus unacum omnibus alijs proficuis & commoditatibus eidem officio ab antiquo quoquo modo pertinentibus sive spectantibus prout aliquis alius pro dicti officij exercicio habuit & percepit. Eo quod expressa menico de vero valore Annuo officij predicti aut vadiorum et feodorum predictorum in presenti minime facta existenta aut aliquo statuto ordinacione seu Restriccione incontrarium facta non obstante. In cuius rei &c.

[The king to all to whom etc. greeting. Know that on account of the good and praiseworthy service which our beloved John Dynham, knight, has often rendered to us and will render in the future, we have given and granted to the same John the office of steward of our duchy of Cornwall, to have, occupy and exercise the said office in person or by his sufficient deputy for the term of the life of the said John. To receive therefor and for exercising the said office the fees and wages due and customary to the same from of old from the issues profits and revenues of the aforesaid duchy for the time being at the terms of Easter and Michaelmas by equal portions with all other profits and benefits in any way appertaining or belonging to the same office from of old as any one else has had and received for the exercise of the said office. That express mention of the true annual value of the aforesaid office or the wages and fees aforesaid has not been made in the present document and notwithstanding any statute ordinance or restriction to the contrary. In witness whereof etc.]

[f 9b] Rex omnibus ad quos &c. salutem. Sciatis quod nos intelligentes quod Isabella Bartlett (filie) & Petronilla Bartlett filie Thome Bartlett defuncti ac heredes Willelmi Bartlett quondam de Comitatu nostro Sussex fatue & idiote existunt & non compotes mencium suarum Ita quod Regimine ipsarum & suarum aut terrarum tenementorum bonorum seu Catallorum suarum non sufficiunt quo pretextu custodia omnium terrarum tenementorum bonorum seu Catallorum earum Isabelle & Petronille predictorum ad nos Racione prerogative nostre Regie pertinet: Nos proinde pro Regimine ipsarum Isabelle & Petronille in hac parte prout convenit ordinare de gracia nostra speciali concessimus & per presentes concedimus dilecto nostro Johanni Audeley Militi domino de Audeley custodiam omnium terrarum bonorum tenementorum & Catallorum predictorum eisdem Isabelle & Petronille & earum alteri aliquo modo spectancium sive pertinencium / Habendum & tenendum prefato Johanni domino de Audeley ad usum earundem Isabelle & Petronille pro sustentacionibus suis iuxta discrecionem ipsius Johannis domini de Audeley pro termino vite ipsarum Isabelle & Petronille & earum alterius diucius viventis absque compoto aliquo inde faciendo. Eo quod expressa mencio de certitudine terrarum Tenementorum bonorum & Catallorum predictorum aut valore eorum in presentibus minime facta existit aut aliquo statuto actu sive ordinacione incontrarium facta edita sive ordinata. In cuius rei &c.

[The king to all to whom etc. greeting. Know that we understanding that Isabel Bartlett and Petronilla Bartlett daughters of Thomas Bartlett deceased and heirs of William Bartlett late of our county of Sussex are simpleminded and idiots and not in possession of their mental faculties so that they are not competent to control themselves or their lands tenements goods or chattels, for which reason custody of all the lands and tenements goods and chattels aforesaid of the same Isabel and Petronilla pertains to us by reason of our royal prerogative; we therefore, as it is fitting to ordain in this respect for the governance of the same Isabel and Petronilla, have of our special grace granted and by these presents do grant to our beloved John Audley, knight, Lord Audley, custody of all the lands goods tenements and chattels aforesaid in any way belonging or pertaining to the same Isabel and Petronilla and to either of them. To have and hold to the same John, Lord Audley to the use of the same Isabel and Petronilla for their support at the discretion of the same John, Lord Audley for the term of the lives of the said Isabel and Petronilla and whichever of them lives the longer without making any account therefor. That express mention of the extent of the lands tenements goods and chattels aforesaid or the value of them has not been made in these presents and notwithstanding any statute act or ordinance made issued or ordained to the contrary. In witness whereof etc.]

Rex omnibus ad quos &c. salutem. Sciatis quod cum nobilis & predilectissimus dominus Edwardus nuper Rex Anglie pater noster vicesimo die Julij Anno Regni sui undecimo per litteras suas patentes concessit Willelmo Evyngton' officium virgebaiuli alias dicti virgarij ad portandam virgam coram dicto patre nostro & heredibus suis ad festum sancti Georgij infra Castrum de Wyndesore tenendum Annuatim cum feodis & vadijs eidem officio debitis prout in eisdem litteris patentibus plenius continetur. Iamque idem Willelmus in voluntatis existit easdem litteras patentes in Cancellariam nostram Restituere cancellandas ad intencionem quod nos officium predictum eidem Willelmo ac dilecto

servitori nostro Edwardo (Hargill) Hardgill' Armigero uni hostiariorum Cam-
ere nostre concedere dignaremur Nos proinde bona & gratuita servica predictorum Willelmi & Edwardi intime ponderantes ac pro eo quod idem Willelmus
easdem litteras patentes in Cancellariam nostram (restitunt)Restituit cancellandas Concessimus eidem Willelmo & Edwardo officium virgebaiuli alias dicti
virgarij ad portandam virgam coram nobis & heredibus nostris ad festum sancti
Georgij infra Castrum nostrum de Wyndesore Annuatim tenendum / habendum & occupandum (dictum) officium illud prefato Willelmo & Edwardo per
(sel) se vel per sufficientes deputatos suos aut sufficientem deputatum suum
pro termino vite eorum & (al) eorum alterius diucius viventis percipiendo in
eodem officio feoda & vadia eidem officio debita & consueta de firmis exitibus
(&) proficuis & Revencionibus de Dominio sive Manerio nostro de Coldekenyngton' in Comitatu Middlesex cum pertinencijs provenientibus per manus
firmarij ballivi Receptoris aut alii occupatis eiusdem dominij sive Manerij pro
tempore existentis aut per manus Vicecomitis Comitatus Middlesex pro tempore existentis unacum omnibus placeis mancionibus proficuis & commoditatibus dicto officio qualitercunque pertinentibus sive spectantibus. Eo quod
expressa mencio de vero valore Annuo feodorum & vadiorum predictorum &
ceterorum premissorum aut de alijs etc donis sive concessionibus per nos aut
per dictum patrem nostrum eisdem Willelmo & Edwardo aut eorum alteri ante
hec tempora factis aut aliquo statuto actu sive ordinacione in contrarium facta
non obstante. In cuius &c.

[The king to all to whom &c. greeting. Know that since our noble and most
dearly beloved father the Lord Edward late King of England on the twentieth
day of July in the eleventh year of his reign by his letters patent granted to
William Evyngton the officer of wand-bearer, otherwise called verger, to
bear the wand before our said father and his heirs on the feast of St George in
Windsor castle, to hold annually with the fees and wages due to the same
office as is more fully contained in the same letters patent, and now the same
William has chosen to return the same letters patent to our chancery to be
cancelled to the intent that we may deign to grant the aforesaid office to the
same William and our beloved servant Edward Hardgill esquire one of the
ushers of our chamber; we, therefore, considering the good and agreeable
services of the aforesaid William and Edward, and because the same William
has returned the same letters patent to our chancery to be cancelled, have
granted to the same Wiliam and Edward the office of wand-bearer otherwise
called verger to bear the wand before us and our heirs on the feast of St.
George in our castle of Windsor annually to hold have and occupy that office
to the aforesaid William and Edward in person or by sufficient deputies or a
sufficient deputy for the term of their life and whichever of them lives the
longer, receiving in the same office the fees and wages due and customary to
the same office out of the rents issues profits and revenues arising from our
lordship or manor of Coldekenyngton in the county of Middlesex by the
hands of the farmer bailiff receiver or other occupier of the same lordship or
manor for the time being or by the hands of the sheriff of the county of
Middlesex for the time being with all places mansions profits and benefits
appertaining or belonging to the said office in any way whatever. That
express mention of the true annual value of the fees and wages aforesaid and
the other foregoing or of the other etc. gifts or grants made by us or our said

father to the same William and Edward or either of them before this time has not been made, and notwithstanding any statute act or ordinance made to the contrary. In witness whereof etc.]

[f 10] Rex Omnibus ad quos &c. salutem. Sciatis quod nos de gracia nostra speciali ac ex certa sciencia & mero motu nostris Concessimus & licenciam dedimus pro nobis & heredibus nostris quantum in nobis est dilecto nobis Patricio Bermyngeham Armigero fratri & heredi Johannis Bermyngeham defuncti qui de domino Edwardo nuper Rege Anglie patre nostro tenuit in Capite die quo obijt quod idem Patricius absque probacione etatis sue in omnia dominia Maneria terras tenementa feodi firmas Redditus servicia hundreda feoda visus franciplegij Curias letas turnos vicecomitum liberatates franchesias ferias mercata jurisdicciones feoda militum patronatus Abbatiarum & prioratuum aceciam advocaciones ecclesiarum vicariarum Cantariarum Capellarum prebendarum hospitalium & aliorum beneficiorum ecclesiasticorum quorumcunque parcos warrennas wreccum maris boscos agistamenta pannagia porcorum molendina aquas liberas piscarias ac omnia alia possessiones & hereditamenta quecunque infra terram nostram Hibernie de quibus prefatus Johannes aut aliquis antecessorum suorum fuit seisitus in dominico suo ut de feodo qualitercunque talliato die quo obijt & que per & post mortem prefati Johannis ad manus ipsius patris nostri aut nostras aliquo modo devenerunt seu devenire debuerunt prefatoque Patricio descenderunt aut descendere Revertere Remanere pertinere seu spectare debent aut deberent licite & impune ingredi & seisire ac ea sibi & heredibus suis ac heredibus de corpore suo exeuntibus prout ipse in eisdem post mortem predicti Johannis aut alicuius (ann) antecessorum suorum hereditabilis existit Retinere habere & tenere possit unacum exitibus & proficuis inde a tempore mortis predicti Johannis receptis ac omnia eadem exitus & proficua prefato Patricio a tempore predicto proveniencia licet omnia terra & tenementa ac alia premissa superius Recitata sint in manu nostra racione alicuius officij sive non concedimus damus & liberamus per presentes eidem Patricio de dono nostro absque aliquo compoto seu aliquo alio nobis vel heredibus nostris inde Reddendo solvendo seu faciendo & absque aliqua inquisicione seu aliquibus inquisicionibus inde pretextu aliquorum brevium nostrorum de diem clausit extremum sive aliquorum aliorum brevium aut mandatorum nostrorum seu aliter per vel post mortem predicti Johannis aut alicuius antecessorum suorum de Dominijs Manerijs terris & tenementis predictis seu ceteris premissis cum pertinencijs capiendis vel faciendis aut aliqua liberacione eorundem extra manus nostras quovis modo prosequendorum vel impetrandorum. Nolentes quod predictus Patricius vel heredes sui racione ingressus & seisine (eorum) suorum huiusmodi per nos vel heredes nostros Justiciarios Eschaetores Vicecomites aut alios ballivos seu ministros nostros vel heredum nostrorum quoscunque molestentur inquietentur impetantur vexentur perturbentur in aliquo seu graventur / nec quod ijdem executores vicecomites ballivi & Ministri nec eorum aliquis de dominijs manerijs terris & tenementis predictis ac (ceters) ceteris premissis aut aliquibus ceterorum premissorum vel in aliqua parcella eorundem in aliquo intromittant vel intromittat Sed quod ijdem Patricius & omnes Escaetores vicecomites ballivi & Ministri & alij officiarij nostri quicunque habeant & quilibet eorum habeat tot & talia brevia & alia waranta quot & qualia eis & eorum cuilibet pro exoneracione sua in hac

parte erga nos & dictos heredes nostros necessaria fuerint & oportuna. Homagio & fidelitate ac Relevio ipsius Patricij nobis in hac parte debitis nobis semper salvis Et ulterius concessimus (etc) pro nobis & heredibus nostris predictis prefato Patricio quod ingressus seisina & possessio per ipsum Patricium de & in Dominijs Manerijs terris & tenementis predictis ac ceteris premissis vigore & auctoritate concessionis & licencie nostrorum supradictorum habite & optente sibi & heredibus suis predictis tanti vigoris in lege existant & (vit) virtutis ac si Dominia Maneria terre ac tenementa ac cetera premissa in manus nostras capta & seisita inquisiciones que inde post mortem predicti Johannis aut alicuius antecessorum suorum rite & debite capte facte & in Cancellariam nostram retornate ac liberacio eorundem dominiorum Maneriorum **[f 10b]** terrarum & tenementorum ac ceterorum premissorum per predictum Patricium extra manus nostras secundum cursum Cancellarie nostre in forma debita prosecuta fuissent. Et quod hoc sit adeo validum prefato Patricio heredibus & assignatis suis & huiusmodi valoris & effectus erga nos & heredes nostros prout esset una bona sufficiens & legalis liberacio per ipsum Patricium in hac parte extra (cances) Cancellariam nostram predictam per cursum communis legis debite prosecuta & habita ac nobis de omni eo quod ad nos pertinere debet seu deberet in hac parte satisfactum esset & contentatum / et quod nos & dicti heredes nostri ad seisiendum & capiendum Dominia Maneria terras & tenementa predicta ac cetera premissa vel aliqua eorundem in manus nostras racione alicuius iuris vel tituli quod vel qui nobis vel eisdem heredibus nostris per vel post mortem predicti Johannis aut alicuius antecessorum suorum competit seu competere poterit simus exclusi imperpetuum per presentes Et insuper perdonavimus Remisimus & Relaxavimus eidem Patricio omnimodas intrusiones & ingressus in hereditatem suam in parte vel in toto post mortem dicti Johannis absque debita (procuc) prosecucione seu liberacione inde extra manum Regiam ac omnimodas transgressiones offensas mesprisiones contemptus fines forisfacturas Redempciones impeticiones & alia malefacta quecunque per ipsum Patricium ante hec tempora facta sive perpetrata Aceciam omnimoda compota prestita arreragia firmarum & compotorum nobis per ipsum Patricium qualitercunque debita & pertinencia ac omnimodas acciones sectas querelas demandas & execuciones quas nos versus ipsum Patricium racione premissorum habemus vel habere poterimus in futuro Et ulterius de uberiori gracia nostra concessimus & licenciam dedimus prefato Patricio quod ipse pro termino vite sue seipsum extra dictam terram nostram Hibernie possit absentare & quod ipse medio tempore per servientes deputatos sive Attornatos suos omnia exitus proficua & commoditates de omnibus Dominijs Manerijs terris & tenementis predictis ac ceteris premissis proveniencia ad eius usum & proficum Recipere ac eadem exitus (&) proficua & commoditates sibi in Regnum nostrum Anglie seu in dicta terra nostra Hibernie ad libitum suum habere Recipere & occupare possit absque impeticione vel impedimento nostri aut heredum nostrorum vel aliquorum officiariorum seu ministrorum nostrorum quorumcunque. Eo quod expressa mencio de vero valore Annuo premissorum aut alicuius eorum aut de alijs donis sive concessionibus eidem Patricio ante hec tempora factis in presentibus minime facta existit aut aliquo statuto actu ordinacione sive provisione in contrarium facta edita ordinata sive provisa non obstante. In cuius &c. Teste &c.

[The king to all to whom etc. greeting. Know that we of our special grace and certain knowledge and free volition have granted and given licence for us and our heirs as far as in us lies to our beloved Patrick Bermyngeham esquire, brother and heir of John Bermyngeham deceased who on the day he died held in chief of the Lord Edward late King of England our father, that the same Patrick lawfully and with impunity may enter without proof of age and be seised of all lordships manors lands tenements fee farms rents services hundreds fees views of frankpledge courts leets sheriffs' tourns liberties franchises fairs markets jurisdictions knights' fees patronage of abbeys and priories and also the advowsons of churches vicarages chantries chapels prebends hospitals and other ecclesiastical benefices whatever parks warrens wreck woods agistments pannage for pigs mills waters free fisheries and all other possessions and hereditaments whatever within our land of Ireland of which the said John or any of his ancestors was seised in his demesne as of fee however entailed on the day of his death and which through and after the death of the aforesaid John came or should have come to the hands of our father aforesaid or to ours in any way and descended or ought to descend revert remain appertain or belong to the aforesaid Patrick and that he should retain hold and possess the inheritance as it stood on the death of the aforesaid John or any of his ancestors, to himself and his heirs and the heirs of his body with the issues and profits received from the time of the death of the said John and all those rents and profits due to the said Patrick from that time; all the lands and tenements and other premises recited above which are in our hand by reason of any office or not we grant give and release by these presents to the same Patrick as our gift without any account or anything else to be rendered paid or done to us or our heirs therefor and without any other inquisition or inquisitions therefor by reason of any writs of ours of diem clausit extremum or any other writs or mandates of ours or otherwise procured or sought through or after the death or the said John or any of his ancestors concerning the lordships, manors, lands and tenements abovesaid or the rest of the foregoing with their appurtenances taken, made or otherwise released from our hands by whatever means. We are unwilling that the abovesaid Patrick or his heirs by reason of their entry and seisin of this kind should be harmed accused impeached harassed disturbed or troubled in anything by us or our heirs justices escheators sheriffs or other bailiffs or ministers whatever of us or our heirs or that the same executors sheriffs bailiffs and ministers or any of them should interfere in any of the lordships manors lands and tenements aforesaid and other premises or in any part of them, but the same Patrick and all escheators sheriffs bailiffs and ministers and other officers of ours whatever are to have and each of them is to have so many and such writs and other warrants as are necessary and opportune for each of them for his exemption in this matter towards us and our said heirs, always excepting the homage and fealty and relief of the same Patrick owed to us in this respect. And further we have granted for us and our heirs aforesaid to the aforesaid Patrick that the entry seisin and possession by Patrick himself of and in the lordships manors lands and tenements aforesaid and other premises by the power and authority of our grant and licence aforesaid had and obtained by him & his heirs aforesaid shall have as much power and virtue in law as if the lordships manors lands and tenements and other premises had been taken and seised into our hands and inquisitions therefor after the death of the said John or any of his ancestors rightly and duly taken and made and returned to our chancery and release obtained in due form of the same lordships manors lands and tenements and other premises by the aforesaid Patrick out of our hands according to the course of our chancery. And this is to be as valid for the aforesaid Patrick his heirs and assigns and of such power and effect towards us and our heirs as if there was a good sufficient and legal release by the same Patrick in this respect duly procured and had outside our chancery aforesaid by course of common law and we are satisfied and contented in all that should appertain to us or might have done so in this respect and we and our said heirs are excluded for ever by these presents from seizing and taking the lordships manors lands and tenements aforesaid and other premises or any of them into our hands by reason of any right or title applicable to us or the same our heirs by or after the death of the aforesaid John or any of his ancestors or which ought to be applicable. And moreover we have pardoned, remitted and released to the same Patrick all manner of trespasses and entries into his inheritance in part or in whole after the death of the said John without due prosecution or release therefor out of the king's hand and all manner of trangressions offences misprisions contempts fines forfeitures reliefs impeachments and other misdeeds whatever made or perpetrated by the same Patrick before this time. And also all manner of accounts payments arrears of rents and accounts by the said Patrick to us in anywise owing and appertaining and all manner of actions suits complaints demands and executions which we have against the same Patrick by reason of the premises or ought to have in future. And further of our more abundant grace we have granted and given licence to the aforesaid Patrick that for the term of his life he may absent himself from our said land of Ireland and in the meantime he may receive to his use and profit through his servants deputies or attorneys all issues profits and benefits arising from all the lordships manors lands and tenements aforesaid and other premises and have receive and occupy the same issues profits and benefits in our realm of England or in our said land of Ireland at his pleasure without impeachment or impediment of us or our heirs or any of our officers or ministers whatever. That express mention of the true annual value of the premises or of any of them or of other gifts or grants made before this time to the same Patrick has not been made in these presents and notwithstanding any statute act ordinance or provision made issued ordained or provided to the contrary. In witness whereof etc. Witness etc.]

xxj die Maij.

Rex Omnibus ad quos &c. salutem. Sciatis de gracia nostra speciali ac ex certa & mero motu nostris ac ex assensu & consensu Carissimi Avunculi nostri Ricardi Ducis Gloucestrie protectoris & defensoris Regni nostri Anglie / Damus & per presentes concedimus dilectis nobis Ricardo Williams & Thome Beynam Armigeris officium Constabularij Castri nostri de sancto Briavello in Foresta nostra de (Deane) Dene in Comitatu nostro Gloucestrie Habendum & occupandum officium predictum prefatis Ricardo & Thome per se vel per sufficientem deputatum suum sive sufficientes deputatos suos pro termino vite ipsorum Ricardi & Thome & utriusque eorum diucius viventis Percipiendum annuatim in & pro officio predicto feoda & vadia eidem officio ab antiquo debita & consueta eisdem Ricardo & Thome & eorum utrique diucius viventi [f11] per manus Receptorum Balliorum Firmariorum aut aliorum occupatorum Dominij nostri de Newelond in Foresta predicta pro tempore existentium ad termos Pasche & sancti Michaelis per equales porciones Unacum omnibus alijs feodis proficuis & commoditatibus officio predicto ab antiquo qualitercunque debitis & consuetis Eo quod expressa mencio de valore annuo feodorum vadiorum proficuorum & commoditatium predictorum in presentibus minime existit aut aliquo statuto actu ordinacione restricione sive provisione aut aliqua re materia vel causa quacunque non obstante In cuius etc Datum etc

[The king to all to whom etc. greeting. Know that of our special grace and of our certain and mere motion and with the assent and agreement of our dearest uncle Richard Duke of Gloucester protector and defender of our realm of England we give and by these presents grant to our beloved Richard Williams and Thomas Beynam esquires the office of constable of our castle of St. Briavel in our Forest of Dean in our county of Gloucestershire to have and occupy the aforesaid office to the aforesaid Richard and Thomas in person or by a sufficient deputy or by sufficient deputies for the term of life of the same Richard and Thomas and whichever of them lives the longer. To receive annually in and for the aforesaid office the fees and wages due and customary to the same office from of old to the same Richard and Thomas and whichever of them lives the longer by the hands of the receivers, baillifs, farmers or other tenants of our lordship of Newland in the abovesaid forest for the time being by equal portions at the terms of Easter and Michaelmas, together with all other fees, profits and revenues whatever due and owed in the aforesaid office of old. That express mention of the annual value of the aforesaid wages, fees and revenues is not made in these presents and not withstanding any statute, act, ordinance, restraint or provision or any thing, matter, or cause whatever. In witness of which etc. Given etc.]

Edwardus etc. Sciatis quod nos de fidelitate circumspeccione & industria dilecti nobis Thome (Ful) Fouleshirst Armigeri plenius confidentes de gracia nostra speciali / ac ex assensu precarissimi fidelissimique Avunculi nostri Ricardi Ducis Gloucestrie protectoris & defensoris durante (minore etate) minore etate nostra Regni nostri Anglie / ordinavimus & constituimus eundem Thomam Constabularium Castri nostri Cestri infra Comitatum nostrum palatinum Cestrie / Ac officium huiusmodi Constabularie Castri predicti eidem Thome commisimus per presentes Habendum & occupandum per se vel per sufficientem deputatum suum durante vita eiusdem Thome Fouleshurst cum omnibus & omnimodis vadijs feodis & emolumentis dicto officio Constabularie ab antiquo debitis sive consuetis seu eidem officio rite spectantibus adeo amplioribus modo & forma prout aliquis alius officium predictum ante hec tempora exercens habuit & percepit in eodem In cuius etc

[Edward etc. Know that we, fully trusting in the faith, discretion and industry of our beloved Thomas Fouleshirst, esquire, of our special grace and with the assent of our dearest and most faithful uncle, Richard, Duke of Gloucester, protector and defender of our realm of England during our minority, have appointed and made that Thomas constable of our castle of Chester within our county palatine of Chester, and by these presents commit the office of constable of the aforesaid castle to Thomas. To have and occupy in person or by a sufficient deputy during the life of Thomas Fouleshurst with all and all types of wages, fees and emoluments due or owed to the said office of constable of old, or pertaining of custom to that office, in as full a manner and form as anyone exercising the aforesaid office before this time had and received. In witness etc.]

Rex Omnibus etc salutem Sciatis quod nos bona laudabilia & fidelia servicia que dilectus (nib) nobis Morganus Kidwelly etc ordinavimus constituimus deputavimus & assignavimus ac per presentes ordinamus constitimus deputamus & assignamus ipsum Morganum nostrum (generalem) attornatum generalem in omnibus Curiis nostris de Recordo in Regno nostro Anglie & Wallie Habendum exercendum & occupandum officium illud generalis attornati nostri eidem Morgano pro termino vite sue percipiendo in fine pro officio illo durante vita sua vadia feoda proficua regarda eidem officio debita pertinentia et spectantia Damus autem & tenore presencium concedimus eidem Morgano plenam potestatem & auctoritatem faciendi ordinandi & deputandi taes Clericos & officarios sub ipso in qualibet Curia Curiarum predictarum quales aliquis alius officium illud ante hec tempora habens sive occupans habuit fecit ordinavit aut deputavit aut facere ordinare sive deputare consuevit Eo quod expressa mencio etc

[The king to all etc. greeting. Know that we, for the good, laudable and faithful service which our beloved Morgan Kidwelly etc. have ordained, made, deputed and appointed Morgan our attorney general in all our courts of record in our realm of England and Wales. To hold, exercise and occupy that office of our attorney general to that Morgan for term of his life, receiving for that office during his life all wages, fees, profits and rewards owing, pertaining and belonging to that office. We give, moreover, and by these presents grant to the same Morgan full power and authority to make, appoint and depute such clerks and officers under him in any court of the aforesaid courts as anyone holding or occupying that office before this time made, appointed and deputed and was accustomed to make, ordain or depute. That express mention etc.]

Edward etc To our auditors beyng or hereafter to be of Southtwales & of the marches of the same etc Where we by our lettres patentes bering date the first yere of our Reigne have graunted amonges other thinges to our right trusty & welbeloved Cousyne Herry duc of Bukingham the offices of Justice-shippe & Chambreleynshippe in Southtwalles & thoffice of Constableshippe & Capteynshippe of the Castelle of Abrustwith & of diverse other Castelle & Townes in Suthtwales and also the Constableshippe of alle other our Castelle there and in the Countees of Salop & Hereford and the Stewardshippe of alle the Castelle lordshippes Maners landes & tenementes in Suthtwales or in the marches thereof or in the seid Countees of Salop & Hereford and also the office of Fostershippe & maistershippe of the Game of alle our Forests & Chaces in Suthtwales etc ut supra (aswelle) suche as byne now voide frome the date of the seid lettres patentes and the Residue of the same frome the tyme that they shalbe void to the seid duc for terme of his lyff as in the lettres patentes etc Wherfore we wolle that ye allowe to the same duc for the premisses suche and as large Fees wages & rewardes as William late Erle of Pembrok or John late Erle of Worcestre or any other occupieng the seid offices in the same had & perceyved Also alle maner reperacions of the premisses costes in theschequer there costes of messengers riding or goynge on erandes cariages & portages of money expenses necessarie done or to be done by the seid deputees by their othes after the due ordure of accompt ye do make due allowaunce and that ye allowe to the seid duc & alle suche officers as he shalle make in any of the premisses fees wages etc to their offices due and the same allowaunces be made frome yere to yere during the liff of the seid duc of the Revenues etc And these our lettres shalbe unto you sufficient warraunt of discharge in that behalve etc

[f11b] Edward etc To our auditors beyng or hereafter to be of Northtwales Suthtwales and of the marches of Wales greting Where we by our lettres patentes bering date   have graunted amonges other thinges to our right trusty etc Herry duc of Bukingham the offices of Constableshippes Stewardships & Resseyvourships of our Castelle maner & Towne of Monmouthe & of alle other Castelles etc in SuthtWales Northtwales & marches of the same whiche byn parcelle of our duchie of Lancastre and also the Fostershippe & maistershippe of Game of Hodenak in Suthtwales & of alle our Forests etc in Northtwales Suthtwales & marches of the same Wherfore we wolle that ye allowe to the seid duc or his deputes for the seid offices such and as large Fees etc (ut in precedente) as is contened in the other warrant on the other side etc

(Edward etc)
A like warraunt to the auditors of Northtwales Suthtwales & the marches of Wales to allowe to the seid duc wages etc for the Constableships Steward-shippes and Resseyvorshippes of Uske & other Castelle lordshippes etc in Northtwales Suthtwales & marches of the same & of Salop & Hereford beyng parcelle of therldome of Marche and wages of Forstershippes & maister of Game of the forest of Trewyk & of alle Forestes chases etc in Northwales Suthtwales Marches of the same & in the said Countees etc

A like warraunt to thauditors of Northwales & marches of the same to allowe to the seid duc suche & as large Fees wages etc for the Justiceshippe & Chambreleyneshippe of Northwales & Constableshippes & Capteyneshippes of the Castelle & Towne of Conwey & other Castelles in Northtwales and also of Stewardshippes Forstershippes & maister of Game of alle Castelles lord-shippes Forestes chaces within the same etc

Edward etc To our auditors of Suthtwales etc greting Where by our severelle lettres patentes bering date the   day of Maij anno primo amonges other thinges have graunted etc Cousyne Herry duc of Buckingham thoffice of Chambreleynshippe of Suthtwales & Northwales and the oversight of oure subgettes now being or hereaftere to be in South Wa(s)les North Wales and in the Merches of Wales / and in the Counte of Salop Hereford Somerset Dorset and Wilteshire / and also powere & auctorite by his discrecione in oure name for oure defence and the defence of oure Realme and for the defence & keping of oure peax of & in the said parties to assemble oure said Subgettes defencibly arreied and therein conveie or sende to suche place or places & fro tyme to tyme as shalbe thoughte to the same Duc expedient & necessarie in that behalve / as in the said lettres patentes made at large is exspressed / We considering that the said Duc shalle bere & sustene gret costes & expenses in executing the said auctorite & powere to him committed have graunted to the said Duc that he have & Reteigne in his owne handes of suche money as he shalle Resceyve to oure use by reasone of the said office of Chambreleynship or of any other office the whiche he hathe of oure graunte suche summe or summes of money as he shalle expende or layout in executing the said auctorite to him committed in forme abovesaid Wherfore we wolle & charge you & every of you that ye & every of you allowe unto the said duc upon accomptes to be made by him or in his name or by his depute or deputees or otherwise suche summe or summes of money as the said duc shalle expend or be charged with by reason of the execucione of the said Auctorite conteyned in the said lettres patentes thereof by us to him made / according to the tenure & effecte of the same lettres patentes fro yere to yere & tyme to tyme / unto the tyme ye have from us otherwise in commaundement / And these oure lettres shalbe to you & every of you sufficient warraunt & discharge in that behalve

[f12] Edward etc To oure Auditors of Northwales now beyng & hereafter to be and to everich of thaim greting / Where we by oure severelle lettres patentes bering date the   day of Maij the first yere of oure Reigne amonges other thinges have graunted unto oure right trusty & righte entirely beloved Cousyn Henry Duc of Bukingham thoffices of Chambreleynship of Northwales & Suthwales and the oversight of oure subgettes now beyng & hereafter to be in Northwales Suthwales and the marches of Wales And also in the Countees of Salop Hereford Somerset Dorset & Wilteshire and also power & auctorite by his discrecion in oure name for oure defence / and the defence of this oure Realme and for the defence & keping of oure peas in the said parties to assemble oure said subgettes defensibly arreied and thaim convey & sende unto suche place or places and from tyme to tyme as shalbe thought unto the same duc expedient or necessary in that behalve as in the same lettres patentes more at large is expressed / We considering that the said duc shalle bere & sustene etc ut antea

Rex &c. Omnibus &c. salutem. Cum nos per litteras nostras patentes quarum data sunt   die Maij ultima preterita inter alia concessimus predilecto Consanguineo nostro Henrico duci Buckingham officia Camerarij in Suthwallia Northwallia Habendum & occupandum officia illa eidem duci per se vel per sufficientem deputatum suum aut sufficientes deputatos suos ad terminum vite sue ac per alias litteras nostras patentes quarum data est die & (die &) anno supradictis concesserimus prefato duci supervisionem omnium subditorum nostrorum in Northwallia Suthwallia & marchijs Wallie ac in Comitatibus Salop Hereford Somerset Dorset & Wilteshire qui nunc sunt & qui imposterum

erunt ac potestatem & auctoritatem ad eos defensibiliter arraiatos iuxta discrecionem ipsius ducis nomine nostro pro negocijs nostris convocandos et
(quo) coadunandos ac ipsos sic coadunatos & arraiatos nomine nostro pro
securitate seu defencione (Re) nostra Regni nostri vel parcium illarum aut
conservacione pacis nostre vel alijs negocijs nostris ad quemcunque (loce) seu
quecunque loca infra idem Regnum ducendos seu mittendos de tempore in
tempus iuxta discrecionem ipsius ducis prout in litteris illis plenius continetur
Sciatis quod nos custagia onera & expensas que dictus dux in execucione
premissorum habebit & subibit considerantes concessimus ac per presentes
concedimus eidem duci quod ipse habeat & (teneat) Retineat de tempore in
tempus in manibus suis proprijs de Receptis per ipsum ad usum nostrum
racione predicte officia Camerarij in Northwallia & Suthwallia ac eorum
alterius imposterum fiendis & percipiendis seu racione aliquorum aliorum
officiorum que idem dux habet ex concessione nostra tales & tantas pecuniarum summas quales idem dux in execucione predicti auctoritatis & mandati
sibi ut prefertur commissi & facti solvet faciet seu aliquo modo subibit Eo quod
expressa mencio de vero valore annuo seu certitudine premissorum aut de alijs
donis seu concessionibus eidem duci per nos ante hec tempora factis in presentibus minime facta existit aut aliquo alio statuto actu ordinacione seu restriccione incontrarium facta edita sive ordinata aut aliqua alia re causa vel
materia quacunque non obstante. In cuius &c.

[The king etc. to all etc. greeting. Since by our letters patent dated the
day of May last past among other things we granted to our dearly
beloved kinsman Henry Duke of Buckingham the offices of chamberlain in
South Wales and North Wales to have and occupy those offices to the same
duke in person or by a sufficient deputy or deputies for the term of his life and
by our other letters patent given on the day and year as above we granted to
the aforesaid duke supervision of all our subjects in North Wales South
Wales and the Welsh Marches and in the counties of Shropshire Hereford
Somerset Dorset and Wiltshire who now are and in future shall be and the
power and authority to summon and assemble them in defensive array at the
discretion of the same duke in our name for our business and when the same
have been thus assembled and arrayed in our name for the security or
defence of ourselves our kingdom or those parts or the preservation of our
peace or other business of ours to lead them or send them to any place or
places within the same realm from time to time at the discretion of the same
duke as is contained more fully in those letters. Know that we considering the
costs burdens and expenses which the said duke will have and incur in the
execution of the foregoing, have granted and by these presents do grant to
the same duke that he may have and retain from time to time in his own
hands from the receipts made and received to our use by reason of the
aforesaid offices of chamberlain in North Wales and South Wales or either of
them henceforwards, or by reason of any other offices which the same duke
holds by grant from us, such and so great sums of money as the same duke
shall pay make or in any wise incur in the execution of his aforesaid authority
and mandate committed and made to him as aforesaid. That express mention
of the true annual value or exactitude of the premises or of other gifts or
grants made by us to the same duke before this time has not been made in
these presents and notwithstanding any other statute act ordinance or re-

32

straint made issued or ordained to the contrary or any other thing cause or matter whatever. In witness whereof etc.]

[f12b] Rex Omnibus ad quos &c. salutem / Sciatis quod nos considerantes bona & laudabilia servicia que predilectus Consanguineus noster Henricus Dux Buckingham nobis impendit & impendere desiderat de gracia nostra speciali ac ex certa sciencia & mero motu nostris constituimus & ordinavimus ipsum ducem Constabularium Senescallum & Receptorem Castri Manerij & ville nostre de Uske in marchijs Wallie ac omnium aliorum Castrorum dominiorum Maneriorum villarum terrarum & tenementorum nostrorum que sunt parcelle Comitatus nostri marchie in Northwallia Suthwallia & marchijs Wallie ac in Comitatibus Salop' & Hereford' / ac officia Constabularij Senescalli & Receptoris Castrorum dominiorum Maneriorum villarum terrarum & tenementorum illorum & eorum cuiuslibet eidem duci damus & concedimus / Constituimus eciam & ordinavimus prefatum ducem custodem sive capitalem foreste & Chace nostre de Treweke ac omnium aliarum forestarum & Chacearum nostrarum parcellarum Comitatus predicti in Northwallia Suthwallia marchijs Wallie & Comitatibus predictis ac officia custodis sive Forestarij forestarum & Chacearum illarum eidem duci damus & concedimus / Habendum & exercendum officia predicta Scillicet illo officia eorundem que modo vacant a die date presencium litterarum nostrarum & omnia dicta alia officia modo plena & non vacancia a tempore quo ex quacunque causa primo vacaverint prefato duci ad terminum vite sue per se vel sufficientem deputatum suum aut sufficientes deputatos suos unacum vadijs feodis Regardis proficuis & commoditatibus officijs illis seu eorum (aliquo) alicui ab antiquo debitis & consuetis per manus Receptoris ballivi seu firmarij Castrorum dominiorum Maneriorum terrarum & tenementorum predictorum & cuiuslibet inde parcellarum ac in manibus ipsius ducis dum ipse Receptor eorundem extiterit Retinendis. Et ulterius dedimus & concessimus prefato duci potestatem & auctoritatem de tempore in tempus faciendi & constituendi omnes & omnimodas Senescallos eschaetores ballivos itinerantes forestarios prepositos Ringildos ballivos & omnes officiarios & ministros in predictis Castris dominijs Manerijs villis forestis Chaceis & eorum quodlibet necessarios & consuetos. Et quod huiusmodi officiarij sive ministri sic per ipsum ducem constituendi habeant & percipiant vadia feoda Regarda proficua & commoditates officijs illis & eorum cuilibet debita & consueta / ac quod idem dux habeat potestatem auctoritatem ad mandandum & percipiendum per litteras suas sive warrantum suum sub sigillo suo Cancellario nostro predicti Comitatus marchie qui pro tempore fuerit ad faciendum & exequendum omnia & singula ad officium cancellarij illius pertinencia sive incumbencia et quod huiusmodi littere sive precepta sint eidem Cancellario sufficiens warrantum de & pro omnibus que idem Cancellarius iuxta formam & efficium litterarum sive preceptorum illorum fecerit seu executere fecerit absque aliquo alio warranto per nos eidem Cancellario in ea parte fiendo. Eo quod expressa mencio &c.

[The king to all to whom etc. greeting. Know that we, considering the good and praiseworthy services which our dearly beloved kinsman, Henry, Duke of Buckingham, gives to us and desires to give, of our special grace and certain knowledge and mere motion, have appointed and ordained the same duke constable, steward and receiver of our castle, manor, and town of Usk in the Welsh Marches and of all our other castles, lordships, manors, towns, lands and tenements parcel of our earldom of March in North Wales, South Wales, and the Marches of Wales and in the counties of Shropshire and Hereford, and we give and grant to the same duke the offices of constable, steward, and receiver of those castles, lordships, manors, towns, lands, and tenements and any of them. Likewise we have appointed and ordained the aforesaid duke keeper or head of our forest and chase of Treweke and of all our other forests and chases parcel of the aforesaid earldom in North Wales, South Wales, the Marches of Wales and the aforesaid counties, and we give and grant to the same duke the office of keeper or forester of those forests and chases. To hold and exercise the aforesaid ofices, namely those offices of the same which are now vacant from the date of these our present letters and all the other said offices now filled and not vacant from the time when they first become vacant for any reason, to the said duke for the term of his life in person or through a sufficient deputy or deputies with the wages fees rewards profits and easements owed from of old and due to those offices or any of them by the hand of the receiver bailiff or farmer of the castles lordships manors lands and tenements aforesaid and any parcel thereof and to be retained in the hands of the same duke as long as he continues receiver of the same. And further we have given and granted to the aforesaid duke power and authority from time to time to make and appoint all and all manner of stewards escheators itinerant bailiffs foresters reeves rhingylls bailiffs and all officers and ministers in the aforesaid castles lordships manors towns forests chases and any of them as are necessary and customary. And such officers or ministers thus appointed by the same duke shall have and receive the wages fees rewards profits and easements owing and customary to those offices and any of them and the same duke shall have power and authority to direct and command by his letters or by warrant under his seal the chancellor of our said earldom of March for the time being to do and execute all and singular pertaining to or incumbent upon the office of that chancellor and such letters or commands shall be sufficient warrant to the same chancellor of and for everything that the same chancellor shall do or cause to be done according to the form and effect of those letters or commands without any other warrant made by us to the same chancellor in that respect. That express mention etc.]

Edward etc To oure trusty & welbeloved William Catesby Chaunceler of oure Erledom of the Marche greting / Where we by oure lettres patentes bering date the   day of Maij the first yere of oure Reigne have graunted unto oure righte trusty & righte entierly beloved (Cousj) Cousyne Henry duc of Bukingham power & auctorite that he by his lettres or warraunt under his seale may commaunde oure Chaunceler of oure said Erldome to do & execute al thinges to thoffice of Chauncelership thereof in any wise appertenyng or **[f13]** belonging as the same oure lettres patentes is expressed more at large / We wolle & charge you that ye obeie & execute al suche commaundementes as oure said Cousyn by his lettres or warraunt under his seale shal directe unto you concernyng youre said office of Chauncelership or thexecucione or due exercise of the same without any othre warraunt had of us thereof according to the tenure & effecte of the same lettres (of) or warraunt of oure said Cousyn unto tyme that ye from us have otherwise in commaundement And these oure lettres shalle be unto you sufficient warraunt & discharge in that behalve / Yeven under oure Prive seale etc

Rex &c. omnibus ad quos &c. salutem Sciatis quod de gracia nostra speciali ac ex mero motu nostris dedimus & concessimus ac per presentes damus & concedimus predilecto & fideli Clerico nostro Thome Langton custodiam omnium temporalium Episcopatus Menevensis simul cum advocacionibus ecclesiarum prebendarum Capellarum Cantariarum & aliorum beneficiorum ecclesiasticorum quorumcunque in manibus nostris per mortem bone memore Ricardi Episcopi Menevensis vacancium existencium / Habendum custodiam predictam prefato Thome a tempore mortis predicti Ricardi nuper Episcopi absque aliquo nobis inde Reddendo seu compoto inde faciendo quamdiu in manibus nostris Remanere contigerint Et ulterius quod quamquam in parliamento domini Edwardi nuper Regis Anglie progenitoris nostri apud Westmonasterium tento de Communi Consilio eiusdem progenitoris nostri inter alia provisum sit & ordinatum quod omnes illi qui impetraverint in Curia Romana Decanatus Archidiaconatus preposituras vel alias dignitates officia Capellas vel alia beneficia ecclesiastica quecunque ad collacionem donacionem presentacionem vel disposicionem ipsius progenitoris nostri vel alterius laicalis patroni de Regno suo spectancia vel impetrarent extunc huiusmodi beneficia per que dampnum preiudicium vel impeticio fuerit vel extunc fieri posset eidem progenitori nostro vel subditis suis in personis hereditatibus possessionibus iuribus vel bonis quibuscunque aut legibus usibus consuetudinibus franchesijs & libertatibus eiusdem Regni & Corone unacum omnibus manutentoribus Consiliarijs abettatoribus & alijs sibi auxiliantibus & fautoribus scienter tam ad sectam ipsius progenitoris nostri quam partis seu alterius cuiuscunque de Regno invenientis plegium & securitatem de prosequendo contra eos in isto casu penas in statuto predicto contentas incurrerent / Nos tamen ob sinceras dileccionem & affectacionem quas ad personam predicti predilecti Consiliarij nostri Thome Langton' Clerici nunc Menevensis electi gerimus & habemus considerantesque quod bona beneficia necnon Maneria terras tenementa Redditus & alias possessiones eidem Episcopatui pertinentes in tantum diminuta sunt & subtracta tantamque dilapidacionem patiuntur & Ruinam quod idem nunc electus cum gradum Episcopatus illius super se assumpserit statum & dignitatem suas ac alia onera eidem Episcopatui incumbencia honorifice uti debiat sustentare minime valeat seu manutenere De gracia nostri speciali ac ex certa (cient) ciencia & mero motu nostris et ut idem electus statum honorem & dignitatem Episcopatus illius decentius & honorificencius sustentare valeat & manutenere concessimus & licenciam dedimus pro nobis & heredibus nostris quod idem nunc electus procuratorem [f13b] seu procuratores suos usque Curiam Romanam transmittere valeat & destinare et quod ipsi quandam provisionem quod idem ellectus postquam in Episcopatum loci illius sit consecratus Ecclesiam parochialem de Pembrig' diocesis Hereford' nostri patronatus quam dictus Thomas iam tenet unacum dicto episcopatu habere & tenere ad terminum vite sue in commendam possidere possit in Curia Romana apud sedam apostolicam nomine ipsius electi prosequi ac litteras apostolicas sibi sub hoc fieri impetrare & eas in hoc Regnum nostrum Anglie transportare

& conducere ac transportari & conduci facere ac debite (execucione) ex-
ecucioni demandari valeant & valeat licite & impune absque impedimento
arrestacione seu gravamine quocunque nostri aut officiariorum seu ministrorum nostrorum quorumcunque. Eo quod expressa mencio &c.

[The king to all to whom etc. greeting. Know that we of our special grace and
mere motion have given and granted and by these presents give and grant to
our dearly beloved and faithful clerk Thomas Langton custody of all the
temporalities of the bishopric of St Davids with advowson of churches
prebends chapels chantries and other ecclesiastical benefices whatsoever in
our hands being vacant by the death of Richard, Bishop of St Davids, of
happy memory. To hold the aforesaid custody to the said Thomas from the
time of the death of the aforesaid Richard late bishop and without paying
anything to us therefor or making account therefor as long as they chance to
remain in our hands. And further although in the parliament of the Lord
Edward late King of England our ancestor held at Westminster it was
provided and ordained among other things by the common council of our
same ancestor that all those who should petition in the Roman curia for
deaneries archdeaconries provostships or other dignities offices chaplaincies
or other ecclesiastical benefices whatever pertaining to the collation gift
presentation or disposition of the same our ancestor or other lay patron of his
kingdom or should thenceforth petition for such benefices by which loss
prejudice or impeachment should arise or might henceforth arise to the same
our ancestor or his subjects in their persons hereditaments possessions rights
or goods whatsoever or to the laws uses customs franchises and liberties of
the same kingdom and crown with all supporters counsellors abettors and
others assisting and knowingly favouring them, either at the suit of the same
our ancestor or on the part of any other of the kingdom finding pledge and
security to proceed against them in this case, should incur the penalties
contained in the aforesaid statute: we however on account of the sincere love
and affection which we bear and have to the person of our aforesaid dearly
beloved counsellor Thomas Langton clerk now elected to St Davids and
considering that the goods benefices and also manors lands tenements rents
and other possessions belonging to the same bishopric are so greatly dim-
inished and reduced and suffer such dilapidation and ruin that the same now
elect, when he takes upon himself the office of bishop, will not be able to
support or maintain as he ought his state and dignity and other burdens
incumbent on the honour of bishop, of our especial grace and of our certain
knowledge and mere motion and in order that the same bishop elect may be
able to support and maintain fittingly and honourably the state honour and
dignity of the episcopate, we have granted and given licence for ourselves
and our heirs that the same now elected may send and direct his proctor
or proctors to the Roman curia and that they should make certain provision that the same elect after he has been consecrated to the bishopric of
that place should be able to hold the parish church of Pembridge in the
diocese of Hereford in our gift which the said Thomas now holds, to have and
hold it in commendam for the term of his life and that they should proceed in
the Roman curia at the apostolic see in the name of the same elect and cause
apostolic letters to be made to him for this and that they should be able to
transport and bring them into this our realm of England and to have them

transported and brought and put into due execution, and that he shall be able
to do so lawfully and with impunity without any impediment arrest or harm
from us or any of our officers or ministers. That express mention etc.]

Rex Omnibus &c. Sciatis quod Thomas Adersey habens ex concessione
domini Edwardi nuper Regis Anglie patris nostri officia Ballivorum Burgi sive
ville nostre de Chestrefeld ac dominij nostri de Scaresdale in Comitatu Derbie
unacum officio vocato Kingesbaillywik eorundem burgi & dominij pro termino
vite sue prout in dictis litteris etc. in voluntate existat litteras illas nobis in
Cancellariam nostram restituendi ibidem cancellandas ad intencionem quod
nos officia predicta dilecto nobis Nicholao Knyveton armigero in forma sequente concedere dignaremur. Nos considerantes etc. dedimus & concedimus
eidem Nicholao officia ballivorum burgi sive ville nostre de Chestrefeld ac
dominij nostri de Scaresdale in Comitatu Derbie unacum officio vocato kinges-
bailliwyk eorundem burgi & dominij habendum &c. per se vel per &c. pro
termino vite sue simul cum omnibus & singulis commoditatibus libertatibus &
dimissionibus firmarum ad dicta Burgum & dominium spectancibus adeo plene
sicud aliquis alius ballivus eorundem &c. habendo & percipiendo de & in
officijs illis talia vadia regarda &c. dictis officijs debita &c.

[The king to all etc. Know that Thomas Adersey, having by grant of the Lord
Edward late King of England our father the offices of bailiffs of our borough
or town of Chesterfield and our lordship of Scaresdale in the county of Derby
with the office called king's bailiwick of the same borough and lordship for
the term of his life as in the said letters etc., is now minded to return those
letters to us in our chancery there to be cancelled to the intent that we may
deign to grant the offices aforesaid to our beloved Nicholas Knyveton
esquire in the following form: We considering etc. have given and granted to
the same Nicholas the offices of bailiffs of our borough or town of Chesterfield and our lordship of Scaresdale in the county of Derby with the office
called king's bailiwick of the same borough and lordship. To hold etc. in
person or by etc. for the term of his life with all and singular easements
liberties and remissions of rents belonging to the said borough and lordship
as fully as any other bailiff of the same etc. having and receiving of and in
those offices such wages rewards etc. owing to the said offices etc.]

Edward etc to the keper of the park of Wodham ferrers in Essex his depute or
deputees greting And forsomoche as we for diverse consideracions us moving
and by thadvyse of our most entierly beloved Oncle the duc of Gloucestre etc
have appoynted our trusty servaunt John Reynford to have the keping of the
seid parc during our pleasure We therefore wolle & charge you that ye incontynent upone the sight of these advoide your enterresse of keping the same
fromhensfurthe not entermytting therewith but suffring the same our servaunt
or his deputees to occupie the same peasibly without any interupcione as ye
wolle answere unto us at your perilles Receyving therefore our lettres for your
discharge in that behalve yevene etc xxij day of Maij Anno primo

Rex Omnibus ballivis & fidelibus suis ad quos &c. salutem. Sciatis quod de
gracia nostra speciali ac ex certa sciencia & mero motu nostris perdonavimus
Remisimus & Relaxavimus Johanni Mewtis de villa nostra Calis' Clerico alias
dicto Johanni de Meautis nuper de London Gentilman alias dicto Johanni de
Mewtise nuper de Kensyngton in Comitatu Middlesex' gentilman Alias dicto
Johanni de Mewtice villa Westmonasterij in Comitatu Middlesex' yoman seu
quocunque alio nomine censeato omnimoda murdra felonias transgressiones
cogniciones feloniarum conspiraciones contemptus manutenencias negligen-
cias extorciones concelamenta forisfacturas impeticiones decepciones & offensas ac alia molestaciones quecunque per ipsum Johannem ante presentem diem
qualitercunque facta sive perpetrata unde indictatus rettatus attinctus con-
victus appellatus vel adiudicatus existat aut per Jurium processum vel aliquo
alio modo indictari rectari attinctari convinci appelari vel adiudicari contigerit
quoquo modo infuturum ac sectam [f14] pacis nostre que ad nos versus ipsum
Johannem pertinet seu pertinere poterit accionibus predictis seu alicuius earundem. Et insuper perdonavimus Remisimus & Relaxavimus eidem Johanni
omnimodas execuciones & penas mortis racione alicuius veridicti sive iudicij
pro aliqua felonia sive cognicione feloniarum aut racione aliquorum premissorum seu alicuius eorundem super eum Redditas sive adiudicatas vel Redd-
endas sive adiudicandas ac omnimodas penas & puniciones quas occasionibus
predictis seu earum aliqua erga nos incurrere deberet Aceciam utlagate sique
in ipsum Johannem hijs occasionibus seu earum aliqua fuerint promulgate &
formam pacem nostram ei inde concedimus. Ita tamen quod stet recto in Curia
nostra si quis versus eum loqui voluerit de premissis vel aliquo premissorum. In
cuius &c. Teste &c.

[The king to all his bailiffs and faithful people to whom etc. greeting. Know
that of our special grace and certain knowledge and mere motion we have
pardoned remitted and released to John Mewtis of our town of Calais, clerk,
alias John de Meautis late of London gentleman alias John de Mewtise late of
Kensington in the county of Middlesex gent. alias John de Mewtice of the
town of Westminster in the county of Middlesex yeoman or by whatever
name he is known, all manner of murders felonies transgressions cog-
nizances of felonies conspiracies contempts maintenances negligences extor-
tions concealments forfeitures impeachments deceptions and offences and
any other hurts in any wise made or perpetrated by the same John before the
present day for which he is indicted accused attainted convicted charged or
condemned or by process of law or in any other way might in the future
happen to be indicted accused attainted convicted charged or condemned,
and breach of our peace which pertains or should pertain to us against the
same John by the abovesaid actions or any of them. And moreover we have
pardoned remitted and released to the same John all kinds of executions and
penalties of death by reason of any verdict or judgment for any felony or
knowledge of felonies or by reason of the other premises or any of the same
given or passed or to be given or passed upon him, and all kinds of penalties
and punishments which on the aforesaid occasions or any of them he ought to
incur towards us. Also we grant to him the form of our peace for outlawry if it
has been pronounced on the same John on these occasions or any of them.
Providing always he stands trial in our court if any wishes to speak against
him on the premises or any of them. In witness etc. Witness etc.]

Rex &c. Omnibus ad quos &c. salutem. Sciatis quod nos de gracia nostra speciali ac de fidelitate circumspeccione & industria dilecti & fidelis nostri Roberti de Sancto Laurencio Militis domini de Houth' plenius confidentes Dedimus concessimus & per presentes damus & concedimus eidem Roberto / Officium Cancellarij nostri terre nostre Hibernie ac ipsum Robertum Cancellarium nostrum terre nostre predicte constituimus & ordinavimus ac per presentes constitimus & ordinamus / Habendum occupandum & exercendum officium illud per se vel per sufficientem deputatum suum pro termino vite eiusdem Roberti cum omnibus vadijs feodis Regardis iuribus auctoritatibus Jurisdiccionibus emolumentis libertatibus proficuis & commoditatibus eidem officio pertinencibus ac ab antiquo debitis & consuetis / tam ampliori modo & forma prout aliquis alius in officio predicto ante hec tempora habuit percepit sive occupavit / Percepiendo de nobis indies & Annuatim vadia feoda & Regarda predicta de exitibus & proficuis Revencionibus & emolumentis hanaperij nostri Cancellarie nostre infra terram nostram predictam provenientibus sive crescentibus per manus Custodis sive Clerici hanaperij predicti vel eius deputati pro tempore existentis / ac de exitibus & proficuis & Revencionibus Manerij sive Dominij nostri de Cromelyn cum (sup) suis pertinencijs in Comitatu Dublin' infra terram nostram predictam provenientibus sive crescentibus per manus ballivorum Receptorum firmariorum prepositorum tenencium sive aliorum occupatorum eiusdem Manerij sive Dominij pro tempore existencium ad festa Pasche & sancti Michaelis Archangeli per equales porciones / Necnon de custumis & Coquettis nostris de Corijs pellibus lanutis & alijs mercandisis & Rebus quibuscunque custumabilibus in portubus Civitatis nostre Dublin' & ville nostre de Drougheda in terra nostra predicta provenientibus per manus Collectorum Custumariorum firmariorum aut aliorum occupatorum eorundem Custumarum & coquettarum pro tempore existencium Aceciam de feodi firma ville nostre de Drougheda in terra nostra predicta (p) crescente sive proveniente per manus Maioris Vicecomitis seu (aliorum) aliquorum aliorum officiariorum eiusdem ville pro tempore existencium ac [sic] predicta festa Pasche & Sancti Michaelis equis porcionibus Damus autem universis & singulis officiarijs ministris & ligeis nostris tenore presencium firmiter in mandatis quod eidem Roberto officium predictum per se vel per huiusmodi deputatum suum debite exercendo intendentes sint respondentes obedientes & auxiliantes prout deccet Eo quod expressa mencio &c. tam infra regnum nostrum Anglie quam terram nostram Hibernie predicte ante hec tempora facta edita sive provisa non obstante. In cuius &c.

[The king etc. to all to whom etc. greeting. Know that we of our special grace and having full confidence in the fidelity, discretion and industry of our beloved and faithful Robert of St Laurence, knight, Lord Houth, have given and granted and by these presents do give and grant to the same Robert the office of our chancellor of our land of Ireland and we have appointed and ordained the same Robert to be our chancellor of our said land, and by these presents do appoint and ordain him, to have occupy and exercise that office in person or by his sufficient deputy for the term of the life of the same Robert with all wages fees rewards rights authorities jurisdictions emoluments liberties profits and easements pertaining to the same office and owing and customary from of old in as ample a manner and form as any other in the aforesaid office before this time had, received or occupied, receiving from us henceforward and annually the wages fees and rewards aforesaid from the issues profits revenues and emoluments coming or growing out of the hanaper of our chancery within our land aforesaid by the hands of the keeper or clerk of the hanaper aforesaid or his deputy for the time being, and produced or growing from the issues and profits and revenues of the manor or lordship of Cromelyn with its appurtenances in the county of Dublin within our land aforesaid by the hands of the bailiffs receivers farmers reeves tenants or other occupiers of the same manor or lordship for the time being at the feasts of Easter and Michaelmas by equal portions. Also from our customs and cockets arising from hides, skins, fleeces and whatever other merchandise and things are subject to customs dues in the ports of our city of Dublin and our town of Drougheda in our aforesaid land by the hands of the collectors of customs farmers or other occupiers of the same customs and cockets for the time being. And also growing or produced from the fee farm of our town of Drougheda in our land aforesaid by the hands of the mayor sheriff or any other officer of the same town for the time being at the aforesaid feasts of Easter and Michaelmas by equal portions. And we give to all and singular our officers ministers and lieges by the tenor of these presents the firm command that they shall be attentive responsive obedient and helpful as is fitting to the same Robert in the due exercise of the aforesaid office in person or by such deputy. Notwithstanding that express mention etc. both within our realm of England and in our land of Ireland aforesaid made issued or provided before this time. In witness whereof etc.]

[f14b] Rex Omnibus ad quos &c. salutem. Sciatis quod nos laudabilia servicia que Ricardus Huddelston' Miles ante hec tempora nobis impendit indiesque impendere non desistit considerantes de gracia nostra speciali ordinavimus & constituimus ipsum Ricardum Receptorem nostrum omnium dominiorum Maneriorum terrarum & tenementorum in Comitatibus Cumbria & Lancastria que nuper fuerunt Thome Marchionis Dorset / Et eundem Ricardum constituimus & ordinavimus Magistrum Forestariorum aceciam Senescallum omnium predictorum Dominiorum Maneriorum terrarum & tenementorum. Et prefato Ricardo officia predicta unacum officio Ballivi de Copelande cum (omnimodos) omnibus vadijs feodis proficuis Regardis Avantagijs commoditatibus & emolumentis quibuscunque eisdem officijs & eorum alicui pertinentibus sive spectantibus dedimus & concessimus & per presentes damus & concedimus / Habendum tenendum & occupandum eidem Ricardo officia predicta & eorum quodlibet per se vel per sufficientes deputatos suos ad terminum vite ipsius Ricardi cum omnibus vadijs feodis proficuis Regardis avantagijs commoditatibus & emolumentis eisdem officijs & eorum alicui appendentibus accidentibus sive pertinencibus. Et ulterius de ubriori gracia nostra concedimus eidem Ricardo quandam Annuitatem viginti marcarum Habendum & percipiendum sive retinendum in manibus suis proprijs vel per manus suas proprias de exitibus proficuis & Revencionibus Dominiorum Maneriorum terrarum & tenementorum predictorum ac ceterorum premissorum / Eo quod expressa mencio de vero valore Annuo premissorum aut de alijs donis sive concessionibus eidem Ricardo per nos ante hec tempora (facter) factis aut aliquo statuto actu ordinacione sive restriccione incontrarium facto non obstante. In cuius &c.

[The king to all to whom etc. greeting. Know that we, considering the praiseworthy services which Richard Huddelston, knight, has paid to us before this time and does not cease to pay, of our special grace have ordained and appointed the same Richard our receiver of all the lordships manors lands and tenements in the counties of Cumberland and Lancaster which were late of Thomas Marquis of Dorset. And we have appointed and ordained the same Richard master of the forests and steward of all the aforesaid lordships manors lands and tenements. And we have given and granted and by these presents do give and grant to the aforesaid Richard the offices aforesaid together with the office of bailiff of Copelande with all wages fees profits rewards advantages easements and emoluments whatever appertaining or belonging to these same offices and any of them. To have, hold and occupy the offices aforesaid and any of them to the same Richard in person or by his sufficient deputies for the term of the life of the same Richard with all wages fees profits rewards gains easements and emoluments attached, accruing or pertaining to the same offices and any of them. And further of our more especial grace we have granted to the same Richard a certain annuity of twenty marks to hold and receive or retain in his own hands or through his own hands from the issues profits and revenues of the lordships manors lands and tenements aforesaid and the other premises. That express mention of the true annual value of the premises or of other gifts and grants made by us to the same Richard before this time or any statute act ordinance or restraint to the contrary notwithstanding. In witness whereof etc.]

Rex Omnibus &c. Salutem. Sciatis quod nos de gracia nostra speciali ac ex certa sciencia & mero motu nostris Concessimus Johanni Josselyn Officium (auditorum) Auditoris omnium Castrorum dominiorum Maneriorum terrarum & tenementorum Reddituum & possessionum quorumcunque nuper Henrici Bourghchier Militis Comitis Essex' iam defuncti que ad manus nostras devenere seu devenire debent racione minoris etatis Henrici Bourghcher Militis Consanguinei & heredis prefati Henrici Bourghcher Militis nuper Comitis Essex' videlicet filij Willelmi Bourghchier militis nuper Domini Bourghchier Filij prefati Henrici Bourghchier nuper Comitis Essex'. Habendum & occupandum officium illud prefato Johanni Josselyn ac eius sufficientibus deputatis durante minore etate eiusdem Henrici Consanguinei & heredis predicti Henrici Bourghchier nuper Comitis Essex' / Ac ulterius quamdiu in manibus nostris fore contigerint Percipiendum annuatim in & pro execucione officij predicti Feoda & Wadia eidem officio ab antiquo debita & consueta per manus Receptoris ballivorum prepositorum Firmariorum aut aliorum officiariorum eorundem pro tempore existencium ad Festa Sancti Michaelis Archangeli & Pasche per equales porciones unacum omnibus alijs proficuis & emolumentis quibuscunque dicto officio spectantibus adeo plene large & libere prout aliquis alius officium illud ante hec tempora habuit sive occupavit. In cuius &c.

[The king to all etc. greeting. Know that we of our special grace and of our certain knowledge and mere motion have granted to John Josselyn the office of auditor of all the castles lordships manors lands and tenements rents and possessions whatsoever late of Henry Bourghchier, knight, Earl of Essex, now deceased which came to our hands or ought to come by reason of the minority of Henry Bourghcher, knight, kinsman and heir of the aforesaid Henry Bourghcher, knight, late Earl of Essex viz. the son of William Bourghchier, knight, late Lord Bourghchier son of the aforesaid Henry Bourghchier late Earl of Essex. To have and occupy that office to the aforesaid John Josselyn and his sufficient deputies during the minority of the same Henry kinsman and heir of the aforesaid Henry Bourghchier late Earl of Essex. And further as long as they shall happen to be in our hands to receive annually in and for the execution of the aforesaid office the fees and wages owing and customary from of old to the same office by the hands of the receiver bailiffs reeves farmers or other officers of the same for the time being at the feasts of Michaelmas and Easter by equal portions together with all other profits and emoluments whatever belonging to the said office as fully largely and freely as any other had or occupied that office before this time. In witness whereof etc.]

Edwardus &c Dilecte (nobis) in Christo nobis Abbisse Monasterij de Wilton' salutem. Cum ad nos & progenitores nostros longa consuetudinis consuetudinis [sic] & a tempore cuius contrarij hominum memoria non existit iure (Corone) Corone nostre ac racione fundacionis Monasterij predicti denominacio (eiusdem) cuiusdam mulieris bone & vertuose Condicionis que estimatur divino famulatui inservire spectat & notorie agnoscitur pertinere que vestre Religioni iuxta ipsius merita imperpetuum Divinis obsequijs valeat famulare / Vobis igitur tenore presencium Emmam (Dac) Daccomber nominamus cupientes quatenus eam iuxta morem preteri temporibus inter vos in ea parte hactenus usitatis admittere curetis. In cuius &c.

[Edward etc. to our beloved in Christ the abbess of the monastery of Wilton, greeting. Since by long prescript of custom and from the time of which the memory of man runs not to the contrary, the presentation of a certain woman of good and virtuous condition, who is considered to be devoted to the religious community, belongs to, and is publicly recognised to pertain to, us and our ancesters, by right of our crown and by reason of the foundation of the aforesaid monastery; which woman should be able to serve your community. Therefore by the tenor of these presents we nominate to you Emma Daccomber desiring that you will cause her to be admitted amongst you according to the custom of times past as you have been used to do in this respect. In witness whereof etc.]

Edwardus &c. Omnibus &c. salutem. Sciatis quod nos de gracia nostra speciali ac bona & gratuita obsequia dilecti Armigeri nostri Alveredi Cornburgh nobis ante hec tempora ad suos grandes Custus & expensas multipliciter impensa intime contemplantes Concessimus eidem Alveredo officium Contrarotulatoris cunagij nostri Stanij in Comitatibus Cornubie [f15] & Devonie. Habendum occupandum & exercendum dictum officium per se aut sufficientem deputatum suum vel per sufficientes deputatos suos a die date presencium durante vita ipsius Alveredi percipiendo annuatim ad festa Sancti Michaelis Archangeli & Pasche per equales porciones in & pro dicto officio Contrarotulatoris tunagij vadia feoda & regarda eidem officio spectancia Sicut Thomas Vaghan Miles qui dictum officium nuper habuit & occupavit habuit & percepit per manus Receptoris generalis ducatus nostri Cornubie pro tempore existentis de exitibus & proficuis eiusdem ducatus eo quod expressa mencio de vero valore annuo vadiorum feodorum & regardorum predictorum seu de alijs donis & concessionibus per nos seu aliquem progenitorum nostrorum eidem Alveredo factis [aut aliquo statuto actu ordinacione sive restriccione incontrarium facto] edito sive ordinato non obstante. In cuius &c. Teste meipso apud Turrim nostram Londoniensis xix° die mensis maij. Anno primo Regis Edwardi v^{ti}.

[Edward etc. to all etc. greeting. Know that we, of our special grace and closely considering the good and agreeable services of our beloved esquire, Alfred Cornburgh, often done to us before this time at his great cost and expense, have granted to the same Alfred the office of controller of our coinage of tin in the counties of Cornwall and Devon, to have, hold and exercise the said office in person or by his sufficient deputy or deputies from the date of these presents during the life of the same Alfred, receiving annually at the feasts of Michaelmas and Easter by equal portions in and for the said office of controller of the coinage such wages fees and rewards belonging to the same office as Thomas Vaughan, knight, who lately held and occupied the said office had and received by the hands of the receiver general of our duchy of Cornwall for the time being from the issues and profits of the same duchy. That express mention of the true annual value of the wages fees and rewards aforesaid or of other gifts and grants made to the same Alfred by us or any of our ancestors [any statute, act, ordinance or restriction to the contrary made] issued or ordained not withstanding. In witness whereof etc. Witness myself at our Tower of London on the 19th day of May in the first year of King Edward V.]

Rex Omnibus ad quos &c. salutem. Sciatis quod nos de fidelitate & circumspeccione dilecti Clerici nostri Walteri Felde plenius confidentes de gracia nostra speciali ac ex advisamentis precarissimi Avunculi nostri Ricardi ducis Gloucestrie protectoris & defensoris Regni nostri Anglie durante juniore etate nostra ac aliorum dominorum de Consilio nostro fecimus ordinavimus & constituimus ipsum Walterum magnum Elemosinarium nostrum ac officium Elemosinarij nostri eidem Waltero per presentes damus & concedimus dantes & concedentes ipsi Waltero potestatem & auctoritatem faciendi & exequendi omnia & singula que ad officium Elemosinarij nostri pertinent in tam ampla forma prout aliquis alius officium illiud aliquo tempore preterito exercens Racione eiusdem officij fecit seu executus fuit. Habendum occupandum & exercendum officium predictum prefato Waltero per se vel per sufficientem deputatum suum aut sufficientes deputatos suos ad terminum vite sue cum omnibus & singulis vadijs feodis & Rebus eidem officio pertinentibus sive spectantibus. Et ulterius damus & concedimus eidem Waltero ad eundem terminum vite sue omnia & omnimoda bona & catalla quorumcunque personarum felonum de se & cuiuslibet persone felonis de se tam infra libertates quam extra infra Regnum nostri Anglie inventa & invenienda forisfacta & forisfacienda aut nobis tam nunc quam infuturum quovismodo pertinencia quam omnimoda deodanda que nobis infra Regnum predictum tam infra libertates

quam extra pertinent aut unquam post primum diem Regni nostri nobis pert-
inuerunt aut pertinere debebunt aut contingent ullo modo quamdiu ipsum
Walterum Elemosinarium nostrum fore contigerit. Et volumus & concedimus
eidem Elemosinario nostro quod bene liceat sibi aut deputatis & servientibus
suis omnia & singula huiusmodi bona & Catalla felonum de se & deodanda
ubicumque inveniri poterint tam infra libertates quam extra capere & seisire
levare & collegere / Ac per presentes Assignavimus prefatum Elemosinarium
nostrum & deputatos suos ac eis auctoritatem committimus in hac parte ad
terminum vite ipsius Walteri ad inquirendum de tempore in tempus vijs &
modis quibus melius scire poterint de huiusmodi bonis & catallis ac (deodandis) deodandis & ad eadem seisiendum capiendum & levandum per se sive
deputatum suum aut deputatos suos sufficientes ubicumque infra Regnum
predictum fuerint inventa tam infra libertates quam extra et ad ipsa sic levata &
collata per se ubi melius sibi videbitur pro nobis in Elemosinam distribenda
Absque Compoto seu aliquo alio inde nobis vel heredibus nostris reddendo seu
solvendo. Mandamus autem & precipimus universis & singulis vicecomitibus
Maioribus ballivis Coronatoribus Escaetoribus Constabularijs ac omnibus alijs
officiarijs ministris nostris tam infra libertates quam extra & eorum cuilibet
tenore presencium quod prefato Elemosinario nostro ac deputatis suis predictis in execucione premissorum supportantes sint intendentes confortantes auxiliantes & defendentes sub periculo quod incumbit. In cuius Rei &c.

[The king to all to whom etc. greetings. Know that we, fully trusting in the
faithfulness and discretion of our beloved clerk Walter Felde, of our special
grace and on the advice of our dearest uncle Richard Duke of Gloucester
protector and defender of our realm of England during our minority and of
the other lords of our council have made ordained and appointed the same
Walter our great almoner and by these presents give and grant to the same
Walter the office of our almoner, giving and granting to the same Walter
power and authority to do and perform all and singular that pertains to the
office of our almoner in as ample a form as any other exercising that office at
any time past did or performed by reason of the same office. To have hold
and exercise the aforesaid office to the aforesaid Walter in person or by his
sufficient deputy or deputies for the term of his life with all and singular wages
fees and things pertaining or belonging to the same office. And further we
give and grant to the same Walter for the same term of his life all and every
kind of goods and chattels of any suicides and of any suicide within the
liberties or without found and to be found forfeit and to be forfeit within our
realm of England or in any way belonging to us now or in the future and all
manner of deodands which belong to us within the aforesaid kingdom both
within the liberties and without or ever have belonged to us since the first day
of our reign or ought to belong or may come to us in any wise as long as the
same Walter shall happen to be our almoner. And we will and grant to our
same almoner that it shall be lawful for him or his deputies and servants to
take and seize levy and collect all and singular such goods and chattels of
suicides and deodands wherever they may be found both within the liberties
and without,. and by these presents we have assigned to our aforesaid
almoner and his deputies and commit to them authority in this respect for
the term of the life of the same Walter to seek out from time to time by what
ways and means he may best have knowledge of such goods and chattels and

deodands so as to seize take and levy the same in person or by his deputy or sufficient deputies wherever they may have been found within the aforesaid kingdom both within the liberties and without and when he has thus collected them and brought them together where it shall seem best to him, to distribute them for us in alms, without account or anything else to be rendered or paid therefor to us or our heirs. And we order and command all and singular sheriffs mayors bailiffs coroners escheators constables and all our other officers and ministers both within the liberties and without and any of them by the tenor of these presents that under peril they should support assist strengthen aid and defend our aforesaid almoner and his aforesaid deputies in the execution of the premises. In witness whereof etc.]

[f15b] Edward etc To oure trusty & welbeloved Chapleyn Maister Henry Bost Maister of oure Callage called the kinges halle within oure universite of Cambrigge and [sic] his absence to his depute there and to every of them greting / We let you wit that in Consideracione of the good & vertuouse disposicione of oure welbeloved maister Hugh Fraunce maister of Arte and of the good & acceptable service that the said Maister Hugh hathe done unto the most famouse prince of the most blessed memorie the late king my lord & Fader whome god assoile / We by thadvise of oure derrest Oncle the duc of Gloucestre protector & defensor of this oure Royaume during oure yong Age / have yoven & graunted unto him the Rome & place of a felowe whiche shal happen furst & next to falle & be voide within oure said Collage be it by dethe Resignacion or in what manere it shal fortune to be voide Wherfore we wolle & charge you that whensoever the said Rome so shal happen to be voide ye admitte take & Receyve the said Maister Hugh unto the same / to have & enyoie it for terme of his lyff with alle duetees & commoditees belonging & apperteynyng or of right ought to belong or apperteyne unto a felowe there / Any benyfice or benefices or other promocione to the yerely valew of xx li or under notwithstanding Yeven etc

Please it youre highness in consideracione of the true & feithefulle service whiche youre humble subgett William Brenner hathe done and during his lyff entendethe to do unto youre most noble grace to yeve & graunt unto him the portershippe of youre Castelle of Beestone parcelle of youre Erledome of Chestre within youre Counte of Chestre whiche office is now in youre graciouse gifte & disposicione by the decesse of Robert of Deyne that late had the same to have occupie & enyoie the said portershippe unto the said William by him selfe or his sufficient depute for terme of his liff with the wages of ij d by the day. To be had & perceyved at the Receipt of youre eschequere at Chestre aforsaid by the handes of youre Chambreleyn of Chestre for the tyme beyng at the termes there usuelles by evin porciones / and with al other profites commoditees & advailes to the same office in any wise belonging in as ample forme as the said Robert or any other persone or persones the same office have had & exercised in tyme passed / That expresse mencione of the profites and comoditees & advaile is not herin specified Eny statute acte or ordenaunce made to the contrarie notwithstanding / And thereupon to have youre graciouse lettres patentes undere the seale of youre Countie palatyne of Chestre to be made in

due & effectuel forme and he shal ever pray to god for youre most Royalle
astate

[f16] Rex / Omnibus ad quos &c. salutem / Supplicavit nobis dilectus Clericus
noster Johannes Gourle ut cum quedam Cantaria unius Capellani in Ecclesia
parochiali de Kemsey in Comitatu Wygorn' ab antiquo fundata de certis possessionibus & Redditibus in villis de (Kemsy) Kemsey & Norton' dotata tam propter
exilitatem proficuorum eiusdem Cantarie quam propter negligenciam & in-
curiam Capellanorum diversorum ibidem temporibus Retroactis deserviencium
a possessionibus & Redditibus predictis quasi desolata Remaneat & destructa
quod Capellanus aliquis Cantariam illam admittere ad deserviendum eidem Cantarie per magnum tempus non Curavit dictusque Johannes premissis pie com-
paciens mediante licencea nostra emendare proponata Ita quod Capellanus qui
ad altare beate Marie in Ecclesia de Kemsey predicta Celebratur pro anima fundatoris Cantarie predicte ordinandus existit habeat sibi & successoribus suis Redditus & possessiones unde dicta Cantaria primitus fuit fundata et ut idem Johannes tanti operis pietatis fiat particeps et dicta Cantaria melius imposterum valeat
sustentari eandem Cantariam de certis terris et possessionibus cupiat (ag)
augmentari velimus licenciam Regiam ad hoc impartiri & concedere eidem
Johanni quod ipse duo Mesuagia sexaginta Acras terre sex Acras prati &
quinque Acras bosci cum pertinencijs in villa & parochia de Kemsey dare possit
& assignare Johanni Carpenter nunc Capellano in dicta Ecclesia de Kemsey
celebranti / Habendum & tenendum sibi & successoribus suis Capellanis divina
pro anima fundatoris dicte prime Cantarie ac salubri statu nostro & prefati
Johannis Gourle dum vixerint & animabus eorundem cum ab hac luce
migraverint. Necnon pro anima Ade Moleyns nuper (Ca) Cisestrensis Episcopi
ac animabus patris & matris dicti Johannis Gourle & parentum suorum &
omnium fidelium defunctorum in dicta Ecclesia de Kemsey singulis diebus
celebraturis / Nos consideracione premissorum concessimus & licenciam dedimus pro nobis & heredibus nostris quantum in nobis est eidem Johanni Gourle
quod ipse predicta duo Messuagia sexaginta Acras terre sex Acras prati &
quinque Acras bosci cum pertinencijs in villa & parochia de Kemsey dare possit
& assignare prefato Capellano / Habendum sibi & successoribus suis Capellanis
Cantarie predicte divina pro Statu & animabus predictis in dicta ecclesia
parochiali de Kemsey ad altare predictum singulis diebus celebraturis imperpetuum. (Et i) Et eidem Capellano quod ipse predicta Mesuagia terram pratum
& boscum cum pertinencijs ei sit per prefatum Johannem Gourle danda &
assignanda ab eodem Johanne Gourle Recipere possit & tenere sibi & successoribus suis predictis divina ut predictum est singulis diebus celebraturis imperpetuum et quod idem Capellanus eiusdem Cantarie & successores sui Capellani
eiusdem Cantarie terras tenementa Redditus & possessiones quecunque ad
valorem quadraginta solidorum per Annum ultimum Reprisas que de nobis in
Capite non tenentur de quacunque persona sive quibuscunque personis ea eis
dare concedere legare vel assignare volente seu volentibus perquirere &
(percipere) Recipere possint & possit / Habendum & tenendum sibi & successoribus suis Capellanis predictis in sustentacionem suam imperpetuum / Et
eidem persone sive eisdem personis & eorum cuilibet quod ipsi & quilibet
eorum terras tenementa Redditus & possessiones huiusmodi usque ad Annuam
valorem supradictam prefato Capellano Cantarie predicte pro tempore exist-

enti & successoribus suis predictis in forma predicta dare concedere legare vel assignare possint & possit Tenore presencium similiter licenciam damus specialem **[f16b]** Statuto de terris & tenementis ad manum mortuam non ponendis edito non obstante. Nolentes quod idem Johannes Gourle vel success-ores sui aut prefatus Capellanus vel successores sui predicti racione premissorum per nos vel heredes nostros Justiciarios Escaetos vicecomites aut alios ballivos seu ministros nostros quoscunque occasionentur molestentur in aliquo seu graventur / Salvis tamen Capitalibus dominis feodi illius servicijs inde debitis & consuetis aut aliquo alio statuto actu ordinacione sive Restriccione in contrarium edito sive facto seu aliqua prosecucione alicuius inquisicionis virtute brevis nostri de ad quod dampnum non obstante In cuius &c.

[The king to all to whom etc. greeting. Our beloved clerk John Gourle has besought us that since a certain chantry of one chaplain in the parish church of Kemsey in the county of Worcester founded of old and endowed from certain possessions and rents in the towns of Kemsey and Norton remains almost desolate and ruined on account of the small income of the same chantry and on account of the neglect and want of care of divers chaplains there in times past serving it from the possessions and rents aforesaid, because no chaplain has accepted to serve at that chantry for a long time, and he the said John taking pious compassion on the premises proposes amend-ment by means of our licence, that the chaplain who celebrates at the altar of the blessed Mary in the church of Kemsey aforesaid for the soul of the founder of the aforesaid chantry might have granted to him and his successors the rents and possessions whence the said chantry was first endowed and in order that the same John might be a sharer in so great a work of piety and that the said chantry might be the better supported for the future he desires that the same chantry should be increased by certain lands and possessions and that we should will that the royal licence for this purpose should be granted and conceded to the same John that he might be able to give and assign to John Carpenter now a chaplain celebrating in the said church of Kemsey two messuages, sixty acres of land, six acres of meadow and five acres of wood with appurtenances in the town and parish of Kemsey. To have and hold to him and his successors, chaplains celebrating the divine rites every day in the said church of Kemsey for the soul of the founder of the said first chantry and for our health and that of the aforesaid John Gourle while we live and for the souls of the same when they have died,also for the soul of Adam Moleyns late Bishop of Cirencester and the souls of the father and mother of the said John Gourle and his relatives and all the faithful departed. Considering these premises, we have granted and given licence for ourselves and our heirs as far as in us lies to the same John Gourle that he may give and assign the aforesaid two messuages, sixty acres of land, six acres of meadow and five acres of wood with appurtenances in the town and parish of Kemsey to the aforesaid chaplain to hold to himself and his successors, the chaplains celebrating the divine services of the chantry aforesaid for the estate and souls aforesaid in perpetuity in the said parish church of Kemsey at the altar aforesaid each day. And to the same chaplain that he may receive and hold to himself and his successors aforesaid celebrating divine service each day for ever as abovesaid the aforesaid messuages land meadow and wood with appurtenances to be given and assigned to him by the aforesaid John Gourle from the said John Gourle and that the same chaplain of the same chantry and his successors, the chaplains of the same chantry, shall be able to purchase and receive lands tenements rents and possessions whatever to the value of forty shillings a year after reprises which are not held of us in chief from any person or persons wishing to give grant bequeath or assign them to them. To have and to hold to him and his successors, the chaplains aforesaid, for their maintenance in perpetuity. And similarly by the tenor of these presents we give special licence to the same person or persons and any of them to give grant bequeath or assign lands tenements rents and possessions of this kind up to the annual value aforesaid to the aforesaid chaplain of the aforesaid chantry for the time being and his successors aforesaid in form aforesaid notwithstanding the statute against putting lands and tenements into mortmain. And we will that the same John Gourle and his successors or the aforesaid chaplain and his successors abovesaid should not be interfered with, molested or harmed in aught by reason of the foregoing by us or our heirs, justices, escheators, sheriffs or other bailiffs or any of our ministers. Excepting however the services owing and customary therefor to the capital lords of that fee, or any other statute act ordinance or restraint to the contrary issued or made or any prosecution of any inquisition in virtue of our writ of ad quod damnum not withstanding. In witness whereof etc.]

Edward by the grace of God etc To thofficers fermors tenauntes & inhabitantes of the lordshippes landes & tenementes called Gower landes in Wales greting / And let you wit that by thadvise of oure derrest Oncle of Gloucestre protector of this oure Royaulme during oure yong Age We have committed the Rule & oversighte & governaunce of the said lordshippes landes & tenementes to oure entierly beloved Cousyne Henry duc of Bukingham to have to him during oure pleasure with putting in & out of of [sic] Thofficers there Wherfore we wolle & streitly charge you & every of you that incontynent upon the sighte hereof ye do advoide your (seff) selff from the possession & occupacion of any office belonging the said Gowers landes and accept & take oure said Cousyne as Rulere overseer & governor of the same / and suffre suche his servauntes as he wolle depute undere him peasibly to occupie without interupcion / and to him & his said deputees in executing the same geve youre aides & assistences supporting & obeieng them in alle thinges as appertenethe This be not failled upon the feith & Alliegeaunce ye bere unto us Yevene the xxvj^{ti} day of Maij the first yere of the Reigne of King Edward the fyfte

please it youre highenes of youre most noble grace Inconsideracionᵥ of the feithefulle service whiche youre humble servaunt Richard Tilles Clerk Countroller of youre most honerable household hathe heretofore done unto the most famouse prince of blessed memorie youre fader late king / and during his lyff intendethe to do unto youre said highenes to geve & graunt unto youre said servaunt thoffice of Countroller of youre Werkes within this youre Royaulme now beyng voide by the dethe of Sir John Kendale late one of the Almesse knightes within youre Collage of Wyndesore / to have occupie & exercise the said office by him selfe or his depute or deputees sufficient during oure pleasure with wages & fees & other libertees & commoditees to the said office of olde tyme due & accustumed and in as ample maner & forme as the said John or any other persone or persones beforetymes the said office occupieng have had & enyoied in & for the same And he shal pray to god for youre most noble & Royalle astate

please it youre most noble grace in consideracione of the true & feithefulle service whiche youre humble servaunt Waltier Hungerford one of the squiers for youre body hathe done unto the most famouse prince of noble memorie the late king youre Fader whome god assoyle and during his lyff entendethe to do (to) unto youre grace to geve & graunt unto him that Annuyte of xx marc whiche Edmund Hawte late had in youre lordshippe of Melton in youre Counte of Kent to have & enyoie the said Annuyte of xx marc unto youre said servaunt for terme of his lyff to be had & perceyved yerely of thissues and Revenues of the lordshippes forsaid by the handes of the Receyvor bailief fermors [f17] or other occupiers there for the tyme beyng at the termes of Seint Michelle tharchangelle & pasche by evyn porcions and he shal pray to god for (the preservac) youre noble persone & astate Royalle

Mekely besichithe youre highenes youre humble & true liegeman John Cotington that it wold please the same youre highenes of youre most noble & habundaunt grace in consideracion of the true & feithfulle service that youre said besechere hath done aswele unto the most excellent & Christien prince of noble memorie youre Fadere whose soule Jhesu have mercy as unto youre highenes and unto the righte highe & mighti prince Richard duc of Gloucestre youre uncle protector & defensor of this youre Royaulme and his lyff during entendeth to do / to graunt unto him by youre gracious lettres patentes in due forme to be made the office of parkershippe of youre parke of Whitemede lyeng within youre Forest of Deane in the same parisshe Which office one William Slatter now goone to the see with Sir Edward Wodevile late had / To have & occupie the said office of parkereship by him or by his depute sufficient for terme of the lyff of youre said besechere with alle maner Fees wages profites Rewardes & commoditees to the said office of olde tyme due and accustumed / That expresse mencion of the (verraye) verray valewe of the said office herein is not expressed or any statute Act ordenaunce or commaundement had or made to the contrarie notwithstanding / And youre said besechere shalle dayly pray to god for youre most high & noble Astate

Rex Omnibus ad quos &c. salutem. Sciatis quod nos de gracia nostri speciali ac ex certa sciencia & mero motu nostris perdonavimus Remittimus & Relaxavimus Thome Trigot & Willelmo Johnson omnimodas donaciones Alienaciones & perquisiciones de manerijs de Bouden & Haverbergh cum pertinencijs in Comitatu Leycestrie ac de quodam redditu Centum solidorum per annum in Holtwell & Abbeketelby cum suis pertinencijs in eodem Comitatu que nuper fuerunt Thome Scrop' de Massham militis defuncti / et que de nobis tenentur in capite per servicium militare ante hec tempora factas absque licencia Regia unacum exitibus & proficuis inde ante hec tempora preceptis. Et ulterius de ubriori gracia nostra concessimus eiodem Thome Trigot & (Iohanni) Willelmo

Johnson omnia & omnimodos exitus proficua & Revenciones Maneriorum & Redditum predictorum cum pertinencijs ante hec tempora provenientia et nobis ex causis supradictus seu earum aliqua debita aut aliquo modo nobis ante hec tempora pertinencia / Habendum & (pert) percipiendum tam per manus suas proprias quam per manus vicecomitum Escaetorum ac nuper vicecomitum & nuper Escaetorum Comitatus predicti seu aliorum occupatorum Maneriorum & Redditum predictorum cum pertinencijs pro tempore existencium adeo plene & integre sicut nos ea haberemus si presens concessio nostra eis inde facta non fuisset / Eo quod expressa mencio de vero valore annuo Maneriorum & redditum predictorum vel certitudine premissorum aut de alijs donis sive concessionibus per nos eisdem Thome Trigot & Willelmo Johnson seu eorum alteri ante hec tempora factis in (premissis) presentibus minime facta existit / aut aliquo statuto actu ordinacione seu restriccione in contrarium facta edita sive ordinata vel aliqua re causa vel materia quacunque non obstante. In cuius rei &c.

[The king to all to whom etc. greeting. Know that we of our special grace and of our certain knowledge and mere motion have pardoned remitted and released to Thomas Trigot and William Johnson all kinds of gifts alienations and acquisitions of the manors of Bowden and Haverbergh with appurtenances in the county of Leicester and a certain rent of one hundred shillings per annum in Holtwell and Ab Kettleby with their appurtenances in the same county which were lately of Thomas Scrop of Massham, knight, deceased, and which are held of us in chief by knight service, made before this time without the royal licence with the issues and profits therefrom prescribed before this time. And further of our more especial grace we have granted to the same Thomas Trigot and William Johnson all and every kind of issues, profits, revenues of manors and rents aforesaid with appurtenances arising before this time and owing to us from the aforesaid causes or any of them or in any way pertaining to us before this time. To have and receive by their own hands or by the hands of sheriffs escheators and past sheriffs and escheators of the aforesaid county or other occupiers of the manors and rent aforesaid with appurtenances for the time being as fully and completely as we would have them if our present grant thereof had not been made. That express mention of the true annual value of the manors and rent aforesaid or the extent of the premises or of the other gifts or grants made by us to the same Thomas Trigot and William Johnson or either of them before this time has not been made in the premises or any statute act ordinance or restriction made issued or ordained to the contrary or any other thing cause or matter whatever notwithstanding. In witness whereof etc.]

Rex Omnibus ad quos &c. Sciatis quod nos de gracia nostra speciali ac ex certa sciencia & mero nostris concessimus & per presentes concedimus dilecto & fideli nostro Willelmo Stanley Militi Custodiam omnium Dominiorum & Maneriorum terrarum tenementorum Reddituum Reversionum & serviciorum ac aliorum possessionum & hereditamentorum quorumcumque cum pertinencijs unacum feodis militum advocacionibus Ecclesiarum Cantariarum vicariarum & aliorum beneficiorum Ecclesiasticorum quorumcumque Curiis letis visibus Francplegij ferijs mercatis parcis warennis Franchesijs libertatibus proficuius

50

ac alijs commoditatibus quibuscumque eisdem Dominijs Manerijs terris tenementis ac ceteris premissis seu eorum alicui pertinencibus sive spectantibus
que nuper fuerunt Rogeri Dutton Armigeri qui de nobis tenuit in Capite ut de
Comitatu nostro Cestrie die quo obijt et que per sive post mortem eiusdem
Rogeri / ac racione minoris etatis Laurencij filij & heredis eiusdem Rogeri ad
manus nostras devenerunt seu devenire debuerunt aut debent & in manibus
nostris ad huc (existent) existunt. Concedimus eciam eidem Willelmo custodiam
& maritagiam dicti Laurencij absque (dispargacione) disparagacione / Habendum & tenendum Custodias & maritagium predicta prefato Willelmo Stanley a
duodecimo die mensis Aprilis ultimo preterito usque ad plenam & legittimam
etatem prefati heredis unacum exitibus & proficuis omnium dominiorum
Maneriorum terrarum & tenementorum predictorum ac ceterorum premissorum
cum pertinencijs medio tempore perceptis sive provenientibus Et si contingat
predictum Laurencium obire antequam ad plenam & legitmam etatem (prefati
heredis) suam pervenerit herede suo infra [f17b] etatem existente tunc volumus
& per presentes concedimus quod prefatus Willelmus Stanley habeat custodiam
omnium dominiorum maneriorum terrarum & tenementorum predictorum ac
ceterorum premissorum cum pertinencijs ac custodiam & maritagium huiusmodi heredis a tempore mortis predicti Laurencij quousque idem heres ad
plenam & legitimam etatem suam pervenerit. Et sic de herede in heredem
quousque aliquis heres heredum predictorum ad suam plenam & legitimam
etatem pervenerit. Et ulterius quamdiu dominia maneria terre & tenementa &
cetera premissa cum pertinencijs in manibus nostris contigerit remanere / Ac
prefatus Willelmus Stanley effectum maritagij alicuius heredum predictorum
debite fuerit assecutus Et quousque debita & legalis liberacio omnium dominiorum maneriorum terrarum & tenementorum predictorum ac ceterorum
premissorum cum pertinencijs extra manus nostras habeatur absque aliquo
compoto seu raciocinio sive aliquo alio nobis vel heredibus nostris inde
reddendo seu faciendo Inveniendo tamen interim prefatis heredibus com-
petentem sustentacionem iuxta gradus sui exigenciam / Eo quod expressa
mencio de vero valore annuo seu aliquo alio valore dominiorum maneriorum
terrarum & tenementorum ac ceterorum premissorum seu alicuius eorum aut
de alijs donis sive concessionibus per nos eidem Willelmo Stanley ante hec
tempora factis in presentibus minime facta existit / Aut aliquo statuto actu sive
ordinacione incontrarium facto edito seu proviso in aliquo non obstante. In
cuius &c. Teste.

[The king to all to whom etc. Know that we of our special grace and of our
certain knowledge and mere motion have granted and by these presents
grant to our beloved and faithful William Stanley knight the custody of all
lordships and manors lands tenements rents reversions and services and
other possessions and hereditaments whatsoever with appurtenances with
knights' fees advowsons of churches chantries vicarages and other ecclesiastical benefices whatever court leets views of frankpledge fairs markets parks
warrens franchises liberties profits and other easements whatever pertaining
or belonging to the same lordships manors lands tenements and other
premises or any of them which were late of Roger Dutton esquire who held
of us in chief as of our earldom of Chester on the day he died and which by or
after the death of the same Roger and by reason of the minority of Laurence
son and heir of the same Roger came into our hands or should have come or

ought to come and are in our hands. We also grant to the same William the custody and marriage of the said Laurence without disparagement. To have and hold the custody and marriage aforesaid to the aforesaid William Stanley from the twelfth day of the month of April last past to the full and legal age of the aforesaid heir with the issues and profits of all lordships manors lands and tenements aforesaid and the other premises with appurtenances received or arising in the meantime. And if it happens that the aforesaid Laurence should die before reaching his full and legal age and his heir is under age, then we will and by these presents grant that the aforesaid William Stanley shall have custody of all the lordships manors lands and tenements aforesaid and the other premises with appurtenenances and the custody and marriage of such an heir from the time of the death of the aforesaid Laurence until the same heir reaches his full and legal age. And so from heir to heir until some heir of the aforesaid heirs reaches his full and legal age. And further as long as the lordships manors lands and tenements and other premises with appurtenances happen to remain in our hands and the aforesaid William Stanley shall have duly accomplished the effect of the marriage of any of the heirs aforesaid, and until due and legal delivery of all lordships manors lands and tenements aforesaid and the other premises with appurtenances is had out of our hands, it is to be held without any account or reckoning or any of them being made or rendered to us or to our heirs therefor. Finding in the meantime however competent subsistence for the said heirs demanded by their status. That express mention of the true annual value or any other value of the lordships manors lands and tenements and the other premises or any of them or of other gifts and grants made by us to the same William Stanley before this time is not made in these presents and any statute act or ordinance made issued or provided to the contrary in anything notwithstanding. In witness whereof etc. Witness.]

(Edward by the grace of God King of England & of Fraunce & lord of Irland To all Constables baillies Receyvors Ryves and to alle other inhabited within the lordshippes of Tilney Islington Barton with theire appurtenaunces / and to Thoccupiers of the landes & tenementes in Marsheland in oure Counte of Norffolke and to every of them greting / We late you wit that by thadvise(s) of oure derrest Uncle the duc of Gloucestre protector & defendor of this oure Royaulme during oure yong Age We have yeven unto oure trusty & welbeloved squier Robert Brandon Thoffice of Stewardship of alle the lordshippes landes & tenementes forsaid / To have & to holde the same during oure pleasure with al maner wages fees prouffites commodites & availles to the said office in any wise belonging / Wherfore we wolle & charge you that unto oure said squiere in executing this oure pleasure ye be obeieng aiding helping & assisting / Not failling thus to do upon the feithe & (le) liegeance ye bere unto us Yeven undere oure signet at oure (Cite) Toure of London the xxix[ti] day of Maij the first yere of oure Reigne)

[see new entry f18b]

Rex Omnibus ad quos &c. salutem. Sciatis quod nos certis de causis & consideracionibus nos & Consilium nostrum moventibus de gracia nostra speciali dedimus & concessimus ac per presentes damus & (concessimus) concedimus dilecto nobis Johanni Ambrosio de Nigrono Mercatori de Janua quod ipse per se Factores sive Attornatos suos indigentos vel alienigentos habeat & percipiat summam tricentarum octuaginta & quatuor librarum septem solidorum & sex denariorum legalis monete Anglie de Custumis & subsidijs nostris provenient-em de quibuscunque lanis pannis laneis tam in grano quam sine grano stannis qualdis aluminibus vinis pannis de serico de bonis suis proprijs/ et de quibus-cunque alijs bonis & mercandisis de primis aliquo tempore post datam presen-cium per ipsum Johannem Ambrosium Factores & Attornatos suos predictos aut per aliquos alios mercatores sive aliquem alium mercatorem de dicta nacione de Janua in Regnum nostrum Anglie in portus nostros London' Sande-wici & Southampton' & in eorum quemlibet in quibuscunque Galeis Carvacis navibus vel vasis aut in quacunaque Galea Carvaca nave vel vase adducendis seu ab eodem Regno nostro extra portus predictos vel eorum aliquem educendis de tempore in tempus nobis qualitercunque pertinentibus sive spectantibus quousque predicto Johanni Ambrosio aut factoribus sive Attornatis suis pre-dictis de dicta summa tricentarum octuaginta & quatuor librarum septem solidorum & sex denariorum debite satisfactum fuerit & plenarie contentatum per manus Custumariorum subsidariorum nostrorum in portibus predictis & eorum quolibet pro tempore existentium per indenturas inde inter prefatum Johannem Ambrosium aut factores sive Attornatos suos predictos aut eorum aliquem et Custumarios sive Collectores Custumarum & subsidiorum pre-dictorum in portibus predictis & eorum quolibet pro tempore existentes / ubi mercandisam predictam aut [f18] aliquam inde parcellam sic adduci vel ut predictum est educi contigerit adduccionem et educcionem illas de tempore in tempus debite conficiendas per quam quidem indenturarum alteram partem has litteras nostras patentes ac brevia nostra superinde Custumarijs sive Collectori-bus nostris in portubus predictis & in eorum quolibet pro tempore existentibus dirigendas volumus & concedimus quod tam idem Custumarij sive Collectores & eorum quilibet quam prefatus Johannes Ambrosius ac Factores & attornati sui predicti & eorum quilibet de omnimodis pecuniarum servicijs Custumarum & subsidiorum nostrorum predictorum in forma predicta habendis & per-cipiendis erga nos & heredes nostros omnino exonerentur & acquietentur im-perpetuum In cuius Rei &c.

[The king to all to whom etc. greeting. Know that we, for certain causes and considerations moving us and our council, have of our special grace given and granted and by these presents give and grant to our beloved John Ambrose de Nigrono merchant of Janua [Genoa] that he in person or through his agents or attorneys native or foreign shall have and receive the sum of three hundred and eighty-four pounds seven shillings and sixpence of lawful money of England arising from our customs and subsidies from whatever wool and woolen cloth both dyed and undyed tin woad alum wines silken material of his own goods and whatever other goods and merchandise out of the first to be brought at any time after the date of these presents by the same John Ambrose his agents and attorneys aforesaid or any other merchants or merchant of the said nation of Janua into our realm of England to our ports of London Sandwich and Southampton and any of them in whatever galleys carracks ships or vessels or in whatever galley carrack ship or vessel or to be taken from our same kingdom out of the ports aforesaid or any of them from time to time pertaining or belonging to us by whatever right, until due satisfaction and full payment has been made to the aforesaid John Ambrose or his agents or attorneys aforesaid of the said sum of three hundred and eighty-four pounds seven shillings and sixpence by the hands of our customers and subsidy-collectors in the aforesaid ports and any of them for the time being according to indentures therefor between the aforesaid John Ambrose or his agents or attorneys aforesaid or any of them and the collectors of customs and subsidies aforesaid in the aforesaid ports and any of them for the time being where the merchandise aforesaid or any part thereof may as aforesaid happen to be brought in or taken out, such import and export being duly made from time to time and according to the other part of these indentures we will and grant that these our letters patent and our writs on this account be directed to our customers or collectors in the aforesaid ports and in any of them and also the aforesaid John Ambrose and his agents and attorneys aforesaid and any of them may be forever exempted and acquit towards us and our heirs of all kinds of money rent, customs and taxes of ours aforesaid to be had and received in the form aforesaid. In witness whereof etc.]

Rex &c. salutem. Sciatis quod nos bona & laudabilia servicia per dilectum Armigerum nostrum Willelmum Slefelde multiplicite nobis impensa intime contemplantes necnon imposterum impendenda sperantes de gracia nostra speciali ac ex certa sciencia & mero motu nostris concessimus & per presentes concedimus eidem Willelmo officium Thesaurarij ville nostre Cales' & march-iarum ibidem tam in eadem villa quam in alijs locis Comitatus & dominijs eorundem marchiarum / Habendum tenendum occupandum & exercendum officium thesaurarij predicti eidem Willelmo per se vel per suum sufficientem deputatum A nono die Aprilis ultimo preterito & deinceps quam diu se bene gesserit in eodem officio / Percipiendo annuatim in & pro officio predicto bene & fideliter occupando & exercendo vadia feoda & proficua eidem officio debita & consueta / Aceciam pro custubus & (expensis expncis) expensis pro passagio & repassagio suis ultra mare & pro mora sive expectacione sua in Regno nostro Anglie / unacum custubus & expensis per prefatum Willelmum infra villam & marchias predictas circa operaciones nostras facien-das in tam amplis modo & forma prout maior & societas mercatorum Stapule apud Cales' nuper Thesaurarij ville & marchiarum ibidem in eodem officio habuerunt & perciperunt de exitibus revencionibus & proficuis ville & march iarum predictarum per manus suas proprias / Et ulterius ex ubriori gracia nostra speciali concessimus & per presentes concedimus eidem Willelmo custo-diam hospicij sive domus nostre in dicta villa Cales' cum omnibus pertinencijs eidem officio hospicio sive domui nostre qualitercunque spectantibus. Haben-dum sibi dictam Custodiam quamdiu officium Thesaurarij predictum occu-paverit. Eo quod expressa mencio de vero valore annuo officij predicti seu aliquo premissorum aut de alijs donis sive concessionibus nostris pro nos ante hec tempora eidem Willelmo factis in presentibus minime facta existit / Aut aliquibus statutibus actibus ordinacionibus sive restriccionnibus incontrarium factis ordin-atis seu provisis aut aliqua re causa vel materia quacunque non obstantibus. In cuius &c.

[The king etc. greeting. Know that we, carefully considering the good and praiseworthy services often rendered to us by our beloved esquire William Slefelde and hoping that such will be rendered in the future, of our special grace and of our certain knowledge and mere motion have granted and by these presents grant to the same William the office of treasurer of our town of Calais and the marches there both in the same town and in other places of the county and lordship of the same marches. To have hold occupy and exercise the office of treasurer aforesaid to the same William in person or by his sufficient deputy from the ninth day of April last past and henceforward as long as he bears himself well in the same office, receiving annually in and for the good and faithful occupying and exercising of the office aforesaid the wages fees and profits owing and customary to the same office. And also for the costs and expenses for his passage and return across the sea and for his delay or wait in our realm of England with the costs and expenses for the aforesaid William in the town and marches aforesaid about the performance of our business in as ample a manner and form as the master and company of the merchants of the Staple at Calais late treasurers of the town and the marches of the same place had and received in the same office out of the issues revenues and profits of the town and marches aforesaid by their own hands. And further of our more especial grace we have granted and by these presents grant to the same William the custody of our hospice or house in the said town of Calais with all appurtenances in any way belonging to the same office hospice or house of ours. To have the said custody as long as he occupies the aforesaid office of treasurer. That express mention of the true annual value of the office aforesaid or any of the premises or of our other gifts or grants made to the said William by us before this time is not made in these presents. And notwithstanding any statutes acts ordinances or restraints made ordained or provided to the contrary or any other thing cause or matter whatever. In witness whereof etc.]

Rex &c. Omnibus &c. salutem / Sciatis quod nos considerantes gratuita servicia per Thomam Fowler Armigerum ac Aliciam Hulcote viduam dilectam & fidelem servientem precarissime matris nostre Elizabeth' Regine Anglie & francie & domine Hibernie ante hec tempora multipliciter impensa de gracia nostra speciali ac ex certa sciencia & mero motu nostris concessimus & per presentes concedimus eisdem Thome & Alicie Manerium de Wauenden' alias dictum Manerium de Wavenden cum pertinencijs in Comitatu Bukinghamia / Quod quidem Manerium cum pertinencijs Johannes Hulcote defunctus nuper vir predicte Alicie tenuit ad terminum vite sue ex concessione domini Edwardi nuper Regis Anglie quarti patris nostri / Habendum & tenendum Manerium predictum cum pertinencijs prefatis Thome & Alicie & Assignatis suis a festo Pasche ultimo preterito pro termino vite eorundem Thome & Alicie & Alterius eorum diucius viventis absque Compoto seu aliquo Alio inde nobis Reddendo solvendo seu faciendo / Eo quod expressa mencio de vero valore annuo seu aliquo alio valore Manerij predicti vel alicuius inde parcelle aut de alijs donis sive concessionibus per nos eisdem Thome & Alicie seu eorum alteri ante hec tempora factis in presentibus minime facta existit / Aut aliquo statuto Actu ordinacione vel restriccione quacunque incontrarium facto edito sive ordinato aut aliqua alia re causa vel materia quacunque non obstante. In cuius &c. Teste &c.

[The king etc. to all etc. greeting. Know that we, considering the gracious services often rendered before this time by Thomas Fowler esquire and Alice Hulcote widow the beloved and faithful servant of our dearest mother Elizabeth Queen of England and France and lady of Ireland, of our special grace and of our certain knowledge and mere motion have granted and by these presents grant to the same Thomas and Alice the manor of Wauenden alias the manor of Wavenden with appurtenances in the county of Buckingham. Which manor with its appurtenances John Hulcote deceased late husband of the aforesaid Alice held for the term of his life by the grant of the lord Edward the fourth late King of England our father. To have and hold the manor aforesaid with appurtenances to the aforesaid Thomas and Alice and their assigns from the feast of Easter last past for the term of the lives of the same Thomas and Alice and whichever of them lives the longer without account or anything else to be rendered paid or done therefor to us. That express mention of the true annual value or any other value of the manor aforesaid or any part thereof or of other gifts or grants made by us to the same Thomas and Alice or either of them before this time has not been made in these presents and notwithstanding any statute act ordinance or restraint whatever made issued or ordained to the contrary or any other thing cause or matter whatever. In witness whereof. Witness etc.]

[f18b] Edward etc To alle Constables Baillies Receyvors Ryves and to alle other inhabited within the lordshippes of Tylney Islyngton Barton with theire appurtenaunces and to thoccupiers of the landes & tenementes in Merssheland in oure Counte of Norffolk and to every of them gretting / We lat you wit that by thadvise of oure derrest Uncle the duc of Gloucestre protector & defendor of this oure Royaulme during oure yong Age We have yevene unto oure trusty & welbeloved squiere Robert Bandon thoffice of Stewardship of alle the lordshippes landes & tenementes forsaid / To have & occupie the same during oure pleasure with the wages of tene poundes by yere to be had & perceyved yerely of thissues & Revenues of the said lordshippes landes & tenementes by the handes of the Receyvor or other occupiers there for the tyme being at the termes of seint Michelle tharchaungelle & pasche by even porcions Wherfore we wolle & charge you alle & every of you that unto oure said squier in executing this oure pleasure ye be obeieng aiding helping & assisting Not failling thus to do upone the feith and (alle) liegaunce ye bere unto us. Yevene etc the ij^{de} day of Juyne Anno primo

Rex Omnibus &c. salutem. Sciatis nos ex mero motu & sciencia (nostra) nostris constituisse Thomam Tremaill' unum servientem nostrorum ad legem necnon concessisse eidem Thome officium unius servientum nostrorum ad legem / Habendum occupandum & exercendum dictum officium necnon essendum unum servientum nostrorum ad legem quam diu nobis placuerit capiendo & percipiendo Annuatim pro officio illo exercendo eidem Thome vadia feoda vesturam & regarda dicto officio debita pertinencia seu emergencia prout (alijc) alij servientes ad legem pro (huis) huismodi officio exercendo percipient seu habere vel percipere debent. In cuius Rei testimonium &c.

56

[The king to all etc. greeting. Know that we of our mere motion and knowledge have appointed Thomas Tremaill one of our serjeants-at-law and granted to the same Thomas the office of one of our serjeants-at-law. To have occupy and exercise the said office and also to be one of our serjeants-at-law   as long as it pleases us, the same Thomas taking and receiving annually for exercising that office the wages fees clothing and rewards owing or pertaining to or arising from the said office as other serjeants-at-law receive for exercising such office or ought to have or receive. In witness whereof etc.]

Rex Omnibus &c. Sciatis nos de gracia nostra speciali ac ex certa sciencia & mero motu nostris concessimus Johanni Vavasour servienti ad legem ad essendum unum servientum nostrorum ad legem. Habendum & exercendum officium predictum quam diu se bene gesserit / capiendo pro eodem officio talia vadia qualia ad eundem officium pertinet &c.

[The king to all etc. Know that we of our special grace and from our certain knowledge and mere motion have granted to John Vavasour serjeant-at-law to be one of our serjeants-at-law. To have and exercise the aforesaid office as long as he conducts himself well, receiving for the same office such wages as pertain to the same office etc.]

A like bill for Roger Towneshende de verbo in verbum etc.

Rex Omnibus ad quos &c. salutem Sciatis quod nos de gracia nostra speciali ac ex certa sciencia & mero motu nostris / Necnon de avisamento Consilij nostri perdonavimus Remisimus & relaxavimus Philippo Legh del Bothes in Comitatu Cestrie Gentilman alias dicto Philippo Legh nuper del Bothes in Comitatu Cestrie Gentilman / alias dicto Philippo Legh de Knottefford Bothes in Comitatu Cestrie Gentilmon / alias dicto Philippo Legh nuper de Knotteford Bothes in Comitatu Cestrie Gentilman alias dicto Philippo Legh de Knotteford in Comitatu Cestrie Gentilman / alias dicto Philippo Legh nuper de Knotteford in Comitatu Cestrie Gentilman alias dicto Philippo Legh de (Okyngton) Okynton in Comitatu Derbie Gentilman / alias dicto Philippo Legh nuper de Okynton in Comitatu Derbie Gentilman seu quocunque alio nomine senseatur omnimodas prodiciones Felonias murdras reptus mulierum transgressiones misprisiones contemptus forisfacturas offensas & alia malefacta quecunque per ipsum Philippum ante presentem diem qualitercunque facta sive perpetrata /Ac sectam pacis nostre & omnimodos attincturas execuciones penas & demandas que ad nos versus ipsum Philippum accione premissorum vel alicuius eorundem pertinent. Aceciam utlagarias sique in ipsum Philippum hijs accionibus seu eorum aliqua fuerint promulgate & firmam pacem nostram ei inde concedimus per presentes / Ita tamen quod stet recto in Curia nostra siqua versus eum loqui voluerit de premissis vel aliquo premissorum. In cuius Rei testimonium &c.

[The king to all to whom etc. greeting. Know that we of our special grace and of our certain knowledge and mere motion and on the advice of our council have pardoned remitted and released to Philip Legh del Bothes in the county of Chester gentleman alias Philip Legh late of Bothes in the county of Chester gentleman alias Philip Legh of Knotteford Bothes in the county of Chester gentleman alias Philip Legh late of Knotteford Bothes in the county of Chester gentleman alias Philip Legh of Knotteford in the county of Chester gentleman alias Philip Legh late of Knotteford in the county of Chester gentleman alias Philip Legh of Okynton in the county of Derby gentleman alias Philip Legh late of Okynton in the county of Derby gentleman or by whatever name he is known all manner of charges felonies murders rapes trangressions misprisions contempts forfeitures offences and other evildoings whatsoever of whatever kind made or committed by the same Philip before the present day and the suit of our peace and all manner of attainders executions penalties and demands which concern us in relation to the same Philip by action of the premises or any of them. Also outlawries if any have been promulgated against the same Philip in these actions or any of them and by these presents we grant him our firm peace therefrom. Providing he stands forth in our court if any desires to speak against him on the premises or any of them. In witness whereof etc.]

[f19] Rex Omnibus ad quos &c. salutem. Sciatis quod cum per litteras patentes famosisse principis bone memorie domini & patris nostri nuper Regis Anglie quarum data est apud Westmonasterium x° die Novembris Anno Regni sui decimo octavo recitans per easdem bona & gratuita servicia que dilectus nobis Willelmus Clifford eidem domino nostro impendit indies que (tumc) tunc impendere non desistebat merito contemplantes de gracia sua speciali concessit prefato Willelmo officium Receptoris dominij & hundredi de Middelton' & Marden' in Comitatu Kantie quod ad manus suas Racione forisfacture Georgij nuper Ducis Clarence ac racione cuiusdam actus in parliamento suo apud Westmonasterium vicesimo sexto die Januarij Anno Regni sui decimo septimo tento editi devenit aut devenire debuit / ac ipsum Willelmum Receptorem dominij & hundredi predictorum constituerit per easdem litteras suas / Habendum & occupandum officium predictum prefato Willelmo per se vel per sufficientem deputatum suum A festo sancti Michaelis Archangeli tunc ultimo preterito pro termino vite sue ipsius Willelmi percipiendo annuatim pro officio predicto exercendo viginti marcas pro feodo suo in hac parte pro termino vite sue predicte de exitibus proficuis & revencionibus dominij & hundredi predictorum provenientibus per manus suas proprias ad terminos Pasche & Sancti Michaelis Archangeli per equales porciones / unacum omnibus alijs proficuis commoditatibus & emolumentis eidem officio qualitercunque pertinentibus prout in litteris patentibus illis plenius continetur / Iamque ex parte predicti Willelmi nobis graviter conquerendo accepimus quod littere patentes predicte quo ad feodum predictum in forma predicta percipiendum eidem Willelmo minus sufficientes existunt in lege unde nobis supplicavit prefatus Willelmus ut nos de ubriori gracia nostra alias litteras patentes inde eidem Willelmo in forma sequenti concedere dignaremur. Nos premissa considerantes ac pro eo quod idem Willelmus litteras patentes predictas quo ad feodum predictum in Cancellariam nostram restituit cancellandum / de gracia nostra predicta concessimus & per presentes concedimus eidem Willelmo viginti marcas per annum pro feodo suo pro (excercio)excercicio officij predicti / Habendum percipiendum

& retinendum (an) annuatim eidem Willelmo pro termino vite sue de exitibus proficuis firmis & revencionibus dominij & hundredi predictorum tam per manus suas proprias quam per manus vicecomitis Comitatus Kancie aut aliorum Receptorum firmariorum seu occupatorum eorundem dominij & hundredi pro tempore existencium ad terminos Pasche & sancti Michaelis per equales porciones / unacum omnibus alijs proficuis commoditatibus & emolumentis eidem officio qualitercunque pertinentibus / Et insuper nos certam scienciam habentes quod idem Willelmus dictum officium Receptoris dominij & hundredi predictorum a dicto decimo die Novembris dicto anno decimo octavo hucusque occupavit et ad huc occupat nulla vadia feoda seu Regarda pro inde de nobis habens aut percipiens de eadem gracia nostra concessimus & per presentes concedimus eidem Willelmo tot & tantas denariorum summas ad quot & quantas viginti marce per annum ab eodem decimo die Novembris eodem Anno decimo octavo hucusque se extendunt sive attingunt / Habendum percipiendum & retinendum eidem Willelmo pro exercicio officij illius nomine regardi de exitibus proficuis firmis & Revencionibus dominij & hundredi predictorum provenientibus tam per manus suas proprias quam per manus nuper receptoris nunc Receptoris & ex nunc Receptorum aut aliorum occupatorum eorundem dominij & hundredi pro tempore existencium ad terminos Pasche & sancti Michaelis per equales porciones. Eo quod expressa mencio &c. In cuius &c.

[The king to all to whom etc. greeting. Know that since by letters patent of the most famous prince of happy memory our lord and father late King of England given at Westminster on the tenth day of November in the eighteenth year of his reign reciting by the same that, duly contemplating the good and gracious services which our beloved William Clifford paid our same lord and did not cease to pay thereafter, of his special grace he granted the aforesaid William the office of receiver of the lordship and hundred of Middelton and Marden in the county of Kent which came or should have come to his hands by reason of the forfeiture of George late Duke of Clarence and by reason of a certain act passed in his parliament held at Westminster on the twenty-sixth day of January in the seventeenth year of his reign, and appointed William by the same letters receiver of the aforesaid lordship and hundred, to hold and occupy the aforesaid office to the aforesaid William in person or by his sufficient deputy from the feast of Michaelmas then last past for the term of the life of the said William receiving annually for exercising the aforesaid office twenty marks for his fee in this respect for the term of his life aforesaid out of the issues profits and revenues arising from the lordship and hundred aforesaid by his own hands at the terms of Easter and Michaelmas by equal portions, with all other profits easements and emoluments whatever pertaining to the same office as in those letters patent is more fully contained, and now, grave complaint being made to us on the part of the aforesaid William, we have heard that the letters patent aforesaid are insufficient in law as relates to the receiving of the fee aforesaid in the form aforesaid by the same William, wherefore the aforesaid William has besought us that of our more especial grace we would deign to grant other letters patent therefor to the same William in the following form: We, considering the premises and because the same William has returned the aforesaid letters patent relating to the fee aforesaid to our chancery to be cancelled, of our grace aforesaid have granted and by these presents grant to the same William twenty marks per annum for his fee for exercising the office aforesaid. To have receive and retain annually to the same William for the term of his life from the issues profits rents and revenues of the lordship and hundred aforesaid both by his own hands and by the hands of the sheriff of the county of Kent or of other receivers farmers or occupiers of the same lordship and hundred for the time being at the terms of Easter and Michaelmas by equal portions with all other profits easements and emoluments whatever relating to the same office. And moreover, having certain knowledge that the same William has occupied the said office of receiver of the lordship and hundred aforesaid from the said tenth day of November in the said eighteenth year and still occupies it not having or receiving any wages fees or rewards therefor from us, we of our same grace have granted and by these presents grant to the same William as much money as represents or amounts to twenty marks per annum from the same tenth day of November in the same eighteenth year. To have receive and retain to the same William for the exercise of that office by way of a reward from the issues profits rents and revenues arising from the aforesaid lordship and hundred both by his own hands and by the hands of the late receiver the present receiver and future receivers or other occupiers of the same lordship and hundred for the time being at the terms of Easter and Michaelmas by equal portions. That express mention etc. In witness whereof etc.]

Edward etc To alle Stewardes Auditors and to alle othere oure officers & true liegemen within oure lordshippes of Milten and Merden within oure Counte of Kent / and to every of them greting / And forsomoche as the king oure Fadere of moost blissed memorie whome god assoille yave in his daies by his lettres patentes Thoffice of Receyvorship of the same oure lordshippes to oure trusty & welbeloved [f19b] servaunt William Clifford squiere / We therefore havyng oure said squiere in the good favor of oure grace have eftsones by thadvise of oure derrest uncle etc commaunded him to occupie & enyoie the same his offices / Perceyving therefore wages & profittes accustomed / Wherfore we wolle & charge you & every of you that to him in executing the premisses ye be aiding helping & assisting to youre powers As ye & every of you purpose to advoide oure grevouse displeasure at youre perilles / Yeven etc the xxvj^th day of Maij Anno primo etc

Fiant littere patentes domini Regis in forma que sequetur &c. Rex &c. omnibus &c. salutem Sciatis quod nos de gracia nostra speciali ac ex certa sciencia & mero motu nostris assignavimus ordinavimus & constituimus dilectum & fidelem nostrum Humfridum Starky Capitalem Baronem de Scaccario nostro & eidem Humfrido officium illud per presentes damus concedimus & confirmamus. Habendum tenendum & occupandum officium predictum quam diu nobis placuerit / ac habendum & percipiendum omnimoda feoda Regarda & commoditates eidem officio debita sive pertinencia ad Scaccarium nostrum seu ad Receptum Scaccarij nostri vel heredum nostrorum per manus Thesaurarij & Camerarij eiusdem pro tempore existentium Eo quod expressa mencio ac vero valore Annuo officij predicti in presentibus minime facta existit aut aliquo statuto actu sive ordinacione in contrarium facta non obstante. In cuius Rei &c.

[Let letters patent of the lord king be made in the following form etc. The king etc. to all etc. greeting. Know that we, of our especial grace and of our certain knowledge and mere motion, have appointed ordained and made our beloved and faithful Humphrey Starky chief baron of our exchequer and by these presents we give grant and confirm that office to the same Humphrey. To have hold and occupy the aforesaid office as long as it pleases us and to have and receive all manner of fees rewards and easements owed or appertaining to the same office at our exchequer or at the receipt of the exchequer of us or our heirs by the hands of the treasurer and the chamberlain of the same for the time being. That express mention of the true annual value of the aforesaid office has not been made in these presents and notwithstanding any statute act or ordinance made to the contrary. In witness whereof etc.]

Rex &c. Sciatis quod concessimus & per presentes concedimus Guidoni Fairfax militi officium Capitalis Justiciarij nostri ad omnia & singula placita Corone & assisarum coram nobis apud Lancastriam tenenda & arrainienda necnon ad omnimoda alia placita apud Lancastriam tenenda Habendum & occupandum officium predictum eidem Guidoni quam diu nobis placuerit / capiendo (Recep) & percipiendo in officio predicto feoda vadia & Regarda inde debita & consueta ad festa sancti Michaelis Archangeli & Pasche (p) equis porcionibus per manus Receptoris nostri sive deputati sui ibidem pro tempore existentium. In cuius Rei &c. Teste &c.

[The king etc. Know that we have granted and by these presents do grant to Guy Fairfax knight the office of our chief justice for all and singular pleas of the crown and assizes to be held and heard before us at Lancaster and all other pleas to be held at Lancaster. To have and occupy the aforesaid office to the same Guy as long as it pleases us, taking and receiving in the aforesaid office the fees wages and rewards owing and customary therefor at the feasts of Michaelmas and Easter by equal portions by the hands of our receiver or his deputy there for the time being. In witness whereof etc. Witness etc.]

Rex &c. Sciatis quod concessimus & per presentes concedimus Miloni Metcalf officium alterius Justiciarij nostri ad omnia & singula placita Corone & assisarum coram nobis apud Lancastriam tenenda. Habendum & occupandum officium predictum eidem Miloni quam diu nobis placuerit / capiendo & percipiendo in officio predicto feoda vadia & Regarda inde debita & consueta ad festum sancti Michaelis Archangeli & Pasche equis porcionibus per [manus] Receptoris nostri sive deputati sui ibidem pro tempore existentium. In cuius Rei &c.

[The king etc. Know that we have granted and by these presents do grant to Miles Metcalf the office of our other justice for all and singular pleas of the crown and assizes to be held before us at Lancaster. To have and occupy the aforesaid office to the same Miles as long as it pleases us, taking and receiving in the aforesaid office the fees wages and rewards owing and customary therefor at the feast of Michaelmas and Easter by equal portions by the hands of our receiver or his deputy there for the time being. In witness whereof etc.]

Rex &c. salutem. Sciatis quod nos de gracia nostra speciali ac ex advisamento precarissimi Avunculi nostri Ricardi Ducis Gloucestrie protectoris ac defensoris huius Regni nostri Anglie durante etate nostra iuvenili commisimus dilecto & fideli nostro Willelmo Houghton militi [officium vicecomitis]comitatus nostri Wigorn' cum pertinencijs quam diu nobis placuerit. Ita quod Firmam debitam nobis Reddat Annuatim ac de debitis nostris & omnibus alijs ad officium vicecomitis eiusdem Comitatus spectantibus nobis Respondeat ad Scaccariam nostram. In cuius rei &c.

[The king etc. greeting. Know that of our especial grace and on the advice of our dearest uncle Richard, Duke of Gloucester, protector and defender of this our realm of England during our minority, we have committed to our beloved and faithful William Houghton, knight, [the office of sheriff] of our county of Worcester with the appurtenances as long as it pleases us. Provided that he pays us annually the due farm and answers in our exchequer for the debts due to us and all else belonging to the office of sheriff of the same county. In witness whereof etc.]

Memorandum of a lettre for Dean of the Chapelle to the next dignite in Excestre

[f20] lettres for benyfices (A°) primo die Januarij Anno ij do

Furst a lettre to the Bisshoppe of Chestre for the next advoidaunce of the parsonage of Norden in the same diocesse At the sute of Sir Randolph Brantingham

Item A lettre to the prior & convent of Duresme for the promocione of maister Christofre Tenaunt to the benifice of Gigleswike at the next vacacione thereof

A lettre to the Bisshop of Carlile for to graunt thadvouson of the parsonage of Rothebury in Northumbreland to the Erle of Westmorland for oon tyme oonly at the kinges instaunce yeven at Westminster the xix day of Fevrier Anno ij^do

Item a lettre to Maister John Combes reciting that notwithstanding the kinges priuer lettres to him directed for the promocion of Maister Rauf Scrope to the vicairaige of Payntone. the said Maister John hathe presented himself thereunto by crafty meanes Whereof the kinges grace takithe displeasir and chargeth him to exclude his handes thereof and suffre the said Maister Rauf to enioye it orelles (tak) to appiere afore the king yeven at Westminstre the xx^ti day of Fevrier Anno ij^do

Item a lettre to the Bisshoppe of Bathe for to graunt the parsonage of Saint Nicholas Cold Abbey within the Citie of Londone to Maister John Nause doctor of bothe lawes (within the Citie of Londone) by resignacion etc

A lettre of Recommendacion to John Longvile Squier patron of the Churche of Stoke to graunt thadvouson of the same unto Maister Edmond Chadertone and

William Catesby for the furst vacacion thereof oonly to present thereunto a Chapellain of the kinges yeven at Westminstre the xxvj^ti day of Fevrier

A lettre to (the) dame (W)   Wingfeld for thadvouson of the parsonage of Emertone in the Countie of Bukingham to be graunted to the king (of)

A lettre to Maister John Combe for (gra) the next prebende that fallethe voide within the Churche of Excestre to be graunted to Maister Cowtone

A lettre to Thabbot of Peterburgh for thadvosons of the parsonage of Chere-overton at the sute of Sir Thomas Fitzwilliam / Yeven the xvj day of Avrille

A lettre to Maistre John Combe for to accept and promote Maister Thomas Cowtone aswele unto the Subdenry of Excestre as unto a prebende there whiche Maister Walter Wynsover late had Yeven at Westminstre the ij^de day of May

A lettre to Maister Edward Cheyney parson of the parisshe Churche of Witteney to graunt to Maister David Irland the vicarage etc Yeven etc the xv day of Maye

A lettre to the pryouresse & Convent of the house of Shepey in Kent to present Sir John Norman prest to the vicairaige of Grene voide by the Resignacion of Sir Thomas Elys prest incumbent there Yeven at Kenelworthe the xxij^ti day of May

A lettre to Thabbot of Peterburgh to graunt the parsonage of Eston to suche a Clerc as the king wille name / at the sute of the Maister of Rolles Yeven at Nottingham the viij day of August

[f20b blank]

[f21] Rex etc Omnibus ad quos etc salutem Sciatis quod nos de provida circumspectia & indubitata [unfinished]

> [The king etc. To all to whom etc. greeting. Know that we, on account of the known uprightness and undoubted discretion]

Per regem

Sincere dilecte salutem vobis mandamus quod sub privato sigillo nostro in custodia vestra existente litteras nostras acquietancie fieri faciatis in forma sequente / Noverint universi per presentes nos Ricardum Dei gracia Regem Anglie & Francie & dominum Hibernie recepisse & habuisse die confeccionis presencium de Johanne Abbate Monastrij beate Marie de Ramesey & eiusdem loci Conventu viginti & quinque libras legalis monete Anglie pro feodi firma Residui ferie sive Nundinarum ville sancti Ivonis in Comitatu Huntingdon pro termino sancti Michaelis ultimo preterito ante datum presencium / De quibus quidem xxv li. fatemur nos pro termino predicto (sancti Michaelis ultimo preterito) inde fore solutis / Dictumque Abbatem & Conventum & Successores suos inde fore quietos per presentes / sigillo nostro privato sigillatas, Datum

&c. Et hee littere nostre vobis erunt super hoc sufficiens warrantum. Datum quartodecimo die Octobris Anno Regni nostri primo.

By the King

[Dearly beloved, greeting, we command you to cause to be made under our privy seal being in your custody our letters of acquittance in the following form. Know all men by these presents that we Richard by the grace of God King of England and France and lord of Ireland received and had of John, abbot of the monastery of St Mary of Ramsey, and the convent of the same place on the day of the making of these presents twenty-five pounds of lawful money of England for the fee farm of the residue of the fair or market of the town of St. Ives in the county of Huntingdon for the term of Michaelmas last past before the giving of these presents. For which twenty-five pounds we acknowledge we have been paid for the term aforesaid and we acquit the said abbot and convent and their successors therefor by these presents sealed with our privy seal. Given etc. And these our letters shall be to you sufficient warrant for this. Given on the fourteenth day of October in the first year of our reign.]

A like acquitance to the same Abbot and Convent for xxv li for Ester terme last past / Yove at the Castelle of Pountfret the furst day of Juyn Anno etc primo

Presentacio. Rex &c. Dilecto nobis in Christo Magistro Johanni Combe vicario generali in spiritualibus Exoniensis diocesis salutem. Ad Ecclesiam parochialem de Bery Ferys eiusdem diocesis iam per mortem ultimi incumbentis ibidem vacantem & ad nostram presentacionem pleno iure spectantem Dilectum nobis Jacobum Molyneux Clericum vobis presentamus Affectantes quatenus eundem Jacobum ad dictam Ecclesiam admittere ac ipsum Rectorem in eadem cum suis Iuribus & pertinencijs universis instituere. Ceteraque peragere que vestro in hac parte incumbunt officio valetis cum effectu. In cuius Rei &c.

[*Presentation.* The king etc. To our beloved in Christ Master John Combe vicar general in spiritualities of the diocese of Exeter, greeting. We present to you for the parish church of Bery Ferys of the same diocese now vacant by the death of the last incumbent there and the presentation belonging by full right to us, our beloved James Molyneux, clerk, desiring you to admit the same James to the said church and install him as rector in the same with all its rights and appurtenances. And to carry out the other things which pertain to your office in this respect. In witness whereof etc.]

Presentacio. Rex &c. Reverendo in Christo patri Johanni permissione divina Lincolniensis Episcopo aut eius in absencia vicario suo in spiritualibus generali salutem / ad ecclesiam parochialem de H. vestre diocesis per mortem A.B. ultimi incumbentis ibidem iam vacentem (ad) et ad nostram presentacionem pleno iure spectantem / Dilectum nobis (in Christo) C.D. in decretum bacallarium vestre paternitati presentamus. Rogantes quatenus eundem C.D. ad Ecclesiam parochialem predictam admittere velitis. Ceteraque peragere que

64

vestro in hac parte incumbunt officio pastorali cum favore. In cuius Rei &c.

[*Presentation*. The king etc. To the reverend father in Christ John by the divine favour Bishop of Lincoln or in his absence his vicar general in spiritualities, greeting. We present to your paternity for the parish church of H. in your diocese now vacant by the death of A.B. the last incumbent there and the presentation pertaining by full right to us our beloved C.D. of the degree of bachelor. Asking that you will deign to admit the same C.D. to the aforesaid parish church, and do all that appertains to your pastoral office in this respect. In witness whereof etc.]

[f21b] *Pro proxima advocacione.* Rex &c. salutem. Sciatis quod nos ex certa sciencia & mero motu nostris dedimus & concessimus ac per presentes damus & concedimus / Dilecto A.B. advocacionem pronominatum ac presentacionem proxime & prime vacacionis ecclesie parochialis de Gayton parcelle ducatus nostri Lancastrie que ad nostram propriam spectant donacionem quamsitius ecclesia illa vacaverit sive sit per mortem resignacionem privacionem permutationem aut alio modo quocunque. Habendum & tenendum & percipiendum advocacionem pronominatus & presentacionem predictas cum suis Iunibus & pertinencijs universis quibuscunque prefato A.B. pro proxima & prima vacacione tantum cum omni potestate & auctoritate presentandi personam idoneum ad dictam Ecclesiam cum (sit) sic ut premittitur primo & proximo vacaverit adeo integre plene & libere prout nos in ea parte feceremus si presens concessio nostra facta non fuisset. In cuius.

[*For the next advowson*. The king etc. greeting. Know that we of our certain knowledge and mere motion have given and granted and by these presents do give and grant to our beloved A.B. the advowson, nomination and presentation of the next and first vacancy of the parish church of Gayton parcel of our duchy of Lancaster which is in our own gift, as soon as that church falls vacant, whether through death, resignation, deprivation, exchange or any other means. To have hold and receive the advowson nomination and presentation aforesaid with all their rights and appurtenances to the aforesaid A.B. for the next and first vacancy only with all power and authority to present a suitable person to the said church when it thus first and next becomes vacant as aforesaid, as fully completely and freely as we would do in that respect if our present grant had not been made. In witness.]

Rex &c. Sciatis nos (dedisse) de gracia nostra speciali ex certa sciencia & mero motu nostris Dedisse & concessisse dilecto nobis A.B. & C.D. & assignatis suis advocacionem collacionem donacionem donacionem & liberam disposicionem ac auctoritatem & potestatem conferendi seu donandi cuicunque idonee persone quamcumque prebendam in Ecclesia nova Collegiatus beate Marie Leycestrie proximam vacaturam cum per mortem resignacionem cessionem permutacionem vel dimissionem seu quocunque alio modo huiusmodi prebendam vacare contigerit pro unica & proxima vacacione tunc / et quod bene liceat eisdem (N). A.B. & C.D. ac eorum alteri & assignatis suis auctoritate predicte concessionis nostre (huis) huiusmodi prebendam cum proximo ut predicitur vacaverit idonee persone litterate conferre seu dare / ac omnia & singula que circa premissa necessaria fuerint seu quomodolibet oportuna agere & perimplere adeo plene & integre prout nos feceremus si presens concessio nostra facta non fuisset. In cuius rei &c.

[The king etc. Know that we of our especial grace of our certain knowledge and mere motion have given and granted to our beloved A.B. and C.D. and their assigns the advowson collation donation and free disposition and authority and power of conferring or giving to any suitable person the next vacant prebend in the new collegiate church of St. Mary at Leicester when the prebend becomes vacant through death resignation surrender exchange or dismissal or in any other way for the next and only one vacancy, and the same A.B. and C.D. and either of them and their assigns may by the authority of our aforesaid grant confer or give such prebend when as aforesaid it next becomes vacant to a suitable literate person and do and perform all and singular which is necessary concerning the foregoing or in any way appropriate, as fully and completely as we would do if our present grant had not been made. In witness whereof etc.]

[f22]   Concessiones facte per Regem Ricardum. a xxviij° die Junij Anno Regni sui primo usque

Henrici Duci Bukingham Officium magni Camerarij Anglie pro termino vite

Willelmo Catesby Armigero Officium Cancellarij Comitatus Marchie ac custodie Sigilli eiusdem Comitatus pro termino vite sue

Eidem Willelmo officium unius Camerariarum de Scaccario quod Willelmus Hastings nuper dominus Hastings habuit / pro termino vite sue

Eidem Willelmo Officium Cancellarij Scaccarij domini Regis pro termino vite sue

Willelmo Comiti Arundell Officium justiciarij itinerantis omnium Forestarum parcorum Chacearum et Warennarum citra trentham ac Magistri deductus eorum durante vita sua

Willelmo Houghton Militi. Custodiam Comitatus Wigornie quamdiu domino Regi placuerit

Perdonacio generalis pro Roberto Moorton de Bawtry Armigero

Morgano Kidwelly. officium Attornati generalis domini Regis quamdiu placuerit

Roberto Worthington officium Cirographie de Communi Banco quamdiu domino Regi placuerit

Ricardo Ive officium Clerici Corone Cancellarie Anglie quamdiu domino Regi placuerit

Henrico Harman officia Coronarij & Attornati nostri in Banco (nostro) domini Regis quamdiu (domino Regi) placuerit

Thome Thwaytes officium Thesaurarij villie Calis' pro termino vite sue

Eidem Thome officium alti Ballivi Comitatus de Guysnes in Marchijs Picardie Aceciam officium custodis victualium in Castro de Guysnes pro termino vite

(Ricardo Ive officium Clerici Corone Cancellarie Anglie quamdiu domino Regi placuerit)

Prefate Thome (Thwytes) Thwaytes dominus Rex concessit tam tenementum Toftum placeam sive pasturam vocatur le Chauntevain in domino de Marke infra Marchias Calesis quam placeam sive pasturam ibidem vocatur le Honekyrke cum omnibus et omnimodis terris pratis pascuis et pasturis etc durante vita sua prout patet in billa plenius etc

Antonio de Nigrono mercatori de Janua. dominus Rex concessit quod per se vel attornatos suos habeat et percipiat summam trescentarum octoginta et quatuor librarum septem solidorum et sex denariorum legalis monete Anglie de Custumis et subsidijs domini Regis prout plenius patet in billa signata etc

Johanni Kendale officium Custodis brevium & Rotulorum de Communi Banco pro termino vite sue

[Grants made by King Richard from the 28th day of June in the first year of his reign until

To Henry, Duke of Buckingham, the office of great chamberlain of England for the term of his life.

To William Catesby, esquire, the office of chancellor of the earldom of March, and custody of the seal of the same earldom for the term of his life.

To the same William the office of one of the chamberlains of the exchequer which William Hastings late Lord Hastings held for the term of his life.

To the same William the office of chancellor of the exchequer of the lord king for the term of his life.

To William, Earl of Arundel, the office of itinerant justice of all forests parks chases and warrens on this side of Trent and master of the hunt of the same during his life.

To William Houghton, knight, custody of the county of Worcester as long as it pleases the lord king.

A general pardon for Robert Moorton of Bawtry, esquire.

To Morgan Kidwelly the office of attorney general of the lord king as long as he pleases.

To Robert Worthington the office of chirographer of the common bench as long as the lord king pleases.

To Richard Ive the office of clerk of the crown of the chancery of England as long as the lord king pleases.

To Henry Harman the offices of our coroner and attorney in the king's bench, as long as he pleases.

To Thomas Thwaytes the office of treasurer of the town of Calais for the term of his life.

To the same Thomas the office of high bailiff of the county of Guysnes in the marches of Picardy. Also the office of keeper of victuals in the castle of Guysnes for the term of his life.

(To Richard Ive the office of clerk of the crown of the chancery of England as long as the lord king pleases)

To the aforesaid Thomas Thwaytes the lord king granted a tenement toft place or pasture called le Chauntevain in the lordship of Marke in the marches of Calais and the place or pasture there called Le Honekyrke with all and all manner of lands meadows grazing and pasture etc. during his life as appears more fully in the bill etc.

To Anthony de Nigrono, merchant, of Janua [Genoa] the lord king granted that he or his attorneys should have and receive the sum of three hundred and eighty-four pounds seven shillings and sixpence of lawful money of England out of the customs and subsidies of the lord king as more clearly appears in a signed bill etc.

To John Kendale the office of keeper of the writs and rolls of the common bench for the term of his life.]

To Gartier King of Armes and to othre harauldes and porsuyantz C.li of money to be payed by the handes of Humfrey Stafford Squyer of suche money as he owethe the Kyng for the warde and mariage of the lord Latymere. for the Kinges largesse the day of his Coronacion

[f22b] A lettre of Recomendacion for Elizabeth Bryther to be the Kinges mynchyn at Shaftesbury at the sute of Edward Hardguylle etc

like lettre for Anne Berners to be the Kinges mynchyn at Berking

To William Evyngtone and Edward Hardgille thoffice of vergier within the Castel of Windesore for terme of their lyves etc

To Thomas Stafford Squiere the Stuard of the Forest of Kynfare cum pertinencijs in the Countee of Stafford & the Stuard of the maneire of Stourtone & Kynfare with thappurtenaunces in the same Countee and the Rangeoure of the hayes of Chespell Iverley and Asshewode in the Forest forsaide. and Bailief of Inspell and Iverley. with pondes Fisshings wayfes strayes fynes amerciamentes profuytes of the Courtes there. with therbage and pannage trees and wodes called wyndfalles etc within the Forest and hayes forsaid. yelding for the said pondes & herbage etc xiij s iiij d. at the Kinges Estchequer / to have the premisses during the Kinges pleasure.

To Sir (Hugh) Edmond Hastings knight the Stuardshippe of the Maneire and lordship of Pykeringlythe in Comitatu Eboracensie. and maister Forster of the Forest and Chace of Pykerynglyth for terme of lyfe

Thomas Clerc and Isabell his wyfe. a mese & a tenement whiche they hold & occupie within the Towne and feldes of Emeldone besides the Castel of Dunstanburghe. with certain landes called two husbondes landes. duryng the Kinges pleasure

Thome Metcalf officium Cancellarij ducatus Lancastrie ac Custodiam Sigilli pro eodem officio. provisi etc pro termino vite sue

Eidem Thome officium Cancellarij Comitatus Palatini Lancastrie. ac Custodiam

Sigilli pro eodem officio. provisi etc pro termino vite sue

(Dux Bukingham officium Constabularij Anglie ad terminum vite sue)

Eidem duci officia Senescalli honoris de Tutbury in Comitatis Derbie & Stafford'
necnon Castri ville dominij & Manerij Novi Castri subtus Linam dominiorum
& Maneriorum de Werkesworth' & Assheborn' ac omnium castrorum dominiorum Maneriorum terrarum & tenementorum in eisdem Comitatibus cum
pertinencijs parcelle ducatus nostri Lancastrie aceciam officia Constabularij
Castri de Tutbury magistri forestarij Chacee nostre de Nedewode et magistri
forestarij chacee de [f23] Duffeld Firth' ac ipsum ducem supervisorem honoris
predicti ac omnium Castrorum dominiorum villarum Maneriorum terrarum &
tenementorum (in eisdem Comitatibus parcelle ducatus nostri Lancastrie)
Forestarum Chacearum parcorum & warennarum in Comitatibus predictis
cum pertinencijs parcelle ducatus predicti Necnon magistrum deductus eorundem forestarum Chacearum parcorum & warennarum predictorum / necnon
Capitalis & magni Senescalli honoris predicti ac ceterorum premissorum cum
pertinencijs ad terminum vite sue cum feodis & vadijs eisdem officijs & eorum
cuilibet ab antiquo debitis & consuetis de exitibus & Revencionibus honoris
predicti &c per manus Firmarij tenentis Receptoris seu aliorum officiariorum
& occupatorum &c. et Centum libras legalis monete ad terminum vite sue de
Revencionibus predictis per manus Receptoris eorundem pro tempore existentis &c. ac eciam officium Senescalli dominij de alto Pecco & magistri
Forestarij & supervisoris foreste ibidem aceciam officium Constabularij Castri
infra dominium de alto Pecco predictum / aceciam officium Constabularij
Castri de Donyngton' in Comitatu Leycestrie ac Senescalli Castri dominij &
Manerij nostri de Donyngton in eodem Comitatu parcelle dicti honoris de
Tutbury &c. aceciam potestatem & auctoritatem faciendi &c. de tempore in
tempus (omnes) ad terminum vite sue omnes & omnimodos ballivos Forestarios
parcarios & alios officiarios & ministros &c. prout nos faceremus seu facere de
iure possemus si presens concessio nostra facta non fuisset / ac omnia &
omnimoda officia nunc vacancia &c.

[To Thomas Metcalf the office of chancellor of the duchy of Lancaster and
the custody of the seal provided for the same office, etc. for the term of his
life.

To the same Thomas the office of chancellor of the county palatine of
Lancaster and custody of the seal provided for the same office etc. for the
term of his life.

(The Duke of Buckingham the office of constable of England for the term of
his life.)

To the same duke the offices of steward of the honour of Tutbury in the
counties of Derby and Stafford and of the castle town lordship and manor of
Newcastle-under-Lyne, of the lordships and manors of Werkesworth and

70

Assheborne and all castles lordships manors lands and tenements in the same counties with appurtenances parcel of our duchy of Lancaster and also the offices of constable of the castle of Tutbury master forester of our chase of Nedewode and master forester of the chase of Duffeld Firth. And the same duke is made surveyor of the honour aforesaid and of all castles lordships towns manors lands and tenements forests chases parks and warrens in the counties aforesaid with their appurtenances parcel of the aforesaid duchy. Also master of the hunt of the same forests chases parks and warrens aforesaid, head and chief steward of the honour aforesaid and the other foregoing with their appurtenances for the term of his life with the fees and wages owing and customary to the same offices and any of them from of old out of the issues and revenues of the honour aforesaid etc. by the hands of the farmer tenant receiver or other officers or occupiers etc. and a hundred pounds of lawful money for the term of his life out of the revenues aforesaid by the hands of the receiver of the same for the time being etc. and also the office of steward of the lordship of High Peak and master forester and surveyor of the forest there and also the office of steward of the castle within the lordship of High Peak aforesaid also the office of constable of the castle of Donyngton in the same county parcel of the said honour of Tutbury and also the power and authority to make etc. from time to time for the term of his life all and all manner of bailiffs foresters parkers and other officers and ministers etc. as we would make or could of right make if our present grant had not been made, and all and all manner of offices now vacant etc.]

Eidem duci officium Constabularij omnium Castrorum ac officium Senescalli omnium Castrorum Dominiorum Maneriorum terrarum & tenementorum in Comitatibus Salop' & Hereford' que modo vacant & que imposterum (vacare) vacaverint / aceciam supervisionem omnium (subid) subditorum domini Regis ibidem &c.

Eidem duci Constabularium Senescallum & Receptorem Castri Manerij & ville de Uske in Marchijs Wallie ac omnium aliorum Castrorum Dominiorum Maneriorum villarum terrarum & tenementorum que sunt parcelle Comitatus Marchie in Northwallia Suthwallia & Marchijs Wallie ac eciam Custodem sive Capitalem Forestarij Foreste & Chacee de Treweke / ac omnium aliarum Forestarum & Chacearum parcellarum Comitatus predicti in Northwallia Suthwallia Marchijs Wallie & Comitatu predicto pro termino vite sue etc

Eidem duci officium Capitalis Justiciarij & Camerarij in Suthwallia & Northwallia pro termino vite sue. Dantes ulterius eidem ducem [sic] potestatem & auctoritatem faciendi exercendi & exequendi omnia & singula que ad officia predicta pertinent &c. ut patet antea in Regestro.

[To the same duke the office of constable of all the castles and the office of steward of all the castles lordships manors lands and tenements in the counties of Shropshire and Hereford which are now vacant and hereafter become vacant and also the supervision of all the subjects of the lord king there.

To the same duke the offices of constable steward and receiver of the castle manor and town of Usk in the Welsh Marches and of all other castles lordships manors towns lands and tenements which are parcel of the earldom of March in North Wales South Wales and the Welsh Marches and also keeper or head forester of the forest and chase of Treweke and of all other forests and chases parcel of the earldom aforesaid in North Wales South Wales the Welsh Marches and the earldom aforesaid for the term of his life.

To the same duke the office of chief justice and chamberlain in South Wales and North Wales for the term of his life. Further giving the same duke power and authority to do exercise and perform all and singular that pertains to the offices aforesaid etc. as appears earlier in the register.]

Willelmo Knyvet militi officium Senescalli Castri Manerij & Dominij de Rysing ac officium Constabularij eiusdem Castri / necnon officium (Ragitoris) Rageatoris Chacee de Rising / Habendum &c. quam diu domino Regi placuerit.

[To William Knyvet, knight, the office of steward of the castle manor and lordship of Rising and the office of constable of the same castle and the office of ranger of the chase of Rising to hold etc. as long as the lord king pleases.]

To Maister John Gunthorpe keper of the kinges prive Seel . fro the xth day of May . the furst yere of the kinges Reyne . xx . s by the day . aslong he shal occupie . that office . payable (as) in divers portes ut patet in billa

To Jamys Metcalff thoffice of Coronere of the marsshalse of the kinges houshold during the kinges pleasure

To Guy Fairefax knighte thoffice of Chieff Juge of Lancastre during the kinges pleasure

To Miles Metcalff thoffice of one of Juges of Lancastre during the kinges pleasure

[f23b] To Thomas Molyneux Thoffice or offices of the kinges serieaunt & Attorney at lawe in alle his Courtes within the Counte [pl] palatyne of Lancastre during the Kinges pleasure

To Robert Brakenbere Armigero thoffice of Constable of the Toure of Londone for terme of his lyfe

Eidem Roberto Officium Magistri et operatoris monetarum ac Officium

Custodis Cambij infra turrim London durante vita sua

[To the same Robert, the office of master and maker of the money and the office of keeper of the mint within the Tower of London during his life.]

To Maister John Payne Bisshoppe of Mythe in Irland the keping of the temporaltees thereof during the vacacion without accompt etc

To Herry lord Grey an Annuite of C marc to be perceived of thoneure and lordshippe of Pountfreit during the kinges pleasure

To Herry duc of Bukingham thoffices of Constable Stuard and Receivor of the Castelles maneirs and Townes of Monmouthe and Kydwelly in South Wales . and . of alle the Castelles lordships Townes etc in North Wales Southe Wales and Marches of Wales parcelles of the duchie of Lancastre / and thoffices of maister Forster and maister of the game . within alle Forestes and Chaces in South Wales . and of alle othre the kinges Forestes and Chaces in North Wales South Wales . and marches of Wales . of the said Duchie for terme of his lyfe

A prive Seel to the Tresourer and barons of theschequer for to discharge the Custumers of Bristowe of xxij li xij d anempst John Forster of Bristowe / according to the graunte and promysse of King Edward the iiij[th]

To Thomas Bayene . to be under Clerc of the parliament during the kinges pleasure

Herry duc of Bukingham thoffice of Stuard of the Towne of Chestrefeld & of the maneire and lordshippe of Skaresdale in the Countee of Derby for terme of his lyfe

Johanni duci Norffolk officium Capitalis Senescalli ducatus Lancastrie in partibus australibus citra Trentham pro termino vite sue

Thome Pylkington militi Officium vice Comitis Lancastrie & Comitatus palatini ibidem . quamdiu domino Regi placuerit

[To John, Duke of Norfolk, the office of chief steward of the duchy of Lancaster in the south parts this side Trent, for term of his life.

To Thomas Pilkington, knight, the office of sheriff of Lancaster and of the county Palatine there as long as it pleases the lord King.]

[f24] Willelmo Byller officium Feodarij honoris ac dominij de Tykhill' quam diu placuerit

[To William Byller the office of feodary of the honour and lordship of Tykhill during pleasure]

To John Verney . the keping of the park of Donyet in the Countee of Somerset . during the kinges pleasure

To Thomas Trygot and William Johnson a generalle pardone for almanere Alienacions grauntes and purchaces of the maneire of Brendone and Haver-bertus with thappurtenaunces in the Countee of Leycestre etc

Carolo Belfeld officium custodis parci de Yghtenyll' infra Forestam de Penmill' in Comitatu Lancastrie quamdiu placuerit

Roberto de sancto Laurencio militi domino de Houth' officium Cancellarij terre Hibernie quam diu domino Regi placuerit

Johanni Duddele Armigero officium Senescalli omnium dominiorum manerior-um terrarum & tenementorum de ducatu Lancastrie infra Comitatus Berkshire & Southampton quamdiu placuerit

[To Charles Belfeld the office of keeper of the park of Yghtenyll' within the forest of Penmill' in the county of Lancashire during pleasure.

To Robert de St. Laurence, knight, Lord Houth, the office of chancellor of the land of Ireland as long as the lord king pleases.

To John Duddele, esquire, the office of steward of all the lordships, manors, lands and tenements of the duchy of Lancaster within the counties of Berkshire and Southampton during pleasure.]

Robert (Couty) Coort Receivor of the duchie of Lancastre in the Countees of Dorset Southampton Wilteshire Berkshire Gloucestre and Oxonford to contynue the same his office during the kinges pleasure

Johanni domino le Scrope militi Officium Camerarij ducatus Lancastrie (and) ad terminum vite sue.

Thome Bryan Armigero ad firmam dominium de Balyngham in partibus Picardie cum omnibus terris etc . habendum quamdiu Regi placuerit Reddendo

74

per annum xx libras ad Scaccariam Calesie etc

Eidem Thome officia Ballivi de Sandegate and Hamme(s) ac Receptoris ibidem quam diu placuerit

Johanni Sapcote Armigero officium Receptoris generalis ducatus Cornubie cum portagio monete eidem officio pertinente quamdiu placuerit.

Edwardo Hastings militi Custodia omnium maneriorum &c. que fuerunt Thome Salvan (militis) Armigeri et Racione minoris etatis Radulphi filij et heredis dicti Thome in manus domini Regis cum maritagio eiusdem &c.

[To John lord le Scrope, knight, the office of chamberlain of the duchy of Lancaster for the term of his life.

To Thomas Bryan, esquire, at farm, the lordship of Balyngham in the parts of Picardy with all lands etc. To hold as long as the king pleases. Paying twenty pounds annually to the Calais exchequer, etc.

To the same Thomas the offices of bailiff of Sandgate and Hamme and receiver there during pleasure.

To John Sapcote, esquire, the office of receiver general of the duchy of Cornwall with the porterage belonging to the same office during pleasure.

To Edward Hastings, knight, custody of all the manors etc. which were Thomas Salvan's esquire, and in the hands of the lord king by reason of the minority of Ralph, son and heir of the said Thomas, with the marriage of the same etc.]

[f24b] To John Duc of Norffolk the Castelle & lordshippe of Farley

Ricardo Huddelston militi officium Receptoris omnium dominiorum maneriorum terrarum & tenementorum etc in Comitatibus Cumbr' et Lancastrie . que nuper fuerunt Thome Marchionis . Dorset . ac Magistrum Forestariorum aceciam Senescallum eorundem quamdiu domino Regi placuerit

[To Richard Huddelston, knight, the office of receiver of all the lordships manors lands and tenements &c. in the counties of Cumberland and Lancashire which were late of Thomas, Marquis of Dorset, and master forester and steward of the same as long as the lord king pleases.]

George Willerby Squier . otherwise goldsmythe a generalle pardone

Thome Sapcote(s) officium Receptoris . dominiorum Castrorum etc que fuerunt Mathei Gourney in Comitatibus Dors' Somers' et Wilt' quamdiu domino Regi placuerit

> [To Thomas Sapcote the office of receiver of the lordships castles etc. which were of Matthew Gourney in the counties of Dorset, Somerset and Wiltshire, as long as the lord king pleases.]

Garard Caniziani and Elizabeth his wyfe a generalle pardone

John Josselyne thoffice of Auditor of alle the landes & tenementes late Henry Bourchiere knighte Therle of Essex knighte during the nonne age of Henry Cousyn & heire of the said Erle and aslong the same the premisses shalbe in the kinges handes with fees & wages to the same due & accustomed etc

Thomas Kebelle Thoffice of Attorney generalle of the Duchie of Lancastre during the kinges pleasure

Maister William Lacy thoffice of Clerk of the Kinges Counsaille with xl marc of Fee quam diu placuerit domino Regi

To the (Counte) Therle of Surrey the Stewardshippe of the duchie of Lancastre in the Counte of Norffolk quam diu etc

A licence to Edward Bramptone to shippe as moche wolles upon the kinges Custumes as shalle amount to the summe of CC li

To my lord prince the lieutenauntshippe of the land of Irland for the space of iij yere

Thomas Hunt Thoffice of Clerk of the kinges werkes within England during the kinges pleasure with wages of ij s by day and vj for his Clerk etc

Roberto Mannyng officium provisoris omnium lathamorum plumbarum & omnium aliorum operiorum & laboratorum ac omnimodi Suffurarum pro (operibus) operacionibus nostris in palacium de Westmonsterio & Turrim London quamdiu etc

> [To Robert Mannyng, the office of purveyor of all masons, plumbers and all other workmen and labourers and all kinds of building supplies for our works for the palace of Westminster and the Tower of London during etc.]

To the vicount Lisle the ferme of the lordships & maners Astley Wydington & Higham in the (D) Counte of Warrewic during oure pleasure

[f25] Willelmo Berkeley militi Custodiam occupacionem et gubernacionem Insule (Vecte) de Wyght' Castrorum et dominij de Caresbroke alias dicti Carsbroke infra eandem insulam ac omnium Castrorum etc in eadem insula. durante beneplacito domini Regis.

Willelmo Uvedale Armigero Custodiam Castri et ville de Portchestre Portesmouth' et Patrie ibidem necnon supervisionem et gubernacionem ville de Portesmouth' et placee Regis ibidem quamdiu domino Regi placuerit.

Thome Tyrell' Armigero annuitatem xl librarum percipiendam de Revencioni-bus dominij de Witheresfeld cum pertinencijs in Comitatu Essex' quousque prefato Thome providatur officium conveniens ad valorem huiusmodi annuitatis.

Willelmo Langley nuper valecto vestiarij illustrissimi principis Edwardi iiij^{ti} Officium janitoris & custodis gaole Castri de Northampton' ac prisonariorum in eodem pro tempore existencium cum herbagio infra idem Castrum & le Bascourt alias dictum Castel Orcherd' eidem Castro annexum cum proficuis fossati Castelli prati castelli vocati Castell' Medewe pistarie aquarum currencium per eadem prata habendum quamdiu domino Regi placuerit.

Nicholo Baker alias Spycer Officium Senescalli dominiorum de Sodbury Barton hundredi Erlescourt honoris Gloucestrie & Fairford cum pertinencijs in Comitatu Gloucestrie & dominij de Sherston' in Comitatu Wiltes quamdiu &c.

Alueredo Corneburgh' Officium Controtulatoris tunagij nostri Stanni in Comitatibus Cornubie & Devonie habendum quamdiu &c.

Johanni Frith' Officium janitoris exterioris porte Castri nostri de Windesore habendum quamdiu &c.

Johanni Mody & Agneti uxori eius Annuitatem quinque librarum percipiendum de exitibus sive de firma manerij de Merston' Meysy in Comitatu Wiltes' per manus firmarij &c. quamdiu &c.

[To William Berkeley, knight, the custody, occupation and rule of the Isle of Wight, of the castles and lordship of Caresbroke, alias Carsbroke, in the same island and of all castles etc. in the same island during the lord king's good pleasure.

To William Uvedale, esquire, custody of the castle and town of Portchester Portsmouth and the country there and also the supervision and rule of the town of Portsmouth and the king's estate there, as long as the lord king pleases.

To Thomas Tyrell, esquire, an annuity of £40 to be received from the revenues of the lordship of Witheresfeld with its appurtenances in the county of Essex until a suitable office to the value of such an annuity is provided for the aforesaid Thomas.

To William Langley, late yeoman of the wardrobe to the most illustrious prince Edward IV, the office of porter and keeper of the gaol of Northampton Castle and the prisoners in the same for the time being, with the herbage within that castle and le Bascourt otherwise called Castle Orchard adjoining the same castle, with the profits of the moat of the castle, the meadow of the castle called Castle Meadow and the fishery of the waters running through the same meadows, to hold as long as the lord king pleases.

To Nicholas Baker, alias Spycer, the office of steward of the lordships of Sodbury, Barton hundred, Erlescourt of the honour of Gloucester and Fairford with its appurtenances in the county of Gloucester and of the lordship of Sherston' in the county of Wiltshire as long as etc.

To Alfred Corneburgh the office of controller of our tonnage on tin in the counties of Cornwall and Devon, to hold as long etc.

To John Frith the office of porter of the outer gate of our castle of Windsor, to hold as long etc.

To John Mody and Agnes, his wife, an annuity of five pounds, to be received from the issues or farm of the manor of Merston Meysey in the county of Wiltshire by the hands of the farmer etc. as long etc.]

[f25b] Johanni Hay Annuitatem decem librarum de exitibus manerij et dominij de Shepton subtus le Whichewood durante iuniore etate Edwardi Comitis Warrewik

[To John Hay an annuity of £10 from the issues of the manor and lordship of Shepton under Whichewood during the minority of Edward Earl of Warwick.]

To Robert Haringtone knighte thoffices of Bailly Stuard & the keping of ij parkes of Loughburghe . and xx li annuite of thissues and prouffites of the same lordship for terme of his lyf.

To Thomas Fulshurst squier thoffice of maister of the game of the park of Blakmere . in the Counte of Salop

78

Gardiano et Conventui Fratrum Minorum Oxoniensis quinquaginta marcas percipiendas annuatim ad Scaccarium quamdiu nobis placuerit etc

Henrico Davy officium Custodis Manerij Gardini nostri palaciatis & warreni Cuniculorum de Shene pro termino vite sue

[To the warden and convent of the friars minor in Oxford fifty marks taken yearly from the Exchequer as long as it pleases us etc.

To Henry Davy the office of keeper of our manor and garden, paliser and keeper of the warren of coneys at Shene for term of his life.]

To Thomas Kebelle thoffice of generalle Attorney of the duchie of Lancastre aswel within England as in Wales during the kinges pleasure with suche wages and fees as Nicholas Sharppe late havyng the said office in & for the same had & perceived at the festes of the Nativite of oure lord and pentecost / of the Revenues of the said duchie by the handes of the Receyvor of the same for the tyme beyng

To John Josselyn thoffice of Auditor of accomptes of alle Castelles lordships maners landes & tenementes late Henry burghchier knight Erle of Essex decessed to have & occupie during the nonne Age of Henry Cousyn & heire of the forsaid Henry (Henry) late Erle of Essex and over that aslong as it shal happen the premisses to be in the kinges handes with the fees & wages (thereto due) to the said office of olde due & accustumed etc

To George Danyelle thoffice of Baillieff of the lordships of Cokeham and bray within the Counte of Berkshire / To have & enioie the said office by him or his sufficient depute during the kinges pleasure with the wages fees & al othere profites commodities & advailes to the same office of olde tyme due & accustumed etc

To Richard Rugge squier Thoffice of baillieff of Patyngeham in the Counte of Stafford / To have & occupie by him. or his depute during the kinges pleasure with the wages & fees of two penyes by day etc

To John Talbot one of the squiers of the kinges houshold thoffice of keping of the parke of Hampstede within the Countie of Berkshire To have & occupie the same by him or his depute sufficient during the kinges pleasure with the wages fees profites commoditees & advailes the same office due & accustumed etc

[f26] Vicomiti Lovell' officium Constabularij de Walingford ac Castri de Walingford ac officium Senescalli honoris de Walingford sancti Walerici ac

quatuor hundredorum & dimidij de Chilterne / Habendum &c. per se vel per
deputatum suum sive deputatos suos sufficientes pro termino vite ipsius
Francisci / Percipiendo &c. feoda & vadia eisdem debita & consueta de exitibus
& proficuis honoris predicti per manus Receptoris de Walingford sive honoris
illius &c. ac feoda & vadia debita & consueta Annuatim de eisdem exitibus etc
pro locumtenente suo ad gubernandum predicta officia in absencia ipsius
Francisci per manus eiusdem Receptoris / Et ulterius eidem Francisco potestatem & auctoritatem ordinandi & constituendi de tempore in tempus durante
vita sua omnes & omnimodos officiarios & ministros de & in predictis honore
hundredis &c.

Vicomiti Lovell' officium (of) Capitalis pincerne nostri Anglie / habendum
gaudendum & occupandum idem officium per se vel per suum deputatum sive
per suos deputatos sufficientes pro termino vite ipsius Francisci / Percipiendo
in & pro officio illo exercendo Centum libras sterlingorum tam de custumis &
prisis vinorum quam de omnibus alijs exitibus proficuis & commoditatibus
nobis quoquomodo emergentibus sive coestentibus de & in officio predicto tam
per manus ipsius vicecomitis quam alicuius alterius persone qui pro tempore
officium illud exercebit &c.

Thome Lynom officium Solicitarij domini Regis Habendum quam diu domıno
Regi placuerit Percipiendo annuatim pro occupacione officij (predictam) predicti a xxvj^{to} die Junij ultimo preterito decem libras sterlingorum de magnis
Custumis nostris in portu Civitatis nostre Londoniensis per manus Custumariorum sive Collectorum eorundem pro tempore existencium ad Festa sancti
Michaelis & Pasche per equales porciones unacum omnibus alijs proficuis
libertatibus &c. / Aceciam eidem Thome Annuitatem xx li. percipiendam
eidem Thome A predicto xxvj° die Junij quam diu domino Regi placuerit de
magnis Custumis nostris supradictis per manus Custumariorum sive Collectorum
eorundem pro tempore existencium ad festa predicta. Eo quod &c. In cuius
&c.

[To Viscount Lovell the office of constable of Wallingford and the castle of
Wallingford and the office of steward of the honour of Wallingford St.
Valery and four and a half Chiltern hundreds. To hold etc. in person or by his
sufficient deputy or deputies for the term of life of the same Francis.
Receiving etc. the fees and wages due and customary for the same out of the
issues and profits of the aforesaid honour by the hands of the receiver of
Wallingford or of that honour etc. and the fees and wages due and customary
annually out of the same issues etc. for his lieutenant to control the aforesaid
offices in the absence of the same Francis, by the hands of the same receiver.
And further to the same Francis, the power and authority to make and
appoint from time to time during his life all and all manner of officers and
servants of and in the aforesaid honour, hundreds etc.

To Viscount Lovell the office of our chief butler of England, to have enjoy
and occupy the same office in person or by his sufficient deputy or deputies
for the term of life of the same Francis. Receiving in and for the exercise of

that office one hundred pounds sterling from the customs and prises of wines and from all other issues profits and easements in any way arising or existing of and in the aforesaid office by the hands of the viscount himself or any other person who for the time being shall exercise that office etc.

To Thomas Lynom, the office of solicitor of the lord king, to hold as long as the lord king pleases, receiving annually for the occupation of the aforesaid office from the 26th day of June last past ten pounds sterling out of our great customs in the port of our City of London by the hands of the customers or the collectors of the same for the time being at the feasts of Michaelmas and Easter by equal portions, with all other profits, liberties etc. Also to the same Thomas an annuity of £20 to be received by the same Thomas from the aforesaid 26th June as long as the lord king pleases, out of our great customs aforesaid by the hands of the customers or collectors of the same for the time being at the aforesaid feasts. That etc. In witness etc.]

To Alexander Mathewson thoffice of Baillishippe of the Towne of Wedersfeld in the Counte of Essex / To have the same office during the kinges pleasure with the wages of ij d by the day / And with alle the proffites & commoditees etc

To William Bracher the keping of the parke of Okehampton within youre Counte of Devone / To have the same during the kinges pleasure with wages to the same office accustumed

Johanni Duci Norffolk . officium Admiralli Anglie Hibernie & acquitanie pro termino vite sue

Eidem Duci Dominium & Manerium de Lavenham cum membris & pertinencijs suis in Comitatu Suffolk Dominia & Maneria de Canfeld Stansted Monfichet Crepping Crustwich' Langdon' Estonhall Vauce Dodynghurst Fyndgreth' Bomsted Helion Beaumond & Bentley cum omnibus membris & pertinencijs cuiuslibet eorum in Comitatu Essex / Dominium & Manerium de Batelesmere cum membris & pertinencijs in Comitatu Kancie dominium & manerium de Hynkeston' in Comitatu Cantebrigg' / Dominia & Maneria de Roseneythyn Helston' Deny Predannok Poledewe Etheron' Dawneth Rilleton Tresedoron' Helleton' Hermena Newland Hamatethy Park Trewige Wigtobham Penhall' Nansirgh Trebighyn' magna Hendred & Scrobhender cum omnibus membris & pertinencijs suis in Comitatu Cornubie Dominia & Maneria de Britford Wellewe Rustishall Chepenham Teffount Bremilshawe Upton Skydmore Upton Parkes Wermynster & Wynerburstok in Comitatu Wiltes' / Et dominium de Hungerferd in Comitatu Berk' / Ac Castrum dominium & manerium de Farlegh in Comitatibus Somers' & Wiltes'. Habendum sibi & heredibus masculis suis de domino Rege per servicium unius feodi militis

[To John, Duke of Norfolk, the office of admiral of England, Ireland and Aquitaine, for the term of his life.

To the same duke the lordship and manor of Lavenham with its members and appurtenances in the county of Suffolk, the lordships and manors of Canfield, Stansted Mountfitchet, Crepping, Crustwich, Langdon, Estonhall, Vauce, Doddinghurst, Fyndgreth, Bumpstead Helion, Beaumont and Bently with all the members and appurtenances of any of them in the county of Essex, the lordship and manor of Batelesmere with its members and appurtenances in the county of Kent, the lordship and manor of Hinkston in the county of Cambridge, the lordships and manors of Roseneythyn, Helston, Deney, Predannack, Poldhu, Otheron, Dawneth, Rilleton, Tresederon, Helleton, Hermena, Newland, Hamatethy Park, Trewige, Wigtobham, Penhall, Nansirgh, Trebighyn, Magna Hendred and Scrobhender with all their members and appurtenances in the county of Cornwall, the lordships and manors of Britford, Wellewe, Rustishall, Chippenham, Teffount, Bremilshawe, Upton Skydmore, Upton Park, Warminster and Wynerburstok in the county of Wiltshire, and the lordship of Hungerford in the county of Berkshire, and the castle, lordship and manor of Farlegh in the counties of Somerset and Wiltshire. To hold to him and his male heirs of the lord king by the service of one knight's fee]

[f26b] Eidem duci Norffolk a Festo Pasche ultimo preterito quam diu domino Regi placuerit omnia exitus proficua & Revenciones dominiorum & maneriorum de Middelton' Berton' Bendich' Stowbedon' Hillyngton Tylney Islyngton' Clencheverton' Wygnall' cum (py) piscarijs Scaleshowe Reyham Scales Scretebye hundrede de Fre brigge Heklyng Hekwold & Wilton' in Comitatu Norffolk Dominij & manerij de Wardilyngton' in Comitatu Suffolk Dominiorum & maneriorum de Berkeway Rokehey & Newsell' in Comitatu Hertfordie & Dominij & manerij de Haselyngfeld in Comitatu Cantebrigge dominij & manerij de Wodham Ferres in Comitatu Essex unacum feodo militis &c. ut patet in billa.

Rex (etc) Archiepiscopis &c. salutem. Ea est maximi solaris luminis claritas simul & caritas quod ubi (de) diffundit in cetera siderea corpora / id quidquid habeat luciditatis & fulgoris non ideo minus tamen sol ipse resplendit nec detrimentum quantumlibet in sua virtute suscipit aut decore libet aspicere / ipsum luminare maius tanquam Regem constitutum in medio procerum / ipsasque maiores minoresque Stellas sua ordinatissima claritate totam ipsam celestem Curiam exornare / Qui procul dubio forma exemplari permoti Videntes vocacionem in qua vocati sumus ut videlicet cuntis mortalibus huius Regni favente altissimo presidere atque prefici debeamus / convertimus nostri oculi interioris intuitum ad huius pernobilis rei publice suorumque membrorum immensitatem id maximopere precaventes ne in (tantes) tantis que nobis incumbunt solicitudinibus ij qui in partem ipsarum sustinendam necessarij nobis forent deesse modo quolibet viderentur / Et quia inter ceteras quaslibet nobis subiectas provincias nulla magis quam Wallie principatus tum (probter) propter situm angularem tum propter linguam & mores populi ab alijs regnicolis abhorrentes / singularem sub nobis dominiumque immediatum exposcit cui Cestrens' Comitatus pene contiguus ac confinalis existit / Nos ideo maiorum nostrorum vestigia insequentes Carissimum primogenitum nostrum Edwardum cuius optima indoles ac preclare quibus pro sue etatis modulo singularitate preditus est nature dotes ingentem atque faventem deo indubitatam future probitatis spem nobis portendunt de Consilio & assensu prelatorum ducum & Baronum Regni nostri Anglie dictorum principatus & Comitatus donis prerogativis atque insignijs statuimus decorare ipsumque principem Wallie & Comitem Cestrie fecimus & creavimus / atque facimus & creamus / Atque eidem Edwardo nomen stilum titulum Statum dignitatem & honorem principatus & Comitatus eorundem dedimus concessimus atque damus & concedimus & per presentem Cartam nostram confirmamus / ac ipsum de dictis principatu & Comitatu ut ibidem proficimus presideat & presidendo dictas partes dirigat & defendat per cincturam gladij tradicionemque & posicionem serti in capite & anuli aurei in digito necnon virge auree in manu investimus ut est (mores) moris. Habendum sibi & heredibus suis Regibus Anglie imperpetuum / Quare volumus & firmiter precipimus pro nobis & heredibus nostris quod predictus Edwardus filius noster habeat nomen stilum titulum dignitatem & honorem principatus Wallie & Comitatus Cestrie predictorem sibi & heredibus suis Regibus Anglie ut predictum est imperpetuum / Hijs testibus &c. Datum etc.

[To the same Duke of Norfolk, from the feast of Easter last past for as long as the lord king pleases, all the issues profits and revenues of the lordships and manors of Middleton Barton Bendish Stow Bedon Hillington Tilney Islington Clenchwarton Wygnall with the fishponds Scaleshowe Raynham Scales Scretebye the hundred of Fre Brigge Hickling Hekwold and Wilton in the county of Norfolk, of the lordship and manor of Wardilyngton in the county of Suffolk, of the lordships and manors of Barkway Rokehey and Newsells in the county of Hertford and of the lordship and manor of Hasling-field in the county of Cambridge, of the lordship and manor of Woodham Ferrars in the county of Essex with a knight's fee etc. as appears in the bill.

The king to the archbishops etc. greeting. The clarity and charity of the sun's light is so great that when it is poured on the other heavenly bodies the sun shines with no less light and splendour, nor does it suffer any diminution of its strength, rather it is pleased to be seen, to shine as a king in the midst of his nobles and to adorn the greater and lesser stars in the whole court of heaven with his outstanding light. Which without doubt we should take as an example seeing the vocation to which we are called, that is, by the favour of the almighty to govern and be set at the head of all the mortals of this realm. We have turned the gaze of our inward eye to the greatness of this noble state and of its members, having great care that, in the great anxieties which press upon us, those who are necessary to support us should not now seem to be lacking. And since among the provinces subject to us none requires separate and immediate rule under us as much as the principality of Wales, because of its remote position and because of the language and customs of the people, remote from those of other areas, and the county of Chester which almost adjoins and borders it. We therefore, following the footsteps of our ancestors and with the assent and advice of the said prelates, dukes and barons of our realm of England, have determined to honour our dearest first born son Edward, whose outstanding qualities, with which he is singularly endowed for his age, give great and, by the favour of God, undoubted hope of future uprightness, as prince and earl, with grants perogatives and insignia and we have made and created, and do make and create, him Prince of Wales and Earl of Chester. And we have given and granted and do give and grant to the same Edward the name style title state dignity and honour of the same principality and earldom and by this our present charter we confirm them and have placed him at the head of the said principality and earldom, as in the same charter, to have the charge of those parts and govern them and defend them. And we invest him as the custom is by the girding on of the sword, the handing over and setting of the garland on his head, and of the gold ring on his finger, and of the gold staff in his hand, to have and hold to him and his heirs, kings of England, for ever. Wherefore we will and firmly decree for us and our heirs that the said Edward our son shall have the name style title dignity and honour of the principality of Wales and the earldom of Chester aforesaid to him and his heirs Kings of England as aforesaid for ever. With these witnesses etc. Given etc.]

Margaret Basset Therbage & paunage of the parke of Claredon and a tenement in the Towne there to the yerely valewe of xiij s iiij d / during the kinges pleasure

[f27] Ricardo (Vaghan) Vaughan Manerium sive dominium de Aber in (Comitatu) Commoto de Uphaugh infra Comitatum de Caernarvan ac villiam de Vike infra dictum Comitatum / Aceciam Dominium sive Manerium de Kemmes in Comitatu Anglesey cum omnibus terris & tenementis &c. Habendum &c. a festo Apostolorum Petri & Pauli ultimo preterito pro termino vite sue Reddendo inde annuatim domino Regi ad Scaccariam de Caernarvan decem libras sterlingorum ad festa Sancti Michaelis & Pasche per equales porciones. Eo &c.

Ricardus &c. salutem.   Sciatis quod nos de fidelitate circumspeccione & industria dilectorum & fidelium nostrorum Johannis Dynham Militis Domini de Dynham Magistri Johannis Cooke Archideaconi Lincolniensis Ricardi Tunstall' militis Johannis Scott militis & Thome Thwaytes militis plenius confidentes de advisamento Consilij nostri eisdem quinque quator tribus aut duobus dedimus & concessimus ac per presentes damus & concedimus mandatum potestatem & Auctoritatem ad recipiendum in manus & obedienciam nostras villam & Castrum nostrum de Guysnes cum omnibus membris & pertinencijs suis de Radulpho Hastinges nuper locumtenente nostro ibidem / Ac ad tradendum & liberandum villam & Castrum predicta cum membris suis Johanni Blounte Militi domino de Mountioye / Habendum & tenendum custod-

84

iam regimen & gubernamen ville Castri & membrorum predictorum quam diu
nobis placuerit / Ac ad tradendum & liberandum prefato Radulpho litteras
nostras gracie Remissiones & perdonacionis generalis / ac litteras confirmacionis
nostre de & super donacionibus & concessionibus terrarum possessionum
officiorum & feodorum eidem Radulpho per bone memorie Regem Edwardum
quartum fratrem & predecessorem nostrum factis / Necnon de & super vadijs
suis ac omnium aliorum stipendiarum & soldariorum dicti Castri de Guysnes /
Aceciam pro quibuscumque reparacionibus refeccionibus & fortificacionibus
dicti Castri nostri per ipsum Radulphum suis sumptibus & expensis ibi factis &
nondum sibi allocatis cum dicto Radulpho tractandum appunctuandum (&)
communicandum & concludendum / Ceteraque omnia & singula que in
premissis necessaria fuerint seu quomodolibet oportuna pro nobis & nomine
nostro facienda exercenda & exequenda eciam si de se mandatum exigant
magis speciale. (Dabunt) Damus autem universis & singulis Capitaneis Maioribus officiarijs nostris ac alijs ultra mare ubilicet constitutis & alijs quorum
interest in hac parte tenore presencium firmiter in mandatis quod eis quinque
quator tribus aut duobus in execucione premissorum intendentes sint assistentes
& obedientes in omnibus diligenter. in cuius.

Johanni Barker officia Ballivi dominiorum Maneriorum & hundredorum de
Bampton' in Comitatu Oxoniensi & Shrivenham cum eorum pertinencijs in
Comitatu Berks. Habendum &c. durante minore etate Georgij Comitis Salop /
ac quamdiu dicta dominia maneria & hundreda cum pertinencijs in manibus
nostris aut heredum nostrorum remanere contigerint &c.

Ricardus &c. Reverendo in Christo patri Johanni Lincolniensis Episcopo
salutem / ad Ecclesiam parochialem de Calverton vestre diocesis per mortem
ultimi incumbentis eiusdem iam vacantem & ad nostram presentacionem
notarie spectantem / dilectum nobis in Christo Edmundum Chaderton Clericum
vestre paternitati presentamus / supplicantes eidem paternitati vestre quatinus
ipsum Edmundum in rectorem dicte Ecclesie de Calverton dignemini admittere
& ipsum in eadem instituere ceteraque ulterius peragere que vestre paternitati
incumbunt in hac parte.

[To Richard Vaughan the manor or lordship of Aber in the commote of
Uphaugh in the county of Carnarvon and the town of Vike within the said
county. Also the lordship or manor of Kemmes in the county of Anglesey
with all lands and tenements etc. To hold etc. from the feast of the apostles
Peter and Paul last past for the term of his life. Paying therefor annually to
the lord king at the exchequer at Carnarvon ten pounds sterling at the feasts
of Michaelmas and Easter by equal portions. That etc.

Richard etc. greeting. Know that we on the advice of our council and having
full confidence in the loyalty discretion and diligence of our beloved and
faithful John Dynham, knight, Lord Dynham, Master John Cooke, arch-
deacon of Lincoln, Richard Tunstall, knight, John Scott, knight, and Thomas

Thwaytes, knight, have given and granted and by these presents do give and grant to the same five, four, three or two of them mandate power and authority to receive into our hands and allegiance our town and castle of Guisnes with all its members and appurtenances from Ralph Hastinges late our lieutenant there and to hand over and deliver the town and castle aforesaid with its members to John Blount, knight, Lord Mountjoy. To have and hold the custody rule and guidance of the town castle and members aforesaid as long as it shall please us. And to hand over and deliver to the aforesaid Ralph our letters of remission, of grace and general pardon and letters of confirmation of and concerning the gifts and grants of the lands possessions offices and fees made to the same Ralph by our brother and predecessor King Edward the fourth of happy memory. Also of and for his wages and those of all the other mercenaries and soldiers of the said castle of Guisnes. Also for any repairs reconstructions and fortifications of our said castle made there by the same Ralph at his own costs and expenses, and not yet allowed to him, which are to be discussed, settled, agreed and concluded with the said Ralph. And all and singular other matters which shall be necessary in the premises or in any way fitting to be done exercised and performed for us and in our name even if they require a more especial commission. And we give a firm command to all and singular our captains mayors officers and others stationed anywhere beyond the sea and others concerned in this matter by the tenor of these presents that they should be diligently attentive helpful and obedient in all things to these five four three or two in the execution of the premises. In witness of which etc.

To John Barker the offices of bailiff of the lordships manors and hundreds of Bampton in the county of Oxford and Shrivenham with their appurtenances in the county of Berks. To have etc. during the minority of George, Earl of Shrewsbury, and as long as the said lordships manors and hundreds with their appurtenances happen to remain in the hands of us or our heirs, etc.

Richard etc. To the reverend father in Christ, John, Bishop of Lincoln, greeting. We present to your paternity our beloved in Christ Edmund Chaderton, clerk, for the parish church of Calverton in your diocese now vacant by the death of the last incumbent of the same which by common knowledge is in our presentation, beseeching your paternity that you will deign to admit the same Edmund to be rector of the said church of Calverton and induct him into the same and do everything further which pertains to your paternity in this respect.]

Henry Birkehede the office of the keping of the parke of Colcombe / and bailieff of the lordship of Colitone within the Countie of Devone for terme of his liff

To John Taillor alias Vale nuper de Basingstoke / a generalle pardone

86

Ricardus &c. Dilectis & fidelibus (suis) Johanni Dynham militi domino Dynham Jacobo Tirell militi Johanni Sapcote Armigero Alveredo (Corneburgh) Cornborugh Thome Aleyn' Roberto Coorte & Thome Sapcote salutem. Sciatis nos de fidelitate & circumspeccione vestris plenius confidentes ordinasse constituisse & assignasse vos prefatos Johannem Jacobum Johannem Alveredum Thomam Robertum & Thomam quorum vestrum vos prefatos Alveredum Cornborugh Thomam Aleyn' Robertum Coorte & Thomam Sapcote unum esse volumus assessores nostros ad dimmittendum & assessandum omnia & singula terras & tenementa nostra infra Comitatum nostrum Cornubie assesssabilia quibuscumque personis idonijs & sufficientibus ad terminum viginti unius annorum vel infra termino ille incipiente ad Festum sancti Michaelis Archangeli proxime futurum / Percipiendo quilibet eorum qui dictis sessionibus interesse contigerit talia vadia qualia alij assessores sive comissionarij **[f27b]** in casu consilii ante hec tempora habere & percipere consueverint de exitibus proficuis & revencionibus ducatus nostri Cornubie predicti per manus generalis Receptoris nostri eiusdem ducatus pro tempore existentis / Mandantes omnibus & singulis ballivis prepositis Firmarijs tenentibus & officiarijs nostris quibuscunque dicti ducatus quod prefato Johanni Jacobo Alveredo Thome Roberto & Thome quorum prefatos Alveredum Thomam Robertum & Thomam unum esse volumus intendentes sint assistentes auxiliantes & faventes in omnibus prout decet. In cuius &c.

[Richard etc. to the beloved and faithful John Dynham, knight, Lord Dynham, James Tirell, knight, John Sapcote, esquire, Alfred Cornborugh, Thomas Aleyn, Robert Coorte and Thomas Sapcote, greeting. Know that we, fully trusting in your loyalty and discretion, have ordained, appointed and assigned you, the aforesaid John, James, John, Alfred, Thomas, Robert, and Thomas our assessors, of whom we wish you the aforesaid Alfred Cornborough, Thomas Aleyn, Robert Coorte and Thomas Sapcote to be one, to demise and assess all and singular our lands and tenements liable to assessment within our county of Cornwall by any suitable and sufficient persons for the term of twenty-one years within that term, beginning at the feast of Michaelmas next. Each one who shall happen to take part in the said sessions receiving such wages as other assessors or commissioners have been accustomed to have and receive in case of counsel before this time out of the issues profits and revenues of our duchy of Cornwall aforesaid by the hands of our receiver general of the same duchy for the time being. And commanding all and singular our bailiffs reeves farmers tenants and officers of the said duchy to be obedient, helpful, attentive and favouring in all things as is fitting to the said John, James, Alfred, Thomas, Robert and Thomas of whom we wish the aforesaid Alfred, Thomas, Robert or Thomas to be one. In which etc.]

To Sir Richard Harecourt the Warde & mariage of Richard Fynes Son & heire of Henry Fynes lord Say with the keping of alle lordshippes maners landes & tenementes etc

The Henry Braythwayt oon of the yomen of the Coronne the (king) keping of the parke of Fulbroke within the Counte of Warrewyk / To have the same /

(during the kinges pleasure for terme of lyff) for terme of liff

To William Browne oone of the Clerkes of the kinges Chapelle the coride or Sustentacione within the monastery of Beauley / To have the same for terme of his lyff etc

To John Stokes the yongere therbage & pannage of the gret parke of Henly in (Aden) Arderne in youre Counte of Warrewyk / To have the same for terme of his liff without any thing therefore yelding or paieng etc

To Kateryne Hastinges Wedowe the warde & mariage of Edward Hastinges son & heire of Sir William Hastinges lord Hastinges with the keping of alle (maners) Castelles lordshippes Maners landes tenementes etc Ut patet in billa etc

To Hamond Hassalle to be one of the iij serieauntes at lawe within the Counte palatyne of Chestre during the kinges pleasure

To Richard Williams and Thomas Beynam and to aithere of them Thoffice of Constable of seint Brevelles in youre forest of Deane / during the kinges pleasure.

To John Nesfeld squiere Thoffice of Constable of the Castelle of Hertford for terme of his lyff

To Richard Champney other wise Gloucestre (herulde) heraulde to be king of herauldes in parties of Wales with twenty pounde Fe during his liff / to be perceived of the Fee ferme of the Citee of Londone & of the Countie of Middlesex etc Ut patet in billa

To Walter Hungerford the keping of the parkes (of) called West parke and home parke within the lordshippe of Corsham / in the Countie of Wilteshire for terme of liff

To Thomas Paterik the Bailliefshippe of the lordshippe of (Wormynghay) Wormynghay within the Countie of Norffolk / during the kinges pleasure

To David Vaghan the ferme of alle the Towne of (Cayus) Cayrus within flyntshire parcelle of Therldom of Chestre with thappertenaunces for the terme of xxj yeres / paying yerely asmoche as was answerd to theschequere of youre

88

Countie palatyne of Chestre in the xxjj^{ti} yere of king Edward the iiijth

To John Sydborowe Thoffice of baillieff of (Riding) Rysing in the Counte of Norffolk during the kinges pleasure

To John Abelle Thoffices of porter of the Castelle of Hertford and the keping of the parke of Racheford During the kinges pleasure

[f28] To Frere Thomas Jonys of the freres minors of Worcestre the medowe called Digley lieng undere the Castelle there during the kinges pleasure without any thing therefore yelding etc

To Thomas Otter Thoffices of Bailieff the lordshippe of brayles with the keping of the warrenne of Connes there / and bailieff of the hundred of Chadlington During the kinges pleasure

To Maister Thomas Barowe to be the Maister of the Rowles for terme of his liff etc

To John Huddelstone the Stewardshippe of the lordshippes of Elmeley Kelmerton Crome Pedille & Lidney in the Counte of Worcestre / and to the same John the Maister Forster of the parke of Elmeley during the kinges pleasure

To Thomas Arundelle knighte the warde & (of) mariage of (Johanne) William Pole (late the wiff of) Cousyne & heire of Johanne Pole late the wiff of John Pole

To William Tirwhite the Stewardship of Castre in Lincolnshire for terme of his lyff with x li Fee etc

To John Grey (k) of Wilton knighte xl li to be had & perceived fro the fest of pasche last past for terme of his lyff of the fee ferme of the Quene hythe in London etc

To thancresse of Saint Elynes within Pountfreit an Annuytie of xl s to be taken yerely during hir lif of thissues etc of thonnor of Pountfreit by the handes of the Receivor generalle etc

To Richard Dentone an Annuyte of V marc to be taken yerely during (his lif) the kinges pleasure of thissues etc of the lordship of Penrethe in the Countie of Cumbreland by the handes of the Receyvor etc

To Thomas Warnare of Colsulle in the Countie of Warrwick / A generalle pardone

To John Grene of the same in the same Countie a generalle pardone

To John Castelle the baillieff of Glatton & Holme during the kinges pleasure

To John (Felde) Feelde the baillieff of the duchie of Lancastre within the Countie of Norffolk during the kinges pleasure

To John Colvell the parkership of Gymmyngham within the Countie of Norffolk during the kinges pleasure

To Sir Robert Stireppe an Annuite of ten markes yerely to be perceived of the lordship of Thikhill During his lyff

To the friers (of) Augustynes of Thikhille an Annuite of v marc of the same lordship During the kinges lyff etc

To John Egremont knighte an Annuyte of xl li / unto the tyme he be preferd unto summe office or offices of the yerely valewe of xl li

To Thomas Otter thoffice of baillieff of Berkeswelle with the keping of the parke there for terme of his lyff

To John Scot one of the Clerkes of the Chapelle an pencion within the Abbey of Ewisham

To Richard Walker one of the Chappelle the Corredie of Glassenbury during his liff

To Henry Davy Thoffice of kepere of the Manor & Gardyn of Shene & parker of the new parke there with other thinges belonging the same as appereth in the bille for terme of his lyff

To the same Henry the servyng Taillor in the kinges gret warderope at London with xij d. by the day during his liff / Also to the same Henry C s per annum during his liff with his clothing to the same office belonging

[f28b] To the prioresse & Convent of Wilberfosse alle those landes tenementes medowes & woddes with their appurtenaunces whiche sumtyme were Robert Hoton within the lordshippe of Sutton upon Derwent / To have & to hold the same of the kinges gift for evermore

To Thomas Molyneux the warde & mariage of Richard Molyneux son & heire of Sir Thomas Molyneux knighte with the keping of landes & tenementes to the valewe of xx^{ti} li ut patet in billa

To the same Thomas the parkere of Crotathe with the fees thereunto of olde tyme due & accustumed during the kinges pleasure

To the same Thomas Thoffice of Constable of the Castelle of Leverpole and Thoffice of steward of Westderbyshire & Salfordshire / And also Thoffice or offices of Master forstere of the Forest & parkes of Symondeswode Toxtathe & Croxtathe / To have & hold the same offices (d) fro the day of dethe of Sir Thomas Molyneux knight during the yong Age of Richard son & heire of the said Sir Thomas etc

To William Scanceby the Clerk of Statute merchaunt at York during the kinges pleasure

To William Shotere Thoffices of baillieff of the Townes and lordshippes of Skindilby Mandby Bradley and (Grenesby) Greynesbye with alle maner thereunto due & accustumed / During the kinges pleasure

To the Maire etc of the Towne of Hulle that they may shipp yerely during xx^{ti} yeres next ensuyng asmoche merchaindises wolle & wollefelles except wherof the custume & subside of the said merchaundises so shipped in the porte outward / and also the subside of the Retorne of the said merchaundises that shalle come and be conveied into the said port inward shalle amounte to the somme of lx li. Which lx li they shall Reteigne in theire handes to the (sustentacion) sustentacione of the porte & Relieff of the said Maire & burgesses etc

To Sir John Savage knighte an Annuite of xl markes to be takyne yerely during his lyff of the Revenues of the lordshippes of Holt Bromfeld & Yale in the marches of Wayles by the handes of the Receivor of (oure lordships of Bromfeld

& Yale) the same at the Festes of pasche & Michaelmas

A licence to the Duc of Norffolk to by & (puveie) purveie C tonnes of Wyne aswele of the grewing of Fraunce as of other places / & the same to shippe in what (pl) shippes as shalle please him best / of England or of other landes / & this licence to endure for a hoole yere

A like licence to Alexander Galyene of Londone Grocere for C tonne of Wyne

To Johanne Langley late wiff of William Langley squiere & to Thomas Quadring Citicene & mercere of Londone the warde & mariage of John Langley sone & heire of the said William Langley . with the keping of alle the lordships maners landes tenementes rentes & services to the said William of late belonging.

To Harman Goldsmythe borne in Estfreisland to be densen

To Sir John Jurdan prest A generalle pardone

[f29] To William Fletchere the keping of the parke of Beskwoode during the kinges pleasure with wages & fees thereto due & accustumed

To Randolph Chalmondley the Ferme of Norbury & Althurst within the Countie of Chestre during x yeres / he finding suerte at theschequiere there to answere for the (ferme) like ferme as John Erington had heretofore at termes there usuelle etc

To Henry Pulley an Annuytee of six poundes & twenty pennys to be takyn yerely fro the fest of the Natyvyte of seint John Baptiste of the Revenues of the lordship of Harom unto the tyme he be proferred to ane office of more valewe

To Lambart Tymanson borne in Holand to be from hensfurth dennesyn

To Maister William Beverley the prebend that Maister Thomas Danet had in the free Chapelle of seint Stephyns with almaner libertees to the same belonging

To William Catesby Thoffice of Steward of the lordshippes or maners of Daventre Higham Ferys & of the Fee called Perverls Fee & of alle other Castelles lordshippes maners landes & tenementes in the Counte of North-ampton parcelle of the duchie of Lancastre for terme of his lyff with the wages

& fees to the same office due & accustumed etc

To Sir John Conyers knighte the maners & lordshippes of Al(d)burghe & Cateryk / & alle landes & tenementes in alburghe Cateryk Crakepot & Swaledale with alle there appurtenaunces To have & hold the same for terme of his lyff / frely of the kinges gift

To Jamys Metcalff The Maister Forstere of Wynsladale Radale & Bisshopdale & the keping of the parke of Wodhalle / To have & hold the same offices for terme of his lyff with the wages & Fees for the Maister Forstership of x li / and for the parkereshippe ij d by the day

To George Birde The Countrollere of the Towne & port of Newcastelle with alle maner fees and advauntages thereunto due & accustumed etc

To Sir William Evers knighte an Annuyte of x li to be takyne yerely during his lyff of the Revenues of (of Pyky) Pikeringlithe in the Countie of York

To Richard Middeltone one of the squiers of the kinges body l marc yerely during his lyff of thissues & profittes of the (the) Countes of Bedford & Bukingham

To Geoffrey (Watton) Warton to be one of the kinges serieaunt at Armes for terme of his lyff / and for the same office xij d by the day fro the ix[th] day of Aprile last past ut patet in billa

To John Lewes to be one of the kinges serieaunt at Armes / and for the same office xij d by day (of) from the fest of pasche last past during his lyff of the the issues & proffites of Kingston upon Hulle

To Adam Nelsone Thoffice of Messagere of the duchie of Lancastre & usshere or keper of the Counselle House ordeyned for the same during the kinges pleasure with the fees thereunto belonging etc

To Richard Pottyere the Attornyshipe of the duchie of Lancastre in the Chauncery of England during the kinges pleasure with v marc of Fee etc

To (Henrey) Henry Drercum Thoffice of Baillieffship of Snettersham with the keping of the warren there during the kinges pleasure with Fees & wages accustumed etc

To John Tenche Thoffice of baillefshippe of (Fetforde) Thett(e)ford during the kinges pleasure & with Fees thereunto accustumed

[f29b] To Therle of Surrey Thoffice of Steward of alle the lordships maners landes & tenementes of the duchie of Lancastre with thappurtenaunces in the Countie of Norffolk with wages thereunto accustumed

To (the) Olyver Sheres Thoffice of Baillieff of Methewold with the keping of the warren of the same with fees thereunto accustumed during the kinges pleasure

The fundacione of the Collage of Seint William of York / new confermed

To Maister Robert Goseborne the parisshe Churche of Whitechurche by resignacion

To David ap Jenkyns thoffice of keping of the kinges warderop within the Castelle of Pountfret with the wages of vj d. by the day during pleasure

(To Sir William Evers an Annuite of x li. to be takyne yerely during his lyff of the Revenues of Pykerynglythe)

To Piers Cartmaille yoman of the Corowne for the fee of the same vj d. by the day of the fee ferme of Norwiche for terme of his lyff

To the priour & Convent of (Morb) Monkebrettone advocacione of the Churche of Dertone / & licence to appropre the same to theim & theire Successors

To Maister John Gylys an Annuite of xl li during his lyff of the Fee ferme of Coventre

To Sir Roger Middeltone the parisshe Churche of Warton

To the Ministere & Convent of Seint Robertes of Knaresburgh a warraunt to the Tresorere & Barons of theschequiere for an halfendelle of an halff of an hoole disme

To Sir Richard Huddelstone the next advoidaunce of the Churche of Aldingham

94

To John Goodmane the Corody or sustentacione within Thabbey of of Cerne

To the lord Stanley Thoffice of Constable of England with the fee of C li / for terme of his liff etc

To Thomas Fowlere the Stewardship of the lordshippes of Bukingham Hakmersham & Birkhille / for terme of his lyff etc

Rex &c. Omnibus ad quos &c. salutem. Sciatis quod nos memorie reducentes multimoda placabiliaque & laudabilia servicia & obsequia nobis per predilectum Consanguineum nostrum Willelmum Comitem Huntyngdon' impensa & que eundem Comitem nobis infuturum impendere speramus & confidimus / eundem Comitem suis exigentibus meritis & premissorum consideracione constituimus fecimus & ordinavimus Capitalem Justiciarium nostrum Southwallie ac eidem Comiti officium Capitalis Justiciarij nostri Southwallie damus & concedimus per presentes. Habendum & occupandum officium illud eidem Comiti per se aut per deputatum suum aut deputatos suos sufficientes quam diu nobis placuerit cum vadijs feodis proficuis commoditatibus & emolumentis eidem officio ab antiquo debitis consuetis seu qualitercunque spectantibus in tam (ar) amplis & eisdem modo & forma prout Willelmus nuper comes Pembrochie pater dicti Comitis aut aliquis alius officium illud ante hec tempora occupavit & exercuit aut habuit & percepit in & pro eodem. Eo quod expressa mencio &c.

[The king etc. to all to whom etc. greeting. Know that we, remembering the manifold pleasing and praiseworthy services and attentions rendered to us by our dearly beloved kinsman William, Earl of Huntingdon, and which we hope and trust that the same earl will render to us in the future, in accordance with his merits, and considering the foregoing, have appointed, made and ordained the same earl our chief justice of South Wales, and by these presents we give and grant to the same earl the office of our chief justice of South Wales. To hold and occupy that office to the same earl in person or by his sufficient deputy or deputies as long as it pleases us, with the wages fees profits easements and emoluments due and customary from of old to the same office or in any way belonging to it, in as ample and in the same manner and form as William, late Earl of Pembroke, father of the said earl, or any other occupied and exercised that office before this time or had and received in and for the same. That express mention etc.]

[f30]	To Sir Thomas Bowles knight	xx marc	for terme of theire lyffes
	To John ap Jenkyn	xx li	to be perceyved of the
	To William Lewes	x marc	lordship of Uske in South
	To Morgan Gamage	x marc	Wales by the Receivor
	To William Herbert of Raglande	xx li	bailly fermors or other
	To Robert ap Jenkyn	C s	occupiers of the same for
	To Thomas ap Morgan	xl marc	the tyme being at the
Annuytees	To Thomas Kemys of Shuothampton	C s	festes of pasche & Seint
	To Morgan Rede	x marc	

	To Edward ap Jenkyn	x marc	Michel yeven the xij day
	To John Morgan	x marc	of Novembre Anno
	To Thomas Kemys of Kerwent	C s	primo
	To Morys Lence	C s	

	John Vaghan	xl marc	for terme of theire lyffes
	John Thomas	x li	to be perceyved of the
Annuytees	Richard Llewellyn ap Morgan	C s	lordship of bergevenny
	David Philip	C s	by the Receivor bailly fermors or other occupieres for the tyme being at the festes of pasche & Seint Michell etc

	To Hopkyn ap Howel	x li	of the lordshippe of Mon-
Annuytes	To Philip Herbert	xx marc	mouthe for terme of
	To William Herbert		theire lyffes by the
	squier for the body	xl marc	handes of the Receivor
	To John Hewes	x marc	bailly fermors or other
	To William Serieaunt	x marc	occupiers for the tyme being at the festes of pasche & Seint Michell etc

	To William Kemys	x marc of Newport	for terme of
Annuytees	To Walter Endreby	xx marc of Kidwelly	theire lyffes by
	To Walter Wynston	C s of Ewes	the handes of the Receivor bailly or other occupiers there etc at the festes of pasche & Seint Michell

To Sir John Elringtone knighte the Steward & bailiff of the lordshippe of Enfeld the keping of the park of Enfelde / and Maister of the gam aswele of the parke as of the chace of Enfelde / with the making of alle officers within the same for terme of his liff with the fees & wages of olde tyme due & accustumed etc

To Thomas Tunstalle squiere thoffice of Constable of the Castell of Conwey with the Captaynship of (your) the Towne of Conwey / and to have undere him the nombre of xxiiij soldiours for the terme of his liff / with the wages & fees to the same office & captaynship due & accustumed / and to have for every of the said soldiors iiij d. by day

To Sir Richard Huddelstone knighte a like graunt for terme of his liff of the Constableship & Captayneship of the Castelle & Towne of (Bew) Beaumaris Anglesey .

To John Kendale one of the yomene of the Coronne (viij d) vj d by the day for the fee of the Coronne / To have & perceive the same fro the first day of July last past / of the Revenues of the fee ferme of Rochestre etc ut patet in billa

[f30b] Richard etc To the tresorere & Chambreleyns of oure Eschequiere greting Where we have appointed and named oure trusty & welbeloved Thomas Wortley knight to be Shereff of the Countie of Stafford for this yere next ensuyng / In the whiche office we understande he shalle have & sustene gret losses costes & charges without oure grace especialle be shewed unto him in that behalve / We not willing him to sustene any hurt therein / wolle & charge you that ye do strike out a taille at the Receipt of oure said Eschequiere in due forme to be levied for the same Thomas Wortley upone him selff as Shireff of oure said Countie conteignyng the summe of C li to be taken of us by wey of reward / And that taille so leveied ye deliver unto him without prest or other charge to be sett (unto) upon him for the same in any wise / And thise oure lettres shalbe unto you warraunt sufficient & discharge Yeven etc

A like graunt to Thomas Fowlere squiere to be Shireff of Bedford & Bukingham for the yere next ensuyng / and to have assignement of lxx by taille etc

To Robert Dymmok Shereff of the Countie of Lincolne / not to be accomptable in the Eschequiere but by appriement / by his othe or by the othe of his deputie

To Roger Wake squiere to be shereff of Northampton for this yere next ensuyng And to have assignement of C li as apperethe by his bille

To Garter king of Armes / his patent of king of Armes new confermed

To John Lightefote Thoffice of baillieff of Sotheray in the Forest of Wyndesor for terme of his lyff.

Humfrey Beaufo to be Shereff of the Counties of Warrewyk & Leicestre for the yere next ensuyng / and to have assignement of Clx li. by taille or tailles

John Bamme to be Shereff of Kent for the yere next ensuyng / & to have oone Assignement of C li by taille or tailles etc

John Sturgeon Shireff of the Counties of Essex & Hertford for the next yere / and to have ane assignement of Ciiij^{xx}xviij li. by taille etc

Adrian Lapping Thoffice of keping of the manere & parke & bailiefshippe of Somersham in the Countie of Huntyngdon

Sir William Hussey Chieff Juge A licence for the fundacion of A Chauntre in olde Sheforde / and to mortesse thereunto the valewe of xx li of lande

Rauff Willoughby Shereff of Norfolk & Suffolk for the yere next and to have ane assigement of a hundreth & sixti poundes by taille etc

Nicholas Palmere Thofffice of waterbailly in the port of Dertmouth during pleasure

Richard Wilsone his olde patent of Serieaunt at Armes new confirmed

John Smyth Surgeon / to have a prive seale directed to the Tresorere & Chambrelayns of Theschequiere for the contentacione of iiij li. xj s. iij d. according to his lettres patentes

To Gervaux Cressy an Annuyte of vj li. xiij s. iiij d. during his liff of the Revenues of the Counties of Bedford & Bukingham

A warraunt to the Tresorere & Chambreleyns of theschequiere to pay C li to the gromes & pages of the kinges Chambre

Sir John Babington to be Shereff of the Counties of Notingham & Derby with an assigement of C li by taille

John Wake to be Shireff of the Counties of Cambrigge & Huntyngdon with an assignement of C marcs by taille etc

[f31] Herry Erle of Northumberland hath the lordship of Holdernes with thappurtenaunces in the Countie of York unto him and Alane his Sone and to theires masles of the same Alane for ever

Johanne the late wiff of Sir John Peysemersshe knight hath an Annuitee of xx marc graunted unto hir for terme of hir lif oute of the manoire of Cranborne

William Milsham Thoffice of baillieff of the lordship of Cheylesmore & kepere of the parke there for terme of his lyff with wages & Fees due & accustumed

John Payntor one of the kinges serieaunt at Armes xij d. by the day (fro) from the first day of August last past for terme of his lyff / of the ferme or issues & profites of the subside & ulnage of the cloth in the Countie & Citee of York & in the Towne of Hulle

Warraunt to Thauditors of Richemond Fee to allowe Leonard Thorneburgh feodarie of the same the summe of xx li. of the kinges reward etc

To the Warden & Convent of friers Minors in the universite of Cambrige An Annuyte of xxv marc to be perceived yerely at the king Eschequiere etc

John Baratayne the Shereff of Oxon & Berks with an Assignement of iiii^{xx}x li by taille

Thomas Barow Maister of the rolles one Tune of Wyne to be taken in the porte of London

Sir John Taillor to be the kinges (Ar) Amnere

To William Nettiltone yoman of the Coronne vj d. by the day of the Revenues of Bedford & Bukingham

To George Chenewe Thoffice of keping the northe parke of the Leghe with the keping of the northelaundes within your Kent for terme of his lyff

To have George Ratclyff prest recommended to the parsonage of Warmworthe of the diocese of Duresme

To John Arundelle prest deane of Excestre a generalle pardon

To John Lawton Thoffice of the Countroller of alle the writtes fines Amercia-mentes & alle other before the Justices in the Countie of Chestre

Sir Thomas Fulshurst an Annuyte of xx marc to be perceived of the Revenues of Tutburye for terme of his lyff

To the Maire & his bretheren of New Castelle an Annuyte of xl li. during the kinges pleasure to be perceived of the fee ferme of the said Towne towardes the buylding of the bregge there yerely by the oversighte of Maister Alexander Lighe & George birde

Thomas Morley one of the kinges serieauntes at Armes xij d by the day from the first day of August last past for terme of his liff / of the fee ferme of Norwiche

(Henry Dawney yoman of Corone thoffice of Baillieff of the Towne of Swafham market for terme of his lyff with the wages and fees of olde tyme due & accustumed)

George Box the bailliefship of Wakefeld during the kinges pleasure

Sir Thomas Burghchiere A generalle pardone

Robert Skerne A generalle pardon

The prior & Convent of the friers precheors of Oxenford quinquagenta marcis Annuatim de exitibus Comitati nostri Cornubie

   [The prior and convent of the friars preachers of Oxford 50 marks annually from the issues of our county of Cornwall]

Henry Dawney thoffice of Baillieff of the Towne of Swafham market within the Countie of Norffolk for terme of his lyff with the wages & fees of olde tyme due & accustumed etc

[f31b] Philip Knighton thoffice of one of the foure Messengers of theschequier for terme of his lyff with the wages of iiij d. ob. by the day and a gowne yerely out of the warderobe such as yeomen of the Chambre have (at) ayenst the fest of Christenmesse

William Litley Thoffice of baillieff of the hundrethe of Fallesley in the Countie of Northampton for terme of his lyff

Maister Thomas Bemesley an Annuite of xl li. for terme of his lyff from the fest of pasche last past to be had & perceived of the Counties of Bedford & Bukingham

Maister William Hobbys A like annuite of xl li for terme of his lyff from the said Fest of pasche / (f) to be had & perceived in forme folowing that is to say (of) de munitis particulis seriauntie (xvj li) of the Countie of Bedford & Bukingham xvj li / and of the revenues of the said Counties (xxvj l) xxiiij li

Sir John Pikering knight the ferme of the lordship of Oswoldkirke in the Countie of York for the terme of his lyff

Thomas Bank to be one of the kinges serieauntes at Armes with the wages of xij d by the day to be had & perceived of thissues & revenues of London for terme of his lyff

Richard Warmyngton thoffice of the Artillerie within the Towne of Calais with the wages of xij d by the day & vj d for a yomane under him for terme of his liff

A warraunt to the Tresorere & barons of the Eschequiere to discharge John Hays in his accomptes of the summe of CCClxvij li. xj s. vij d. / whiche somme he hathe laid out & delivered to oure handes / Datum viij° die Decembris Anno primo

Thomas lord Stanley an Annuite of C li to be perceived during his lyff of the Revenues of the duchie of Lancastre

Rauff Assheton knighte An Annuite of xx li. during his lyff of the said duchie

Maister William Billere the kinges promotere with xx marc fee to be taken in the kinges Eschequiere by the handes the Tresorere of the same for terme of his lyff

To the deane of Windesore a (an) warraunt direct to the Chauncelere for the confirmacion of alle the olde grauntes of the said Collage of Windesor

To John Forstere Thoffice of baillieff of the lordship of Langton (next) besides Malton in the Countie of York with the Fees of ij d. by the day during the kinges pleasure

Nicholas Hedelam Thoffices of portere of the Castelle of Sherefhoton the keping of the warderoppe within the same / and parkereship of the same for everiche of theim ij d. by the day for terme of his lyff

Sir William Parkere knighte the maner & lordshippe of (penlt) Pentlow hall within the Countie of Suffolk (to hi) with thappurtenaunces to him & his heires for ever

William Sankey to be one of the serieauntes at Armes for terme of his lyff with the wages & Fees of xij d. by day to be perceived of the Countie Palatyne of Lancastre

To William Sapcottes the Manoire of Stokedole with thappurtenaunces within the Countie of Northampton late belonging unto Sir Thomas Lewknor to have the same Manere during his lyff without any thing therefore payeng

Olyver Guyen Thoffice of baillief of Wassingborowe Fulbek & Ledenam

Richard Metcalff An Annuyte of liij s. iiij d. of the lordshippe of Middelham unto the tyme he be promoted unto an office of bettere valewe

A like graunt to Otywell Metcalff of xl s.

A nother to Piers Metcalff of xl s.

[f32] To Roger Wake certen landes & tenementes in Hertwelle & Rede with thappurtenaunces within the Countie of Northamptone which late were Anthony Wodevile to the valewe of xx li

To William Wake squiere the halfvendele of the manoire of Dalingtone in the Countie of Northamptone to the yerely valewe of xx marc / to him & his assignes

To Friere John Bury the keping of the Chapelle within the Toure of Suthampton with ten poundes for his solde to be taken of the Custumes & subside of (your) Suthampton during his liff

To Maister William Dawbeney Thoffice of serchere in the porte of London & other portes thereunto belonging during the kinges pleasure

To Henry lord Grey Thoffices of (portership) Constable of the Castelle of Puesey & of the honnor Egill / and Maister Forstere of the Chace of Asshedowne and of alle chaces parkes & (weri) werennes within the said lordship & honnor for terme of lyff

(To Sir (Edward Hast) Edmond Hastinges knighte to be Shereff of Yorkeshire / to (with) have ane assignement of CCClx li. by taille or by tailles etc)

To Sir Edmond Hastinges knight to be Shereff of Yorkshire / and to have assignement of CCCxl li by taille

William Eustace one of the serieauntes at Armes with the wages of xij d. by day to be had by the handes of the Shereff of Londone for terme of his lyff

William Clerk to be Constable of the Castelle of Briggenorth for terme of his lyff

Richard Hansard Thoffice of Constable of the Castelle of Odeham the portere of the same Castelle parker & warrener of the same lordship with the Steward-ship of the same for terme of his lyff with wages & fees thereunto due & accustumed

John Huton the Constable (with) of the Castelle of Suthampton for terme of his lyff with the wages & fees thereunto due & accustumed And (an Annuyte of) x li for his fee of the custume of Suthampton   Th

To Sir Rauf bigod an Annuitie of xl li to be taken at Sherefhoton

To Sir Rauff Bigot a pardon for his Amerciementes of the Shereffwyk of York

To Maister Edmond Chattertone to be Clerk of the Hanuper for terme of his lyff

Thomas Horde squiere to be Shereff of the Countie of Salop for the yere next following / and to an assignement of C li. by taille

To John Morice otherwise Turk the Coride or sustentacione within the Monastery of malmesbury for terme of his liff with alle maner rightes thereunto belonging

Nicholas Rigby the place & ferme to the yerely valewe of ix li. called Stanlige in the Countie of Wilteshire late belonging to Richard Beauchamp for terme of his lyff

To Tharchebisshoppe of Canterbury A generalle pardone

To John Papde An Annuyte of xx li. to be perceived yerely during his lyff of the honnor of Pountfret

To Henry Hixe Thoffice of portership of the Castelle of York with the wages of ij d. by the day to be perceived yerely of the lordship of Sherefhoton during the kinges pleasure

To   Nightingale Thoffice of keping of the gaole within the Castelle of York with alle maner Fees & wages to the same belonging during the kinges pleasure

To Thomas Hargille Thoffice of Baillieff of Newport Pannelle (and) with the membres & keping of the parke of Tikforde with the wages & fees of vj d. by day to be had & perceived yerely during his lyff of thissues of the said lordship

To Roger Hartlington Thoffice of Baillieff of (Bovetracie) Bovitracie with the keping of the parke there with the wages & fees of iiij d. by day for terme of his lif

To Chestre Herault of Armes with xx marc fee to be perceived of the duchie of Cornewaille for terme of his lyff

To John Otter Thoffice of keping of the parke of Dartington with the Fisshe-garthe & were nighe adioynyng to the same / with the fees of iiij d. by the day for terme of his liff

[f32b] To Sir John Batmane prest an Annuelle Fee of vij marc to be takene of the honnor of Pountfret / and he to syng at Towton Chapelle / for terme of his lyff and so after (him in) his decesse in like wise etc

William Crawcestre yoman of Corone a Tenement with thappurtenaunces in the Towne of Waturfulford called Roos halle late belonging Thomas lord Roos / for terme of his lyff

Richard Laurence those six poundes yerely whiche Thabbot & Convent of Salop were wont yerely to pay for the wode called Lethywode and whiche John (Bestne) Besteney late oon of the serieauntes of Armes with the king that dede is of his graunt had / to have to the said Richard for terme of his lyff

Doctoure Roby the Fre Chapelle of oure lady of Gissemond besides Newcastelle upon Tyne being voide by the decesse of Maister Lumley

Edmund Dalton / a yerely Annuyte of x li of the Revenues of the lordshippe of Sherefhoton for terme of his lyff by the handes of the Receivor fermors baillieffes or other occupiers for the tyme being

A generalle pardon to William Gawge squier etc

[cross] To Thomas Elrington Thoffice of porter of the Castelle of (penv pen) Pevensey in Sussex for terme of his lyff with the wages due & accustumed

Annuytees to the persones following for terme of theire lyffes of thissues & Revenues of the Counte of Lancastre by the handes of the Receyvor there for the tyme being first to Sir Piers Lighe x li. Sir Alexander Houghton x li Sir Richard Langton x li. Sir Richard Shirburn x li. (and) Sir Henry Kighley x li. / Sir Richard Bolde x li. Sir Henry Tarboth x marc. Sir William Farington x marc. Sir Thomas Talbot x marc Sir William Stanley of Hoton x li / John Biron x li George Bothe x li. William Troutbek x li / Thomas Pole x li. Robert Dokenfeld x marc / William Warde v marc Roger Lever v marc Elys Prestwyche v marc Thurston Andreton v marc Thomas Maynwarynge v marc William Davenport x marc William Lathom v marc Edmund Grenehalghe v marc Piers Orelle v marc Piers Worthington v marc George Clifton v marc Richard Heyton v marc Roger Hilton v marc Humfrey Savage v marc and Henry Traford v marc

Sir Roger Kynastone knighte Thoffice of Constable of the Castelle of Hardlaghe in Northwales during his lyff with xx souldeors undre him with the wages and fees to the said office due & accustumed and taking for every souldeor iiij d. by the day by the handes of the Chambreleyn of Northwales for the tyme being

Geoffray Franke Thoffice of keper of the lawnde within the Forest of Galtresse for terme of his lyff with the wages & fees of x li. to be perceyved of the lordshippe of Sherefhoton by the handes of the Receyvor there etc

[f33] Richard Diconson oon of the yeomen of Corone thoffice of oon of the iiij forsters of the forest of Galtresse during the kinges pleasure with the wages of

iiij d. by day to be perceyved of the lordshippe of Sherefhotone by the handes of the Receyvor there for the tyme being etc

John Barsworthe thoffice of oon of the iiij forsters of the Forest of Galtresse during the kinges pleasure with the wages of iiij d. by the day ut supra

Thomas Rawe thoffice of oon of the foure forsters of Galtresse ut supra

John Ratcliff serieaunt of the pantrie thoffice of huissher of the parliament Chambre For terme of his lyff . with the wages fees profites and advailes thereto belonging / etc

Thomas Thornton thoffice of oon of the iiij forsters of Galtresse during the kinges pleasire with the wages of iiij d. by the day ut supra

Thomas Edwardes yeman of Corone an Annuyte of (x) C s. for terme of his lyff to be hadde and perceyved from Michellmas last of the Revenues of the lordship of Busby in Clyveland by the handes of the fermors Receivor baillieff or other occupieres there for the tyme being at the festes of pasche & Seint Michell etc yeven the xvj day of decembre

John Piers the Maister of the Vyneyerde or of the Vynes besides the castelle of Wyndesore for terme of his lyff / with fees of vj d. by day to be taken by the handes of the Constable of the Castelle there etc

A warraunt to the prive seale to be directed to the keper of the gret Warderobe / to deliver to the Barons Chauncelere Remembrauncieres & Clerk of the pipe suche & asmany clothinges furres & lynynges ayenst the Fest of Christymesse & pentecost next comynge & so furthe yerely / as the were used to have in king Edward dayes

Sir John Asteley knight his lettres patentes of confirmacione upon his olde grauntes of annuyte of xl li. to be taken of the ferme of the Citie of Wynchestre

Like lettres of Confirmacione to the same Sir John of an Annuyte of lx li. to be takyne of the Receit (of) by the handes of the Tresorer & Chambreleyns etc

John Hope an Annuyte of v marc to be takyn of Therledom of Marche unto the tyme that he be promoted to office landes & tenementes of the same valewe for terme of his lyff

106

A like Annuyte to John Llody etc

John duc of Norfolk a Mese with thappurtenaunces called the Toure in the parisshe of Seint Thomas Thappostle to him & his heires masles late the duc of Somerset etc

William Brewer an Annuyte of xl s. of the kinges landes & tenementes in the Counte of Somerset etc

William Bracher thoffices of baillieff & parker of the lordshippe & parke of Barington with the keping of the Maner there with the wages & fees of iiij d. by the day for terme of his lyff and also an Annuyte of xl li. of the said lordship unto the tyme that he have to him & his heires masles of the kinges graunt landes & tenementes to the same valewe

Thomas Danyelle yeman of Corone thoffices of bailly of Hatfeld and the keping of the parke called Innynges parke / as long as the temporaltees of the bisshopriche of Ely is in the kinges handes

[f33b] Thomas Calbrond Thoffice of portere of Beston Castelle in the Countie of Chestre for terme of his lyff with alle maner fees wages etc

To William Combershalle Thoffice of Baillieff of Dove Court & Harewiche in Essex for terme of his lyff with alle maner fees & wages

To Maister John Harington an Annutye of xx li to be takyne by the handes of the Chambrelayn or Tresorere of the kinges Eschequiere / for the office Clerkship of the Counselle afore the lordes etc for terme of his lyff.

To John Cotington Thoffice of parkereship of Whitemede parke in the Forest of Deane with the wages & fees of iiij d. by the daye to be perceived of the Revenues of the same Forest for terme of his lyff etc

To Robert Clerc to be one of the kinges serieauntes at Armes with the wages of xij d. by the day to be perceived of the Revenues of the Counties of Norffolk & Suffolk for terme of his lyff

(Th) To John Alfegh A generalle pardon

Thomas Lovelle Gent Thoffice of Spigurnelle in the Chauncery with the fees & wages thereunto accustumed for terme of his lyff

Roger Harlakynden A generalle pardon

To Nicholas Brytte to be one of the kinges serieauntes at Armes & to have the fee of xij d. by day to be perceived of the fee ferme of the Citee of London for terme of his lyff

To John lord Audeley A generalle pardon

To the Wardene of the Grey Friers at Wynchestre the kinges halfendele of the lordship of Pyrye nighe Wynchestre with alle thinges thereunto belonging with the mylne undere the Castelle of Wynchestre during the nonne Age of therle of Warrewyk / paying therefore yerely to the king sex poundes sterlinges at the Fest seint John Baptist & Christynmesse

A warraunt to the prive seale to charge Jamys Songere late under shereff of the Counties of Essex & Hertford to deliver to John Kirkeby alle his goodes & catalles late by him seased etc / or elles to appere afore the kinges Counselle at Westminstre on the utas of seint Hillary upon payne of ij^C li

To Sir Richard Huddelstone knighte the Maister forstere of the Forest of Snowden in North Wales for terme of his lyff with fees accustumed

To John Fulthrope the keping of the Manoire of Grenewiche with alle Gardyns belonging the same for terme of lyff / with wages & fees accustumed

To (John) Thomas Greynefeld A generalle pardone

Bartilmewe Darvyveyre knight An Annuyte of C li. for terme of his lyff / videlicet 1 li. xiij s. iiij d. tam de firma exitibus & proficuis ballive hundredorum de (W) Estflegge Westflegge Happing Taverham Blofeld Walsham & Humliard in Comitatu Norffolk quam de alijs firmis finibus exitibus &c. Comitatibus Norffolk & Suffolk per manus vicecomitis eorundem pro tempore &c. ad terminos Michaelis & Pasche &c / ac undecim libras x s. iiij d / tam de Minutis particuliis serieancie Comitatum Somerset & Dorset quam dc alijs firmis &c. eorundem Comitatum provenientibus per manus vicecomitis eorundem Comitatum ad eosdem terminos &c. [f34] vij li. xvj solidos & quinque denarios / inde habendos percipiendos tam de Redditibus seriancie Comitatus Wilteshire quam de alijs firmis (etc) finibus exitibus &c. eiusdem Comitatus provenientibus &c.

per manus vicecomitis dicti Comitatus ac x li. inde habendas & percipiendas tam de cremento ville de Allerwas per manus Receptoris firmarum &c. eiusdem &c. Necnon xx li. inde habendas & percipiendas de custumis & subsidijs in portu ville Gippewici provenientibus per manus Collectorum Receptorum sive Custumariorum eorundem &c.

[To Bartilmewe Darveyveyre, knight, an annuity of £100 for term of his life viz. £50. 13. 4 from the farm, issues and profits of the bailiwick of the hundreds of East Flegg, West Flegg, Happing, Taverham, Blofield, Walsham and Humliard in the county of Norfolk and from other farms, fines, issues etc. in the counties of Norfolk and Suffolk by the hands of the sheriff of the same for the time being etc. at the terms of Michaelmas and Easter etc. and £11.10.3 from the small items of the serjeanty of the counties of Somerset and Dorset and other farms etc. proceeding from the same counties by the hands of the sheriff of the same counties at the same terms etc., £7.16.5 to be had and received from the rents of the serjeanty of the county of Wiltshire and other farms, fines, issues etc. proceeding from the same county etc. by the hands of the sheriff of the said county and £10 thereof had and received from the increment of the town of Allerwas by the hands of the receiver of the farms etc. of the same etc. and £20 thereof to be had and received from the customs and subsidies arising in the port of the town of Ipswich by the hands of the collectors, receivers or customers of the same etc.]

Reynold (bray) Bray a generalle pardon

David Vaghan thoffice of mobershippe within the Counties of Carnarvon & Anglesey for terme of his lyff

Warraunt to the Tresorere and barons of theschequiere to make an assignement by taille or tailles to John Belle late of the baillieffes of Cambrigge / of the summe of xiiij li xj s v d

William Norton the keping of the manor & parc of Henley in the Heth for terme of his lyff

To the Maire & Commonalte of the Towne of Plynmouthe towardes the walling of the said Towne C marc yerely during the kinges pleasure of the Custumes there

To Richard Williams Thoffices of Stewardship of the lordship of Urchenfeld and Constable of the Castelle of Goderyche in the marche of Wales with the making of the maister serieaunt and portere apperteynyng to the said offices / during the nonne Age of Therle of Shrewesbury .

To William Hungate the Corodie or sustentacion within the monastery of Eynesham late in the handes of William Newarke

To William Herbert Secretarie to my lord prince an Annutie of xl marc for occupieng of the said office / to be perceived of the honnor of Pountfret for terme of liff

To John Hawkyn thoffice of keper of the parke called Horsfirthe parc with the fees & wages accustumed to be perceived of the lordship of Writhille during the kinges pleasure

To the Maire & his bretheren of Tynby there Chartre confirmed with a penaltie of C li. they that brekes it / Halff thereof to the king & the other to the reparacion of the Towne walles / and that no man entremete theim with the almoushouses of seint Johns & seint Danyell / and that the Towne may enioye alle suche lyvelode as hereafter shalbe yeven to the reparacione of the Towne Walles

To Richard Williams Thoffices of Constable & Steward of the Castelle Towne & lordshippe of Pembroke the Constable of the Castelle of Tynby chieff Forstere of the Forest of Coydrathe the Constable & Steward of the Castelle Towne & lordshippe of Haverford West with the botellershippe there / Thoffices of Constable & Steward of the Castelle Towne & lordshippe of Gilgarran with the Stewardship of Llanstephan and Trayne with auctorite forto make & deputie the Court Clerkes and porters of & in every of the Castelles above specified for terme of lyff

[f34b] Henry Savile Thoffices of (of) baillieff of the lordshippe of Epworthe within the Isle of Axiholme The keping of the manor / The keping of the Gardyns there within the said manor / and thoffice of Approwere of the harbage & pannage of the parkes within the same Isle / for terme of lyff

Thomas Savile Thoffices of parkere of Belgrave within the Isle of Axiholme & palicere of the same for terme of lyff

John Fitzherbert & Thomas Babingtone the ferme of lede mynes of Werkesworthe within the Countie of Derby for x yeres / paying therefore yerely vj li xiij s. iiij d. at the fest seint Michell etc.

Richard Fitzhughe lord Fitzhughe thoffice of keping of the Forest of Hey & of the parke of Petertone besides Briggewatere for terme of lyff

John Fitzherbert the yongere the baillieff of the Newe Franchise of the duchie of Lancastre in the Countie of Derby during the kinges pleasure payeng therefore yerely lxxiij s. & iiij d. etc

Robert Gedney the keping of the parke of Melwode within the Countie of Lincolne & palicere of the same during his lyff / and ane Annuytee of x marc to be taken of the lordship of Epworthe etc

Robert Harwod of Sandewiche Ane Annuytee of v marc / to be takene of the Custume of the said Towne of Sandewiche / unto the tyme he be promoted to an office of more valewe

Margarete Choke an licence to founde a Chaunterye of one preste in parisshe Churche of Longasshetone nyghe bristolle .

Robert Warmyngtone Tresorere of the werrys of Calais during the kinges pleasure

To Sir Edmond Shawe a warraunt directed to the Tresorere & Chambreleyn of the Eschequiere for the payment of D marc

To John Walcote of London mercere A like warraunt to the Tresorere & Chambleyns of the Receipt for the contentacion of lxxiiij li. xj s. jd.

A Warrant directed to the Tresorer & Barons of theschequier to acquite & discharge the late baillieffes of Gloucestre of xxxij li. x s.

Jamys Aker of Holande borne / to be denysyne

Richard Eggecome A generalle pardone

Jamys Mounjoye Thoffice of portere of the Castelle called Symme Revelle within the Forest of Deane / with thoffice of bedelle within the same Forest during pleasure

George Hiet Thoffice of ridere of the Forest of Deane with thoffice called Ale Cunnere in the parisshe of Newlond during pleasure

Thomas Rydley Thoffice of Captaynship of the Isle of Guernesey for terme of lyff

Thomas Graftone a tenement in calais whiche was William Waynesworthe / and that Philip Harbene now dede had of the graunt of king Edward the iiijth /for terme of the lyff of the said Thomas

Richard Gould & other the ward & mariage of John Asshe sone & heire of Jamys Asshe with the keping of alle landes maners tenementes etc

Alexander Baynham knighte A generalle pardone

[f35] Henry Long late Shireff of the Countie of Wilteshire a pardone for the same

Sir William Courteney knight late Shireff of the Countie of Devone warraunt directed to the Tresorere & Chambreleyns of theschequiere for to remitte & release the said Sir William of C marc

The Maire & Burgesses of Temby theire grauntes made to theim by Henry the sext & Humfrey duc of Gloucestre new confirmed by king Richard the iij^{de}

Robert Nighttyngale & Marion his wiff an Annuyte of C s. to be takyne yerely during her lyff of the Fee ferme of New Castelle upon Tyne

To The (Shireffes) Tresorere and Barons of Theschequiere to discharge Thomas Pereson and Miles Grenebank late Shereffes of the Cite of York of the summes of xxv li. parcelle of the fee ferme of the said Citee and lxiij s. iiij d. the Buchere penys and of xx li. by theim paid to the Chambreleyns of the said Citee / and ix li. ijs. vj d. to John Newton Maire of the said Citee etc

(A licence for Henry Frese theldere to (bring) lade a Gascoigne Wyne in any ship of the partes of zeland & braband)

A licence graunted to Henry Frise theldere to lade certen Wynes & merchaundises in a ship of the partes of zeland or braband of the portage of C Tonnes for one hoole yere to endure after the date herof / yevene the xxx^{ti} day of Januarij Anno primo

William Bowdelere an Annuyte of vj li. & xx d. during his lyff to be taken of thissues proffites & Revenues of the lordshippe of Clatton

John Webbe Thoffice of porter of the Castelle of Vyse in the Countie of Wilteshire & the keping of the parke there for terme of his lyff with the fees & wages thereunto due & accustumed

Thomas Wyntershulle & Richard Westbroke the keping of the parke of Wytteley Asshehurst in the Countie of Surrey for terme of theire lyffes & aithere of theim langer lyvyng with the Fees of iiij d. by the day

Nicholas Cromer of Londone squiere A pardone.

My lord prince his patent of xx li. for his creacione of Therle of Sarum new confirmed

A prive seale direct to The tresorere & barons of Theschequiere for the discharge Constantyne Dazelle & other of the summe of C marc by them forfacted etc

John Sapcottes squiere the landes & tenementes of Jamys Tregurreye the kinges Ideote / in the Countie of Cornewaille

Ris ap Thomas an Annuyte of xl marc to be taken yerely during his lyff of the Countie of Carmardyne

A prive seale direct to the Tresorere & Chambrelayns of Theschequiere for the payment of CCCxl li. unto Loweys de Gremaldes for certen harnesses by the king of him boughte at Sandewiche

A prive seale directed to the Tresorere & Chambreleyns for (to content to) the discharging of Thomas Totothe Receivor of the lordship of Freston in Lincolne-shire & William Tirwhite (of the summe) for an Annuyte (giv) of xx li. graunted to the said William out of the same lordship etc

A warraunt direct to the same totothe Receivor of the said lordship to content & pay unto the said William Tirwhite the summe of x li. for the part of his annuyte of the same lordship for (terme of) the halff yere (of) at Michilmesse last past

[f35b] To Sir John Savile knighte the lieutenant or Captaigneship of the Isle of Wighte for terme of his lyff / with etc ut patet in billa

William Mirfeld Thoffice of keping of the Castelle of Porchestre & of the Foreste & warren there / And also the supervisore & guvernor of (of) the Towne of Portesmouth & of the place there / with other ut patet in billa for terme of lyff

Maister David Hoptone a pardon generalle

John Cartingtone the warde & mariage of John Thornetone son of Sir Roger Thornetone knighte with the keping of alle Maners Castelles etc

John Hotone squiere for the kinges body Thoffices of Constable of the Castelle of Crischirche / & the Stewardship of the lordshippes or Maners of Crischirche & Ryngwold / for terme of his lyff

The same John Hoton the keping of the parke called the New parc & keping of the manor within the same within the New Forest in the Countie of Suthampton

William Evington his patent of king Edward of the Newe parke of Wyndesore new confirmed for terme of his lyff

Robert Bukstede his patent of king Edward confirmed of the keping of the Manere lordship & parke of Ditton for terme of his lyff

Henry Norries Thoffice of portere of the Castelle of Brekenok for terme of his lyff

Thomas Englisshe Thoffice of Rent gaderere in the Towne of Caleis for terme of his lyff

Thomas Hunt Thoffice of the Clerc of the kinges Warkes for terme of his lyff Ut patet in billa

Thomas Maymond the Bailliefshippe of Oustone for terme of his lyff etc

Sir John Morgane an Annuyte of xl li. of the lordshippe of Newport for terme of his lyff

Thomas ap John the portershippe of (Ne) the Castel of Newport with the keping of the Conyes there

A discharge to Driew (Britnelle) Britonelle of the summe of lx li. / by him delivered to Thomas Fouler

William Birmyngeham an Annuyte of C s. for terme of his lyff of the lordship of Whitchirche

Thomas Cole thoffice of serieaunt Furrier for terme of his lyff with the wages of xij d. by day

John Cornysshe thoffice of parker of Hatfeld Brodeoke with iij d. by day for terme of his lyff . and with therbage there and wynd fallen wodys and an Annuyte of x marc to be takyn of the same lordship

[f36] The lady Ferys & other the warde and mariage of Thomas Ferys her sone with the keping of al the landes etc

Robert Smalwode parker of Langley Marise for terme of his lyff

William Avery An Annuyte xx marc for terme of his lyff of (Cokeham and) Cokenham & bray

To my lord prince & Geoffrey Franke the next advoidaunce of the Cherche of Metheley

John Smythe An Annuyte of vj li. xiij s. iiij d. during the nonne Age of Therle of Warwic or as long as the lordship of Flamston shall Remayne in the kinges handes

Thomas Eliot a general pardone

Edward Gower the keping of the Maner of More with alle the Gardyns and the parke & warene there / and keping of a tenement called Baggesworthe Hethe with ij gardyns to the same belonging for terme of his lyff

William Hewet an Annutye of v marc to be takyn of the custumes of Sandewiche unto tyme he be promoted to office or other to the same valewe for terme of his lyff

Robert Vasy thoffice of Baillief of Burley within Newforest in the Counte of Suthampton for terme of his lyff

Thomas Aleyne the Corody of (p) Spalding

Thomas Everley thoffice of oon of the Serieauntes of Armes with fee etc

Maister Thomas Hotone Clerc of the parliament during his lyff

Henry Lokwode baillieff of Thriske for terme of his lyff

John Molle the fee of the Corone / of the Fee ferme of Pennokshire

The same John and Joyes his wyff & (h) either of them longer lyvyng an Annuyte of xx marc of the Custumes of Sandewiche etc

Richard Forster baillieff of the hundred of Godlaxtone and the fees & profites commyng of the same for terme of his lyff without any accompt yelding

To the same Richard thoffice of baillieff and keping of Wytlesmere & warennes & wodes of Glatton and Holme / and keping & apprower of al the Swannys in the Counte of Huntingdon Cambrigge Lincolne and Northampton belonging the ducherie

John Stapiltone Raunger of the forest of Milchet with vj d. by day for terme of his lyff

[f36b] Jamys Hyde the keping of the Manoire parke woodes and warene of Caversham and (theire) of the feire there aslong as the lordshippe of Caversham shalbe in the kinges handes / and An Annuyte of x marc of the same lordshippe

The Tresorer and Chambreleyns of theschequier to allowe the Maior and merchauntes of the Staple M^{l}Cxx li.

Thomas Bawdrippe the Constableshippe of Newport for terme of his lyff and l marc for the of squier for the body to be perceyved there /

Richard Mountfort an Annuyte of v marc / of the lordshippe of Birdhal during the nonne Age of the lord Latymer

Rouland Harper Riding forster of Newforest in the Countie of Suthampton for terme of his lyff

Richard Vaghan to be deynsyne

Thomas Ussher baillieff of Swafham and Richemond fee in the Counties of (Noff) Norffolk and Suffolk / and keping of the Conyes of Swafham for terme of his lyff

Robert Bolman An Annuyte of C s. to be takyn in theschequer unto he be promoted to office or offices of the same valewe or above

Maister Henry Sharp thoffice of prothonatorie in the Chauncery as long as he wele behavethe him etc

John More king of Arms in the Northe parties / xx li. for terme of his lyff

John Water alias York herauld the lordshippe of Bayhalle to the valieu of C s. / and an Annuyte of viij li. vj s. viij d. of the Revenues of the lordshippe of Huntingfeld in the Countie of Kent for terme of his lyff

Thomas Holme alias Claranceux king of Armes in the Southe parties xx li. of the Custumes and subsides of Excestre & Dertmouthe / and xx marc of Annuyte of the lordshippe of Walden in the Countie of Essex for terme of his lyff

Gloucestre Herald to him (&) his heires & assignees forever the Maner of Olde Oven in Kent with all landes tenementes & other belonginging the same / late Sir John Fogge

John Wood squier the keping of the Coigne & money of gold & silver in the Toure of Londone and elleswhere in (Lo) England

[f37] John Norrys A generalle pardone

John White alle the landes & tenementes within the Towne of Tymbe called the mayne fugatife landes Waterwynshille & Regonclose with ij wynde mylles & a wattere mylle / to valew of x li. for terme of his lyff

William Sankey squier thoffice of one of the serieauntes at Armes with the fee of xij d.

Jamys Erle Douglas CC li. of Annuyte for terme of his lyff

John Duc of Norffolk Thoffice of Chieff Steward of the duchie of Lancastre in the southe parties for terme of his liff

Richard Willoughby Thoffice of Constable of the Castelle of Nethe / with the wages accustumed / & an Annuyte of xl marc

Edmond Hastinges knighte An Annuyte of C marc for terme of his lyff to be taken of the baillieffwyk of souke & the liberties of Pikering in the Countie of York

Waltier Graunt thoffice of keping of the Castel of Maxstok and the keping of the parke of the same / for terme of his lyff late belonging the Duc of Bukingham

Dan William Cerff the parsonage of Fulbek in the diocese of Lincoln etc

lettres of warraunt to Thauditors of the Counties of Chestre and Flynt to allowe Sir William Stanley Chambrelein & Shereff there xl li. whiche the he standethe charged with for certain arreraiges of (certain) chieff Rent & other that Thomas Salesbury the yonger (stande) standethe endented unto the king

Richard Swansey the baillifshippe of (Swansey) Hawnes in the Countie of Bedford and the keping of the parke there for terme of his lyff etc

Kateryn Arundelle wyff of Thomas Arundelle knighte a yerely rent or pencione . C li. (of) going out of alle & singuler Maners landes & tenementes whiche late were John Chydyok knighte (etc) for terme of (her) lyff of the said Thomas etc

118

Robert Swifte thoffice of parker of Lytelhay in the Counte of Essex for terme of his lyff etc

(William Baynard thoffice of keping of your waren and wodes of Sherston for terme of his lyff etc)

A (n allow commaundement &) discharge to the Tresorer and Barons of theschequer for thallowance of xx li. (parcell) parcelle of the summe of Cxx li. of the fee ferme of Northampton to John Bukby and John More late baillieffs of the same

A (parrdon) pardon to John Isley etc

Robert Roo thoffice of keping of the Maner of Somborne and keping of the parke there for terme of his lyff etc

[f37b] William Porter . thoffice of parker of Hertford & warrenner of Hertford-ingbury with the profites of the Conyes for terme of his lyff without any accompt etc

Rauff Banastre the Maner & lordshippe of Ealding with thappurtenaunces in the Countie of Kent / to him & his heires masles forever / yelding the Rents services & duetees going out of the same / and also to Thomas Jebbe for terme of his lyff iiij li. yerely / and after the decesse of the said Thomas the same iiij li. to be paied yerely to the king & his heires for ever as Castelle warde to the Castelle of Rouchestre etc

Johanne Mountfort oon of his daughters of Thomas Mountfort knighte x marc yerely for terme of (his) hire lyff of the honour of Pountfret etc

John Dudley thoffice of Sheref of the Countees of Surrey & Sussex for the yere now next ensuyng / with assignament by Taille or Tailles of xl li.

John Squier Maister Carpenter of the werkes in the Castel of Wyndesore for terme of his lyff

Thomas Sutton thoffice of Busby & Faceby in the Counte of York for terme of his lyff etc

Thabbot and Convent of Basingwerke x marc yerely for the sustentacione & salarie of a prest at the Chapelle of Seint Wynefride / to be perceyved (of) at theschequer of Chestre by the handes of the Chambreleyn etc

John Tenaunt thoffice of porter of the Castelle of Rouchestre for terme of his lyff with the wages of iiij d. by the day etc

A warraunt to the prive seale to make out lettres of warraunt to the Custumers of the portes of Excestre & Dertmouthe to content Mathewe Andrewe of Topsham the summe of xlv li. for v Tonne wyne and xx li. stokfisshe (with other) whiche Charles Dynham with other spent & emploied (upon) in the kinges nedes upon the see in Recountring of the kinges Rebelles etc

Richard Scopeham oon of the yeomen of Corone Thoffice of keping of (youre) the Toure nighe unto theschequer within the Towne of Westminstre for terme of his lyff etc

John Busshe grome of the hal / thoffice of baillieff of Eston in the Countie of Northampton during the nonne Age of the heire of the duc of Clarence etc

William Okebourne thoffice of baillieff of Enfeld with an Annuyte of xl s. yerely for terme of his lyff etc

[f38] Richard Goughe secundary Clerc of the kychyn / the Amobreiship with thoffice of Raglarship within the Countie of Merionethe and with the Raglership of the Advoures in the said Countie for terme of his lyff etc

Rauff Sill Thoffice of Baillieff of the Towne & libertee of (Tombrigge) Tonne-brigg and Thoffice of Chambreleyn of Tonnebrigge for terme of his lyff

William Haymond Trumpet an Annuyte of x markes for terme of his lyff of the fee ferme of Bardport

Hugh Taillor an Annuyte of sex markes for terme of his lyff / to be taken of the lordship of Bergevenny

Warraunt to the Receivor of (the Duchie of) Pountfret for the contacion of the summe of xl li for the buylding of the Chapelle of Towton

120

Rauff Banastre the keping of the parkere of Everley & warren there for terme of his lyff with the Fees of iiij d by the day

John Lightefote Thoffice of Bagshote Bailly in the Forest of Wyndesore with the fees of vj d by the day for terme of his lyff

To the Maire & (his B) Citizens of York the king hath graunted lx li yerely of the Fee ferme of the said Citee & to theire successors for ever / and also have graunted unto the said Maire & his successors to be chieff serieaunt of Armes / and for (thexersic) thexercising of that office to have xviij li v s yerely / and also the king hath remitted & relessed aswelle to the said Maire & his successors / as to the Shireff there & his successors alle the residue of the said fee ferme without any accompt (th) making or any other thing therefor yelding

To the (We) Felosshippe of the Wexchaundelers of London / the King hath graunted theim to be incorperate for theim & theire successors for ever / and to purchesse landes to the valewe of fyve markes

To Rauff Salvane the king hath graunted (a new) and yeven licence to entre into the manor & lordship of Dancastre / and the same to have & to holde to him and to his (his) hires of his body lawfully begotten for ever / as his olde & just enheritaunce

To Maister Henry Bost / the king confirmeth such grauntes & lettres patentes as he had of the provostship of the Collage of Etone

To the Maire & his Felosship of the Stapille of Calis a discharge direct to the (B) Tresorere & barons of Theschequiere of the summe of M^{l}M^{l}CCCliij li x s iiij d ob q for the custumes & subsides of certen wolles Shipped to calais wardes (with) whiche for fere & daunger of Ennemys Retorned home to Londone Agen

To William Alayne the king hath confirmed suche graunt as he had of thoffice of bailly of Fynchampstede within the Forest of Wyndesore during his liff / and suche graunt as the said William had of thoffice of keping of the Manor of Esthampstede & of the newe parke there within the said Forest / and also hathe confirmed unto him suche graunt as he had of vj d by the day of the Fee of Coronne paied (it) of the Rentes of the serieauntie of Wilteshire and of alle other proffites & Revenues comyng of the said Countie

[f38b] To Thomas Wyntershille the king hathe confirmed such lettres patent as he hath of Thoffice of serieaunt of the kinges herttes houndes graunted unto

him by king Edward the iiijth during his lyff

To Robert Whittelbury the king hath graunted an Annuyte of x marc to be taken yerely during his lyff of thissues proffites & Revenues of the lordship of Brigstok within the Countie of Northampton

To John Nesfeld (squi) the king hath graunted to be squier for his body for terme of his lyff / for thexercising thereof to perceive yerely l marc of thissues proffites & fermes of the Counties of Somerset & Dorset

To Thomas Cressy the king hath confirmed such lettres patentes as he hath of Thoffice of keping of the beddes within the Castelle of Windesore to him graunted by king Edward the iiijth during his lyff

To John Talbot the king hathe graunted the keping of the parke of Hamstede Marshalle / and the baillishippe of the lordship there for terme of his lyff

To John Smythe the king hathe graunted to be one of the serieauntes at Armes (w) during his liff with the fee of xij d. by the day to be taken of the Custumes (of) & subsides of the port of Ippiswiche

To John Wainflete the king hathe graunted to be one of his serieaunt at Armes for terme of his liff with the wages of xij d. by the day to be takene of thissues of the Counties of Bedford & Bukingham

To William Davenport squiere a licence to put certen his lyvelode in feoffment

To John Broune of Cottone & John Byritone Thoffice of Steward or Ridere of the Forest of Morff in the Countie of Salop for terme of theire lyves & aither of theim langest lyvyng

To Thrustayn Hatfelde the king hathe confirmed such graunts as he had (of) for the fee of the Coronne (by b) to him graunted by king Edward iiijth for terme of his liff And Also suche grauntes as he had of the olde parke of Pleysshe for terme of liff

To Roger Dynley an Annutye of xx^{ti} markes / to be had & perceived yerely of thissues proffites & Revenues of Pountfret for terme of his liff

To Edward Burton the king hathe confirmed suche graunte as he had for the fee of the Coronne of king Edward the iiij[th] for terme of his lyff

To Carles Belfeld Thoffice of bailly of Chesterford in Essex & keping of the parke there for terme of his liff / with the wages & Fees etc And also an Annuyte of C s. / to be teken yerely of thissues & Revenues of the said lordship

To William Crawcestre / a tenement in Waturfulford in the Countie of York called Roos halle for terme of his liff

To John Stanbrige the king hath confirmed suche grauntes as he had of the keping of the logee of Immeslowe in the Forest of Shirwod & to be one of the Forsters there during his lyff

To Thomas Lovelle & Agnes Lovelle his modere the lordshippe of Polstedehalle in Burnham with thappurtenaunces in the Countie of Norffolk / to theim & aithere of theim longest lyvyng

[f39] To Thomas Bawdewyn Thoffice of bailly of Cosham & keping of the parkes there for terme of his lyff

To the lord Zouche / the Warden of your Forestes of Gillingham & Selwod with the keping of the parke of Gillingham for terme of lyff

To Edmond Verney the king hathe confirmed his grauntes of (the keping) the Steward of the lordship of Yerdley in the Countie of Wigorn / and of the keping of the parke of Claredon in the Countie of Warrewic / as long as the said (lordshi) landes shalbe in the kinges handes

Thomas Rede Thoffice of one of the Forsters in Bernewode for terme of his liff

To William Porter the king hathe confirmed (f) his (f) graunte of the Fee of Coronne to him made for terme of his lyff

To Henry Sewalle to be one of the knightes of Wyndesore for terme of his liff

To John Graysone the Bailliship of the lordship of (Some) Soham in the Countie of Cambrige & the keping of the warrene there for terme of his liff .

To William Staverton the king hath confirmed his grauntes to him made of Thoffice of Batilbaly in the Forest of Wyndesore / and of the parkership of Moot parke within the same Forest for terme of his lyff / by king Edward the iiijth

To Rauff Dowelle thoffice of keping of the herber within London / & the Receivor of the same for terme of his liff

To Thomas Fitzwilliam (the) An Annuytee of xx markes to be takyn of the lordship of Bolingbroke for terme of his lyff

To Edward Skelton the king hathe confirmed his graunte of one of the serieauntes at Armes with the wages thereunto accustumed for terme of his liff

To the same William Stavertone the king hath confirmed his graunte made to him of thoffice of Steward of the lordshippe of Caversham & Assherigge & the bailly of Assherigge for terme of his lyff

To the prior & Convent of Mounkebrettone licence to mortice the parisshe churche of Derton

To Edward Hargille the king hathe confirmed his grauntes made unto him of an Annuyte of / ix li. ijs. vj d. / to be takyn of the fee ferme of Norwiche during his lyff

To the same Edward the king hath also confirmed his grauntes of thoffices of Steward of the lordshippe of (Medre) meore & parkere of the parke there for terme of liff

To the same Edward the king hathe also confirmed his graunte of the Rangeor of the Forest of Whitewode for terme of his liff

To the same Edward the king hathe also confirmed his graunte of the keping of the parke of Fremantille for terme of his lyff

To John Scot squiere the king hath confirmed his graunte to him made of (l) fyfty markes / for terme of his lyff / by king Edward the iiijth

To Thomas Sapcot Thoffice of Eschetor & Feodere of the Cornvaile during the kinges pleasure

124

[f39b] To John Langford the king hath confirmed his patent made unto him for the fee of the Coronne for terme of his lyff

To the same John the king hath confirmed his graunte of thoffice of Rangeor of the Forest of Waltham for terme of his liff

To John Pikering an Annuyte of foure markes of thissues of the Countie palatyne of Cestre for terme of his liff

A discharge to John Ambrose for the nonne payment of the subside certen wyne direct to the tresorere & Chambreleyns of Eschequiere

Robert Leget his patent of Chief mason in the Castelle of Wyndesore new confermed for terme of his lyff etc

John Hame the bailliship of Eccleswalle & Cradnelle in the Countie of Hereford during the nonne Age of George Erle of Shrewesbury

Moresse of Prise thoffice of portryve of Pristane in the marche of Wales for terme of his liff

Robert Brynt A generalle pardone

Thomas Berwyk thoffice of Constable of the Castelle of Rouchestre for terme of his lyff

John Leventhorpe / the bailliship of Erlescourt with the keping of the parke there for terme of his liff

William Cheyne thoffice of bailly of Stallage of Penwithe & Kerye in the Countie of Cornubie for terme of his liff

John Cheverelle a generalle pardone

John Wyngfeld A generalle pardone

John Wyngfeld yongere a generalle pardone

Sir Richard Harecourt knighte the warde & mariage of Nicholas Asshton with the keping of alle landes Maners etc

Garter king of Armes & to other kings of Armes / the king hathe graunted to be corporate / & licence to purchesse xx li worth of land / And also a place in Londone called coldearbere etc

Thomas Worley / the king hathe confirmed his patent made to him by king Edward the iiij[th] a tenement in Londone in distaff lane called the Lambe / for terme of his liff

Henry Abyngdon / the king hathe confirmed his graunt made unto him by king Edward the iiij[th] for terme of his liff of an Annuyte of viij li. to be taken of Hadeley Ree & Leth Ree in the Countie of Essex

John Nightingale / the king hath confirmed thoffice of keping of the parke of Clyff with the harbage & pannage within the same parke for terme of his liff

[f40] Sir Jamys Tirelle / Steward of the Duchie of Cornewaille for terme of liff

Robert Allerton / the king hathe confirmed unto him thoffice of Serchere of the porte & Towne of Calais during his liff

Nicholas Russelle the king hath confirmed unto him An Annuyte of x marc for terme of his liff / takene of thissues proffites & Revenues of the lordship of Yarkehille in the Countie of Herford

Hugh Hurltone thoffice of Surveior of the kinges werkes & Reparacions of his castelles lordshippes & manors (of) within the Counties of Chestre & Flynt for terme of liff with the fee of iiij d. by day

Edward Pargate of Canterbury A generalle pardone

William Catesby / the warde & mariage of Anthony acton Son & heire of John Acton with the keping etc

William Wyndesore the king hath confirmed unto him an Annuyte of x marc during his liff to be taken of the fee ferme of the hundredes of Kestesgate Holeford & Crestone with the feires & markettes within the Towne of Wynchecombe

Richard Hevyn / the king hathe graunted unto him an Annuyte of C s. to be takene of the lordshippes Wigmore Beaudeley & Clebury for terme of lif

Geoffrey Whitford / the king hathe confirmed to him thoffice of Ringille within the Countie of Flynt during his liff

Roger Wilkynson / the king hathe graunted (the) to him thoffice of baillieff of Shelford within the Countie of Notingham during his liff with iiij d. by day

William Stanley knighte the king hathe graunted xx li. yerely during the nonne Age of Edward Erle of Worcestre to be taken of the feeferme of the Towne of Cambrige

Therle of Arundelle the king hathe confirmed unto him Thoffice of Constable of the Castelle of Dovere / and the Wardenship of the V portes during his liff

John Traybone / the king hathe confirmed unto him an Annuyte of x li. to be taken during his liff of the feeferme of the Citee of Worcestre

The lord Greystok / An Annuyte of C li. to be taken during his liff of thissues & Revenues of the lordship of Tikhille

John Alday the king hath confirmed unto him An Annuyte of x li. to be taken during his liff of the fee ferme of Quenehyghe

Nicholas Burton / the king hath confirmed unto him thoffice of bailly of the Towne of Dovere during his liff

Sir Thomas Everyngham / the king hath graunted unto him the leiftenantship of the Towre of Risebanke during his liff

[f40b] Richard Scopham the king hath graunted vj d. by day for the fee of Corone to be taken yerely during his liff of thissues proffites & Revenues of the ulnage of sale clothes within the Countie of Kent

Thabbot of Gloucestre / the king hath to him & his Successors for ever xx li. to be takene yerely of the fee ferme of gloucestre (for ever)

Walter Rufford the king hathe confirmed unto him thoffices of keping of the parke of Abburley & baillieff of the hundred of Dodington and of the lordship of Shrawley in the Countie of Worcestre during the nonne Age of Edward Erle of Warrewic

The priour of the house of Monkebrettone / the king graunteth to him & the Convent there & theire successors for ever thadvoson of the patronage of the parisshe Church of Derton / & A Licence unto theim to impropre the same

John Newman prest / the king hath graunted unto him the Chauntery in the parisshe Churche of brales

Roger Pye / the king hath confirmed unto him vj d. by day for the fee of the Corone to be taken during his liff of the fee ferme of Pynnokshire

Sir Cristofre Warde / the king hathe graunted the stewardship of the lordship of Warplestone & of the lordship of Whitley in the Countie of Surrey for terme of liff with the fee of lx s. by yere

William Duket / the Free chapelle of seint Leonardes besides the Towne of Kirkeby

Thomas Wrangwys / An Annuyte of xx marc to be taken during his liff of the lordship of Sherefhotone

Robert Rokeley & William Rokeley his Son thoffice of Rangeour of the Forest of Lee / otherwise called the forest of Rutland with the wages of ij d. by day / for terme of liff and aither of theim longest lyvyng

John Belle & Robert his son thoffice of parkere of Casteldonyngtone in the Countie of Leycestre / with wages of iiij d. by day & bally of the same with iij d. by day for terme of theire lyves & aithere of theim langere lyvyng

William Tunstalle the lordship of Shirburne in Hertfurthlith in the Countie of York for terme of his lyff

The same William for the fee of one of the squiers for the kinges body an Annuyte of fyfty markes yerely during his liff to be taken of the honnor of (Th) Tikhille for the fest of the concepcion of oure lady last past

128

John Goyne an Annuyte of x marc / to be taken for terme of liff / of the lordship of Uske .

William Fletchere the king hath confirmed to him Thoffice of keping of the parke of Beskwod / with the wages of iiij d. by day to be takyn yerely during his liff of the serieaunt Rent of the Counties of Notingham & Derby

[f41] Johanne Ingaldesthorp late wiff of Sir Edmond Ingaldesthorpe knight the king hath confirmed an Annutte of Cxj li. ij d ob.qr. / to be taken yerely during here lyff of the subside & unlnage of the cloth in the Counties of Norffolk Suffolk & Essex

To the Maire & Barons of Sandewiche / the king hath graunted C li. yerely during his pleasure to be emploied of the mending of the walles by the oversighte of John Aldare Nicholas Burton John Crafford & William Salman

The Ankeresse of Westminstre the king hath confirmed unto here an Annuyte of vj marc to be taken yerely during his liff of thissues prouffites & Revenues of Notingham

Adame Dale thoffice of porter of the Castelle of Scardesburghe with xl s. Fee for terme of liff to be takene of the fee ferme there

Humfrey Curtney An Annuyte of xx marc / to be taken yerely during his liff of the Revenues of the duchie of Cornewale

A warraunt to the Tresorere of Calais to content & pay yerely to Richard Chainley the summe of xx li. unto the tyme the summe of C li. be fully content & paied / And to the Tresorere & Chambleyns of the Eschequiere to allowe the same

John Broune & Thomas Riddelle / the king hathe confirmed unto theim thoffice of keping of the parke of Biltone in the Forest of Knaresburgh for terme of theire lyffes & aithere of theim longest lyvyng

The same John / the king hathe confirmed unto him Thoffices of keping of the parke of Hay & palicere of the same for terme of lyff

Richard Copeland / the baillieff of the lordship of Estgarston & haywarde of Colynghorne (fo) in the Countie of Wilteshire for terme of lyff / with the wages

& fees due etc / And also an Annuyte of v marc for terme of his liff to be taken of the lordship of Estgarston

George Cheynewe / the king hathe confirmed an Annuyte of C s. for terme of his liff to be taken of the ferme of the hundred of (Ryngeswolde) Ringeslowe Dunhamford & Blenegate in the Countie of Kent / Also hath confirmed unto him his graunte of the manere of Brendbradfeld in the Countie of Suffolk with alle his appurtenaunces for terme of his liff / late the lord Roos

William Tavernere prest / the pensione & sellery which Sir Thomas Rawson had in the Chapelle of seint Elyn in Pountfret

Philip Curtney / an Annuyte of xl li. / to be taken during his liff of the Revenues of the duchie of Cornewaille

[f41b] Robert Coke / thoffice of portere of the Castelle of Pevesey for terme of his liff with alle maner wages etc

Roger Dyneley the keping of the parke called Scolys parc in the Countie of York for terme of his liff / with the wages of ij d. by day to be takyn of the lordship of Scolys etc

John Curteney / an Annuyte of xl marc / to be takene for terme of his liff of the Revenues of the duchie of Cornewaille

William Curteney an Annuyte of xx li. / to be taken for terme of his liff of the Revenues of the duchie of Cornewaille

Maister Thomas Henbury / a Chauntery in the Castelle of Dynbigh in north Wales for terme of his liff

Charles Nowelle / the king hathe confirmed unto him an Annuyte of ix li. ijs. vj d. to be takene yerely during his liff of the Revenues of the Countie palatyne of Lancastre

The lord Mountjoye / the lieutenantship of the Castelle of Guysnes & governer of the Towne & Countie aforsaide for terme of his liff

(Sir) Jamys Blount / the lieutenant of the Castelle of Hampnes for the terme of

130

xx yeres / with wages & fees due & accustumed

Thomas (Ch) Cancelere / the warde & mariage of John Torney son & heire of Philip Torney / with the keping of alle maners etc

Thomas Thorousby / Thoffice of bailly of the lordship of Donmowe in the Countie of Essex / with the keping of the parke there for terme of his liff / And also an Annuyte of x markes to be taken of the Revenues of the said lordshippe

Adryan Whetehille/ an Annuyte of xl li. for terme of his lyff to be takene (of) aswele of the Custumes the wolle / as of othere Revenues of the Towne of Calais

Margarete the wiff of John Bernard / an Annuyte of xx marc to be takene yerely during here liff of the Revenues of the lordshippes of Salwarp & Wyche in the Countie of Worcestre

Rouland Nicholsone / the king hath confirmed the gadering & receving of the custumes & tolle called Sandgelt of the lordshippes of Marke & oye for terme of his liff without any accompt therefore making

The lord Dynham / the chieff Steward & supervisore of alle Castelles lordships honors Maners & other possessions of the duchie of Cornewaille / as long as he beres him wele / with the fees & wages of C li. / to be taken by the handes of the generalle Receivor of the same

[f42] Edward Kingdone the king hath confirmed unto him vj d. by day for the fee of Coronne / to be takene during his liff of the fee ferme of Birdport / Also Thoffice of baillieff of the lordship of Chewyk for terme of his lyff / with the wages & fees due & accustumed / Also the Fisshing or keping of the watere of Exe for terme of his lyff without any accompt therefore yelding etc

(Maister) William Dawbeney / An Annuyte of x li. / unto the tyme he be promoted to offices of xx li. for terme of his lyff / to be takene yerely of (a) the ferme of a mese in Watford in the Countie of Northampton / and to the same William & Johanne his wiff xx markes by yere for terme of his liff & aithere of theim legere lyvyng to be taken of the fee ferme of Notingham etc

Robert Brews / an Annuyte of x li / to be taken for terme of his liff of the fee ferme of Uippi' in the Countie of Suffolk

Richard Hide an Annuyte of xx li / to be takene yerely during his liff of the lordshippes of Abirley & Shrawley in the Countie of Worcestre

John Hayes / the king hath confirmed unto him / thoffice of Receivor of alle maners lordshippes landes & tenements in the Counties of Cornewaille Devone Somerset Dorset Wilteshire & Suthampton called Sarum landes & Spencere landes / with xx^{ti} markes Fe / As long as the said maners shalle remayn in the kinges handes

Thomas Wade & John Challey / the king hath confirmed unto theim & aithere of theim lengest lyvyng / thoffice of Custumare & Collector of the money comyng of the weghte of wolle within the Towne of Calais with the fees & wages thereunto due etc

Richard Beauchamp otherwise called lord Seint Mount A generalle pardone

Robert Dokunfelde / an Annuyte of xx marc / to be taken yerely during his liff of the Revenues of the Countie palatyne of Lancastre

Sir John Ferrers / an Annuyte of xl marc / to be taken yerely during his liff of the Revenues of the lordship of Warrwyk

The lord Ferrers / thoffice of Maistere forstere & keper of the Chace of Enfelde Estbally Westbailly Southbailly & Rangere of the same / the keping of the parke of Enfelde & palicere of the same / with the wages & fees thereunto due & accustumed / And for the palershippe of the same ij d. by day (of) to be takene for terme of his liff of the lordship of Enfelde

Sir Thomas Burghe thoffice of Steward of alle the lordship maners landes & tenementes in the Isle of Axholme in the Countie of Lincolne with the fee of x li. to be takene of the Revenues of the said lordshippes during his liff

Robert Thorpe / the king hathe confirmed unto him thoffice of Spigurnelle in the Chauncery with the fees & wages accustumed for terme of his liff

[f42b] William Breirley / the king hathe confirmed unto him / C li. yerely to be perceived of the moncy curraunt in the marches of Wales unto the tyme he & his executors be fulle paied of the summe of D li.

A warraunt direct to the Tresorere & Barons of the kinges Eschequier to discharge Sir William Evers knighte late Shireff of the Countie of York of the summe of C marc by reasone of a Recoignaunce etc

A licence to John Magnus for a ship called the John of Scardeburgh of the portage of C tonne to seale to Island / and to endure for an yere

Henry Yong / the king hath confirmed unto him the village of Cansey in the Countie of Guysnes / with landes & tenementes called gaole Waymot in the same village (etc) with other thinges etc

A warraunt direct to the Tresorere & barons of the Eschequiere for discharging of Richard Delabere late Shiref of the Countie of Hertford of the summe of xx li

A licence to Edward Gowere for a ship called the Kateryn of Horwelle of the portage of Cxl Tonnes into Island / for a yere

A licence to Tayte & Edward Grene merchauntes of London for a ship of C Tonnes or undere / for brettayns to sale in to Brettany to endure half a yere

A warraunt direct to the Tresorere & barons of theschequiere forto discharge John Sapcottes late Shireff of the Countie of Cornwaille of alle maner accions sutes & demaundes made or to be made ayenst him by virtue of his office in the Eschequiere

John Challey / the king hathe confirmed unto him certen lecesse made of (the lordshippes of Marke & oye) a pasture called the pasture of Ram de Grave with alle thappurtenaunces / without any thing therefore payng / for terme of his liff

(Richard Whi)
Adryan Whitehille / the king hathe confirmed unto him thoffice of Countrollere of the Towne of Calais with the wages of xx li to be takene of the Custumes of wolle there for terme of lyff

Richard Whetehille of Calais / the king hathe confirmed unto him the lesse of a pasture & watere called calkewell plasshe for the terme of xl yeres in his lettres patentes comprised / paieng therefore yerely xxiij s iiij d / And also hathe confirmed unto him / a ferme (called) of ij (wh) wyndmylnes upon the Castelle hille within Calais & a grounde called Mylhille / and ij warrene of Connes one lieng in the lordship of marke & the other in the lordshippe of Oye for the terme of xl yeres paying yerely for the said ij mylnes x li. & for the ij warrans xlvj s. viiij d. & iij s. iiij d. of incresse

[f43] To the Maire & Citizens of Wynchestre the king hath pardoned relesed & remitted for ever (C marc) xx li. of theire fee ferme yerely

To the Maire & Burgesses of Oxon the king hath pardoned relessed & remitted for ever xx marc of theire fee ferme yerely

To the baillyffes & Burgesses of the Towne of Salop the king hath pardoned remitted & Relessed for ever xx marc of theire fee ferme (f) yerely

To Sir Thomas Everyngham knight / the king hath graunted the Castelle & borow of Barnstaple / the Castelle & Manere of (Toryngto) Toryton the Fee ferme of Toryton & Barnstaple in the Countie of Devone with theire appurtenaunces / late Sir Thomas Seintligers / the maners of Blakford & Pristley and an Annuelle Rent of v marc in Rode in the Countie of Somerset with theire appurtenaunces / Also the Manere of Netherhayforde / and alle landes & tenementes in the Towne of Netherhayford / with theire appurtenaunces in the Countie of Oxon and the manere of Cherington with thappurtenaunces in Berkshire to the said Sir Thomas & hieres masles / by the services due & accustumed

To Sir Thomas Mountgomery knight / the king hath graunted the Castelle lordshippe & Maner of Hyngham at Castelle with thappurtenaunces in the Countie of Essex / the lordshippe & Manere of Hingham Sibbille in the same Countie / the lordshippe & maner of Praiers & alle landes & tenementes called Praiers in Hingham Sibbille The lordshippe & maner of Pevers & alle the landes & tenementes called Pevers in Hingham Sibille aforsaid / the lordship & maner of Gildham / the lordshippe or maner of Colne otherwise called the lordshippe or maner of Erlscolne / the lordship or maner of Hatfelde Brodoke / the lordshippe or maner of (w) Vausesse / the lordship or maner of Ongre / the hundred of Ongre / the hundred of Harlowe with theire appurtenaunces in the Countie of Essex / for terme of his liff without any accompt therefore paieng or yelding / And over this the king hath graunted unto the said Sir Thomas thoffices of Maistere Forster & Maister of the game of alle Forestes chaces & parkes within the said Countie of Essex / and office of Steward of alle lordshippes maners landes (&) tenements & hundredes in the forsaid Countie / for terme of his said liff

To Robert Percy knighte Countroller of the kinges house / Robert Percy yongere his sone Robert Lamptone & John Pullan / the king hath graunted unto theim an Annuyte of xxxv li. to be had & perceived of & in the lordshippe or maner of Clidrowe in the Countie of Lancastre parcelle of the duchie of Lancastre in the Countie aforsaid during the lyff of Thomas lord Stanley

[f43b] To the same Sir Robert Percy / the king hath graunted the Maners of

Camps / Saxtone / Abitone / & Hingestone with thappurtenaunces in the Countie of Cambrige / And the (lordshi) Maners of Scottone & Brereton with thappurtenaunces in the Countie of York / and other landes (&) tenementes Rentes services & inheritaunces with thappurtenaunces in Scottone breretone Staveley Staneley Burtone & Knaresburghe in the Countie of York aftere the decesse of Thomas lord Stanley / to have the same with alle theire appurtenaunces to the said Sir Robert & his heirs masles forever by the services of one knightes fee / Paieng yerely to the king or to his heires xv li. / And also hathe confirmed unto the said Sir Robert & Joys his wiff A gift unto them made by certen feoffes of the lordship of Garboldesham with alle thappurtenaunces / to theim & theire heires masles

Therle of Northumberland / the king hathe graunted / the maners or lordshippes of Torebryane / Slapton / Northam / Dertmouthe / and Cliftone Hardnesshe in the Countie of Devone / the maners or lordshippes of Wroxhalle / Wurdesford Bolet / Rammesham / Cheldefrome / (Sy) Swynetollere / Mapertone / Pomknolle / Netherkentecombe & Hasselbeare / & the (wa) bailly of of keping of the bankes of frome & Stoure etc in the Countie of Dorset the maners or lordshippes of Shokeryk / Bathenesdone / Kingesdone / Somertone Erlethe / Somertone Randolff / Denehed / Stokmychille & ix messuages / CCCiij^{xx} & viij Acres of land / iiij^{xx}xij Acres of medowe / xl Acres of pasture iiij^{xx} Acres of wod / (x)xxvj(j) s. of Rent in Bathennesden Kingesdone Somertone Erlethe Somerton Randolff & thadvosone of the Chirche of Kingesdone in the Countie of Somerset / to him & to his heires / by the services due & accustumed for ever / And also the (Reversion of) ferme & Revenues of the said lordshippes from Michaelmas last past unto the date herof / And also the Reversione of the Maners of foxherde with thappurtenaunces in the Countie of Essex / the maner of Aketone & morewes in Waldyngfelde in the Countie of Suffolk the maner of Chelesfelde with thappurtenaunces in the Countie of Kent the maner of Esthalle nighe chelesfelde & the maner of Asshe nighe Fremyngham with thappurtenaunces in the Kent / the maner of Leiham otherwise called the maner of overburyhalle in Layham & Worstede in the Countie of Suffolk / the maner of buresse with netherhalle & overhalle & a tenement called Ropers in Seintmarieburesse in Essex & suffolk & the maner of Layham in the same Countie of suffolk

[f44] To John Caryngto squie / the Maner of Callylond in Cornewaille of the valew of xl marc / to him & to his heires masles by knighte services / paying yerely to the king xl s. of fee Rent

To Sir Thomas Markynfelde / the king hath gevene the Manere or lordship of Glutton & Farneham with thappurtenaunces to the valewe of xxxiiij li. / the maner or lordshippe of Southbrent / to the valewe of xxxij li. the manore or lordshippe of Stratton to the valew of xvj li / the maner or lordshippe of Yebilton & spekington to the valewe of xj li. / the maner or lordshippe of Chilingtone to the valew of viij li / to him & to his heires masles / paieng to the king vij li. & x s.

To John Aldey / the king hath graunted alle those landes tenementes Rentes & services with thappurtenaunces which late was Sir George Browne in the parisshe of Wynham & Goodmystone in Kent / to the valewe of vj li. xviij s. & iiij d. ob. / to him & to his heires masles / by knighte service payeng therefore yerely to the king x s.

Sir John Huddelston thoffice of parkere of muche Walden in the Countie of Essex . for terme of his liff / with the Fees & wages etc

Robert Pembertone An Annuyte of xx li. / to be perceived yerely for terme of his liff of thissues & Revenues of the Towne of Russhdene in the Countie of Northamptone

William Rosse squiere / the king hathe confirmed unto him / thoffice of vitalere of the Towne of Calais / As long as he berethe wele perceiving yerely for the same office / the fee of ij s. by day for him selff / and for his clerc & ane yoman eithere of theim xij d. by day / and for iij his servauntes eiche of theim vj d. by day / of the Revenues of the lordshippe of Guysnes

To the baillieffes & burgesses of Huntyngdon the king hathe confirmed unto theim alle theire olde grauntes / and over that of new hathe graunted unto them & theire successors for ever to be a body incorperate / and that they shalbe able to purchesse landes / and also hath pardoned & relessed to the said baillieffes & burgesses & to their heires & successors xxj marc yerely parcelle of theire fee ferme / And also that they shalbe discharged (of) from hensfurth of taken of cariages & alle maner graynes & vitailles wod & tymbre / And that they shalle have fre warren within the precincte of theire libertes of the Towne Ut patet in billa

[f44b] *Grantham* To thalderman & Burgesses of Grantham / the king hath graunted that they and theire Successors shalbe Justice of peas within the said Towne and kepe sessions of the peas as oft as it shalbe necessary by the warrant of the Alderman of the same / and that they shalle have a Gaole within the said Towne / and that they shalle have execucione of preceptes & warraunt within the said Towne & soke / And that the shireff of Lincolnshire shalle have no execution thereof within the same / and that they shalle have wekely a market in the same Towne every (Wednesday) Wednesday / and every yere perpetually ij Faires one in the Fest of Seint Nicholas in Wynter & ij daies folowing / and another on passion Sonday & j day folowing with alle libertes to suche faires appurteignyng / And that the same Alderman & burgesse shalle have thordenaunce & assignement of alle stalles & places in the said feire & market /

And the said Alderman & burgesses & their Successors shalle have for ever alle maner Tallages Stallage & proffuytes of the said feires & markettes without any thing therefore paieng or accompt making / Also that neither the said Alderman & burgesses ne any other dwelling within the said Borowe & Souke shalle fromhensfurth be compelled to be enpanelled or passe in any (Attente) Attainctes without the Towne borow or Souke aforsaid / And that the said Alderman & burgesses & any othere dwelling within the said Borow & Souke shalle not be chosen nor compelled to be Shireff of any countie / And that the said Alderman & Burgesses shalle have a comon seale to seale withalle mesures & weightes / And that the Clerk of market shalle not medille in any poynt within theim

To the Clarge of England / the king hathe confirmed unto alle theire libertes as in theire patent to theim made by king Edward the iiij[th] more playnley it apperethe

A warraunt directed to Sir William Hussy knighte chieff justice of the kinges benche & other there to discharge alle prosses made or to be made ayenst John Crokker of Lynham in the Countie of Devon knighte & other his Feloship / by reasone of an indytment certified ayenst them there

To Sir Thomas Broughtone the king hathe graunted the lordshippe of Combe Martyn / that is worth by yere xxix li. xvij s. vj d / the maner of Combe Burgus that is worthe by yere xx li. xvj s. x d. / the maner of Wynkeleytracy that is worthe by yere xxvj li. xvj s. iiij d. / the maner & hundred of Suthmulton burgus that is worthe by yere xxiij li. xiij s. iiij d. in the Countie of Devone / To have & hold the same to to the said Sir Thomas & his heires masles of the king by knighte services / & paieng therefore vij li. x s.

[f45] Henry lord Grey the king hathe graunted unto him the maner of Okeham in the Countie of Rutland to the valewe of iiij[xx]vj li. / the Maner or lordship of (Hengrave in the Countie of Suffolk to the valewe of xliiij li. / the maner or lordship of Haverhille & Hersham in the Countie aforsaid to the valewe of xxviij li.) Langham in the same Countie to the valewe of iiij[xx] li. / the Maner or lordship of Egeston in the same Countie to the valewe of xxviij li. xiij s. iiij d / the maner or lordshippe of Hengrave in the Countie of Suffolk to the valewe of xliiij li. / the maner or lordship of Haverhille & Hersham in the same Countie to the valewe of xxviij li. / to the same lord & his heires masles by knighte services paieng yerely xx li.

Thomas Stafford the maner (of) or lordship of Chellesworthe & Knawelle (to) of the valewe of lxvj s. viij d. / the maner or lordshippe of Bromham of the valewe of xiiij li. xvij s. x d. / the maner or lordshippe of Woderew of the valewe of xxviij li. ij s. / the maner or lordship of (Wad) Whaddene of the valew of xxiiij li. / the maner or lordshippe of Lavyngtone of the valew of xvj li. x s. / the maners or lordshippes of Chesyngbere Wyke abbotes & Wyntersew of the valew of x li. xiij s. iiij d. / and the maners of Wynter(s)wyk Basset & Wynterburne in the Countie of Wilteshire to the valew of iiij li. / to have & holde / to the said Thomas & to his heires masles of the king by knighte service & paieng therefore yerely vij li. x s.

Sir Thomas Markynfeld the Maner or lordshippe of Gluttone of the valew of xxxiij li. / the maner or lordshippe of Southbrent xxxij li. the Maner or lordshippe of Strattone xvj li. / the maner or lordshippe of Yebiltone & Spekyngtone xj li. and the maner or lordship of Chilyngtone viij li. in the Countie of Somerset / to have & holde to the said Sir Thomas & his heires masles / (pai) by knighte service & paieng vij li. x s.

Sir Rauff Asshetone the maners of Melton & Yeffing in Kent of the valew of xxv marc / the maner of Kingesko(ti)th of the same Countie xx li. / the maner of mykilreptone Litil Repton & Assheford in the same Countie xxj li. vj s. viij d. / the maner of (Louthfelde) Lothfelde in Kent xx marc / the maner of Cheryngton in Kent xxv li. / C Acres lande in (Rume) Rumney marsshe in Kent viij li. / the maner of Hertrigge in the parisshe of (Cumbrogh) Cranbroke with thappurtenaunces in the parisshe of forsaid called Gilfordes xij li. / to have & hold the same to him & his heires masles / (p) by knighte services paieng yerely ix li.

Sir Roger Vaghan / the king(h) hathe confirmed unto him a graunt of the Castelle maner & lordshippe of Brilles / the maner of Alexanderstone & the maner of Penkelly with thappurtenaunces / by services thereto due & accustumed

[f45b] William Catesby the maners of Clapthorne & Rowelle & the hundred of Rowelle / the maners of Mikelwolford Litilwolford Litillaford & Waweswotton in the Countie of Warrwik / the maners of Pekhám & Crimerwell & the reversione of ij mesuages vj cotages & sex gardyns in Suthwerk late the duc of Bukingham / the maner of Cleycotone Breyntone Ceyke Lilburn & Newbatelsgrave in the Countie of Northants / and the maner of Broughton Asteley in the Countie of Leycestre late lord Marquis / and sex mesuage in the parisshe of seint Andrews Undershaft in Londone late Sir George Broune / to have the same to him & his heires masles by the service of ane knightes fee / paieng yerely xx li.

Hugh Grymesdiche / The bailif of the hundred de vico malbo in the Countie of Chestre for terme of his lif

John Shaa / The kyng hath confirmed to hym Thoffice of Graver of the coygnyng Irens of gold & silver within England & Calais for terme of his lif

138

Christofre Bentley (an a) an annuite of v markes to bee had of the lordship of Shirif hutone (for term of) unto the tyme he bee promoted

Sir William Stanley The constable of the Castel of Caernervon in Northwales & captainshippe of the towne there during his lif with xxiiij souldeours in his Retinue etc

Sir Richard Tunstal / lieutenaunt undre the king of the castell of Calais during the kinges pleasure

Hugh Shirley — the king hath confirmed his lettres patentes of the fee of the Crowne to bee taken of the fee ferme of the towne of Hereford

John Fortescu squier for the kinges body — hath for the same l markes terme of his lif of the lordshippe of Chesthunt in Hertfordshire and an annuite of x markes of the lordshippe of Flampstede during the noon age of my lord of Warwik

Philip Nowell (an a) an annuite of v markes upone the lordshippe of Midiltone & Merdene unto the tyme he bee Recompensed etc during his lif

John Crowland / A confirmacione of x markes for terme of lif / that is to say v markes of the fee ferme of Dudestone & v markes of the manoir of Bertone

John Priour / x markes for terme of lif that is to say iiij li. of the ferme of Wynchestre & liij s. iiij d. of the manoir of Lokerle

Thomas Paynter Trumpet — x markes for terme of his lif of the Forest of Cornbury

Vincent fynche — xl s. for terme of his lif of the lordshippe of Midilton & Marden in Kent /

[f46] Robert Philpot — an annuite of xxvj s. viij d. for terme of his lif of the lordshippe of Midelton & Merdone

Robert Grene Mynstrel — x markes for terme of his lif of the feferme of Norwiche

William Erl of Huntingdone — the stewardshippe of Uske (&) Carlione Treyleke & Evyas Lacy for terme of lif

Sir Roger Kynastone Thoffices of Shirif & escheitor of Merionneth in North Wales for terme of lif

Sir Thomas ap Morgane / xl li. sterlinges by way of Reward upon the custome of Bristowe

John Hawkyns mynstrell — x markes for terme of lif of the lordshippe of Bartone of the fee ferme etc nyghe gloucestre

Sir Thomas Vaughan — Steward of Breknok for terme of lif / with the wages of xl li. to bee perceyved jde

Erl of Huntingdone & Katerine Plantaginet / an annuite of CCCC markes of the lordshippes of Newport Breknok & Hay

John Cowardyne an annuite of xx li. for terme of lif. of thonor of Tutbury

John Uptone — bailif of the franchise within the Rape of Pevensey and thonnor of the Egle for terme of lif

William Waddenow / The keping of the park of Marshfeld in the Countie of Sussex for terme of his lif

Henry Clegge the bailif of the hundred of Broxone in the countie palatyne of Chestre during his lif

James le Danoys / A merchant A saufconduit to endure viij monethes

Nicholas Lathel clerk of the pipes — xij d. by the day during his lif of the Revenues of the Shires of Bedford & Bukingham

Robert Byrnand — x markes for terme of lif of the lordshippe of Knaresburghe

Robert Wilkinsone — an annuite of xl s. of the lordshippe of Shirifhutone til he bee Recompensed etc

John Savage / an annuite of x markes during pleasure of Pevensey

Rauf Sacheverel (of) An annuite of x markes during pleasure of Pevesey

Morys Berkeley / an annuite of x markes during pleasure of Pevesey

John Thurlby sergeant at armes with xij d by the day during his lif of the duchie of Cornewaill

Robert Markyngfeld / the keping of the park of Holrig in Devoneshire during the kinges pleasure

Giles Brugge / Constable of the Castel of saint briavel for terme of lif / with an annuite of lxvj li. xiij s. iiij d. of the Revenues of the forest of deane

Christofre Wellisborn the Manoir of Esyndone in the countie of Bukingham for terme of his lif

[f46b] Geoffray Whiteford / A confirmacione of vj d. by the day for Fee of the crowne during his lif of the Revenues of Wydennessy in the countie of Lancastre / And also thoffice of parker of Bartone & Shire Old with thoffice of keper of the warde of Bertone / And also al therbage & paunage of the parkes of Bartone and Shire old

Thomas Warde the porter of the Castel of Kenelworthe keper of the parkes & wodes there for terme of his lif

Thomas Stafford / Thoffice of Constable of the castel of the Vise and Steward of Marleburgh Vise Rowde & Chippenham and of the hundred of Chippenham / And thoffice of lieutenant of the forestes of Melkesham Peuesham and Blakemore with the Stewardshippe of Corsham & parker of Ludgarsale with the maister of the game within al the countie of Wilteshire // And also thoffice of Stuward of al lordshippes of the duchie of Lancastre within the same countie / And also stieward of al the lordshippes etc in the same countie of therldome of

Warwick during the noon age etc

William Hanmer / the ward & mariage of Robert Pouleston

Robert Burtone — vj d. by the day during his lif for the fee of the crowne of the Revenues of the countie of York / Also sex poundes xiij s. iiij d. during his lif of the soke of Snayth with therbage of the park of Fyppyng within the same soke / And also thoffice of Bailif of Soke & towne of Snayth aslong as he berith hym wele

George Poleyne — The keping of the park of Crokeham in Oxonford during noone age of my lord of Warwik & an annuite of six poundes there

Hugh Lloid   a prive seal for the payment of the fee of the wode-warshippe of the counties of Caernervan & Merioneth etc

John Shilton / bailif of the towne of Rye during his lif etc

Kateryn Mountferaunt / an Annuyte of xx li. / for terme of here lyff of the Revenues of Bedford & Bukingham

Jamys Saxtone thoffice of keping of the woddes of Litille Salghalle in the Countie of Cestre for terme of lyff / with fee of j d. by day of the Revenues of the Countie of Cestre

William Barbor an Annuyte of xxvj s. viij d. (of) for terme of his liff / of the Revenues of Middeltone & Merdene

Sir Richard Ratclyff / the office of Shireff of the Countie of Westmorland for terme of his liff / with the wages etc

Sir William Petche knighte / the king hathe confirmed unto him an Annuyte of xl li. for terme of his liff (to) of the Revenues of the Countie of Kent

Richard Chomley squier the warde & mariage of Philipp Eggerton with the etc

[f47] William Hanmer squiere / the Custodie of alle the lordships landes maners etc within the Counties of Chestre & Flynt during the nonne Age of Roger

Pulstone / paieng therefore yerely as moche money as Jane late the wiff of the said Roger or any other paied etc

Cristofre Huddelstone the next rome that shalle falle voide in the kinges halle of Cambrigge for terme of liff / any promocion not exceding the yerely valew of C li notwithstanding

Thomas Strangways Thoffices of (keping of) Constable of the Castelle of Plecy & keper of the litille parke & palicer of the same for terme of liff / perceiving for the Constableship ten markes by yere / and for parker & palicer fees & wages accustumed / of the Revenues of the same lordship / and annuyte of ix li. v s. x d. / of the said lordship

Sir Thomas ap Morgan knighte / the warde & mariage of Nicholas Asshetone sone & heire of Edward Asshetone / late (of the) in the handes of Sir Robert Willoughby

William Pye the king hath confirmed Thoffices of keping of bothe parkes of Henley in Arden in the Countie of Warrwik / with thoffice of bailly of Henley for terme of liff with the fees & wages due & accustumed

Roger Holden thoffice of Colfild in the Chace of Suttone / during the nonne Age of Edward Erle of Warrwik with the wages of ij d. by day

Robert Chambre & his wiff An Annuyte of x marc (to be) for terme of theire lyves of (Annuyte of) the lordshippe of Shiptone under Whichewode in the Countie of Oxenford

John Knighte / thoffice of keper of Berwod in the Chace of Suttone in Colfeld during the nonne Age of Therle of Warrwik

Thomas Salesbury the yongere Constable of (Dy) Denby / to have xij Souldiors there / every man xij d. by day during the kinges pleasure

A warrant to the Tresorer & Chambrelains of theschequier for (to contente) the contentacion Edmund Shawe the somme of iiij^{C}xxxj li. x s. x d. parcel of DCClxiiij li. xvij s. vj d. upon the Receyvor of the ferme of fee fermes etc

John Berker / A pardone of tharrerages of xx li. & to be delivered out of prison wherin he remaineth for noon payment thereof

Laurence Duttone & Thomas Duttone / A pardone of (xlv) xlvj li & thereupon a warrant directed to the Chambrelain & auditours of the countie palatine of Chestre

John Sapcote / hath to hym & his heires masles for ever the manoir of Ipplepene with thappertenaunces in Devoneshire / and the lordshippes & manoirs of Netherham & stoke in the countie of Somerset with advousons etc by knyghtes service & the Rent of x (s) markes yerely

Edward Ratclife / the manoirs & lordshippes of Broke & Suthwik within Wiltshire to hym & his heires masles forever by knyghtes service & the Rent of vij li. x s. /

[f47b] Robert Scrop / the manoir of Southmymmes in Middlesex with thadvousons etc to hym & his heires masles forever by knyghtes service & lx s. yerely

Charles Dynham — the lordshippes & manoirs of Halwil & Torre / and all meses landes tenementes Rentes etc in combe otherwise called Illescombe in the parishe of Bykebury Langstone in the countie of Devone etc to hym & his heires masles for ever by knyghtes service & the Rent of

William Herbert The manoire & lordshippe of Tokyngtone with thappertenaunces to hym & his heires masles forever by knyghts service & the Rent of lxxv s.

Sir John Egremond / the manoir & lordshippe of Kempstone in Bedford to hym & his heires masles forever . by knyghtes service & the Rent of lx s

James Hobart an annuyte of x markes for terme of his lif of the fre farme of Ipswhiche

John Nesfeld the maner of Heytredesbury with thappurtenaunces in the Countie of Wilteshire for him and his heires masles

Laurance Savage an annuyte of vij markes vj s. viij d. of the of the landes of thabbot & Convent of our lady of (de) Dieulencres other w(a)ise called thapprowement of Rudhethe in the Counte of Chestre for terme of his lif

Richard Williams the Castelle lordship & maner of Manerbere with thappertenaunces in the counte of Pembroche in Wailles for him and his heires masles by knyghtes service

Christofer Standissh an annuyte of x markes for terme of his lif of the revenous of the Counte palatyne of Lancastre

Sir Jamys Danby Thofice of maister of the (heir) hare houndes for terme of his liff with alle belonging thereto

An acquitaunce to dame Elizabeth stokton late wiff of Garard Canysyane & to his executors for VC marc

George Mountfort an Annuyte of iiij markes during his liff of the Revenues of the lordship of Ryes in Yorkshire

(William) John Belle late Escheator of Surrey & Sussex . a pardone of alle offenses transgressions etc

Philip ap Res / the halff part of the tolle of the Towne of Knyghton in the marche of Wales for terme of his liff

Charles Pilkington / the baillieff of Mansfelde in Sherewod with the keping of the woddes of Thornewoddes & owtwoddes of Notingham in the forest of Shirewod during his liff / with the wages of vj d. by the day of the lordship or maner of Bollesover

Sir Thomas Burghe / an Annuyte of xxxvj li / during the liff of Thomas lord Stanley of the Revenues of the lordshippes of Bolyngbroke Sutton in Holand Ingolmels Thoresby Whathall Stepyng Brotelby & Wadyngton in the Countie of Lincoln

[f48] John Shut / the king hath confirmed unto him vj d. by day for the Fee of the Coronne during his liff / of the fee ferme of Colcestre Also (th) Thoffice of keping of the parke of (Hajd) Hadlegh / with the fees & wages accustumed or iij d. by day / of the said feeferme / Also the portership of the Castelle of Hadliegh in the Countie of Essex / for terme of his liff / or (his) elles iij d. by day of the said Fee ferme

Sir Charles Pilkington / Constable of the Castelle of Notingham porter of the same / Thoffice of Steward & Maister Forster of Shirewod Beskewod & Clipston & of the woddes of Billowe (Bay) Bykelond Rumwood Ouseland & Fulwood in the Countie of Notingham for terme of lyff / with the fee xl marc sterlinges of the maner or lordshippe of Bollesover in Countie Derby / And also for ix Forsters undere him / ix li. / every of theim xx s.

William Clerc / the king hath confirmed the Constableship of Castelle of Bruggenorthe in the Countie of Salop / during his lyff with the wages & fees of vj d. by day of the fee ferme of Bruggenorth

Nicholas Leventhorp / the king hathe confirmed unto him thoffice of generalle Receivor of duchie of Lancastre in alle England & Wales during the kinges pleasure with the wages accustumed etc

Richard Baldere Clerc Maistere of Berking Chappelle / the prebend of Tamworthe in the Churche of seint Edith

The lord Audeley C li. of Annuyte for terme of lyff of the Custumes of

Edward Bourtone vj d. by the day during his lif for fee of the crowne of thonor of Tutbury

Henry Hermane — Thoffice of Crowner or attorney in the kinges benche during his lif with the fees accustomed

William Dobinsone The manoir or lordshippe of Steutley Camoys in the countie of Huntingdone of the yerely valewe of vj li. xiij s. iiij d. to hym & his heires masles by knyghtes service & x s. of fre Rent

Edward Bramptone xv mesuages xviij tenementes xj cotages iiij toftes thre croftes viij gardenis v vergers of land vj acres of medow xj acres of pasture xxvj s iiij d of Rent in the towne & feldes of Northamptone the manoirs of Russhetone Oghtone great Tyvone Eginytone Arodone litel Willoughby Barton Erls Hanging Houghtone old Wynkle Wyndlyngburghe Assheby Marreys Stanwig in the said Countie late belonging to Sir Thomas Tresham knyghte / to the said Edward his heires masles by knyghtes service & chief Rent of lx s.

[f48b] The maire bailiffes & burgeys of cardif / to be incorporat and to have (a warr') certain liberties & fredoms within thaym silf

The priour & chanons of Karlil to have to thaym & thair successors forever two tonnes of Red wyn of Hull by the handes of the chief butteller of England etc for using divine observances / And also to have the tithes of the mylles of Karlil & al thinges within the Citie of Karlil tythable . And that noon officer or minister of the kinges arreste any personne within the procincte of the churche of Karlil . or . jurisdiccione of the same And also that thay may distreigne thaire owne tenauntes within the said citie (witho) orels where without any Rescue to be made by any minister of the kinges / with enioieng thair old liberties

Nicholas Leventhorp the king hathe confermed unto him thoffice of Receyvor of the Castel & lordshippe of Knaresburghe and collectoure of the fermes of the lordes landes there & proffittes & amerciamentes of Alburghe and thoffice of supervisor of (the kinges) alle the workes in the lordshippe afforesaid terme of his lyf with the fees wages proffittes & Regardes unto the same offices due & accustumed / the king hathe confermed also unto the said Nicholas thoffice of keper of the kinges artillerye within the Castel for terme of his lyf with almanere wages fees & proffittes (& commoditees) unto the same office due & apperteining The king hathe confermed also unto the said Nicholas thoffice of Receyvor of the honnor of Pountfret & of the Revenues of the same for terme of his lyf with fees wages proffittes & regardes to the same due & accustumed

Roger Hoptone the king hathe confermed unto him an annuyte of ix li. ij s. vj d. during his lyf of the ferme of the hundred of Kistisgat Holford & Greston with holding of feyres & markettes to be holden in the towne of Wynchecombe in the Countie of Gloucestre by the handes of thabbot & Convent of Wynchecombe

John taillor theldre the king hathe graunted unto him thoffice of parkre of Morelewod in the lordshippe of thornbury in Gloucestreshire during his lyf with the wages & fees of iiij d. by the day of thissues of the said lordshippe by the handes of the Receyvor there

John taillor the yonger the king hathe graunted unto him thoffice of parker of Estwode within the lordshippe of Thornebury aforesaid during his lif with the wages of iiij d. by the day of thissues of the said lordshippe by the handes of the Receyvor there

[f49] Richard Symsone the king hathe graunted unto him thoffice of his attorney of the duchie of Lancastre for theschequier during his lyf with a fee of C s. of the Revenues of the said duchie by the handes of the general Receyvor there etc

Maister Stephen fryon the king hathe directed his lettres unto the Tresourer and chambreleyns of his Eschequier for contentacione or assignement of xxxvj li. resting due unto him of the fee of his office of oone of the Secretaries by the graunt of king Edward the iiij[th] to be had of the kinges yeft in ful paiement of his said duetie

Maister William Talbot the prebende of Chute in the Churche of Sarum

Richard Garnet thoffice of Sergeant of the kinges tentes for terme of his lif withe the wages of xij d. by the day for himself . and (vj d.) iiij d. by day for a yoman undre him C s. for a house to ley the tentes in and (xxxvj s.) xlvj s. viij d. for his Robes . xiij s. iiij d. for his yomans Robes . to be taken of thissues etc of the lordships of Wrytelle Havering Boytone Hadleghe Reyleghe and Roche-forthe in the Countie of Essex . and of the lordships of Tunbrigge Penshurst Myddeltone and Merden in the Countie of Kent by the handes of the Receyvors

John Atkynsone keper of the Armoury in the Towre or elleswhere within England for terme of his lif with the fee of vj d. by the day to be perceived ut supra

John Edwardes / Constableship of the Castel of Uske in Southwales for terme of his lif with the fees and wages accustumed . And an annuytie of xl marces to be perceived by the handes of the Receivor of the said lordship of Uske etc

John Bodman an Annuytie of xl^{ti} poundes to be had of the Custumes of the poort of Bristowe unto the tyme he be promoted to office or land of gretter value

Roger Hertlingtone Thoffice of Baillif of the hundred of Colrigge withe the keping of the parke of Stokenham and the manoir of the same in Devone withe the wages of iiij d. by day for terme of his lif to be perceived of the same lordship and hundred etc

John Cotingtone / to be yomane of the Crowne with the fee of vj d. by day to be perceived during his lif of the Custumes of the poort of Bristowe

John Oter therbage of the out woodes of the lordship of Dertingtone in Devone for terme of his lif without any thing therefore paying

Sir Christofre Warde an Annuytie of xxiiij li. to be perceived for terme of his lif of the Revenues of the milnes of Burgbrig by the handes of the Receivor fermors etc

John Leventhorp yoman of the Crowne hath for his fee of the same vj d. by the day for terme of his lif of the lordship of Wrytel in the Countie of Essex

Thomas Straunge an Annuytie of xx^{ti} marces . of the lordship of Hanslap unto suche tyme as he be promoted etc

William Tankard a warraunt to the Chauncellor of the duchie to discharge him of vj li. that he ought to king Edward the iiij^th for the ferme of Burghbrigge mylles

[f49b] Nicholas Gardyner thexecutor of John Gardener / hathe licence to (mortize) founde a Chauntery in our lady Church of Lancastre and to mortize xij li. of land therto for the fynding of a prest to syng there forever

Morgan Kydwelly / the Stewardship aswele of al the lordships and maners of the duchie of Lancastre in the Countie of Dorset / as of alle othre lordships in the said Countie to the king belonging with the wages and fees accustumed for terme of his lif

Robert Worthingtone thoffice of Cirograph in the Common benche for terme of his lif with the wages and fees accustumed

Sir Laurence Raynford and (Est) Ector his son the parkership of Wykes with the Stewardship and baillifship of Wykes for terme of theire lifes and to the longer lyvere with the wages (of) accustumed and to the said Ector an Annuytie of xx li. of the said lordship of Wikes during his lif

Robert Dupliche a warraunt to the Tresourere and Chambrelains of theschequier to pay unto him C marc of the kinges yeft

Sir Robert Fenes xl li. for terme of his lif of suche money as Thabbot and Convent of Saint Edmondes Bury owe to pay to the king yerely

Humfrey lord of Dacre and of Gyllesland an Annuytie of C marcs during his lif of the Revenues of Cumbreland

John Kighley the Constableship of Okehamptone in Devone and maister Forster and of the game within the parke and chace of the said lordship for terme of his lif with the fee of xx li. of the same lordship

John Broughtone an Annuyte of x li. of the lordship of Mydelham for terme of his lif

Richard Quadring the Baillifship of Totehille in Lincolneshire during the kinges pleasure with the wages of ij d. by day to be perceived of the said lordship and also an Annuytie of C s. during his lif of the said lordship

Andrewe Leke the Baillifship of Framtone Bykker and Bostone in Lincolneshire during the kinges pleasure with the wages of iiij d. by the day of the said
lordships and an Annuytie of C s. during his lif of the said lordships

Maister William Lacy / Clerc of Counsaille during the kinges pleasire with the
wages of xl^{ti} marces of the Revenues of the manoire of Bradwel in Essex

Sir Cristofre Warde . maistership of herthoundes for terme of his lif with the
wages of xij d. by day (by) for himself . the wages of vij d.ob. by day for a
servaunt in the said Office and viij d. by day for ij yomene Ryders in the (Ry)
said Office iiij d. by day for ij (gromes) yomen veantrers viij d. by day for iiij
(gromes) yomen on fote vj d. by day for iiij gromes vj d.ob. for the keping and
expenses of ij horses in the same Office iij s. iij d. for the mete of xl dogges
and xij grehoundes & iij d. by day for iij lerners for terme of his lif of the Revenues of the manore of Trottone in Sussex of the manoire of Bolbrok in the same
Countie . the manoire of Blecchinglee in Surrey the manoirs of Worplesdone &
Wytley in Surrey the lordships of Est Wardelham and West Wardelham in the
Countie of Suthampton

[f50] Sir Cristofre Warde Receyvor of the lordships of Trattone in Sussex of
Wardelham in the Countie of Suthampton of Blecchinleghe in Surrey of
Wropesdone in the said Countie of Wytley in the same Countie of the lordships
of Asshehurst and Bolbroke in Sussex for terme of his lif withe the fees & (wag)
wages accustumed / and also the keping of Trattone and Wardelham forsaid /
with the parkes wareyn of Conyes and wodes with al thappurtenaunces to the
same belonging for terme of his lif without anything therefore yelding

Jaques Hawte the manoire of Mote in the parisshe of Ightham zele Sheborne
and Wrotham to the value of viij li. xiij s. iiij d. & a tenement called Chaltnesse
in the parisshe of Ightham and Wrotham iiij li. and the manoirs or lordships of
Hastingly and Alvelose in the parisshe of Hastinglye and Braborne xij li. xiij s.
iiij d. in Kent To have and hold to the same Jaques to him and to his heirs
masles forever by knightes service and the Rent of xl s. to the king

The lord Scrop of Boltone the manoire of Martok in the Countie of Somerset
the manoir of Bovytracy in Devone . the manoire of Trewynne in Cornewaille .
landes and tenementes in Esternayne in Cornewaille to the value of CCvj li. xj s.
viij d. to him and to his heires masles by knightes service and by Rent of xv li.
x s. And the same lord Scrop an Annuytie of CC marces by the handes of John
Hayes of the Revenues of his Office . for the Office of Constable of the Castelle
of Excestre and the Steward of alle the lordships landes and tenementes
belonging to the said Castelle And to the same lord an Annuytie of Cxxvj li.
xviij s. iiij d. by the handes of the said John Hayes unto the tyme he be
promoted

150

Benet Medeley hathe confermed unto him Thoffice of Baillif of the lordship of Yelverstoft in the Countie of Northhamptone during the nonnage of therle of Warrewik or aslong etc

A warrant to John Hayes to content yerely to Elizabeth Dabeney xl li. during hir lif of his Recept

John Whartone / the Constableship of Becheworthe the Stewardship of Blecchingleghe with the keping of the manoir there and maister Forster of the parkes of the said lordship for terme of his lif with the wages of x li. to be perceived of the lordship of Becheworthe by the handes of the Receyvor etc

Edward Waltone the parkershippe of the South parke of Blecchingleghe for terme of his lif withe the wages of iiij d. by the day (f) to be perceived of the said lordshippe

Thomas Whartone porter of the Castelle of Becheworthe withe the wages of iiij d. by the day for terme of his lif to be perceived during his lif of thissues of the said lordshippe

John Waltone / Baillief of Blecchingleghe for terme of his lif with the wages of iiij d. by the day to be perceived of the said lordship

William Waltone parker of the northparke of Blecchingleghe for terme of his lif withe the wages of iiij d. by the day to be perceived of thissues of the said lordshippe

[f50b] Thomas Baker certain landes and tenementes lying in the Towne of Wellys in the Countie of Somerset late longing to John Saintlowe knighte to the value of vij li. xiij s. iiij d. for terme of his lif without any thing therefore paying

Nicholas Banaster the Baillif of the lordship of Walthambury and keping of the parke of Lytley within the Countie of Essex with the wages of iiij d. by the day & an Annuytie of v marces for terme of his lif of the Revenues of the said lordshippe

Richard Conyers Squier an Annuytie of xxvj li. xiij s. iiij d. to be perceived of the Revenues of the lordship of Barnard Castelle unto the tyme he be promoted etc

William Erle of Notingham ij^Clxvj li. xiij s. iiij d. to be perceived yerely from the fest of Mighelmasse last past during his lif of the Custumes of wolle lether and Shepe skynnes in the port of Londone . provyded alwey that if Elizabeth duchesse of Norffolk dye the said Erle lyving than the said graunt from the dethe of the said duchesse stand voyde etc

John Abelle the manoire or lordship of Hawkystone with thappurtenaunces in the Countie of Cantebrige for terme of his lif of the value of vij li.

Thomas Pontesbury alle landes and tenementes withe thappurtenaunces that was Anthony Wydeviles Erle Ryvers within the Towne and marches of Calais of the yerely value of xxvj li. vj s. viij d. ob. to him and to his heires masles by knightes service and the Rent of xxx s. yerely at the festes of pasche & mighelmas by even porcions

John Fitzherbert Receyvor generalle of alle fee fermes and sommes undre-writen that it to say l li. of the Fee ferme of Bristowe / xx li. / of the fee ferme of Bedford Cv marc of the ferme of Cantebrige x li. of the keping of the sises of brede and ale there / xv li. of the (fee) ferme of Radwel in Essex xij li. of the ferme of the hundred of Dodestone in Gloucestreshire / xl li. of the fee ferme of the manoire of Bartone (and the) iuxta Gloucestre xxxviij li. of the ferme of the hundred of Kestesgate Holford and Graftone with feires and markettes holden in the towne of Winchecombe in Gloucestreshire iij^xx li. of the ferme of Bertone Bristowe xliiij li. of the ferme of Hareford xij li. of the fee ferme of Rouchestre x li. of the manoirs and lordships of Huntingfeld xxxvj li of the Rentes of the Castelle of Rouchestre xv li. of the ferme of the manoire of Fal-wesley in the Countie of Northamptone xx li of the ferme of certaine landes and tenementes in Watford liiij li. of the ferme of Notingham lviij li. v s. of the fee ferme of Norwiche iij^xxli. of the ferme of Gyppyne ix li. xvj s. ix d. of the sur-plesaige of the manoire of Lowestoft and the hundred of Luddingland xx li. and of mylnes and of the kinges medowe iuxta Oxonford x li. of the manoire of God-ingtone in the Counties of Oxonford and Bukingham xl li. of the manoire of Hed-ingtone (w) iuxta Oxonford x li. vj s. viij d. of the fee ferme of Rowley in the Countie of Stafford ix li. of the keping of the manoire of Kynfare and Stortone viij li. of the manoire of Wrokworden in the Countie of [f51] Salop xij li. of the manoire of Forde xlvj li. of the ferme of Suthampton xx li. of the fee ferme of Dorchestre xij li. of the keping of Shaftesbury xij li. of the ferme of Kyngtone in the Countie of Warrwik C s. of the ferme of the Wapentak of Goscote in Leicestreshire Cxvj s. of the ferme of half the Towne of Tamworthe xij li. xviij s. v d. ob. of the fee ferme of the hundred of Framland in the Countie of Leicestre and (of othre that was John Hastinges late Erle) Cx s. of the fee ferme of the honnor of Peverel Borion and Hagonet with the membres in the Counties of Bukingham Northampton and Leycestre and of othre lordships that was John Hastinges Erle of Pembroke to have the same with xx li. fee of the ferme of the same during the kinges pleasire

Raynold Yong thoffice of purveyer of stone lede and other thinges necessary and for cariages of the same at our manoire of Childerne Langley and the logge within the parke with the pale of the same for terme of his lif with the wages of iiij d. by the day to be perceived of the lordships of Writtel Haveryng Boytone Hadleghe Rayleghe and Racheford in Essex and of the manoirs of Tunbrige Penshurst Myddeltone and Merden in Kent

Richard Merley the keping of the parke of Bechewethe with the fee of iiij d. by the day for terme of his lif to be perceived of the same lordship etc

John Crochard the maister Smythe within the Towre of Londone for terme of his lif with viij d. by the day of the lordships of Wrytelle Havering etc ut supra

Thomas Hilles an Annuytie of iiij markes during the nonneage of therle of Warrewik of the Revenues of Caversham in the Countie of Oxonford by the handes etc

John Cotingtone a warrant to thauditors of the Forest of Deane and to the Receivor there to pay to him al suche sommes of money as he is behinde for the parkership of Whitemede from the vj day of April last past unto the date of his (pay) patente after the rate of iiij d. by the day

Edward Vicount Lisle the manoire or lordship of Asteley to the value of xliiij li x s. the manoire or lordship of Bentley Bostus of the yerely of lxvj li. viij d. the manoire of Emeryes to the value of C s. ij d. the manoirs of Wydingtone and Higham to the value of xxiij li. vij s. ij d. in the Countie of Warrwik & Leicestre to him and his heires masles by knightes service and the Rent of vj li. vij s.

To the maister and brethren of thospitalle of Dover called Meyson due certain landes lying in the Isle of Thenet in the parisshe of Birchingtone and Monketone called denne of the value of xxxiij s. iiij d. and a certaine pasture called Archerscourt to the value of xxvj s. viij d. in the parisshe of Ryvers iuxta Dover late longing to Sir George Browne (for) geven to them forever in pure and perpetuel Almoux

James Stokdale the keping of the parke of Bagshote within the forest of Windesore for terme of his lif withe the wages of iiij d.ob. by the day of the ferme of a tenement called the Corowne in Bagshote

[f51b] Sir Cristofre Warde the lieutenantship and Rangership of the Forest of Wolmer and maister of the game of Alice Holt withe the keping of the manoire and parke of Wardelham for terme of his lif with the fee of xx li. vj s. viij d. of

the Revenues of the lordship of Wardelham by the handes of the Receivor etc

The same Sir Cristofor the manoire or lordship of Dadesham in Sussex to the yerely value of xvj li. the manoire of Alkesborne in Essex to the value of iiij li. to him and his heires masles by knightes service and the Rent of xxx s.

The king hathe confermed to therle Douglas v^C li. yerely from the fest of Mighelmasse last past during his lif to be perceived of diverse poortes etc

William Pocche Thoffice of keper of the litil Warderobe in the Towre of Londone for terme of his lif withe the wages of vj d. by the day for himself and vj d. for ij gromes undre him of the Revenues of the (w) lordships of Wrytelle Havering Boytone Hadleghe Raleghe and Racheford in Essex and of Tunbrigge Penshurst Middeltone and Merdene in Kent

John Huddlestone Squier Thoffices of Steward and Baillif of Sudeley withe the keping of the parke and Constable of the Castelle with therbage and pawnage for terme of his lif with the wages of x li. of the Revenues of the said lordship by his owne handes and paying for the said herbage and pawnage v li.

The same John Huddlestone thoffices of Constable and porter of Monnemouthe with the Stewardship of the same for terme of his lif with the wages (of) due and accustumed and a C marc of Annuytie of the said lordship

Waltier Forde an Annuytie of xx li. for terme of his lif of the Revenues of the Countie of Suthampton by the handes of the Shiref etc

Jamys Whitfelde / the keping of the (parke) were called Hornewere within your Ryver of (Ty) Th(y)amys in the parisshe of olde Wyndesore in the Countie of Berkeshire / for terme of his liff without any thing therefore yelding or paieng

Symond Dowsying / thoffice of keping of the Gardynges within the Toure of London for terme of his liff / with the wages of vj d. by day of thissues & Revenues of Wrotelle Havering Boytone Hadlegh Raylegh & Rochefford in Essex / and of Tunnbrigge Penhurst Myddelton & Marden in Kent etc

Thomas Kynaston squier an Annuyte of xl marc for terme of his liff of the Commote of Penllyne in the Countie of Merioneth by the handes of the Ringler of the same

154

William Griffithe the king hathe confermed unto him an Annuytie of xxvj li. xiij s. iiij d. for terme of his lif of the fee ferme of Monnemouthe

[f52] The maire and felauship of the merchantes of the Staple of Calais have a privie seale directed to the Custumers Comptrollers and Weyers of the poort of Bostone to allowe unto the said maire and merchauntes and to every of theim awners of every sak of wolle ij nayles etc

A like warrant directed for the said maire and felisship to the Custumers Comptrollers and Weyers of Yeppeswiche

John Stok Thoffice of Clerc of thordenaunce within England or elleswhere for terme of his lif with the wages of vj d. by the day to be perceived of the lordships of Wrytelle Havering Boytone Hadleghe Rayleghe and Rocheford in Essex and of the manoirs of Tunbrigge Penhurst Middeltone and Merden in Kent etc

John Leventhorp Squier an Annuytie of x li. (for terme of his lif) during the nonneage of Edward Erle of Warewik confermed unto him by the king upon a graunt made unto the said John by king Edward the iiijth of the said Annuytie (of) to be perceived of the Revenues of the lordship of Northwylde in Essex

The prioresse and Convent of Saint Mary of (puy) Pray besides saint Albans (hathe) have confermed unto theim theire graunt of a faire in the fest of the nativytie of our lady

To Richard Barbor a close next adioynyng to (your) the pasture called the lefeld within the lordship of Warrewik during the nonne age of Edward Erle of Warrewik without any thing or accompt making etc

The pryor and Convent of the Frere prechours of Cambrige xxv marc yerely out of theschequier during the kinges pleasire by the handes of the Tresourer etc

Herry Grey the yonger Squier the king hathe confermed unto him Thoffice of the keping of the Armoury within the towre of Londone for terme of his lif withe the wages and fees accustumed to be perceived of the fee ferme of Norwiche

Richard Tylles thoffice of Comptrollere of Werkes during the kinges pleasire with the wages of xij d. by the day for himself and vj d. for his Clerc of the Revenues of Cambrige and Huntingdone

Sir Rauf Asshetone knighte a tonne of wyne yerely during his lif to be had frely of the kinges yeft in Londone by the handes of the chief Botillere of England

John duc of Norffolk maister Forster in alle forestes chaces parkes warennes maners of Desenyng and Hemgrave and of of al othre manoirs landes and tenementes and fisshinges that late was the duc of Bukingham for terme of his lif with the wages accustumed

To the maistre and brethren of Trynitie Gylde of Cheping Nortone a mese and certain landes to the value of xl s. within the Towne of Grete in the lordship of Sudeley forever

Robert Gryme hathe a lettre missive to Richard Pole for to content unto him xlj li. that the Bisshop of Ely toke from him

[f52b] David Goghe of Melleinth the king hathe confermed unto him the Office of Constable of the Castelle of Radnore in the marches of Wales during the kinges pleasire with the fee of x li. and also an Annuytie of C s. to be perceived of the lordship of Elvelle

Sir Roger Kenastone hathe a warraunt to the Chambrelain of North Wales to content unto him the wages of iij^{xx} souldiors after the Rate of iiij d. by the day during the kinges pleasire to be within the Castelle of Hardlaghe

Miles Child to bee oone of the foure messagers in the kinges eschequier for terme of his lif with the wages of iiij d. ob. by the day to bee payed in the Recept by the handes of the Tresourer & Chambrelains etc

William Tyler to be oone of the four messagers in theschequier for terme of his lif with the wages of iiij d. ob. by the day

Sir Roger Kenaston knyghte An annuitie of xl markes during his lif of the Comote of Arduduy in the countie of Merionethe in North Wales

Thomas Woltone Thoffice of Escheator in the Countie of Chestre & attourney in the Countie of Chestre & Flynt for terme of his lif with the wages & fees accustomed

Thomas Redehede Thoffice of porter of the Towre of Londone and keper of the Bulwerk without the West yate of the same towre for terme of his lif with the wages of vj d. by the day of the Revenues of the lordshippes of Writel Haveryng Boytone Hadleghe Rayleghe Rocheford in the Countie of Essex and of the lordshippes of Tonbrige Penshurst Mideltone & Mardene in Kent

John Taillor the manoir or lordshippe of Doddescot & Doddescote more in the Countie of Devone to the value of (x) xviij li. to hym & his heires masles by knyghtes service & the Rent of Cxiij s. iiij d.

William Sadler of Ledes the keping of the manoir of Wokesey with the keping of the park & wodes there for terme of his lif with the wages & fees accustomed And an annuite of xl s. for terme of his lif to be perceyved of the lordshippe of Wokesey

Richard Revel . the keping of the park of Shothil in the countie of Derby with the wages & fees accustomed And annuite of x markes of the lordshippe of Tutbury for terme of his lif

Theobald Ferrount Gonner / an annuite of xij li. for terme of his lif of the Revenues of the lordshippes of Wrotehil Haveryng Boytone Hadlegh Raylegh & Rocheford in Essex and of Tunbrige Penshurst Mideltone & Mardene in Kent

William Tempill . thoffice of yeoman of thordinance for terme of his lif with the wages of vj d. by the day to be perceyved of the lordshippes of Wrotell Haveryng Boyton ut supra

Patrik dela Moyte gonner Thoffice of Maister Gonner within the Towre of Londone for terme of his lif with the wages of xviij d. by the day for hym & xij d. by the day for two mene undre hym to bee perceyved of the lordshippes of Wrotell Haveryng Boytone ut supra

[f53] Richard Tayllor landes and tenementes called Clyste Barnefeldes in Devone to the value of x li. to him and to his heires masles by knightes service and the Rent of xv s.

Robert Downe an Annuytie of xxvj s. viij d. to be perceived of the lordships of Middeltone and Merden in Kent during his lif

William Glasiere an Annuytie of xxvj s. viij d. to be perceived during his lif of the same lordships

Robert Mannyng Thoffice of purveyor of al werkemen and of Stuf for the kinges werkes within the palois of Westmynster and the Toure of Londone for terme of his lif with the wages of x d. by the day to be perceived of the fee ferme of the Towne of Portesmouthe

Garter king of Armes and othre (war) heraulds have a warrant directed to the Clerc of the hanaper to delyver unto theim lettres patentes of certaine grauntes to theim made by the king without fyne or fee therefore paying

Anthony Lupyane Surgeone C s. of Annuytie for terme of his lif of the Revenues of the lordships of Wrytelle Haveryng Boytone etc Ut antea

Thomas Fowler and Alice his wif the king hathe confermed unto them an Annuytie of x li. for terme of theire lyves to be taken of the fee ferme of Kyngesthorp in the Countie of Northamptone and hathe graunted unto the said Thomas after hir decesse the said Annuytie of x li. during his lif

John Brechold seriaunt plommer in the Towre of Londone Westminster Eltham and Shene for terme of his lif with the wages of xij d by the day to be perceived of the (the) lordships of Wrytelle Havering Boytone etc Ut antea

Thomas Fowler and Alice his wif the manoir of (Walv) Wavenden in the Countie of Bukingham to theim and eithre of theim lenger lyving without any thing paying etc

The same Thomas Fowlere the Manoire of Prestone with thappurtenaunces in the Countie of Bukingham and vj mesuages ij^C Acres of lande v^C acres of pasture and xx s. Rent in Prestone and Coveley in the said Countie to him and to his heires masles by the service of old tyme accustumed

William Josephe the keping of the parke of Hathynden in Kent withe the wages and fees accustumed for terme of his lif

William Stokes the Baillifship of Savoy in the Suburbes of Londone for terme of his lif with the wages of ij d. by the day in as ample maner and forme as any othre herebifore had or perceived

John Brakenbury an Annuytie of v marces to be perceived of the lordship of Sherief Hotone for terme of his lif

158

Thomas Fowler Thoffice of Steward of the Townes and lordships of Bukingham Hakmersham and Birkhille (and) for terme of his lif with the fees and wages accustumed

Thomas Grayson the manoire and lordship of Landhilp othrewise called Landylik in Cornewaylle and the manoire or lordship of Lyderant in the same Countie to the value of xx li. to the same Thomas (& his he) for terme of his lif by knightes service and the Rent of xxx s.

[f53b] Thomas Fowler thoffices of Steward of the lordships of Calvertone Whitchurche and Stonystratford for terme of his lif with the wages accustumed

The dean of York Thomas Portingtone & William residentes there and John Hert Clerc have a pardone that they shal pay noo x^{me}nor xvme during theire lifes

Thomas Wentworthe the Constableship of Quynnesburghe for terme of his lif with the wages of xx^{ti} marc to be perceived of the Revenues of Thisle of Shepey by the handes of the Receyvor etc

Thomas Mountford Squier an Annuytie of x li. to be taken yerely during his lif of the Revenues of the lordship of Roclyf by the handes of the Receyvor or grave of the same

the lady of Oxonford a C li. to be had & perceived during the lif of the said Erle of Oxonford that is to saye xl li. of the Custumes of Londone xl li. of the Custumes of Sandewiche xx li. of the Custumes of Pole

John Grey Wyltone the maister of the kinges hawkes and the keping of a place called the mewes nere Charingcrosse in Middlesex for terme of his lif with the fee of C marc for himself and the wages of xx li. for a gentilman sergeant in the said Office and the wages of viij marc for ij yomen in the same Office and for the borde of the same yomen ij s. viij d. every weke / and the wages of xij li. for vj gromes in the said Office and for theire borde every weke viij s. and the wages of iiij marc for ij pages in the same Office and for their borde every weke ij s. iiij d. and x marc for theire lyvere ij tymes a yere and for xviij hawkes every of theim j d. by day for theire mete and for iiij houndes iiij d. by the day to be had(d) & perceived of the Revenues of the lordships of Chesham and Whit-churche in the Countie of Bukingham and of the Castel and manoire of Bukingham of the manoire and lordship of Agmondesham for terme of his lif

Thomas Metcalf the manoir of Wymyngtone in the Countie of Northampton to the value of lxvj li. xiij s. iiij d. to him and to his heires masles by knightes service and the Rent of C s.

John Norman the king hathe confermed unto him to be oon of the iiij messyngers (for) of theschequier for terme of his lif with the fee of iiij d. ob. by the day to be perceived by the handes of the Tresourere and Chambrelains

William Boltone kepar of the parke of Sonnynghille for terme of his lif with the wages of iiij d. by the day of the Revenues of the Castel of Windesore

John Fernelee yoman of the Crowne an Annuytie of ix li. ij s. vj d for terme of his lif of the Countie palatyne of Lancastre

Waltier Amadas the king hathe graunted unto him the Custumes (of) and subsidies of clothe and othre merchandises within the poortes of Excestre and Dertmouthe and the Cokes to them apperteynyng unto the somme of lxx li sterlinges by (h) kyng Edward the iiijth due to him/ be content and payed

[f54] To John Coringtone the manoire of Calelond and thadvouson of the Churche of Saint Sampson in Cornewaille to the value of xviij li. to him and to his heires forever by the service due and accustumed

William Sandford Thoffice of Baillif of Trowbrigge withe the keping of the wareyn there for terme of his lif withe the fees and wages accustumed and an Annuytie of C s. to be perceived of the said lordship by the handes of the Receyvor etc

A warrant to the Chambrelain of Chestre to make the kinges lettres patentes to the Citezens and theire Successors of Chestre for theire discharge of the payment of lxxiij li. x s. j d.ob. yerely during the terme of x yeres after the date herof parcelle of Ciij li. x s. j d.ob. whiche they stande charged to pay to the king yerely for theire fee ferme and Custume Rent Chambre Rent langable Rent (and) etc and nowe during the said x yere to pay but xxx li. Apud Westminsterium iij^{tio} die marcij Anno primo

Edmond Graveley thoffice of chief Carpentere of the kinges (k) werkes within the palais of Westminster the Towre of Londone and elleswhere within England with the wages of xij d. by day during his lif of the Revenues of the lordships of Writtelle Haveryng Boytone etc

Glando Pyroo an Annuytie of ix li. ij s. vj d. for terme of his lif of the Revenues of the said lordships of Writtelle etc

Katheryn Holt wydowe and Richard Botiller a croft conteynyng Dv acre of land iiij^{xx} acres of Arrible land iij^{xx} acres of pasture x acres of mede and x s. of Rent with thappurtenaunces in Kyngesnortone called Fermons in the Countie of Worcestre late James Erle of Wilteshire and than of Waltier Mathewe by the graunt of king Edward the iiij th To have and hold the same to the said Kateryn and Richard from the dethe of the said Waltier for terme of theire lifes and of eithre of theim lenger lyving without any thing or accompt etc

William Nele Gonner an Annuytie of vj d. by the day for terme of his lif of thissues etc of Writtelle Havering Boytone etc Ut supra

Piers Saint Abyne the Bailliship of the lordship of Abwartone Tiernay and Those in Cornewaille for terme of his lif with iiij d. by the day to be perceived of the said lordshippe

Sir James Tyrelle thoffice of Steward of the lordships of Lanemtherry Lanthoes-ant Newport Wenloke and (Koiv) Kevoethmeredith in Wales & the marches for terme of his lif withe the wages fees proffites etc accustumed and to make Officers in the said Offices undre him

Peter Saintabyne the manere of Trenay in the parisshe of Saint Nyet in Cornewail of therely value of xxiij li. xiij s. iiij d. to him and his heires masles by knightes service and the Rent of xviij s.

A warrant to the Custumers Countrollers and Weyors in the porte of Hull that nowe bein or hereafter shalbe to allowe unto the maire and merchauntes of the staple and to every owner of the same ij nayles of wolle in every sak wighte without any custome or subsidie

[f54b] John Strangways Squiere the king hathe confermed unto him an Annuytie of xx li. during his lif of thissues & Revenues of Pykring and Pykeringlithe by the handes of the Receivor etc

William Kelley hathe confermed unto him thoffice of chief plummer within the Castelle of Windesore during his lif withe the wages and fees accustumed to be perceived yerely of thissues of the said Castelle by the handes of the Constable or his deputie there for the tyme being

Thomas Lynome the manoire of Colmeworthe in the Countie of Bedford of the value of xxxiiij li. xij s. iiij d. to him and his heires masles by knightes service and the Rent of l s

John Walkere an Annuytie of xx^ti marc during his lif of the Custumes of the poort of Suthampton and othre Crekes to the same lying by the handes of the Custumers

John Hille Thoffices of Warennere and keper of the wodes within the lordship of Kyrtlingtone for terme of his lif with the wages and fees accustumed and an Annuytie of xl s. of thissues of the said lordship by the handes of the Receivor

Thomas Mauncelle Squier an Annuytie or Annuelle Rent of x li. during his lif of thissues of the manoire or lordship of Aldeborne in the Countie of Wilteshire by the handes of the Receivor etc

Thinhabitauntes of the lordship of Brekenok in Wales and of the grete Forest there have a licence to have fre entre & outgoing with theire Catelles cariages goodes and other merchandises thrughout the Forest of Devynnok without any interrupccione or any thing therefore paying forevermore

Vincent Tentler Armourere the king hathe confermed unto him to be his Armourere during his lif with xx^ti li. fee by the handes of the Tresourere and Chambrelains of theschequiere

John lord Dynham the Stewardship of the Burghe and manoire of (Bradnigh) Bradnynthe & of al other landes and tenementes in Devone parcel of the duchie of Cornewaille and the keping of al tynne pyttes withe the fee of xx li. to be taken of the Revenues of the Burghe and manoire of Bardnynche

The same lord Dynham Thoffice of Ryder and maisterforster of the forest of Dertmore with the fee of x marc of the (lordship) duchie of Cornewaille during the kinges pleasire

Sir Thomas Thwaytes a C li. yerely from the vj th day of August last past unto the somme of CClxxiij li. x s. be fully content unto him of the Revenues of the Towne and marches of Calais

Sir Thomas Wortley the manoire or lordship of Mawdeley in the Countie of Stafford to the value of of xlij li. the manoire or lordship of Shobeholt and Bankers in Kent to the value of xl li. to him and his heires masles by knightes service and the Rent of viij li.

162

[f55] The lord Powes an Annuytie of C li of the lordships of (Uske) Mountgomery Kery and Kedeweyne in the marches of Wales during his lif

John lord Dudley the Stewardship of our Forest of Kynfare in the Countie of Stafford and of the manoire of Stourtone and Kynfare in the said Countie and the Raungership of the kinges haies of Chaspel Ivereley and Asshewode . and the bailliship of Chaspelle and Ivereley forsaid for terme of his lif withe (the wages of) wayfes strayses etc and herbage and pawnage yelding to the king for the forsaid waters diches etc xiij s. iiij d. to the eschequiere (w) And with the wages and Rewardes accustumed to the said Offices and every of theim

John Dightone the Bailliship of Aytone in the Countie of Stafford during his lif withe the wages accustumed

Herry Crokehille the Bailliship of Blomhille and Dorlastone in the Countie of Stafford during his lif with the wages and fees accustumed

Rauf Bukland and John Langley to take for to pay theire fynaunce the somme of xl li. of the Custumes in the poortes of Excestre and Dertmouthe

Sir Thomas Wortley knighte Constable of the Castelle of Stafford Steward of alle lordships landes & tenementes late longing to the duc of Bukingham and maister of the game of al chaces forestes woodes parkes and al othre places within the said Countie late longing to the said duc for terme of his lif withe the fee of C li.

John Benet of Londone a pardone general

Sir Thomas Wortley Steward of the lordship of Scaresdale and of the Towne of Chesterfeld in the Countie of Derby for terme of his lif withe the wages and fees accustumed

William Bayldone the keper or baillif of the manoire of Stafford for terme of his lif with the wages and fees accustumed

Christofre Wandesford an Annuytie of x li. to be taken during his lif of the Revenues of the Castel & lordship of Pykringlithe

Robert Broune hathe a prive seale directed to the chieff Justice of the kinges Benche & other his felowes / to surceasse of making out of any processe ayenst him / for a fyne levied ayenst him / for a frae made by him upon John Hawkyns of London draper

Richard Pok / the baillieffship of Epworthe and belton within the Isle of Axholme in the Countie of Lincolne & keping of the Garden there / and Storere and apprower aswele of Therbage & paunage of your parkes within the lordshippes of Epworthe as of Watters & other (Ryvers) Revenues of the said lordshippe for terme of his liff / with the wages to the said offices of baillieff & keping of the Gardyne / Fees & wages accustumed / and for approwere xl s. by yere of the Revenues of the said lordship

Sir Rauff Hastinges knighte an Annuyte of xl li. during the kinges pleasure of the Revenues of the Towne & marches of Calais

[f55b] Sir Humfrey Talbot knighte / hathe confirmed unto him an Annuyte of xl li. / of the Revenues of the lordshippes of Blakmer & Whitchurche in the Countie of Salop during the nonne Age of George Erle of Salop And also hathe confirmed unto him / a house with thappurtenaunces within the Towne of Calais whilk Sir John Scot late dwelled in during the nonne Age of Edward Erle of Warrwik

Thomas Belle / the keping of the parke of Stafford for terme of his lyff with the wages & fees accustumed

Robert Wortley the bailly of Stafford Grene within the Countie of Stafford For terme of his liff / with the wages & Fees due & accustumed

Sir Edmond Shaa / a warrant directed to the Tresorer & Chambreleyns of theschequier to deliver severelle tailles to the said Sir Edmond for the Contentacion of CCCC marc by him to the king lent to be levied of the first & secunde half of a disme / to the king in the province of Canterbury in the Archdeaconries of Norwiche & Norffolk / etc

Thomas Sayville / Thoffice of keper of the manoire of Epworthe within your Isle of Axholme in the (your) Countie of Lincolne for terme of his lif with the wages and fees of xl s. yerely of the Revenues of the lordship of Epworthe by the handes of the Receyvor etc

A saufconduyt to John Petelle / William Caen Johan de Lannoy Oliver le Beuf & Gaufryde Petel merchauntes of Britaigne theire factors and attorneys to come into England or any othre place of the kinges obeissaunce with a ship of Britaigne of the portaige of xxxiiij (li) tonnes or undre laden withe gascoigne wyne or any othre wynes goodes and merchandises laufulle and a maister xv maryners & a page for the saufguyding of theire said Ship . and the same ship at theire pleasire to recharge with almanere merchandise in England to the staple of Calais not apperteynyng and to departe with the same to any outward parties provyded alway that the king be payed of his Custumes and that the said Bretaignes hurt not the kinges liege people by (reason) color of the said sauf conduyt

A proteccione Royal to Jevan ap Tudre ap Owyne for the terme of vij yeres

William Carlisle the king hathe confermed unto him thoffice of Baillief of the lordship of Flamstede withe the wages and fees accustumed . with thoffice of Collector of alle issues and proffites of the lordship of Flamstede with the wages and fees to the said office Accustumed and also an Annuytie of six marces of thissues of the same lordship during the nonneage of Edward Erle of Warwick by the handes of the Receivor etc

George Longvile & John Kendale (the keping) the keping of a Rent owing to the Castelle of Northampton at the Fest of pasche of the (ferme) Fee of Chokes in the Counties of Northampton Bedford Bukingham Lincoln & Leicestre / that is to say of every fee x s. and the prise . in the Towne of Northampton belonging to the Constable of the said Castelle and therbage within the said Castelle & without in the Dykes & a medow belonging to **[f56]** the same Castelle / to have to the same John & George fro Michilmesse last past during vij yeres / paieng yerely therefore xj li / and the keping of the honnor of Peverelle Bonone & Hagenet in the Countie of Bukingham Northampton & Leicestre & of the Castelle & honor of Huntyngdon with the membris in the countie of Huntingdon & in the Countie of Cantebrig Bedford Bukingham & Northampton that was John Hastinges late Erle of Pembroke / to have to theim from the said Fest / during the terme of vij yeres yelding to the king yerely by the said space Cx s (atte) at the fests of Estre and Mighelmasse by even porcions

A generalle pardone (V) to William Cruse

Richard Boyvile Squier the king hathe confermed unto him an Annuytie of xx li during the nonneage of Edward Erle of Warrwik of thissues & Revenues of the lordships of Prestone and Uppyngham

James Aker of Holand Borne made denizine

John Coke Thoffice of Baillif of the hundred of Edusbury within the Countie of Chestre for terme of his lif with almaner issues proffites etc without any accompt or other thing etc.

Sir Thomas Burghe the king hathe confermed unto him xl li yerely of the money commyng of the fermes Rentes and Revenues of the honor and lordship of Bolingbroke in the Countie of Lincolne parcel of the duchie of Lancastre / by the handes of the Receyvor Fermors Collectors etc for terme of his lif

Thomas Arundel lord Matravers iij^C marces for terme of his lif that is to say a C marces of the Custumes of Suthampton and CC marces of the subsidie called Tonnage and poundage that is to wite iij s of the tonne and xij d of the pound / in the port of Londone by the handes of the Custumers Collectors etc

A generall pardone to Richard Potter

A generalle pardone to Richard Fisher

Thomas Swayne oon of the felawes within the kinges halle (for t) in Cambrige during his lif

Thomas Sayvile Squier therbage and pawnage of the newe parke of Wakefeld to the value of xij li for terme of his lif without any accompt etc

William Foulshurst thoffice of keping of the woodes called bubney Tystoke Burghalle Alyington asshewoodes and Glasmorehayes within the lordship of Whitchurche in your Countie of Salop during the nonneage of (Edwa) George Erle of Salop with the wages and fees accustumed & with al other profites etc

William Boltone thoffice of oon of the Foresters of the Forest of Wyndesore othrewise called the Ryding forster fro the (Vj) xxvj day of June last past during his lif with iij d by the day of thissues of the Castelle of Wyndesore

John Molle thoffice of keping of the manoire of Penshurst of the parc there called Asshore and Redelef / and Bailyf of the lordship of Penshurst

John lord Audeley an Annuytie of C li for terme of his lif of the Custumes in the poort of Londone by the handes of the Collectors

Herry Everingham an Annuytie of xx^{ti} marces of thissues of Thonnor of Tutbury by the handes of the Receyvor unto suche tyme as he be promoted etc

[f56b] William Botiller Thoffice of Clerc of the Mylnes of Dee in the Countie of

Chestre for terme of his lif with the wages and fees accustumed

Robert Brakenbury the Constableship of the Toure with a C li. fee for terme of his lif to be perceived of the Revenues of Writtelle Havering Boytone etc

To the same Robert the manoirs of Mote Merden Dething Newentone in Kent and alle othre landes tenementes Rentes and services in Townes hamelettes and territores of Mote Merden Dething and Newentone forsaid late Therl Ryvers to the value of xxvj li. xiij s. iiij d. and the manoirs of Crawthorne and Cokerede late John Cheynes (and) Robert Cheynes and Humfrey Cheynes and al othre landes and tenementes in Rumney mersshe late the said Johns Robert and Humfreys of the value of l li. xviij s. j d. and the manoire of Glassingbury and alle othre landes and tenementes in the Counties of Kent Sussex and Surrey whiche was Waltier Robertes of the value of xl li. to the same Robert and his heires masles by knightes service and the Rent of (x) viij li. xvj s

(Ro) The same Robert the keping of the lyons in the said Towre of Londone for terme of his lif with the wages of xij d. by the day for himself and for the mete of every lyone and leobard vj d. by the day of the Revenues of the lordships of Wryttelle Haveryng Boytone etc

(Thomas W) John Fox Thoffice of kepar of the outwoodes of Wodestok during his lif with the wages of iiij d. by the day of thissues proffites and Revenues of the said lordship and the keping of al wylde beestes within the newe Forest nere to Wodestok with the fee of ij d. by the day of the said lordship and thoffice of (pk) oon of the parkers in the parke of Wodestok with the fee of x li. to be perceived of the said lordship for terme of his lif

Richard Croft and Thomas Croft the keping of the parke of Woodstok and porter of the parke and Comptrollers and supervisors of the werkes of the manoire of Wodstoke and keping of the gardyne and the yate of the manoire to them and eithre of theim lenger lyving with the fees and wages accustumed

William Griffithe an Annuytie of xxiij li. v s. during his lif of the Revenues of the fee ferme of Colchestre (for)

Hugh Brice the Clerc of the mynte of mony & chaunge within the Toure of Londone and James his son for terme of his lif with the wages and fees accustumed

Sir Richard Beauchamp and Agnes his wif the manoire of Chareltone to theim and eithre of them lenger lyving and an Annuytie of iij^{XX}xiiij li. for terme of theire lifes and eithre of them lenger lyving of the Custumes of the porte of Bristowe

[f57] John Hotone Squiere the lordships of Besterne Hyde Exbere Lepe Tottone Mynstede Berkeley in the Countie of Suthampton and the lordship of Playtforthe in Wiltshire of the value of C marc to him and to his heires masles by knightes service and the Rent of v li.

The maire baillifes and Burgesses of Dertmouthe xxx li. yerely to be leveyed of the Custumes and subsidies of the poortes of Excestre and Dertmouthe for the maynteynyng of a bollewerk and chaynes of the havone

To the maire and felisship of the staple a warrant to the Custumers Comptrollers and Weyers of the gret Custume in the poort of Londone to allowe theim ij nayles of woll custume fre in every sak

Sir Alexandre Bayneham an Annuytie of xl li. during his lif of the Custumes of Bristowe and also an Annuytie of xl marc after the decesse of Thomas Baynham his fader of the Custumes aforesaid

James Huddlestone the Fery of Portathowe in Northwales for terme of his lif withe the wages and fees accustumed

William Coplowe the kinges Attorney in the kinges benche (during) aslong as he bereth him wele by the handes of the generalle Receyvor of the duchie of Lancastre

Sir Thomas Broughtone / Stewardship of the lordship of Dertingtone and Bovytracy and maister of the game of the parkes there (w) during his lif with the fees and wages of C marc to be perceived of thissues proffites and Revenues of the same lordship

Richard Grene a warraunt to the Chaunceller of the duchie of Lancastre for to discharge him of the somme of vij li. that he aughte to king Edward the iiij th for the ferme of Borowbrig Mylles

Robert Brakenbury thoffice of Receyvor of the lordships of Writtelle Haveryng Boytone Hadleghe Rayleghe Racheforth in the Countie of Essex & Tunbrigge Hadlowe Penshurst Myddeltone and Merdon in Kent for terme of his lif withe the wages and fees accustumed

Thomas Croft the king hathe confermed unto him Thoffice of Steward and lieutenant of the manoire of Woodstok and of the membres for terme of his lif withe the fees and wages accustumed and Thoffice of (Gra) Ranger of the Forest of Shotter and Stowewode in the Countie of Oxonford and the forest of Burnewode in the Countie of Bukingham for terme of his lif with the wages and fees accustumed and Thoffice of waterbaillif of our Towne of Bristowe for terme of his lif with the wages accustumed

Sir Richard Tunstalle an Annuytie of C marces during the lif of the lord stanley of the Revenues of the Towne and marches of Calais

[f57b] William Sherman of your Towne of Ludlowe to have in ferme the lordship of Stauntone Lacy in the Countie of Salop for terme of his lif yelding therefore xxviij li. yerely and an Annuytie of vj marc of the same lordship for terme of his lif

Thomas Sandlands an Annuytie of viij li. for terme of his lif of the ferme of the manoire of Wrakwerden in the Countie of Salop

Robert Merbury Squier an Annuytie of xx^{ti} marces of the lordship of Hanslap in the Countie of Northampton unto suche tyme as he be promoted

Thomas Lowthe an Annuytie of x li. of the Revenues of the lordship of Glattone and Holme in the Countie of Huntingdone unto suche tyme as he be promoted

A prive seale directed to John Hayes to content John Lemplowe of Londone Grocere Thomas Carter waxchaundelere John Short bocher and othre of Londone forsaid the somme of CC li. for vitaill spended in the house of (king) Edward the Vth pretending to be king

[cross] Sir Robert Harringtone the Stewardship of the manoirs or lordships of Lugheburghe Meltone Moubrey Segrave Coldovertone Dalby Chacombe Twyford Wytherley Syleby Mountsorel and of the hundred of Goscote within the Countie of Gloucester withe the wages of x li. of the Revenues of Loughborowe and thoffice of keping of ij parces and warennes there for terme of his lif with the wages accustumed etc

[cross] The said Sir Robert the manoire of Awstwik of the value of iij^{xx}li. unto suche tyme as the lordship of Groby in the Countie of Leicestre nowe in the possessione of Sir John Burgchiere shal by his decesse descende to Thomas late marques Dorset and by his forisfaiture to come to the kinges handes . And over

that an Annuytie of iij^{xx}iij li. (xiij) vj s. viij d. to be perceived of the lordship of Lughborowe

Richard Norreys thoffice of Attorney of your Court in Haltone within Chesshire during his lif with the fees and wages accustumed

Humfrey Lytelbury an Annuytie of xx^{ti} marces to be perceived of the lordship of Bostone unto suche tyme as he be promoted

William Claxtone the manoirs of Godmanstone Wareham and Stoweboroughe in Somersetshire to the value of xl li. vj s. xj d. the maners or lordships of Meryot Bukland beate Marie and Longsuttone in the same Countie of the value of xxvj li (vj s) viij s. ij d. to him and to his heires masles by knightes service and the Rent of C s.

Rauf lord Nevylle an Annuytie of iiij^{xx}li. to be yerely perceyved during the lif of Thomas lord Stanley of the Revenues of the lordship of Barnard Castelle

[f58] The same lord Nevylle the manoirs of Baryngtone & Southepedertone in the Countie of Lincolne of the value of iiij^{xx}xj li. xiiij s. viij d. the manoire or lordship of Illesley in the Countie of Berkeshire of the value of xxvij li. xix s. iiij d. and immediatly after the decesse of Thomas lord Stanley the manoirs and lordships of Cammelle Regine and Kyngesbury in the Countie of Somerset of the value of iiij^{xx} li. ix s. vj d. to him and his heires masles of his body begotene for evermore to be holden of the king by knightes service and the Rent of xv li. yerely etc

Sir Robert Percy the manoire of Camps Saxtone & Abitone in the Countie of Cambruge and the lordships of Scottone and Breretone with theire appurtenaunces after the decesse of Thomas lord Stanley by knightes service to him and to his heires masles and by the Rent of xv li. and also the manoire of Garboldesham & the landes and tenementes in Garboldesham with (thadous) thadvoison of the Churche of the same to the said Robert and Joice his wif and to the heires masles of the said Robert betwix him and the said Joyce begoten And if it happen the foresaid Robert without heires masles betwix him and the said Joyse to dye than the said manoire of Garboldesham landes and tenementes and thadvouson to remayne to the said Robert and his heires masles of his body begotene And also the said Robert hathe the manoire of Maldone Waltons Halle in Purley Flannerswike Jakelottes & Mondene & alle othre landes and tenementes withe the appurtenaunces in Maldone forsaid to him and his heires masles

Sir Thomas Burghe the manoirs or lordships of Ingilby Saxilby and Broxhome in the Countie of Lincolne . the manoirs or lordships of Comptone Wodemancote Charefeld Faylfeld (Cha) in the Countie of Gloucester / and the hundred of Stone and Catesasshe in Somersetshire to him and his heires and the Reversion of the manoire of Clostone Basset in the Countie of Notingham immediatly after the decesse of Thomas lord Stanley

Thomas Banke Thoffice of Weyer otherwise called the paysership of Wolles in your Towne and poort of Bostone in your Countie of Lincolne for terme of his lif with the wages accustumed and an Annuytie of xx^{ti} li. to be perceyved yerely from the fest of mighelmasse last past during his said lif of thissues of the lordship of Bostone

John Cawinefeld the manoire of Rollestone in Wiltshire A valoris vij li. xiij s. iiij d. to hym and his heires masles forever by knightes service and the Rent of x s.

Herry Godmond Thoffice of keping of the woodes and wareyne of Sherstone in the Counte of Wilteshire for terme of his lif withe the wages of ij d. by the day and an Annuytie of v marces to be perceived of the said lordship

[f58b] Sir Thomas Thwaytes A warrant directed to the Tresourer and (Cham) Barons of theschequiere to make unto him allowaunce of the somme of viij^C li. sterlinges payed by him aswele to the kinges handes as to diverse othre persones by his commaundement

Richard Salkeld an Annuytie of of xx li. to be taken from the fest of Saint Mighell last past during his lif of the Revenues of the lordship of Penrethe

Alexandre Quadring the manoire of Grays in Sybille Hingham in Essex of the yerely value of xx^{ti} marces for terme of his lif

John Hargylle the Bailliship and wardership of Moltone in the Countie of (Sutht) Northampton for terme of his lif withe the wages of iiij d. by the day to be perceived of the said lordshippe

John Clapham Thoffice of porter of the Castelle of Penrethe for terme of his lif with the wages of iiij d. by the day of our said lordship from Mighelmasse last past

Sir James Tyrelle and Richard Goldes the warde and mariage of Robert Arundelle treryse son and heire of John Arundelle Treryse Squier with the keping of alle landes and tenementes manoirs etc during his nonnage

Sir John Cave prest (the) keper of our lady of Pewe an Annuytie of x markes unto the tyme he be better promoted

William Myles the manoire of Netherhaven of the value of xx li. ij s. vj d. to him and to his heires masles by knightes service and the Rent of xxx s.

Dame Kateryn Vauce an Annuytie of xx^{ti} marces during hir lif of the lordships of Middeltone and Merden in Kent and of Havering at bowre by the handes of the Receyvors etc

The Burgesses of Scarbugh a warrant to the Tresourer and Barons of theschequiere to discharge theim at theire accomptes of the somme of xlviij li. ix s. due at Mighelmasse last past of theire fee ferme

John Kendalle the keping of the Chaunge within the Towne of Calais and the Royaulme of England from Ester next comyng during the space of ten yeres . yelding therefore yerely to the king xxx li. vj s. viij d.

[f59] the president and felawes of the Quenes Colleige of Cantebrige have a licence to purchase lande not exceding the somme of (x) vij^C li over alle reprises and also advousons of Churches etc and the same to put in mortmayne to theire said College

Robert Conystable of Barneby an Annuytie of x li. (y) for terme of his lif of the lordship of Shiriefhotone

John Leptone Squier an Annuytie of x li. during his lif of the same lordship of Shiriefhotone

Robert Gower a like annuytie of the same lordship

Thomas Gower knighte an Annuytie of a C marces during his lif in forme folowing that is to say of thissues of the lordship of Hundeburtone in the Countie of Yorke xx^{ti} marces / of thissues of the manoire of Scoreby in the said Countie xl marces and of thissues of the lordship of Langtone xl^{ti} marces by the handes of the Fermors Baillieffes etc

Sir John Neville knighte an Annuytee of xlvj li. xiij s. iiij d. during his liff / To be had from Michelmasse last past of the Revenues of Tutbury / yevene the xxvj day of marche Anno primo

172

The same Sir John / a warraunt to the Receivor of Pountefret to pay unto him the somme of xlij li. xviij s. iiij d. of the first money that commes to his handes for the wages of xxx persones in the Castelle of Pountfret / from the kinges Coronacione unto his last being at there

Watkyn Chaundeler the thoffice of baillieff of Olney with the keping of the park there for terme of his liff / with the wages of iiij d. by the day for the baillieff and ij d. by the day for the baillieff / of the same lordship

William Brandone a pardone for his liff onely

John Forde oon of the yomen of the Corone / the fee ferme of the Towne of Shaftesbury in the Countie of Wilteshire to the valewe of Cvj s. viij d. from Michelmasse last past during his liff / yerely to be perceyved by the handes of the Baillyes or inhabitantes of the said Towne and also vj d. by the day for the fee of the Crowne from the said fest during his said lif of the Custumes of Suthampton

Richard Croft knighte an Annuytie of xx^{ti} li of the lordships and manoirs of therldom of the marche within the Countie of Hereford from the fest of Saint Mighel last past for terme of his lif / by the handes of the Fermors Baillies or Receyvors for the tyme being etc

John Kyldale an Annuytie of v marces for terme of his [lif] of the Revenues of Myddelham by the handes of the Receyvor etc

Geffray Franke an Annuytie of liij li. during his lif of the Revenues of Middelham and Shiriefhotone by the handes etc

[f59b] George Portingtone the Bailliship of Multone in Holand in the Countie of Lincolne during the kinges pleasire with the wages of vj d. by the day to be perceived of the same lordship

John Kendale an Annuytie of iiij^{xx} li. yerely during the lif of Jane Stonor moder to Sir William Stonor knighte to be taken yerely in forme folowing that is to wite l li of the Revenues of the lordship of Marleburghe in Wilteshire or of the fee ferme of the said lordship . and xxx li. residue of the ferme of thissues proffites and Revenues of the Chaunge within the Towne of Calais and within the Royaulme of England from the fest of Saint Mighel last past by the handes of the Fermors etc

Piers Hogge the keping of the manoire and lordship of Kyngestone Lacy in the Countie of Dorset and baillif of the hundred of Kingestone Lacy and thoffice of keping of the wareyne with the proffites of the same and thoffice of keping of the kinges Swannys in the waters of Ryngwode & Stoure for terme of his lif withe the wages and fees accustumed And also an Annuel Rent of C s. from the fest of Saint Mighel last past during his said lif of the same lordship

Rauf Willughby Squier the manoire of Willughby Waterlesse in the Countie of Leicestre of the yerely value of lx(x) li vj s. viij d. and the manoire of Estone in the Countie of Wilteshire of the value of xx li. and after the decesse of the lord Stanley the manoire of Ornesby in the Countie of Norffolk of the value of lx li. vj s. viij d. late the Countesse of Richmond . to the same Rauf and his heires masles by knightes service and the Rent of iij li. xviij s. forever etc

John James / his patent new confermed of a C acres land and pasture and iiij acres of medowe iiij acres of wode and xij s. of Rent in Thaxsted and a tenement in Thaxstede of the value of (x) vj s. viij d. for terme of his lif without any thing paying

Rauf Willughby Thoffices of Constable and Steward of the Castelle and lordship of Bukenham in the Countie of Norffolk for terme of his lif withe the wages and fees accustumed

[f60] John Lord Dudley the manoirs or lordships of Darlastone Bentley (an) Tyttensovere and Hertwelle in the Countie of Stafford of the value of xxx li. v s. v d. . the manoir of Pakingtone in the same Countie to the value of iiij li. with the landes and tenementes in Briggenorthe in the Countie of Salop late the duc of Bukinghams of the value of viij li. iij s. x d. and the Reversion of the manoire or lordship of Nortone in le Mores in the said Countie of (Salop) Stafford of the yerely value of xvij li viij s. iij d. of the manoire or lordship of Rokby in the Countie of Warrwik to the value of xliij li. ij s. vij d. late the Counties of Richmond immediatly after the decesse of Thomas lord Stanley . to the said lord Dudley and his heires masles by knightes service and the Rent of (x) vij li x s. from the fest of Mighelmasse last past

Nicholas Spicer Constable of the Castelle of Bristowe for terme of his lif withe the wages of xx li. by yere . and to constitue under him a porter and ij wacchemen to wake aswele by night as by day in the same Castelle for terme of his lif . perceyvyng yerely for the said office of Constable xx li. at the feestes of Ester & myghelmasse by even porcions. And for the wages of the said Gayler ij d. by day and for the wages of the saides ij wecchemen iij d.ob. by the day . of the fee ferme of Bristowe by the handes of the Shireff

The pryor and Convent of Botley in Suffolk have a warrant directed unto the

Tresourere and Chambrelains to discharge them of the Somme of xx li. parcelle of xxxiiij li. ij d.ob.qr. for his last dyme graunted

Sir Marmaduc Constable Steward of the honor of Tutbury and maister Forster of the forest and Chace of Nedewode within the Countie of Stafford . Constable of the Castel of Tutbury and porter there . maister Forster or wardeyne of Duffeld Frithe in Derby Shire . Steward and Constable of the lordship (or) and Castelle of Donyngtone in the Countie of Leicestre . Steward of the lordship and Towne of Assheborne in Derby shire . Steward of the highe peke with the Surveyorship of the same and Constable of the Castelle there and Steward of the lordship of Newcastelle undre Lyne in the Countie of Stafford for terme of his lif with the wages and fees accustumed

[f60b] Sir Marmaduc Constable an Annuytie of iiij^{xx} ix li. xvj s. viij d. of the Revenues of the lordship of Tutbury during the lif of Sir Robert Constable fadre to the same Sir Marmaduc

John lord Dudley an Annuytie of lx li. from the fest of Mighelmas last past during the lif of Thomas lord Stanley of the honnor of Tutbury

John lord Dudley an Annuytie of C li. (d) from the fest of Mighelmasse last past of the Custumes of the Citie of Londone during his lif

Edmond Hoggesone thoffice of porter of the Inner yate of the Castelle of Carlisle with the wages of iiij d. by the day to be perceived of the lordship of Perythe for terme of his lif

John Warde an Annuytie of (l) xl li. from the fest of Mighelmasse last past for terme of his lif of the fee ferme of quenehithe

William Bracher the manoires of Chedder lat Sir William Berkleys to the value of xix li. the manoirs or lordships of of Barowe Gurney & Tykenham late the said Sir William in the Countie of Somerset of the value of xxj li. x s. to him and his heires masles by knightes service and the Rent of lx s.

Aprile Sir John Everyngham an Annuytie of lxvj li. xiij s. iiij d. from the fest of Mighelmasse last past unto suche tyme as he be promoted to the value of C marc or better . of thissues proffites and Revenues of the Castel and lordship of Bolyngbroke in Lincolneshire parcelle of the duchie of Lancastre

Richard Kneveton Squiere an Annuytie of v marces during his lif of Thonnor of Tutbury

Robert Fyenderne Squiere an Annuytie of iiij marces for terme of his lif of Thonnor of Tutbury

William Bothe a like Annuytie of the said honnor during his lif

George Stanley Squiere an Annuytie of C s. of the same honnor during his lif

Hugh Egertone Squier an Annuytie of x li. during his lif of the same honor

Nicholas Mountgomery an Annuytie of x li. during his lif of the same honnor

[f61] Rauf Longford a like Annuytie of x li. during his lif of the said honor of Tutbury

Herry Vernone Squier an Annuytie of xx^{ti} marces during his lif of the said honnor

Robert Eyere an Annuel rent of ten marces during his lif of the same honor

William Lilborne the manoire of Edonbrigge in Kent of the value of viij li. to him and his heires masles forever by knightes service and the Rent of xj s.

John Belle a pardone for theschetorship of the Counties of Surrey & Sussex

The Superioure and comens of Waiesford in Irland have theire liberties and fredoms of theire Towne Ratefied and confermed

David Keting the manoire or lordship of Eskir with a water mylne in the Countie of Dublyne in Irland not exceding therely value of xl^{ti} marces during the kinges pleasire without any thing paying etc

Herry Wydehoke thoffice of yomane and keper of the (Ann) Armory & hablimentes of werre in the Towre of Londone for terme of his lif withe the wages of vj d. by the day of thissues of the lordships of Wrotylle Havering boytone Hadleghe Rayleghe & Rocheford in Essex and of Tunbriche Penshurst Myddeltone and Merdone in Kent

John Strangways Squiere an Annuytie of xx^{ti} marces from the xxvj day of Juyne last past aslong as he berethe him wele of the Custumes of Bostone by the handes of the Custumers etc

John Toby an Annuytee or annuell rent of six poundes thirtene shillinges & foure pennys / of the Revenues of Northwithom in Lincolneshire unto the tyme he be promoted by the king to the office or offices of like value or better

Richard Copeland / Thoffices of Bailly and heyward of the hundreth of Uplamborne and Chepinglamborne and bailif of Estgarten and keper of the warenne there within the Countie of Berkeshire for terme of his liff / with the wages & fees accustumed / And an Annuytee of v markes of the Revenues of the said hundrethe & lordshippe for terme of his liff / by the handes of the Receivor of the same for the tyme being

William Myrfeld alle the landes and tenementes with thappurtenaunces in the Towne and fyldes of Colcote & Chelworthe in the Countie of Suthampton lat William Berkleys to him and his heires masles forever by knightes service & the Rent of xx s. vj d.

Sir Thomas Everyngham hathe a warrant to Herry botfisshe maire and eschetor of Calais to make delyvery and payment unto him of al the goodes within his jurisdiccione that late (longed) belonged Peter Johnsone and by him forfaitted to the king for that he made his wille to an Aleyn borne contrary to the statutes therupon ordeyned

[f61b] Thomas Windesore thoffice of Constable of the Castel of Windesore and lieutenaunt of al Forestes parces wareyns & other places to the said Office belonging . for terme of his lif with the wages of xxx li yerely of thissues of the said Castel by the handes of the Receyvor there for the tyme being & with al other proffites etc and also fyfty shillinges for thoccupying of the same Office from the x day of marche last past datum octavo die Aprilis Anno primo

John lord Dynham hathe a warrant to the Tresourer and Chambrelains of theschequiere to make assignement unto him (by) of the somme of C li. due unto him of DC li. to him graunted by kyng Edward the fourth of thissues etc of the lordships of Sampford Courteney Chalnelegh Torbryane & Slapton in Devone by taylle or tailles at the Recept of theschequier to be leveyed of the landes and tenementes late longing to George duc of Clarence in the Counties of Warrwik Worcestre Stafford Northampton & Roteland

the same John lord Dynham hathe the Reversion of the manoirs and lordships of Sampford Povorol the Burgh of Sampford Peverelle the manere of Aller

Peverelle & the hundred of Albertone in Devonshire and the manoire of Bedhamptone with the membres in the Countie of Suthampton after the decesse of Thomas lord Stanley to him and his heires by knightes service and the Rent of x li.

Sir Thomas Dalamare a pardonne for his lif

Mathewe Andrewe a licence to charge a Ship of the portage of xlv tonne or under with almaner goodes and merchandises to the Staple of Calais not apperteynyng as oft as him shal like within a hole yere and with the same to departe to any outward partes there to discharge and to recharge ayen into England (etc) Datum at Notingham x^{mo} Aprilis Anno primo

William Conyers an Annuytie of xx li. during his lif of thissues of the lordship of Myddeham by the handes of the Receyvor etc

Thomas Fowler thoffice of parker of Bekley and the keping of the manoire there in the Countie of Oxonford during his lif withe the wages and fees accustumed to be perceyved of the same lordship

Robert Lilly Thoffice of parker of Stokley in Staffordshire by himself during his lif withe the wages accustumed and pasture for ij horses and ij kyne within the said park And also an Annuytie iiij li. xj s. iij d. during his said lif of Thonnor of Tutbury by the handes of the Receyvor etc

Mathewe Gate the parkership of Rollestone in Staffordshire with the wages accustumed & the pasturing of ij horses & ij keyn . And also an Annuytie of iiij li. xj s. iij d. of the same honnor from mighelmasse last past

[f62] Robert Hunt thoffice of kepar of the woodes and Rede dere of Crowllemos-wode and Rosse in the (Ishe) Isle of Axholme in Lincolneshire during his lif . withe the wages fees & proffites of old tyme due and accustumed to be perceived of thissues within the said Isle

Thomas Fowler Squier (for your body) alle the landes and tenementes Rentes & services with thappurtenaunces called Dyttons landes lying in the Towne & parisshe of Bradden in Northamptoneshire of the yerely value of viij marces late Anthony Widevyles . aslong as the same landes shal Remayne in the kinges handes

John Erle of Lincolne an Annuel Rent of Clxxvj li. xiij s. iiij d. from the fest of Michelmasse last past during the lif Thomas lord Stanley of thissues of the duchie of Cornewaile by the handes of the generalle Receyvor of the same etc

The same John Erle of Lincolne the manoire and lordship of Wodehey in Berkshire of the yerely value of liiij li. manoire of Roos in Yorkshire of the value of lxxij li. and the manoire of Westbury in Wiltshire of the value of xxx li. xiij s. iiij d. And also the Reversion of the manoire of Eydon & of Thorphille with the membris in the Countie of Northampton of the value of lxxiiij li. the manoire of Lammersshe & Colnewake in the Countie of Essex of the value of lix li. x s. the manoire of Billing magna in Northamptonshire of the value of xxiij li. xiiij s. v d. and the manoirs of Basingstoke and Andever in the Countie of Suthampton of the value of xx li. xviij s. after the decesse of Thomas lord Stanley . to him and his heires masles by knightes service & the Rent of xxx li. & xij d.

Sir William Husee knighte the keping of al the landes & tenementes heredita-ments and (possessessions) possessions that late was William Trusselles knighte nowe being in the kinges handes (of Edwa) by reason of the nonnage of Edward Trusselle Son and heire of the said William from the fest of mighelmasse last past during the said nonnage

John Hudlestone thoffice of Steward of our lordships of Monnemouthe Grosmond Whitcastelle & Skenfreithe in the marches of Wales and Constable of the Castelles of Monnemouthe Grosmond Whitcastel & Skenfreithe and also Jailor of the Castel of Monnemouthe during his lif withe the wages fees & proffites accustumed of thissues & Revenues of the same lordships etc and also an Annuytie of C marces during his said lif of thissues of the same lordships etc

Roger Cocques thoffice of Receyvor of the Revenues of the lordships of Mark and Oye with vij parisshes to the same lordships Annexed and also Thoffice of Sercher with the Towne of Calais & the water of Gravenyng aswele within the Scunage in the marsshe as without elleswhere and also thoffice of highe Baillif of the lordships of Marke and Oye with the said vij parisshes therunto Annexed [f62b] during his lif from the xxv^{ti} day of Marche last past And to perceive yerely in the said Offices the wages of xij d. by the day that is to say for thoffice of Receyvor iiij d. and for thoffice of Serchor iiij d. and for thoffice of highe baillif iiij d. of thissues of the said lordships etc by his owne propre handes or by the handes of the fermors tenauntes etc or by the handes of the Tresourer of Calais for the tyme being Togeders withe al othre proffites etc and also al suche sommes of money as be (f) due for thoccupyng of the said office from the said xxv^{ti} day of Marche

Sir Charles of Pylkingtone the manoirs and lordships of Hertyshulle and Hauseley in Warrewikshire of the value of lx li xij s. xj d. And the manoire of Knesale in Notinghamshire of the value of xx li. to him and his heires masles forever by knightes service and the Rent of vj li.

Piers Gerard Squier an Annuel Rent of x marces from the fest of Mighelmasse last past during his lif of thissues proffites and Revenues of oure Countie palatyne of Lancastre by the handes of the Receyvor of the same for the tyme being

Thomas Hoptone Squier Thoffices of Baillif & Warener of Marlowe in the Countie of Bukingham with the keping of the Swannes there during his lif with the wages of iiij d. by the day of thissues of the lordship of Marlowe by the handes of the Receyvor etc And also an Annuytie of x li. during his said lif of thissues forsaid by the said Receyvors etc

Sir Gervays Clyftone the manoire of Radclyf upon Sowre with thappurtenaunces in the Countie of Notinghame and Kynstone in the same Countie and Kegworthe in Leicestreshire by knightes service and the Rent of xl s. yerely. And also the manoire or lordship of Overtone Longvile with thappurtenances in the Countie of Huntyngdone by knightes service and the Rent of xl s. Also to the same Gervays the manoire or lordship of Dolbury and Dolburylyes in the Countie of Derby with thadvouson of the parisshe churches of the same lordships . and of landes and tenements in Etwalle & Wrykesworthe in the same Countie of Derby late the duc of Bukingham by knightes service and the Rent of xx s.

Master John Shirwood the Restitucion (of the Restitucion) of the temporalties in the Bisshopricheche of Duresme

Thomas Everley the king hathe confermed unto him the keping of the manoire of Goodrest in the parke of Wegenok with a gardeyne to the same with iiij d. by the day to be perceived of the lordship of Wyntertone during the nonnage of Therle of Warrwik

[f63] Humfrey Soldsone the keping of the parke of Suttone in the Countie of Warrwik and (pal) keper of the poles there with the wages and fees accustumed during the nonnage of therl of Warrwik And xl s. for keping of the said poles etc

The Bailliefes (and) Burgesses and Commonaltie of Cambrigge have a pardonne of x li. of theire fee ferme forever

Richard Mershtone thoffice of keper of the gaole within the Castelle of York during the kinges pleasire withe the wages accustumed

Gloucester herauld the manoire of Olde Owene in the parisshe of Selling in Kent & other landes and tenementes called Dyngleys in the parisshe of Chilham in the same Countie by knightes service and the Rent of vij s.

Thomas Metley an Annuytie of x li. of thissues of Estone in the Countie of Northamptone unto the tyme he be promoted etc

Sir Robert Percy the keping of alle dominicalle landes of the kinges manoire of Kenyngtone in the Countie of Surrey withe a barne & othre esamentes without the pale there also Conyes rentes and perquisites of Courtes and othre profites whatsoever to the same manoire belonging from the fest of michelmas last past during his lif yelding to the king xx^{ti} marces And over this thoffice of Steward of oure lordship of Kenyngtone and keping of the manoire there . & Conyes and gardyne there during his lif and for thoffice of Steward the wages accustumed and thoffice of keper iiij d. by the day by his owne handes of the said xx marces

Christofir Colyns hathe a warrant to the Tresourere and Chambrelayns of theschequiere to make assignement unto him by taille (our) or tailles in due forme at the Recept of theschequier to him and Thomas Cottone as Collectors of the Subsidie in Londone (of) of the somme of iij li. appointed to the said Christofre (of his) for his Reward and iiij^{xx}xvij li. for habilimentes of werre etc

Morgane Kydwelly the manoire of Fyfehede Wolftone Hammone Holcombe Deverelle alias Deverelle combe Childe Okeford withe thappurtenaunces in the Countie of Dorset. also al landes and tenementes in Fyfehede Wolftone Hammone Holcombe Deverelle & Childockeford late John Mones to him and his heires masles by knightes service and the Rent of Cxiij s.

[f63b] Waltier Chaundellere the lordship of Astone Samford in the Countie of Bukingham to him and his heires masles by knightes service and the Rent of xviij s.

Nicholas Lathelle and Richard Williams the keping of the manoir of (Co) Overhalle withe thappurtenaunces in Cavendisshes in the Countie of Suffolk late Thomas Cavendisshe during the nonnage of Thomas son and heire of the said Thomas (pera) paying yerely therefore x marc

Hugh Annesley an Annuytie of iiij marc of the honor of Tutbury

Sir William Stanes the pension of Saint Bartholomewes

John Kendale Thoffice of keping of the parke of Havering at Bowre and palacere of the same withe the wages of iij d. by the day for the parkership and xxvj s. viij d. for the palacereship with therbage and pannage of the same and Thoffice of oon of the Rangers of the forest of Dean with the wages of vj d. by the day Thoffice of Steward of the lordship of Savoye with the fees and wages

accustumed for terme of his lif
And ix li for the said Office of Rangership in arrerages etc

Sir John Grey the Manoire of Wilsamstede in the Countie of Bedford by knightes service and the Rent of xxxiij s.

William Wake / a warraunt under the privie seale directe to the Tresourere & Barons of the Eschequiere / to discharge him & the baillieff of Watford of x li. / by the said William spended by the kinges commaundement

Master Edmond Chaderton Thoffice of Tresorere & Receivor of the Chambre during the kinges pleasure with fees accustumed

John Sibille Clerc of the mercate of the kinges houshold during (his) the kinges pleasure

Roger Kelsale A pardon

Sir John Seintlowe knight A pardon

John Harecourt(e) of Staunton a pardon

Walter Hungerford of (Hattesbury) Haytesbury A pardon

John Trencherd of Charmynster a pardon

Sir Nicholas Latymer A pardone

Sir William Norrys of Yatendene a pardone

William Uvedale of Wykeham a pardone

John Milwarde An Annuyte of x marc from Michaelmas last past unto the tyme he be promoted to office or lande of Better Valew to be taken of the honnor of Tuttebury

182

[f64] William Catesby the manoire or lordship of Bukeby in Northamptone-
(shie)shire To have and hold the same in fee ferme to him and his heires
forever withe issues proffites and Revenues of the same and knightes service
etc for the somme of lx li. at the fest of Saint mighel and passhe by even
porcions etc

James Frijs phisiciane hathe confermed unto him alle and singuler tenementes
loigges and houses that Christofir Furneys had within the palois of Westminster
that is to say a tenement that Thomas Stok late had to ferme of Herry the vjth &
the logge being betwene the Rounde Toure in the palaice & the lytelle water
Conduyt whiche John Gurney late had to ferme of the same Herry and a house
within the palais whiche John Prudde late had of the graunt of the same Herry .
also a house under the Receipt of theschequier conteynyng in lenghte xlvj fote
with a litel house called the pycherhouse conteynyng in lenght x fote & in brede
vij fote whiche John Randolf Squier late had . and a house within Westmynster
halle in a Toure under a house called Quene Margrettes Counsaille house / for
terme of his lif without any accompt or other thing etc

John Wassheborne Squier an Annuytie of x markes of the Revenues of the
lordship of Elmeley Lovet in Worcestreshire during his lif by the handes of the
Receyvor etc

Sir William Bekwithe knighte an Annuytie of xxti marces during his lif of
thissues etc of the lordship of Knaresburghe in Yorkshire etc

James Erle Douglas hathe a warrant directed to the Tresourere and Chambrelains of theschequiere to content unto him xlij li. xvij s. iiij d by assignement to
be made to him to be leveyed upon the Receyvor or Receyvors of the fee
fermes etc

William Thirkeld hathe confermed unto him Thoffice of serieaunt of Armes
during his lif withe the fee of xij d. by the day of the subsidie and ulnage of
clothes and the (haf) halfendele of forfaitures in the Counties of Oxonford and
Berkshire by the handes of the Receyvors Fermors etc withe liverey clothing
etc

John Robynson purser of the Lucas hathe a warrant directed to the Tresourere
& Chambrelains to content unto him the somme of xxvj li. ix s. in redy money
whiche was by employed upon the vitailling and mannyng of the said Ship

John Grisley knighte an Annuytie of xl li. of thonnor of Tutbury by the handes
of the Receyvor etc during his lif

Bryan Talbot l marces yerely for the fee of Squier for the body during his lif of the Revenues of Bolingbroke etc

[f64b] Sir Charles Pilkingtone hathe a warrant to Sir Gervays Clyftone Shirief of the Counties of Notingham & Derby to pay unto him xvij li. xvj s. viij d. of the Revenues due at Mighelmas last past of the lordship of Bollesover in the Countie of Derby of the kinges Reward And also he hathe a nother warrant to the Tresourer and Barons of theschequier to allowe the same Sir Gervays of the payment of the same in his accompt of the Shiriefwike

James Erle Douglas xx^{ti} marces yerely from the fest of mighelmas last past during his lif of the fee ferme of Notingham by the handes of the Shirief Baillieffes etc

Bryan Talbot hathe confermed unto him Thoffice of Constable of the Castelle of Clyderowe parcelle of the duchie of Lancastre withe the wages of x li. of thissues of the same Castelle from the fest of mighelmas last past during the kinges pleasire

Sir Gervays Clyftone hathe a warraunt to the Tresourer and Barons to allowe unto him the somme of xl li. in his accompt of Shiriefwik of Notingham and Derby shires whiche he hathe paied to the kinges of the Revenues of Bollesovere due at mighelmasse last passed

Sir William Husy knighte chief Justice William Beverley Clerc William Catesby Squier and Edmond Chadertone Clerc have the lordships manoirs and hundredes of Wexcombe Kyndwardstone Burbage Savage Willesford Knouck Strattone ste Margarete Bedwynde Orchestone in the Countie of Wiltshire Cornehamptone Petresfeld Mapulderham Upclatford in the Countie of Suthampton Welles Wareham Sheringham and Wevetone in Norffolk to theim and theire assignes for the terme of vij yeres next ensuyng the fest of Ester last (last) past to content therewithe the dettes of the duc of Bukingham

John Risley Squier landes & tenementes in Swainton alias Swayneston in the Countie of Suthampton late Mighell Skellinges of the value of vij li. vj s. viij d. the manoire of Shiptone Beryng in the same Countie the value xx li the manoire of Surdingtone in the same Countie the value xj li. & alle landes and tenementes in Swatheling Nasshefeld & Grateley in the same Countie late William Halles the value xxxvj s. viij d. to him and his heires masles forever by knightes service and the Rent of iij li.

William Otter thoffice of Ryding Forster in the forest of Waltham during the kinges pleasire withe the wages & fees accustumed

[f65] William Mystelbroke Thoffice of Auditor of alle Castelles lordships landes & tenementes & other possessions of the duchie of Lancastre aswele in the Southparties on this side Trent as in the parties of Southwales from the fest of saint mighel last past during his lif with the wages and expenses in the said office accustumed to be had

William Selby hathe confermed unto him the portership of the Castel of Warrwik and keping of the gardyne there during the nonnage of the duc of Clarence [sic] withe the wages and fees accustumed to be perceived of the lordship of Warrwik . and also he hathe confermed to him a mesuage or an Inne called the Belle in le hope with iij tenementes to the same adioynyng in the parisshe of Saint Mary stronde without Temple barre . and alle landes & tenementes in that parisshe and a mesuage in the parisshe of Saint Clementes without the same Barre late Richard Stucleys to him and to John Hampsterley during theire lifes and the lenger lyver by the service therof due

Sir Harry Perpoint hathe confermed unto him the Stewardship of Mawnsfeld in Notinghamshire withe the wages accustumed of thissues of the same . and also Steward of the lordship of Bolesore & Horseley in the Countie of Derby with the wages accustumed of thissues of the same . And also the parkership of Clypstone & palyser of the same withe the wages and fees accustumed of thissues of the same for terme of (their) his lyf etc

The werkers of clothes of straunge Countrees have theire liberties confermed to theim to duelle in Wales Irland or England under the kinges proteccion etc

Sir Hugh Hastinges knighte the manoire of Wellys in the Countie of Norffolk of the yerely value xxix li. xvij s. ob. the manoire of Wareham in the same Countie of the yerely value of xxiij li. xiij s. vij d. the manoire of Sheringham in the Countie forsaid of the yerely value of x li. xviij s. x d. the manoire of Wivetone in the same Countie of the yerely value of xxxvj li. xvij s. j d.ob. to him and his heires masles for ever by knightes service and the Rent of viij li. xvj s. vij d.

[f65b] William Dampoort maister Coke for the kinges mouthe hathe an Annuytie of xx^{ti} li. during his lif of thissues etc of the lordship of Bolingbroke in the Countie of Lincolne etc

John Wilson Thoffice of Forster of Fulwithe & Harlowe within the forest of Knaresburghe parcel of the duchie of Lancastre for term of his lif withe the fees and wages accustumed of thissues of thonnor of Knaresburghe by the handes of the Receyvor etc with almaner othre proffites etc

Roger Laurence Citezen and taillor of Londone the Rome of oon of the yoman

Taillors in the grete warderobe in Londone with the wages of vj d. by the day and lyvery clothing yerely to be perceived by the handes of the keper of the grete garderobe for the tyme being

Robert Veysy Thoffice of Ryding Forster of the neweforest within the Countie of Suthampton for terme of his lif with the wages and fees accustumed of the Revenues of the said Countie by the handes of the Shirief togeder with al other proffites etc

Herry Smythe thoffice of Bailly of Burley within the neweforest during the kinges pleasire with the wages accustumed of the Revenues of the same Countie by the handes of the Shirief

Thomas Barowe maister mason of the Castelles of Lancastre Clyderhowe and Lytherpole in your Countie of Lancastre and of Halton in Chestershire with the wages accustumed by the handes of the Receyvor of the duchie of Lancastre unto suche tyme as he be promoted

A prive seale to the Custumers of the poort of Suthampton to content unto John Hotone squier for the body xx li. and to Robert Vaysy ten marces of suche money as is growen of the Custumes Apud Dancastre xxviij die Aprilis Anno primo

The bisshop of Saint Assaphe hathe x li. yerely during his lif whiche thabbot and Convent of Welbek for the ferme of the mylnes of Ratford in the Countie of Notingham owe to paye to the king yerely etc

Nicholas Spicer thoffice of Receyvor of the lordship of Monnemouthe and Monnemouthes land in Southwales from the xxvj[ti] day of Novembre last past during the kinges pleasire / with the wages accustumed of the Revenues of the same lordship by his owne handes etc

The same Nicholas the Receivorship of the lordships of Brekenok Newport Uske and Carlione in Southwales from the same xxvj[ti] day during the kinges pleasire with the wages of xx[ti] marces of thissues of the same lordship by his owne handes or by the handes of the baillif

[f66] Sir Cristofre Moresby knight the Stewardship of the manoirs and lordships of Penreth Gamelesby & Queneshames in Cumbreland with the governaunce of the tenauntes there for terme of his lif with the fee of C s. thissues of the said lordships . And also an Annuytie of xxxv li. during his lif of thissues of the said manoirs by the handes of the Reveyvors etc

Richard Hastinges knighte lord Welles an Annuytie of C marces during his lif to be perceived of thonor of Richemond within the Countie of Lincolne by the handes of the Receyvor etc

Richard Spert hathe confermed unto him an Annuel Rent of x li by the handes of the Receyvor of the duchie of Lancastre within the said Countie of Lincolne for the tyme being unto suche tyme as the said Richard be preferred have Office with the fee of xx^{ti} marces for terme of lif

Dawson Clerc a presentacion to the Bisshop of Londone for the parsonage of Debden (by) voyde by the (deth) Resignacion of Master Richard Payne

Sir William Husey knight hath of J Vernam & Humfre [illegible deletion] Belchier for the Custody of alle manoirs land and tenementes that late were Sir William Trusselles the manoire of Wyllastone in Chesshire and al other landes and tenementes called Bruersalghe in the same Countie oonly except during the meyndre Age of Edward son and heire of the said William . (yelding) which yelde therefore to the king yerely Cviij li. The said somme of Cviij li. (from the fest and) from the fest of Seint Martyn in wynter last past during the said nonnage to him and his assignes of the kinges yeft

John Strangways Squier an Annuytie of xx marc from the fest of mighelmasse last past aslong as he bereth him wele of thissues & Revenues of al manoirs landes & tenementes commyng in the Countie palantyne of Lancastre by the handes of the Receyvor etc

Geffrey Whartone an Annuytie of x li. during his lif of the Revenues of the lordship of Bodyam in the Countie of Sussex by the handes of the Receyvor etc

Sir William Husey knighte the manoirs and lordships of Frestone and Bostone in the Countie of Lincolne of therely value of iij^{xx}xiij li. and the Reversion of the manoire or lordship of Uffyngtone in the Countie of Lincolne of the yerely value of l li. (after the) late the lord Roos . after the decesse of Philip lady Roos and the Reversion of the manoire or lordship of Borner in the said Countie of the value of lviij li & the lordship of Enderby in the Countie of Leicestre of the value of xxviij li late the (bas) lady Riche / after the decesse of Thomas lord stanley / to him and his heires masles forever by Knightes service and the Rent of xv li xiij s. vj d

[f66b] John Luthingtone hathe confermed unto him Thauditorship of alle honors Castelles lordships manoirs Townes & tenementes of the duchie of Lancastre aswele in alle Counties in the northparties over Trent as in the Counties of Lincolne Northamptone Warrwik & leicestre according to the

circuite of the chief Steward of the same duchie in the north parties for terme of his lif withe the wages fees proffites & advailles accustumed of thissues etc by the handes of the general Receivor of the same duchie

Item the same John Luthingtone and Richard Grenewey have confermed unto them Thauditorship of Northwales & of Chestre and Flyntshire and of the partes of theim during theire lifes and of him that overlyveth thother with suche wages and fees as John Browne (late Auditor there had) and John Walshe late Auditors there had by the handes of the Chambrelaine Shireffes Escheators Baillieffes Ryngildes & other Officers there for the tyme being & with al other proffites etc

Item the said John Luthingtone hathe confermed unto him Thauditorship of al and singuler Castelles lordships manoirs landes & tenementes longing to the duchie of York and therldom of the Marche within the Royaulme of England during his lif with the fees and wages accustumed of thissues & Revenues of the said Castelles & lordships etc by the handes of the Receyvors Baillifes etc and with al other proffites etc And also thauditorship of the manoirs lordships landes & tenementes of thonor of Richemond during his lif withe the wages accustumed etc of thissues of the same etc And also (Thauditorship) Thoffice of Baillif of Chesthunt & Walthamcrosse & parcar of Chesthunt alias Bran-tyngeshey in the Countie of Hertford and Thoffice of Baillif of Clavering in Essex during his lif with the wages of vj d. by the day that is to wite ij d. by day for the Baillifship of Chesthunt & Walthamcrosse and ij d. by the day for the said (th)office of parker of thissues & Revenues of the manoire of Chesthunt and ij d. by the day for thoffice of Baillif of Clavering of thissues of the lordship of Clavering by the handes of the Baillif etc And over this the same John and Elizabeth his wif of the house and Chambre & al other places within the manoire of Chesthunt (to th) during theire lifes and of eithre of them lenger lyving without any thing therefor paying etc

William Erle of Huntingdone hathe confermed unto him and to his heires the name state and title of the said Erldome with xx li of the fermes of the Counties of Cantebrigge and Huntingdone by the handes of the Shiref for the tyme being

[f67] Robert Brakenbury thoffice of Surveyor of the lordship of Writtel Havering Boyton Hadleghe Rocheforthe in Essex Tunbrigge Hadlow Penshurst Middeltone and Merden in Kent for terme of his lif withe the wages and fees accustumed of the Revenues of the said lordships by the handes of the Receyvors etc & with al other proffites etc

John Broke lord Cobham an Annuytie of sixtene poundes during the lif of Thomas lord Stanley of thissues of (your) the lordships of Middeltone and Merden in Kent by the handes of the Receyvors baillieffes etc

John lord Cobham the Manoire of Ermyngtone with the Burgh of the sam in Devone the hundred of Ermyngtone in the said Countie the manoire of Hode in Dertingtone in the said Countie the manoire of Wolstone alias Wolnastone in Cornewaile with almaner theire appurtenaunces late Sir William Stonor And the Reversion of the manoire of Dertford in Kent after the decesse of Thomas lord stanley . to him and his heires masles by knightes service and the Rent of x li. yerely etc

Robert Brakenbury the manere or lordshippe of Mote Marden Detlyng & Newentone in the Countie of Kent / and the maners or lordshippes of Crathorne & Cokered with thappurtenaunces / and alle other landes & tenementes rentes & services in Rompneymersh in Kent & otherwhere in the same Countie And in the Isle of Oxney and the Towne & parisshe of Hastinges in the Countie of Sussex & otherwhere in the same Countie that late was John Cheneys Robert Cheneys & Humfrey Cheneys / to the same Robert & his heires masles fro the ix day of marche last for ever by knight services & the rent of viij li & xvj s

The same Robert an Annuytie of fourty pounde from the furst day of August (last past) Anno primo during his lif of thissues etc commyng of the mynt within the Toure of Londone by the handes of the keper of theschaunge of money & Cunage there

Sir Robert Myddeltone an Annuytie of xx^{ti} li from Estre Anno primo during his lif of thissues and Revenues of the lordship of Middelham by the handes of the Receyvor Baillif etc

Robert Mannyng thoffice of purveyor of alle plummers and other laborers and werkmen and also almaner stuf for the kinges werkes within the palois of Westminster and the Towre of Londone necessary from the xxvj^{to} day of Juyne last past during his lif withe the wages of x d by the day . to be perceived of thissues etc of the lordships of Wryttel Havering Boytone Hadlegh Rayleghe and Rocheford in Essex and of Tunbrigge Penshurst Middeltone and Merden in Kent by the handes of the Receyvors Fermors etc

John Bigge hathe the manoire of Codbarowe in the Countie of Warrwik of the yerely value of xvj li viij s with thissues of the same during his lif (without)

[f67b] Richard Beauchamp hathe in Recompense of an Annuytie of xl marces to him graunted by king Edward the iiij th of the fee ferme of Gloucestre An Annuytie of lxvj li. xiij s. iiij d. during his lif of the Custumes of Bristowe by the handes of the Custumers

John Harringtone an Annuytie of xx li. during his lif of thissues commyng and growing of your Countie of Lancastre by the handes of the Receyvor etc

John Hastinges an Annuytie of xx^{ti} marces from the furst day of Januarij last past during his lif of thissues of Shiriefhotone by the handes of the Receyvor etc

Waltier Wynter an Annuytie of lx s. x d. from mighelmas Anno primo during his lif of thonor of Tutbury by the handes of the Receyvor etc

John le Germawe of the Bisshopriche of London is made denizin during his lif

William Crawcestre hathe confermed unto him an Annuelle Rent of C s. during his lif of thissues etc of Kilborvene in the Countie of York parcel of the duchie of Lancastre by the handes of the Receyvors etc

The Maire and burgesses of Newcastel upon Tyne and theire successours forever have xl li. yerely of the furst pens of the Custumes within the port there by the handes of the Collectour & Custumers there / for the tyme being . towardes the Repayring of the brigge and walles of the same Towne

Thomas Strikland knighte hath an Annuytie of xx li. of thissues etc of the lordship of Penrethe during his lif by the handes of the Receyvor etc

Wiliam Stevenson Thoffice of Baillif of Esshedalewarde under the Shirief of Cumbreland for the tyme being during his lif with the wages and fees accustumed

George Percy an Annuytie of xl^{ti} marc during his lif of thissues etc of the Countie of Northumbreland by the handes of the Shirief

Sir Thomas Grey of Hortone knighte an Annuytie of x li during his lif of thissues etc of the Custumes of Newcastel upon tyne by the handes of the Custumers

Maister William Beverley the deanry of Wymbourne in the Countie of Dorset for terme of his lif

Herry Robynson Scoler hathe a prive seale to the maister of the Kinges Colleige of Cantebrigge or to his lieutenaunt or deputie to admytte him felawe in the said Colleige with almaner rightes etc Any graunt or benefice or benefices

190

to the yerely value of xl^{ti} li. or undre notwithstanding

A pardone for Thomas Rither of Londone gentilman for his lif

[f68] A licence to Owene Ogle son and heire of Robert Ogle knighte and Isabelle his wif decessed to entre into alle suche landes possessions and hereditamentes as apperteigned to the said Robert & Isabelle and to have and enioy the same to him and his heires forever . and also a pardone upon al contemptes etc don upon the same

Oliver Middeltone An Annuyte of x marc during his lif / of the Revenues of the lordshippe of Middelham by the handes of the Receivor there at Michelmas and Estere

Sir Rauff Crathorne (his) An Annuyte of x li. during his lif to him graunted by the king Edward the iiij th of the Revenues of Pikerynglithe (graunt) new confirmed

William Mistilbroke hathe to ferme the custodie of the manor of Claygate fro Michelmas last past for terme of his lif paying therefore yerely sex poundes thertene shillinges & foure penys & xl d. of increase

(Sir John Beamont prest)

Sir Hugh Lynke prest the parisshe churche of Shirwille of the diocisse of Excestre

William Herbert / thoffice of Maisterforstership of Wyeswode Tryllek and Pennallt in the marches of Wales for terme of his lif

Maistere William Beverley Deane of the kinges Chapelle / the deanery of Wymborne Mynster in the Countie of Dorset

Sir Jamys Tirelle & Sir Thomas Cornewaille The Stewardshippe of the lordshippe of Bealt in Southwales for terme of theire lyves & aithere of them longest lyving / with the Fees & wages of xx markes of the Revenues of the said lordshippe

Sir William Stanley the Conotablechippe (of the Castelle) & Captaigne of

Castelle & Towne of Carnervan with xxiiij soldiours for the saufgard of the same for terme of his lif / To have the same office of Captaigneshippe with the xxiiij soldiours fro the ij^de day of May last past for terme of his lif with like wages & fees as Sir Thomas Mountgomery late had for thoccupieng of the same

Alice Burgh her Annuyte of xx marc to her graunted by king Edward the iiij th. during the nonne Age of Therle of Warrwik to be perceived of the Revenues of the Castelles lordshippes landes & tenementes in the Countie of Warrwik belonging to the said Erle of Warrwik now confirmed

Richard Hansard the Custodie of the lordship Maner & hundrethe of Odeham with thappurtenaunces fro the fest of pasche last past to thende & terme of xx^ti yeres paieng therefore yerely lj li. etc

Sir Thomas Lewkenor a pardon

Sir Jamys Strangways the maner or lordshippe of Dightone in the Countie of York to the valew of (lv) l li for terme of his lif / And an Annuyte of xvij li. xiij s. iiij d. from the fest of pasche last past during his lif of the Revenues of the lordship of Middelham

(John Coket)

Robert Gisborne / the keping of your (ff) game & woodes with the forest of Pambere in the Countie of Suthamptone for terme of his lif with alle maner wages fees etc

Henry Forest / the baillieffshippe of Kymberworth with the keping of the parke there for terme of his lif with the wages of iiij d. by the day / and an Annuyte of xiij li. xviij s. & iiij d. for terme of his said lif / from Michelmas last past during his lif of the Revenues of the said lordship by his owne handes or by the handes of the Receivor

[f68b] Sir William Berkley knighte hath confirmed unto him an Annuytie of x li. to be perceived of the lordshippe of Sulhille in the Countie of Warrwik And also Thoffice of Steward of the said lordshippe of Sulhille with thappurtenaunces / & of the lordshippe of (Edington) Erdingtone in Warrwikshire / and of the lordship of (Purbare) Purrebarre in the Countie of Stafford / Also the (te) office of riding Forstere of the chace of Sutton and Colvyle & of the parke of Sutton during the nonne Age of Edward Erle of Warrwik / for theoffice of Steward of Sulhille iiij li / for the Stewardshippe of Erdingtone xx s / for the Stewardshippe of Purybarre xx s. & for the riding forstership C s / during the nonne Age etc

A commaundement to Therls of Lincolne & Northumberland the Maire of York Sir Richard Ratclyff & other to cast doon alle fisshegarthes in ousse Wherff Aire Derwent & other fresshe watters within the Countie of York / and in especialle oone called golderne garthe in the water of Eyre etc

Edmond Prestwiche / an Annuytie of C s. during pleasure to be takene of thissues & Revenues of the lordship of galford in the Countie of Lancastre by the handes of the Receivor

Richard Harleston & William (Her) Hareby squiers hath the Captaigneship of Jersey & of the Castelle of Mountorgelle during theire lyves & aithere of theim lengest lyving

Robert Appulby thoffice of keping of the prive palois in Westminster with the fees & wages due & accustumed for terme of his lif / and also thoffice & keping of the warderobe within the same palois with the wages & fees accustumed during his liff from Michelmas last

William Lilborne An Annuelle Rent or a fee ferme of viij li. goyng out of certen landes & tenementes in Edenbrigge in Kent now in the halding of Richard Martyn squier / to have the same to him & to his heires masles for ever by knighte service & the Rent of xj s.

John Chester Thoffice of gaugier within the Towne & port of Bristowe during pleasure with fees & wages accustumed

John (Saxby) Saxilby an Annuite of x li fro Michelmas last of the lordship of gret Lighes in Essex unto the tyme he be promoted

Thomas Fraunceys the pencion within thabbey of Thorney now void

Master Andrew Doket president & the felowes of the Quenes College within the universitee of Cambrigge / the maner of Covesgrane in the Countie of Bukingham / and alle alle [sic] the landes & tenementes in Sheldingthorp Market Deping Bragham & Stowe in the Countie of Lincolne Also the maner of Neuton in the Countie of Suffolk / the manor of Stanford in the Countie of Berkshire / (and also Clxx li. every yere everlasting / lx li to be perceived) the manor of bukby in the Countie of (Lincolne) Northamptone [f69] And also Cx li of an Annuyte / to be takene in forme folowing that is to say (of the fee ferme of the lordship & maner of Bukby in the Countie of Northampton / and othere) lx li of the feeferme of the Towne of Aylesbury in the Countie of Bukingham And l li residue of the feeferme of Ramesey in the Countie of Huntingdon

John Hopertone the king hathe graunted unto him an annuyte or annuelle rent of C s of the lordship of Sherefhuton unto he be promoted

John Smythe the king hathe graunted unto him an annuyte or anuel rent of thritty shillinges and v d for terme of his lif

Johannes Coket the [sic] hathe comfirmed unto him thoffice of parkership of Sodbury with herbage and paunage during nownage

Herry Willougby the king hathe graunted unto him thoffice of Constable of the Castelle of Makstoke and steward of the same and maister of the game of the park there for terme of his lif

John Babingtone & William Maleherbe / hathe a warraunt directed to the Custumers of the Custumes & subsides in the poorte of Excestre & Dertmouth to pay unto theim xl marc / whiche the king hath geven unto them towardes theire Ramison / late taken upone the see by brytaygnes

Thomas Asper an Annuyte of x marc during his liff of the Revenues of the lordshippe of Sherefhotone

Roger Hertlingtone alle landes & tenementes within the lordshippe of Stokenham late John Halwell in the Countie of Devone / landes & tenementes called Blakbourneboty in the Countie aforsaid late Sir Thomas Seintleger / landes and tenementes in Quydamptone & Bemertone in the Countie of Wiltshire late Sir William Berkeley / landes & tenementes in Newton & landes & tenementes in Stowford to him & his heires masles by knighte services & Rent of xvj s. viij d .

John Agard the king hathe graunted unto him thoffice of Receivourship of all his lordshippes manours Castelles Townes and landes with thapportenaunces within the Counties of Warwik Worcestre stafford and Northampton late belonging unto his Brother the duc of Clarence during his pleasure with the wages and fees due and accustumed / Yevene etc at Pountefret the x th day of Juyne the first yere of oure Reigne [monogram]

Thomas Wildcotes the baillief of your Towne & lordshippe of Beaudeley during pleasure with the wages & fees thereto due and accustumed

Edward Son & heire of John late Erle of Wilteshire & Constaunce his wif a specialle licence to entre into his landes without provyng of Age etc

194

John Payne of Bristowe & John (Browne) George his felowe have certen lettres to them confirmed of the graunt of king Edward the iiij th / that where by a lettre of marke graunted by the king of Castelle Lyone to oon Petir Ochoa generally upon alle the kinges subgiettes / a Shippe with goodes longing to the said John & John was takene at the Towne of Guypusque / for the whiche the said John & John to have M^{l}M^{l}M^{l}DC Coronnes of iiij s. contented unto them by the Custumers of Londone Sandwiche Southamptone & Bristowe upon the Custumes of the merchauntes of the provynce of Guypusque / notwithstanding the graunt made to them upon the Custumes of alle maner merchandises of men of Castelle Lyon of v^M Corones & vj^M Corones / unto suche tyme as forsaid summe be contented unto the said John & John

[f69b] Sir William Husse knighte Chief Justice of the kinges benche John Catesby knighte oon of the Justices of the Comon place Richard Tunstalle knighte William Catesby squier Robert Wittelbury & Oliver Sutton squiers the warde & mariage of Edward Son & heire of John late Erle of Wilteshire with the keping of alle the Castelles manors lordshippes etc from Michelmas last etc yeven etc the xx day of Juyne Anno primo

William Abbot of Seint Albones & the Convent of the same / hathe to them & their Successors for ever an Annuyte or Annuelle Rent of xl marc (of) to be taken of the fee ferme of the Towne or burgh of Bedford

Richard Spert / An Annuyte of xl marc during his lif to be taken of the proffites of Longbenyngtone in the Countie of Lincolne by the handes of the Receivor etc

John Moylle hathe confirmed unto him an Annuyte of v marc to be taken yerely during his lif of the lordship of Dynbighe / And also an Annuyte of x li / to be taken yerely during his lif (of) at the Receipt of the (Che) Eschequiere of Dynbighe

John Tymperley hathe confirmed unto him an Annuyte of xx li unto the [sic] he be promoted etc of the proffites & Revenues of the Counties of Norffolk & Suffolk

Sir Thomas Wortley (hat) and Johanne his wif (hath) have to theim and aithere of them longere lyving / the keping aswele of lxxviij s. of the residue of the manor of Torneham halle & Thornetone exceding the value of the iij^{de} part of the said maners with the membres (&) as of alle other manors landes & tenementes with thappurtenaunces whatsoever within the Counties of York Lancastre Lincolne Derby within the Citee of London with Courtes letes etc except the manors of Torneham halle & Thorneton with theire appurtenauntes to the said Johanne as afore in her dowre assigned / fro the tyme of the dethe of John Pilkington knighte during the nonne Age of Edward his Son / yelding yerely to the king (xxv li) Cxx li And also a pardone of alle mysprisons fynes amerciamentes etc

Thomas Holt an Annuytie of x li during his lif of thissues etc of the Countie palantyne of Lancastre by the handes of the Receyvor etc

Sir Gervays Clyftone Thoffice of keping of the parke of Foly John within the Forest of Wyndesore for terme of his lif with the wages and fees accustumed of thissues of the Castelle of Windesore etc

John Petite of Londone merchaunt and John Bolle wollemane have a Commissione under prive seale to (be) make due serche of alle maner wolles aswele within Franchises as without within the Royaulme of England etc

Alexandre Sely oon of the seriauntes at Armes with the wages of xij d by the day during his lif of thissues proffites fermes etc of the Counties of Bedford & Bukingham by the handes of the Shirief withe a liverey gowne etc

John Gaynesford a pardone for his lif

Margarete Lancastre hathe the keping of Richard Kyrkely of Assheley in the Countie of Cambrigge with alle his landes and tenementes etc by (reaso) the kinges gyft by reason of the ydiocy of the said Richard

[f70] Nicholas Gaynesford / a pardon for his lif

John Boullare of Homfleur in Normandy hathe a saufconduyt to come into England with a Ship called the Morice of Homflewe laden with almaner wynes & other merchandises and the same discharged to recharge ayein with almaner merchandises of this Royaulme to the Staple of Calais not apperteynyng

John Henbury and Robert Henbury thoffice of Coedership within the lordship of Dynbighe for terme of their lifes and of eithre of theim lenger lyving withe the wages and fees accustumed etc

Sir Thomas Cornewaille knighte an Annuytie of xlti poundes during his lif of thissues etc of the lordships of Pembrige Yerdislond and Orletone within the Countie of Herford by the handes of the Receyvor etc

196

Thomas lord Stanley and George Stanley lord Straunge have the Castelles manoirs & lordships of Hope and Hopedale in the marches of Wales in the Countie of Chestre the manoir(s) & lordship(s) of Northwiche with the pasture of Overmersshe in the said Countie the manoirs & lordships of Westlydford Blakenden Hailesbertre alias Hasebeare in the Countie of Somerset the lordship of Bereford sancti Martin in the Countie of Wilteshire the lordship of Ardingtone in Berkshire the lordship of Steventone in Bedfordshire the lordships of Knotting Collesden & Cottone in the same Countie & al landes & tenementes in Blomeham late Roger Tocotes in the said Counte the lordship of Gaddisden magna in Hertfordshire the Castelle manoire lordship and Soke of Kymbaltone in Huntingdonshire with the manoirs of Swyneshed Hardewik & Tilbroke in the same Countie Also al mesuages landes & tenementes Rents & services in (Macclessffeld) Macclesfeld & Cristeltone in Chesshire late duc of Bukingham the manoirs of Chorley and Boltone in Lancastreshire / landes & tenementes in Brightmede in the said Countie Also the mesuage & al landes & tenementes late Robert Willughbys knighte within the parisshe of Saint Petre by Powleswharf in Londone orelleswhere within the said Citie to theim and theire heires masles forever by knightes service and the Rent of l li yerely

Sir Robert Maners knighte the manoire or lordship of Tremwelle in Cornewaille late Marques Dorset Annui valoris xlv li iiij s. the manoirs or lordships of Kentesbeare & Blakborowe & Charletone in Devone Annui valoris xxxv li. ij s. ij d. for terme of his lif without any accompt etc

Walter Vaghan Thoffice of Steward of the lordship of Elvele in the marches of Wales during the kinges pleasire with the wages accustumed etc

Edmond Talbot and John Forster Custumers of Hull have a prive seale to the Tresourere and Barons to surcesse of almaner processe (till mighelmasse) depending betwix them and Stephan Clampard and John Crochard upon a certain Annuytie to the said Stephen and John graunted by King Edward the iiij th unto mighelmasse terme next commyng Datum apud Pountfreit xxij° die Junij Anno primo

Thomas Stroder Squier hathe the manoire or lordship of Northcote in Cornewaille late Marques Dorset Annui valoris v li. xiiij s. x d. the manoire of Wellingtone in the said Countie Annui valoris ix li. vij s. x d. the manoire of Southhold in Devone Annui valoris iiij li. xvij s. xj d. for terme of his lif without any accompt etc

[f70b] Robert Coort thoffice of Auditor of alle the accomptes of the duchie of Cornewail
and Receivor of alle manoirs lordships landes & tenementes of the duchie of Lancastre & of therldom of Hereford in the Southparties of the Royaulme of England during the kinges pleasire with the wages and fees accustumed etc by his owne handes

William Vaghan Squier an Annuytie of x marces during his lif of thissues etc of the manoire of Galsebury in the Marches of Wales etc by the handes of the Receivor Firmar etc

Robert Cade a generalle pardone

Herry Burghe and Isabelle his wif an Annuytie of xx^{ti} marc for terme of theire lifes and of eithre of theim lenger lyving of thissues etc of the lordship of Middelham / by the handes of the Receyvor etc

the xij governors burgesses and inhabitauntes of the Towne of Beverley have a C li that is to wite xx^{ti} marces yerely of the grete and litell Custumes within the port of Kingestone upon Hull commyng of almaner merchaundises to the Staple of Calais not apperteynyng by theim theire charged or discharged unto the tyme the said Somme of C li be fully paied

John Evers Squier an Annuytie of vj marces during his lif of thissues & profittes etc of the watermylne of Melborne in Leicestreshire per manus Receptoris

Robert Shirborne an Annuytie of x marc during his lif of thissues etc of alle lordships & manoirs of the Countie palantyne of Lancastre by the handes of the Receivor

John Lyvesey an Annuytie of x li of thissues etc of the Countie palantyne of Lancastre unto the tyme he be promoted to landes & tenementes of like value

Richard Rugge an Annuytie of x li during his lif of thissues etc of the lordship of Walsalle by the handes of the Receyvor etc

Roger Breretone thoffice of Baillif of the hundred of Northwiche in the Countie palantine of Chestre for terme of his lif with the wages & fees of iiij d. by the day by the handes of the Chambrelain of Chestre

William Rither yomane of the Crowne vj d. by day for the fee of the same of thissues etc of the Countie of Devone by the handes of the Shirief
And also an Annuytie of xx^{ti} marces of thissues etc of the lordship of Newport Paynelle by the handes of the Receivor during his lif per confirmacionem

John Talbot an Annuytie of xx marc of thissues of the Countie palantyne of Lancastre unto the tyme he have landes & tenementes of like value

Robert Rawdone thoffice of keper of the Forest and Chace of Mogtre alias Moktree within the lordship of Wigmore in the marches of Wales withe the wages of vj d. by the day during his lif of thissues etc of the lordships of Beaudeley Cleberey & Yernewode in the Countie of Salop by the handes of the Receyvor etc

Roger Hertlingtone Thoffice of Steward of the lordships of Stokenham Yealhamptone & Langacre with the hundred of Colrigge in Devonshire during the kinges pleasire with the wages and fees accustumed etc of thissues of the said lordships etc

[f71] Gerald Erl of Kyldare the manoire of Lexlep with thappurtenaunces during his lif without any accompt etc

John Wadingtone an Annuytie of v marc for terme of lif or unto suche tyme as he have landes of like value . to be perceived of thissues of the lordship of Bowland by the handes of the Receyvor etc per confirmacionem

William Dyrling of Bristowe xx li of the Custumes there of the kinges gift .

William Harringtone Squier an Annuytie of x li during his lif of thissues of the lordship of Middelham in the Countie of Yorke by the handes of the Reccyvor

Anthony Baveryne merchaunt of Venyse hathe a prive seale to discharge the Custumers & Comptrollers of Southamptone of taking of any Custumes for (certain) xj ml bowstaves there by him discharged etc

William Croke thoffice of Collector of ancorage wharfage hedesylver & othre custumes in the porte of Calais during his lif withe the wages and fees accustumed etc per confirmacionem

Sir Thomas Fitzwilliam hathe the manoire of Kenwyk in Norffolk during the lif of Sir William Norreys whiche to him apperteygned as parcelle of thenheritaunce of the lady marques Mountague his wif and in the kinges gift by reason of his Rebellione

Thomas Lambe and Katheryne his wif an Annuytie of v marc during (his) theire lifes and of eithre etc of thissues of Middelham etc

John Scot of the Chapelle the free Chapelle of Saint Loye at the Townes ende of Newcastelle undre Lyne during his lif with almaner rightes etc

Thomas Gowere an Annuytie of C marc during his lif that is to wite xl li yerely of thissues etc of the lordship of Hesingwald & Hubye in Yorkshire xx li yerely of thissues etc of the (y) manoire of Yaristhorp in the same Countie and x marces yerely of thissues etc of the lordship of Knaptone in the same Countie by the handes of the Fermors etc

Agnes Bekewithe wydowe is pardonned of xlj s. that she owed the king at myghelmasse Anno primo for the ferme of certaine landes and tenementes called Cleynthalle within the lordship of Knaresburghe

The said Agnes and Thomas Bekwithe hir son hathe an Annuytie of xl s during theire lyfes and of eithre of theim lenger lyving of thissues etc of the lordship of Knaresburghe by the handes of the Receyvor etc

William Bowdeler an Annuitie of vj li xx d during his lif of thissues etc of the lordship of Glattone in the Countie of Huntingdon by the handes of the Receyvor

John Bulle thoffice of porter (of) or gaylere of the Castelle of Clederowe in the Countie of Lancastre with the wages accustumed during his lif

Sir Lawrence Squiere prest the prebend of the Collegiat Churche of oure lady of Laicestre that Sir James Letes had

[f71b] Fraunceys lord Lovelle an Annuytie of x li for the terme of vij yeres fro mighelmas Anno (pr) secundo of thissues etc of the lordships of Cokeham and Bray in Berkshire . And an Annuytie of xl li fro the said fest during the lif of Margarete Harecourt wydowe of thissues of the said lordships . And also an Annuytie of xxiiij li from the said fest during the lif of Anne somtyme the wif of John Stonor Squier of thissues of the said lordships

Anthony Baveryne merchaunt of Venyse hathe a discharge to the Custumers of Londone upon the payment of Custome of vijM^{l}D Bowstaves by him there discharged

Frydeswide Lovelle an Annuytie of C marc during his [sic] lif of thissues etc of thonor & lordship of Walingford in the Countie of Oxonford by the handes of the Receyvor etc the tenauntes Fermors baillieffes Reves and other mynistres aswele of the duchie of Lancastre as of the Countie palantyne of Lancastre have a pardonne of al amerciamentes issues Relevies and alle dettes etc

Launcelet Whartone Thoffice of Bowberere of Mallerstange in Westmorland during the nonnage of Thomas son and heire of Sir William Parre with the wages of (vij) vj marces yerely of thissues of the said Countie by the handes of the Receyvor

Nicholas Rigby thoffice of Baillif of your Towne of Winchelsee during his lif withe the wages accustumed etc

the same Nicholas thoffice of Constable of the Castelle of Bodyham in Sussex with the keping of the parke there late Thomas Lewkenores knighte . during his lif perceyvyng yerely for the said Office of Constable xx li And for the said keping of the parke the wages and fees accustumed etc of thissues of the same lordship

Anthony Baveryne hathe a warrant to the Tresourere and barons of theschequiere to allowe the Custumers of Londone and Suthampton in theire accomptes (of) the Custumes of (xj m^l and vij^{ml} D bowestaves) xviij M^{l}D Bowstaves to the said Anthony geven by the king

William Worsley and William Josephe thoffice of Baillif of the Scunage of the Towne of Calais and Island of Colne during theire lifes and of eithre of theim lenger lyving withe the wages and fees etc accustumed

William Gascoigne knighte an Annuytie of xx li during his lif of thissues etc of the lordship and Castelle of Knaresburghe

[f72] John Sotheworthe maiore of Chestre an Annuytie of x li during his lif of thissues etc of the lordship of Dynbighe And also a nother Annuytie of x li of (thissues and) the fee ferme of Chestre during his lif per confirmacionem

John Busshe in Gilderland borne mad denizine during his lif

Thomas Bisshop of Saint David hathe a prive seale to the Treasourere & Chambrelains of theschequiere to doo levie oon taille or tailles of C li upon the disme of the Bisshopriche of Sarum and to delyver the same to maister John Doges for the said Bisshop in discharging him of the said Disme

John Sambroke Thoffice of oon of Sergeant at Armes during his lif with the wages of xij d by the day of the fee ferme of the Citie of Hereford (with livery etc)

John Somerford and othre tenauntes and seriuntes apperteynyng to William Breretone have a warrant to the Shiref of Chesshire and Auditors of the Countie palantyne of Chestre to allowe and discharge of a fyne of viij li xiij s iiij d to theim pardoned by the king

John Ottere certaine landes and tenementes in Knoylle in Wiltshire and in Kylmantone in the Countie of Somerset to him and his heires masles by knightes service and the Rent of xj s

Thinhabitauntes of the parisshe of Wynanddermere have a warrant to the Receyvor of the the [sic] lordship of Kendale for v marc to theim geven by the king towardes the buylding of theire Churche

To be in the Churche of York the king hathe ordeigned / C / prestes and to sing there in the worship of god oure lady seint George & seint Nynyan ut patet in billa

The king hathe graunted to the Towne of Pountfret to have a mair and other certen libertees as apperethe in theire bille

Gilbert Maners the maners landes & tenementes in Foweytone & Lanteglos in the Countie of Cornubie / annui valoris xij li xiij s iiij d / the maner of Trenowde in the same Countie vij li xvj s viij d / to him & to his heires masles for ever by knighte service & the Rent of xxx s

Sir Richard Huddelston the keping of the parke of Badowe for terme of his liff with the wages & fees thereunto due & accustumed

Thomas Radclyff Thoffices of bailly of Westgate of Excestre otherwise called Exiland / of Topisham / of Colompjohn / and of the hundred of Harigge / to have the same offices & eiche of them from seint Michelle last past during his lif / with the Fees & wages thereunto due & accustumed / and also to have the ferme of the Crane & sellers of Toppisham during his said lif / in as large maner & forme as Richard Cruse occupied the same before this tyme

[f72b] John (Cursene) Coursone squier hathe confirmed unto him an Anutie of C s for terme of his lif to be perceived of thissues profuytes & Revenues of (thonl) thonnor of Tutbury

Thomas Feror & William Tattone Thoffice of Clerc of theschequier of Chestre during the kinges pleasure with the fees of vj d by the day to be perceived at the Eschequier of the Revenues of the Counties of Chestre & Flynte

Richard Lee thoffice of Baillif of the lordship of Wyng within the Countie of Bukingham for terme of his lif withe the wages of iiij d by the day of thissues of the said lordship etc

Sir Richard Corbet knighte an Annuytie of xx li during his lif of thissues etc of the lordship of Dynbieghe per manus Receptoris etc

Thomas Fentone yoman of the Corowne an Annuytie of C s during his lif of thissues etc of the lordship of Barnaycastelle within the Bisshopriche of Duresme by the handes of the Receyvor etc

Richard Clervaux Squier oon Tonne of wyne yerely during his lif of the pryuse wynes of Hulle by the handes of the chief Botiller etc

A warrant to the Tresourere (of) and Chambrelains of theschequiere to stryke out ij tailles at the Reciep in due forme to be leveyed for Richard Laurence yoman of the Juelhouse upon Thabbot & Convent of Shrewesbury upon the ferme or fee ferme of the wode of Lythewood that is to say the oon taille of theim of lx s to be leveyed in termo pasche Anno primo And the other of xxxij s x d to be leveyed upon the Receipt of the said warrant datum xxix th day of Juyl Anno secundo

A licence geven to William Wilcokes & Thomas Fuller to be Comptrollers or Clerkes of Custumes and to bye and selle merchandises . the statute made contrary to the same notwithstanding

John Browne yomane of the Seler hathe the keping of the parke of Haye within the forest of Knaresburghe in the Countie of York during his lif with the fees of iiij d by the day of thissues of the said lordship of Knaresburghe

A warrant to thauditors of the duchie of Lancastre to (allowe) discharge and allowe aswele Richard Knaresburghe as Nicholas Leventhorp Receyvor of the lordship of Knaresburghe of xij li by the said Richard expended by the kinges commaundement of the ferme of mylnes and other Rents in the said lordship of Knaresburghe etc Datum the xxx^{ti} day of Juylle Anno ij^{do}

John Stanford Thoffice of Auditor of alle and singuler Comptes of alle

Castelles landes etc apperteynyng to the Corowne within the Royaulme of England and of alle lordships landes etc late John duc of Norffolk and Margrete duchesse of Somerset also of the Castel of Holt and of lordships landes and tenementes in Bromfeld & Yale [f73] during his lif . perceyvyng for the said landes longing to the Crowne x li of thissues etc of the lordship of Bradwelle in the Countie of Essex Cosham & the manoire of Roude in the Countie of Wiltshire·by the handes of the Collectors baillieffes etc and for thoffice of Auditor(s) of thother landes the fee of xx marces of thissues etc of the lordships & manoirs of Wenge in Countie Bukingham & Syleby in Countie Leicestre by the handes of the Receyvor of the landes of the said late duc . and iij s iiij d for his wages dailly during his lif as oft as he shal Ryde in the said Office . with alle other proffites etc accustumed etc

Thomas Talbot knighte an Annuytie of xl li to him and his heires masles of thissues etc of the Countie palantyne of Lancastre in the Countie of Lancastre by the handes of the Receyvor etc

A specialle graunt made to the maire Constables and felisship of merchauntes of the Staple of Calais & theire Successours that they shalbe in quest or impanelled in any assises etc

A warrant direct to the Receyvor of the duchie of Lancastre to content xx^{ti} marces to Elizabeth Grenehaughe late suster to Sir John Pylkingtone whiche was by him bequethed towardes the mariage of hir children Datum v° die Augusti Anno ij^{do}

A prive seale to the maistre of the Colleige called the Kinges halle to Receyve William Pykering Scoler for a felowe within the same datum iiij^{th} day of August Anno ij^{do}

A licence to the maiere Constables and felisship of merchauntes of the Staple at Calais that they and their Suceessors shal (put) mortise landes and tenementes to the valor of C li by yere over reprises (in mor) etc

to the vicairs of the Cathedralle churche of York thadvouson of the parisshe Churche of Cotyngham in the Countie of York forever

A warrant to the Tresourere and Chambrelains of theschequier to doo levye a tayle for the some of Clx li for the merchauntes of the staple for fulle contentacion of (h) othre sommes to them due and so moche lost by the payment of flemmysshe money

204

Walter Deveraux lord Ferrers . hathe the manoire of Chesthunt with thappurtenaunces in Chesthunt and Waltham in the Countie of Hertford parcelle of
Richemond Fee from mighelmasse Anno primo during his lif without any
accompt etc

Richard Mascy to be oon of the kinges seriauntes at (Armes) lawe in the
Countie palatyne of Chestre & Flynt during the kinges pleasure with the fees &
wages accustumed

[f73b] Alveredo Corneburgh Officium Constabularij Castro de Restormelle et
Officium parcarij de Restormalle necnon totam piscariam aque de Fowey in
Comitatu Cornubie pro termino vite sue cum vadiis consuetis absque compoto
pro piscaria predicta de exitibus etc ducatus Cornubie. Ac officium Ballivi
villarum de Plymmouth Sutton Prior Sutton Pole Sutton Rauf Sutton Vautort
& Estonhous in Comitatu Devonie pro termino vite sue cum vadiis consuetis
Ac Officium parcarij parci de Kirrybullok ac warrenne in parco illo pro termino
vite sue cum vadiis consuetis

[To Alfred Corneburgh, the office of constable of the castle of Restormelle
and the office of parker of Restormelle together with the whole fishery of the
water of Fowey in the county of Cornwall for term of his life with the
accustomed wages and without accounting for the abovesaid fishery, from
the issues etc of the duchy of Cornwall. And the office of bailiff of the towns
of Plymouth, Sutton Prior, Sutton Pole, Sutton Rauf, Sutton Vautort and
Estonhous in the county of Devon for term of his life with the accustomed
wages. And the office of parker of the park of Kirrybullok and warrener in
that park for term of his life with the accustomed wages.]

Thome Tunstalle Manerium sive dominium de Gotherington iuxta Tottnesse in
Comitatu Devonie annuj valoris xl li sibi et heredibus masculis de corpore suo
legittime (procrel) procreatur per servicium militare et Redditum iij li annuatim

[To Thomas Tunstall, the manor or lordship of Gotherington near Tottnesse
in the county of Devon, of the annual value of £40, to him and the heirs male
of his body legitimately begotten, by knight service and a rent of £3
annually.]

John Bottyle yoman of the Crowne an Annuytie of C s during his lif of thissues
etc of the lordship of Barnardes Castelle

A warrant to John Clerk and John Cotone Auditors of theschequiere to here
and determyne thaccompt of Thomas Canceller aswele of al money by him
Receyved and al charges and costs by him doon from the xj day of January
the xxij[ti] yere of king Edward the iiij[th] unto the xj day of Januarij Anno primo
Regis Ricardi tercij And fromthence yerely from tyme to tyme as (he shal) the

buylding of the Chapel of Windesore . the vicairs newe logginges and the Reparacions of the grete manor in the old parke shalbe doone . and to allowe aswele unto him or his deputies (by) the said charges by him (and len) had and doon / as the wages of him and diverse other Artificers there appointed with certain other particuler sommes in the said warrant comprised Datum vj° die Augusti Anno ij^{do}

the tenauntes of the Counties of Caernarvon Anglesey and Merioneth have a warrant to the Chambrelain of North Wales to make unto them suffisaunt lettres of pardonne of almaner dettes and accomptes by them due the day of theire attendaunce etc

John Jervays Thoffice of Chief Junere within the Toure of Londone during his lif with the wages of xij d by the day of thissues etc of the lordships etc of Wrottylle Havering Boytone Rayleghe etc and a gowne of the stute of Squiers of household

Thomas Norresse an Annuytie of iiij marces during his lif of thissues etc of the lordship of Middelham per manus Receptoris

Thomas Bryane chief Juge hathe the manoire of Willesford nighe Uphavyne in the Countie of Wiltshire the manoire of Ovir in the Countie of Gloucestre and the manoire of Calvertone in Countie of Bukingham to him and his heires masles by knightes service and the Rent of xliij s iij d for the said manoire of Willesford and the Rent of xxxj s vj d for the said manoire of Ovir and the Rent xxxix s iij d for the said manoire of Calvertone

[f74] Edward Erle of Kent hathe confermed unto him his lettres patentes of the name stile and title of the said Erldome

Richard Harlestone hathe a licence for a ship of iiij^{xx}tonnes charged with almanere merchandises to goo to outward(es) parties and Recharged there to come ayen (ast as oft) as oft as him shal like within the space of a yere

Elizabeth Brewster hathe a pardonne of almaner fynes amerciamentes issues forfaites etc

John Jacoby of Londone Broker borne in Florence is made denisyne and his heires forever

Richard Kydwelle prest hathe confermed unto him his patent to be oon of the

Chappellayns of the Chauntery of saint Mary within the manoire of Wodestok with x marces of wages during his lif of thissues (there) of the said manoire etc

Thomas Erle of Surrey an Annuytie of M^{l}li during the lif of the duc of Norffolk his fadre of thissues of the duchie of Cornewaille by the handes of the Receyvor

A warrant to John Sapcotes Receyvor generalle of the duchie of Cornewaille to content unto John duc of Norffolk ij^{ml} markes and to Thomas Erle of Surrey M^l marc of thissues of his Receipt without delay etc

Robert of the Seler hathe a licence to charge a ship of his called the (Mary) Trinite gale of the portage of vj^{xx} tonnes with almanere merchandises to owtward parties (outw) adverse or other and to bring into this Royaulme almanere merchandises . as oft etc within oon hole yere Datum ix° Augusti Anno ij^{do}

William Cowper the lordshippe of Okham in the Countie of Surrey of the valewe of xx marc / to him & to his heires masles by knightes services & xx s Rent

Rauff Banaster the manor of Ealding in the Countie of Kent to the valewe of (li).l.li / to him & to his hires masles (&) by knighte service & the Rent of iiij li

Thomas Mering the Maner of Raminardewyke of the valewe of vj li xiij s iiij d the Maner of Ikelford & Pyrtone in the Countie of Hertford / and certen landes & tenementes in Holewelle Arlesey & Eyoon in the Countie of Bedford of the valewe of xiiij li / to him & to his heires masles by knighte service & the Rent of xl s .

Roger Bikley the parkershippe of Fulbroke in the Countie of Warrwik during the nonne Age of Edward son & heir of George duc of Clarence with the fees & wages accustumed

Roger Bikley The Constable of the Castelle (d) of llannandewere in the Countie of Kemerdene for terme of his lif with the fee of xx^{ti} li / of the Revenues of the said lordship

Maister Thomas Babethorpe the parsonage of Bulmere in the Countie of York voyde by the decesse of Maister George Strangways /

[f74b] Randolph Kelchethe an Annuytie of v marces during his lif of thissues etc of the Countie palantyne of (Chestre) Lancastre by the handes of the Receyvor etc

George Dale thoffice of kepar of the manoire of Haverying at Boure otherwise Thoffice of Baillif there . with the keping of the wareyne there during his lif with the wages and fees due and accustumed Also the keping of the yate of the parc of Havering called the Southgate during his lif with the wages and fees accustumed etc per confirmacionem

Maister Walter Lemster Doctor of phisique an Annuytie of xl li during his lif of thissues & proffites etc in the kinges hanaper growing by the handes of the Clerc of the same

Sir John Savage knighte thelder an Annuytie of xx marces during his lif of thissues etc of the Forest of Macclesfeld by the handes of the Baillif there

William Malyverer certain landes and tenementes called Hertanger lying in the parisshe of Berstone in Kent Annui valoris xx s certain landes called Parattes landes lying in the same parisshe annui valoris xlvj s viij d a wynde mylne called Berstone mylne Annui valoris xxvj s viij d certain landes called garardes annui valoris xx s iij acres of land lying in the lordship of Freydefeld Annui valoris xviij d the manoire of Eythorne with thappurtanaunces annui valoris ix marc x s iij d ob a certain rent paied by the tenauntes of the said manoire l s certain landes called Mottes lying in the parisshe of Nonyngtone Annui valoris vj s iiij d a certain mesuage with certain landes lying in Wymlyngiswelde Annui valoris liij s iiij d. An yerely Rent going out of certain landes and tenementes in the parisshes of Wyngeham and Godnestone annui valoris vj li xviij s iij d ob iij acres of land in the parisshe of Dele within thehundred of Cornelo annui valoris v s certain landes in Sibbersweld annui valoris xiij s iiij d xj acres of land lying in Staple called Barnefeld annui valoris viij s iiij d x acres & di. of land lying in Estre annui valoris vj s viij d late George Brown xlij acres land lying in the parisshe of Godnestone annui valoris xxix s certain Rentes and services going out of the same v s vj d a certain Rent which Robert Gervays is bound to yeld yerely vj d the manoire of Kryksale annui valoris liij s. iiij d the manoire of Heppynden late John Fogge annui valoris ix li to him and his heires (f) masles forever by knightes service and the Rent of lx s yerely

Christofir Colyns thoffice of Constable of the Castelle of Queneburghe And the mylne to the said Castel adioynyng during his lif with the wages of xx marces yerely to be perceived of thissues etc of the Counties of Essex and Hertford by the handes of the Shirief

John Hotone hathe xx li and Robert Veysy x marces by a taille leveyed in theschequier by the Tresourere & Chambrelains upon the Collectors of the Custumes in the port of Suthampton of the kinges Reward etc

Thomas Cookesey Squier thoffice of Steward of oure lordship of Henley in Arderne within oure Countie of Warrwik during his lif with the fees and wages of C s of thissues etc of the said lordship Also Thoffice of maister of the game of the parkes of Henley during his lif withe the wages and fees accustumed

[f75] William Belanoyne merchant hathe a licence for a C tonne of gascoigne wyne or othre of his owne goodes or othre . to bring into this Royaulme at his pleasire in a ship or shippes of Britaigne or Hispain

John Parker thoffice of Baillif of the Tollebothe in Lynne during his lif with almanere wages accustumed etc

William Cowper the lordship of Okeham in the Countie of Surrey Annui valoris xx marc to him and his heires masles by knightes service and the Rent of xx s yerely

Richard Page xx li yerely during his lif of the Custumes in the portes of Plymmouthe and Fowey by the handes of the Custumers per confirmacionem

Randolphe Franke thoffices of keping of the warderobe within the Castelle of Notingham and of the parke and logge there called the hermytage . also the keping of the Gaole within the Towne of Notingham . perceyvyng yerely for the said keping of warderobe vj d by the day and for the keping of the parke ij d by day of the fee ferme of the Towne of Notingham by the handes of the Shirief or fermors etc and for the keping of the gaole the wages and fees accustumed with xj li of Reward of the said fee ferme

Richard Triplard merchant hathe a licence for viij^C pece of Tynne to be bought in this Royaulme and shipped and conveyed to outward parties etc at oon tyme or diverse tymes etc

William Staveley and Richard his Son have the money of billes of Aliantes within the Towne of Calais leveyed and perceived during theire lyves and of eithre of theim lenger lyving

Sir James Tyrelle knighte Thoffices of Shirief of your lordship of Wenloke and Steward of your lordships of Newpoort Wenllonk Kovoethmeredithe Lan-enthevry and Lanthocsant in Wales and in the marches of the same during his lif with the wages and fees accustumed and with making also of almanere Officers there undre him etc

Bernard de la force . an Annuytie of xl li yerely at the Receipt of theschequier by the handes of the Tresourere unto the tyme he have landes of like value etc for terme of his lif

John Fitzherbert hathe the manoire of Rotynge in Kent to him and his heires masles by knightes service and the Rent of xv s

John Nesfeld the manoire of Haytesbury in Wiltshire annui valoris lxxviij li xij s vj d. landes and tenementes in litelle Cheveralle annui valoris xviij li xiij s iiij d landes and tenementes in Somerford Maudyte in the Countie aforesaid lxvj s viij d to him and his heires masles by knightes service and the Rent of vij li. x s yerely

Robert Brakenbury is Receyvor generalle of alle landes and tenementes Rentes possessions goodes and catalles in the kinges handes by reason of any atteindure or forfaicture within the Counties of Sussex Kent and Surrey not by the king geven

[f75b] Sir John Savage knighte thelder hathe therbage and pannage of the parke of Northwode outwode & menhey to the yerely value of x marc xx d during his lif without any accompt etc

Thomas Jebbe an Annuytie of iiij li for terme of his lif of thissues etc of the lordship and Manoire of Ealding in Kent by the handes of Rauf Banaster and his heires masles occupyors of the same lordshippe etc

John Wrothe Squier a pardon with a clause in the same of fines amerciamentes and othre dettes and accomptes by him due for that he was Escheytors in the Counties of Somerset and Dorset

John Fyneux an Annuytie of liij li vj s viij d during the kinges pleasire . that is to wite xl li thereof yerely of the ferme of the manoire of Hedingdone with the hundred of Bolyndene without the north yate of Oxonford by the handes of the Fermors or Shirief etc and xiij li vj s viij d of the litell Custumes in the port of Londone by the handes of the Collectors there etc

Sir John Middeltone knighte the manoire or lordship of Wexcombe in Wiltshire and landes and tenementes Rents and services in the towne and territorys of Wexcombe annui valoris xlvj li viij s v d . the hundred of Kingwardstone in the said Countie annui valoris xx li xiij s vj d to him and his heires masles by knightes service and the Rent of C s yerely

John Browne of Bridpoort merchant John Baker and Thomas Yogge merchantes have licence to suche and asmany peces of tynne at oon tyme or diverse etc in the portes of Pole Plymmouth or Fowey and the same to conveye to outward parties without any Custume paying till they be paied of the somme of Cviij li & iij s by the Custumes forsaid according to endentures therupon made betwix the king and theim

A warrant for Edmond Tankard to the Tresourere and Chambrelains of theschequier to content unto him viij li viij s due unto him for pewter vesselle pottes and pannes etc in the dayes of king Edward the iiij th

Edward Bramptone the manoire of Fauxstone annui valoris xx li to him and his heires masles by knightes service and the Rent of xxx s etc

Robert Brakenbury hathe the keping and Stewardship of al his Forestes of Essex in the Countie of Essex during his lif of the graunt of Sir Thomas Mountgomery and per confirmacionem domini Regis with almaner fees etc

Thomas Aleyne is oon of the Auditors of al Castelles lordships landes and tenementes of the duchie of Cornwaille aslong as he bereth him wele withe the wages and fees accustumed etc

Bryan Rouclyf secundary Barone of theschequier hathe the manoire of Forcet in the Countie of York during his lif without any thing yelding etc

John Dort of Londone merchaunt hathe a saufconduyt for a Ship or Shippes of Britayne Spayne or Fraunce of the portage of xij^{xx} tonnes with gascoigne wynes to be charged into this Royaulme and to recharge there with almaner merchandises Stapelle ware except in Recompense of the payment of xxviij li due by George Neville late Archiebisshop of York nowe decessed /

[f76] Maister Piers Puissaunt a saufconduyt for a C tonne of wyne gascoigne or othre to bring in to this Royaulme at oon tyme or diverse tymes etc per unum annum

John Mathewe and William White late Shirieffes of Londone have a dishcarge to the Tresourer and Barons of theschequier to acquyte theim ayemst the king upon theire accomptes (to) yelden of money gadred of alyantes by theim etc

Petre de Salamanca Petre de Valiadolet Diego de Castro Sancio de Valmasedo Fernando de Carione Johanni Pardo Diego de Cadago Alfonso de Lyone Martino de Ordova Gonsalo de Salamanca merchauntes of Spayne they and theire executors to have the somme of CC (& l) li of money of England of the Custumes and subsidies commyng of whatsoever clothes grayned or ungrayned and of othre merchandises whatsoever by theim charged in the port of London or elleswhere in England etc

Robert Strete an Annuytie of xx li sterling of thissues etc of Calais by the handes of the Tresourere there till he have Office or Offices of like value or better etc

John Erle of Lincolne lieutenant of the land of Irland during the kinges pleasire

Richard Cooke hathe the passage or Fery over the water of Mersy betwene the Towne of Lytherpole and the Countie of Chestre with batelles & alle othre proffites etc during his lif

Edward Bramptone an Annuytie of C li from the fest of Estre (last) Anno primo til the terme of xx yere then folowing be complete of the subsidie of iij s of the tonne and xij d of the lb in the port of Londone by the handes of the Collectours etc

John Abbott late of Leycestre a generalle pardonne etc .

Richard Contone a licence for C tonne of gascoigne wyne of his owne goodes or othre in whatsoever ship or shippes of the Royaulme of England or Britaigne Holand Zeland & Flandres or othre outward parties undre the trewes leeg or Amytie paying the Custumes etc

John Cotone of Londone merchant hathe licence for CCCl tonnes or undre of gascoigne wynes or othre merchandises to bring into this Royaulme etc

The king hathe founded a Chauntre in the Chapelle of Hedistastone in the parisshe of Wemme in the Countie of Salop

Richard Walter and Alice his wif of Lydde in the Countie of Kent laborer a pardonne for theire lyves

Sir Alexandre Bayneham knighte an Annuytie of xl li during the lif of Thomas Bayneham his fadre of the Custumes in Bristowe and an Annuytie of xl li during his owne lif of the said Custumes etc

Cristofre Colyns Squier an Annuytie of C li fro Estre Anno primo to the ende and terme of xx^{ti} yere of the subsidie of iij s the Tonne and xij d the lb in the port of Londone by the handes of the Collectors etc

William Frankelyne alias temple maister Carpenter of the kinges werkes within the Counties of Chestre and Flynt with the wages of vj d by the day by the handes of the (Chambrelains there) Shirief of Chestre of the fee ferme of the Towne there and x s for a gowne yerely and xviij li due unto him of his wages and ij howses within the Castelle of Chestre with other regardes etc during his lif per confirmacionem

[f76b] William Nele an Annuytie of xx li during his lif of the fee ferme of Malmesbury with iij hundreds to the same Towne perteynyng by the handes of the Abbot & Convent of Malmesbury & theire Successours or by the handes of the Shirief of the Countie of Wiltshire for the tyme being

Alianore Wentworthe wydowe an Annuitie of xx li sterling of thissues etc of the lordships of Myddeltone and Merden in Kent by the handes of the Receyvor etc during hir lif etc

Sir Richard Radclyf hathe the manoire of Tyvertone annui valoris liiij li xiij s vj d the Burghe of Tyvertone & hundrede annui valoris xxiij li xvj s viij d. the Manoire or lordship of Chalveleghe annui valoris xxvj li iiij s viij d the Manoire of Colytone & hundrede there annui valoris xxxiiij li xiij s viij d the manoire of Musbury annui valoris xxviij li xiij s iiij d the Burghe of Colyford annui valoris C s the manoire of Whitford annui valoris xxvj li vj s v d the manoire of Sampford Courtenay annui valoris xxvj li x s iiij d the manoire of Colom John annui valoris xxij li iiij s viij d the manoire of Faveway annui valoris viij li xx d the manoire of Nortone Dawney annui valoris xvij li x s viij d. the manoire of Whympill annui valoris xxvj li x s the manoire of Gatcombe annui valoris xxj li the manere of Iwerne Courtnay annui valoris xl li the manoire of Ebbertone annui valoris xxj li the manoire of Crukerne annui valoris iiij^{xx}x li x s the manoire of Misterton annui valoris xx li x s the manere of Bereford annui valoris xxx li landes and tenementes in the townes & hamlettes of Gesberkirke Surflet Quadring and Pinchebek annui valoris xxxij li the manoire of Mertone annui valoris xviij li the manoire of Aylesbere annui valoris xxiij li vj s viij d the manoire of Wibertone annui valoris xviij li the iij^{de} parte of the manoire of Skendewy annui valoris xiiij li the Manoire of Manby annui valoris xx li the manoirs of Bradley & Graynesby annui valoris xxiiij li to him and heires masles (and) by knightes service and the Rent of l li yerely

Thomas Frisley a tenement with thappurtenaunces lying in the parisshe of Saint Mighelle in Wodestrete within the Citie of Londone for terme of his lif with almanere advauntages etc

Thomas Crawford the vergeorship of the Towne of Sandewiche with the keping of the Castelle there during his lif with almanere wages fees etc

Thomas Erle of Surrey an Annuytie of a M^{l}C li yerely during the lif of John duc of Norffolk of the Revenues of the duchie of Cornewaille by the handes of the Receyvor etc

John (Bow) Boxwelle Corser a licence for a . C . ambling horses to shippe over see within the space of ij yeres

James Fryse phisician an Annuytie of xl li during his lif that is to wite xx li of thissues etc of the lordship of Wigmore by the handes of the Receyvor and xx li of the fee ferme of Ludlowe by the handes of the Baillif per confirmacionem

[f77] Maister William Duffeld hathe the iiijth prebende of of [sic] lady of Leicestre by the decesse of maister John Billesdone

Jenyn Huissher an Annuytie of xxvj s viij d during his lif by the handes of thabbot of Persshore and thoffice of keping of Myddilbailifwik within the Chace of Crosselaund in the Countie of Gloucestre with the wages and fees accustumed during the nonnage of Edward Erle of Warrewik

Kateryn duchesse of Bukingham an Annuytie of CC marc (during hir lif) during the kinges pleasire of thissues of the lordship of Tunbrigge in the Countie of Kent by the handes of the Baillif etc

John Kendale yoman of the Crowne hathe the Rent of certain landes & tenementes lying in Dertford and Wylmyngtone in your Shire of Kent called Grawnisome Rent of the yerely value of vj li the Charges deduc for terme of his lif without any thing etc

Thomas Danyelle thoffice of mason of the werkes aswele within the Toure of Londone as elswhere within the Royaulme of England during his lif with the wages and fees accustumed of thissues etc of Wrottelle Havering etc with lyvere clothing after the sute of Squiers of household out of the Warderobe

Marcelle Mawres hathe a warrant to the Tresourere and barons of theschequiere to surcesse ayenst him almaner processes for his homage to be made to the king for that he was borne in Utrighte etc

Guille Vielle Johan le Cachoure Perrenot Durant Johan Viel & Symon le Prevost have a saufconduyt for (v) oon Ship of the portage of lx tonne with maister xxxij maryners and ij pagettes or within with almaner wynes etc

John Broke and Richard Noneley have a warrant to Sir Thomas Thwaytes Tresourere of Calais to content unto them CClxx li sterling money at the vj day of octobre next to come due by the king for wynes of them boughte

Bryan Talbot squier for the body hathe a warrant to the Receyvor of the lordship of Bolingbroke to content him l marc due of his fee for the yere ended At Estre Anno primo

John Frithe thoffice of gayler of thutter gate of the Castelle of Windesore during his lif with the wages of iij d by the day de exitis dicti Castri etc per manus Constabularij etc

Thomas Burgchier late Constable of Windesore hathe a warrant to the Tresourere and Barons of theschequier to allowe him in his accompt made of thissues of the said Caster . iij d by the day which he payed John Frithe from the fest of Saint Mighelle the xxij^{ti} yere of Edward the iiijth unto the xxvj day of Juyne than next ensuying for his Office of gayler of thutter gate there

John Wodeward an Annuytie of (v)iiij marc of thissues etc of the lordship of Hanslap in the Countie of Bukingham quousque etc

[f77b] William Dayson an Annuytie of v marc of thissues of the lordship of Hanslap in the Countie of Bukingham quosque etc

Nicholas Spycer hathe a warrant to the Tresourere and Barons of theschequier to allowe John Stephens shirief of Bristowe in his accompt the somme of xiiij li iij s vij d ob qr whiche he paied the said Nicholas for his wages of Thoffice of Constable of the Castel of Bristowe . and for the wages of a jayler and ij wacchemen

The same Nicholas hathe a prive seale to the maire of Corke to attache Richard Galny and Richard Barry Citezins there and theim kepe in sure warde unto the tyme thay have paied unto him the somme of lxviij li xv s

Alianore Duttone the wif of Piers Duttone hathe a (warrant) prive seale to thescheator of the Countie palatyne of Chestre to ammove his handes from the possessione of suche landes and tenementes as was seised to the kinges behouf upon an outlary of the said Piers . and he thereof nor seased at the day of promulgacion as evydently it is proved

Sir Richard Richard [sic] Cutteler prest the parsonage of Nethe in the diocise of Landaf by (b) the dethe of David Bragham

Richard Pole Squier for the body thoffices of Steward of the lordship of Rysing . Constable of the Castel there and maister of the game or Ranger of the Chace there with the wages and fees accustumed . and xiiij li of reward for thoccupying of the same ante datum of thissues thereof etc

Humfrey Savage an Annuytie of of x li fro Estre Anno primo during his lif of thissues etc of the Countie palantyne of Lancastre

Septembre Anno ij do Rauf Willughby Squier for the body thoffices of Constable of the Castelle of Bukenham . Steward of the lordship there and the keping of the parke there during his lif perceyvyng yerely for the said Office of Constable . x marc . the Stewardship v marc and the parkership ij d by day of thissues of the same lordship with al other proffites etc

The same Rauf an Annuytie of xvj li vj s iiij d of thissues of the Castelle of Bukenham during the lif of Thomas lord Stanley

Kateryn Ratclyf an Annuytie of x li during hir lif of thissues etc of the lordship of Olney in the Countie of Bukingham

[f78] John de Peler Trumpeter an Annuytie (d) of x mare during his lif of the ferme(s) of the hundredes of Kyftesgate Holford & Grestone by the handes ot Thabbot and Convent of Winchecombe per confirmacionem etc

Geffray Whitford thoffice of Escheator of Anglesey in Northwales during his lif with the wages and fees accustumed of thissues of his Office by his owne handes etc

John Cletone an Annuyte of v marces of thissues etc of (y)oure lordship of Dinbighe bi the handes of the Receyvor quousque

David Lyonhille Sargeant at Armes during his lif with xij d by the day of the fee ferme of the Citie of Londone by the handes of the Shirief etc with livere etc

John Rowel ij d by the day during the nonnage of Edward Son of George duc of (Cal) Clarence of thissues etc of the manoir of Yerdeley (of) in the Countie of Worcestre per confirmacionem etc

Nicholas Baker and Elizabeth his wif have the manoire of Beltone in the Countie of Somerset late James Erle of Wiltshire during theire lifes and of eithre of theim lenger lyving

Johanne Forest and Edward (his) her son an Annuytie of v markes during theire lyfes and of eithre of theim lenger lyving of thissues of the lordship of Barnardcastelle by the handes of the Receyvor etc

A warrant to the Custumers of Excestre and Plymmothe to pay to Herry Rede of the Custumes there xxiiij li to be employed by the kinges commaundement and a warrant thereupon to the Tresourer and barons of theschequier to allowe the said Custumers

Thomas Beestone prest the parsonage of Ratlesdene in the diocese of Norwiche by the Resignacion of maister William Duffeld

Maister Edmond Chadertone the parsonage of Almondesbury in the diocese of Yorke

Rauf Grenne & Nicholas Suthworthe have Thoffice of Approwere of the fennes parcelle of the duchie of Lancastre within the Countie of Lincolne during theire lifes & eithre of theim etc with the wages and fees accustumed etc yelding yerely the agistementes and issues etc

The said Nicholas Thoffice of Baillif of Tonworthe in the Countie of Warrwik with the keping of the parke there during the nonnage of Edward Son of George duc of Clarence with the wages of ij d by day & ij d by the day for (of) thoffice of parker of thissues of Tonworthe

The same Nicholas the manoire of Fritewelle in the Countie of Oxonford & alle landes and tenementes in Friteswel forsaid during his lif by the service thereof due per confirmacionem

[f78b] John Bausson and John de la Roche of Fraunce have a Sauf conduyt for the Margret of Humflete of the portage of xxxij tonnes to come into England with almaner wynes and other merchandises during half a yere

Edmund Coppingdale owner of the trinitie coppingdale of Hulle of the portage of CCC tonnes and Richard York John Willesby and Robert Chapmane owners of the Antony of Hul of the portage of CCl tonnes have licence to goo to Bourdeux for oon tyme and there charge theim with almanere wynes etc

Robert White of Beverley merchant hath a licence for a Ship called John Bridlingtone to Bourdeux for oon tyme in like manere

John Bohun and Anne his wif have a special graunt of the king that the same John shal not be Reputed or trouble herafter for an Idyot as he heretofore hathe ben

William Dawne hathe a Saufconduyt for a Ship of iiij^{xx}xv tonnes or diverse shippes of the same portage charged with almaner merchandises to oure Staple etc to come into this Royaulme with wynes as oft etc during a hole yere

Herry Clyfford an Annuytie of xx li of thissues etc of Beltone in Lincolneshire quousque etc

Elizabeth duchesse of Norffolk the tenement and al mesuages in Chelchehith late Richard Beauchamp Bisshop of Sarum during hir lif (without) for the service of a Rede Rose

Thomas Hoddlestone hath a licence for the Mary of Hulle of iiij^{xx}x tonnes to go to Bourdeux for wyne for oon tyme etc

Margret Bussel hath a licence for the Mary Bussel of the portage of iiij^{xx} tonnes to goo to Bourdeux for wyne for oon tyme etc

Thomas Thoresby William Cobbe & Robert Braybroke have the ferme of Rysing in Norffolk with the keping of the warenne there for the terme of vij yeres for the Rent of . l . li

John Delamere and John Feisere of Fraunce merchantes have a saufconduyt for a half yere for a ship called the Antony of Rouen of the portage of xxxvj tonnes to come with wynes and other merchandises into England etc

218

Sir Marmaduc Constable knighte hathe the manoire of Boseworthe in the Countie of Leicestre and the manoire of Braunstone in the same Countie to him and his heires masles by knightes service and the Rent of ix li xj s

Blewmantel landes and tenementes Rents and services late Thomas Bynburys in the Townes and parisshes of Andever Walop and Herfordbrigge for terme of his lif without any accompt

[f79] A (priv se) prive seale to dame Elyner Delves and Rauf hir sone whereby they be charged to Receyve no Revenues of the enheritaunce of the said dame Elyner otherwise than is conteigned in Recoignoissaunce made betwene theim and James Blount and Robert Shefeld

William Scopeham hathe certain tenementes landes medowes & pastures lying in the Towne and feldes of Manby in Lincolneshire during his lif without any accompt etc

Thabbot and Convent of Leicestre have licence to have a faire at Leicestre in the fest of Saint Leonard within the said Abbey and in the parisshe of saint Leonard ij day before the said fest and ij dayes after forever etc

William Barnefeld hathe a licence for xij Ambling horses and asmany Calve Skynnes and wollen clothes as wol extende to the (w) value of CCCC Frankes for the Redemyng of Robert Harding lying prysoner in Fraunce for the said somme etc

Nicholas Middeltone Thoffice of keper of the Warde of Millehay in Derbyshire during his lif with the wages of xxx s v d by the yere of thissues of thonor of Tutbury with an Annuytie of liij s iiij d of the said issues by the handes of the Receyvor etc

Roger Dean thoffice of kepar of the warde called Holand warde in Derby shire / with like wages and Annuytie of the said honor during his lif

Richard Yorke a licence for the Peter of Hulle of the portage of iiij^{xx} tonnes for oon tyme to bring in wyne to this Royaulme fro Bourdeux

William Turnor an Annuytie of x li during his lif of thissues etc of Wakefeld in Yorkshire by the handes of the Receyvor etc

John Somerby of Bridlingtone in Yorkshire hath a licence for oon tyme to goo to Bourdeux with the George of Hulle of the portage of C li to charge the same there withe wyne etc

Frere Bewik an Annuytie of C s in way of Almoux during his lif of thissues of Pountfreit etc

A prive seale to the Tresourere and barons of theschequiere to allowe from tyme to tyme the Shiriefes of Londone of the payment of the fee by theim paied to Sir John Catesby for the keping of the palois of Westmynster and the flete etc

Richard Yorke John Daltone John Burgh John Rudde and John Hopkinsone have a warrant to the Tresourer and Barons to allowe the merchauntes of Staple of CC markes (of) in theire accomptes of the Custumes and subsidies commyng of the merchandises which the king hathe geven them for the waughting of theire shippes

[f79b] *Pro prebenda.* Rex &c Episcopo Sarum seu ipsius in spiritualibus vicario generali. Quia nos dilecto & fideli Clerico nostro A.B. prebendam de C. in ecclesia Cathedrali Sarum predicta vacantem et ad nostram donacionem racione temporalium eiusdem ecclesie nunc in manibus nostris existencium pleno iure hac vice (spectan) spectantem donavimus intuitu caritatis vobis mandamus quatinus ulterius in hac parte faciatis quod vestrum est / et ad vos pertinet Racione iurisdiccionis in spiritualibus. In cuius Rei &c.

[The king etc. To the bishop of Salisbury or his vicar general in spiritualities. Since we have given to our beloved and faithful clerk A.B. the prebend of C. in the cathedral church of Salisbury aforesaid now vacant and pertaining to our gift by full right on this occasion by reason of the temporalities of that church being in our hands we command you of your charity to do further in this matter what pertains to you by reason of your jurisdiction in spiritualities. In witness of which etc.]

John Grenehille the keping of the Gawle of Mikill dene & litille dene in the Countie of Gloucestre otherwise called the Gawle by nethe the Wodde / during his lif / without any thing therefore paying etc

John Moole & John Barton hath a prive seale directed to the Tresourer & barons of theschequier to allowe theim xj li by them paid to Randolf Fraunke whiche the king gave him for thoccupieng of his office afore the date of his patent

Charles Ledanoys Jamys Ledanoys & John Broquet / hathe a saufconduyt of for a Ship of Cxx tonne during half a yere / tociens quociens

Blewmantille otherwise called John Brice / alle the landes & tenementes Rentes & services with theire appurtenaunces which late were Thomas Bynbury within the Townes & parisshinges of Andever Walop & Hertfordbrigge within the Countie of Suthampton for terme of his lif

Robert Fenton of Scardburg a pardon that he shalle not be put in Assisses & othere

Loweys Bonvese borne in the parties of Itale to be dynzene for terme of lif

Sir Thomas Wortley shiref of (Buk) Stafford hathe prive seale to the Tresourer & Barons / to suffre him to accompte by his deputie

Thomas Fowler Shireff of Bedford & Bukingham hath a like prive seale

John Sapcotes generalle Receivor of the duchie of (Lancast) Cornewaille hathe a prive seale directed to him / to pay to the duc of Norffolk the summe of M^lM^l marc for oon tyme / according to the kinges graunt

Thomas Yare & John Lewington merchauntes of Scotland / hath a saufconduyt for a ship of lx towne [sic] with xij serviauntes within the same to come & goo asoft as shall please theim / for a yere

Thomas Barow Clerc & Richard Barow / An Annuite of lxx s / to be takene during their lyves & aither of theme langer lyving of the ferme of Meles in Skignes in the Countie of Lincolne

The Bisshoppe of Worcestre Agnes Beaupe wedue late wif of Piers Beaupe Edward Beaupe John Beaupe Olyver Cambre & Hugh Brithyn / hathe licence to founde a Chauntery of a prest to sing at the Aweter of oure lady & seint Gabrielle within the parisshe Church of seint Laurence at Ludlowe / and to mortisse thereunto land of the value of x marc

Richard lord Fitzhugh hathe an Annuyte of C li / for terme of his lif to be taken of the Revenues of Tikhille

[f80] The Churche of York hath a graunt for a C prestes etc

John Holgrawe / Thoffice of the iiijth Baron of Theschequier during the kinges pleasur with fees & wages & accustumed

William Catesby Thoffice of the Chanceler of Therledom of Marche during his lif / with the fee of xl li of the Revenues of the said Erldom

Thomas Hartgille the porter of the Castelle of Queneburghe in the Countie of Kent & the keping of the warderop within the same with a grome under him / with the wages & fees of iiij d by the day / and xl s for the wages of the Grome of the profittes & Revenues of the lordshippes of Milton & Mardene in Kent. for terme of lyff

Thomas Thuresby Thoffice of baillief of Dunmowe with the keping of the parke there and an Annuytee of ten markes to be taken of the said lordship during his lif

William Mistilbroke & John Hewyk / the Auditors of alle landes & tenementes called Warrewyklandes Salesburylandes & Spencerlandes in the Counties of Stafford Derby Warrewik Salop Gloucestre Hareford Wigorn Northampton Roteland Oxonford Berkshire Hertford Essex Middlesex with the Citee of London Kent Southampton Wilteshire Somerset Dorset Devone Cornewaille & in the Isle of Wighte during the kinges pleasure

William Mistilbroke & Richard Lussher / Auditors of the principalite of Southwales in the Counties of Kermerdyne & Cardygan / and of Pembroke Westhaverford / of Tallaghan & Walwynescastelle Bergevenny Cardyf / of Newport Hay & Brekenok during the kinges pleasure / etc

Sir Henry Wentworth knighte the warde & mariage of Thomas Sampson Son & heire of Thomas sampson squier with the keping of the manor of Sprowton with thappurtenaunces in the Countie of Suffolk etc

John Wedon Thoffice of Baillief of the Towne of Chessham in the Countie of Bukingham with the wages & fees accustumed during the kinges pleasure

Brian Metcalf an Annuyte of x marc to be had & perceived during his lif of the Revenues of the lordship of Middelham

James Pemberton hathe confirmed unto him the keping of the parc & Gardyn of the maner of Eltham / and of the new parke of Horne within the lordship of Eltham for terme of his lif

Edmund Talbot squier hath confirmed unto him an Annuyte of vj li xiij s iiij d to be taken during his lif of the Revenues of Ticle

The same Edmund hathe an Annuytie of xx li to be taken during his lif of the Revenues of Cotingham / in recumpence of the Wapentake of Staneclif whiche he had of king Edward graunt for terme of lif

Richard Musgrave / an Annuyte of xl li during his lif of the Revenues of Ticle by the Receivor handes

Richard Watsone / An annuyte of iiij markes during his lif of Revenues of the lordship of Sherefhotone

Sir (Rich) John Huddelstone hathe confirmed unto him an Annuyte of fyfty markes to be taken & perceived during his lif of the lordship of Barnolswyke

William Lee Thoffice of keping of the Counselle Chambre dore at Westminster & hussher of the Receipt of theschquier for terme of liff with the wages & fees accustumed

[f80b] Thinhabitauntes of the Baronie of Kendale to be fre of tolle & other with the duchie of Lancastre

the same tenantes & inhabitauntes to be fre in alle Citees & other places in England

John llod of Ludlowe an Annuite of v marc fro Michelmas last during his lif of the Revenues of the lordship of Stauntone

William Creting prest a pardone

Sir William Husee knighte a warrant to the Receivor of Bolingbroke to content him the summe of xlv li for beafes by him delivered for thexpenses of the houshold

John Couper thoffice of baillief of Sutton in the Forest of galtresse in the Countie of York for terme of his lif with the wages & fees accustumed

John (Hew) Huys gentilman An Annuyte of ten markes from Michelmas during his lif of the Revenues of Munmouth

Christofer Metcalf & William his Son the keping of the parke of Wanlesse within the lordship of Middelham for terme of theire lyves and aither of theim langest lyvyng with the fees due & accustumed

David ap Guillin Morgan Thoffice of Steward of the lordshippe of Hay and Glynbugh & Constable of the Castelle of Hay for terme of his lif with the wages of x marc / and also an annuyte of xl marc to be perceived of the Revenues of the said lordship for terme of his said lif

Sir Thomas Pilkington an Annuytee of C marc to be perceived yerely during his lif of the Revenues of the duchie of Lancastre

Richard Mynors Thoffice of Steward of the Commotes of Cardigan & Cantremawre in south Wales for terme of his lif with wages & fees accustumed

John Llod hath warraunt direct unto the Receivor of Dynbighe to pay unto him the summe of xx marc which the king hath yeven him

Thomas Bromley an Annuyte of v marc yerely during his lif to be perceived of the Revenues of Dynbighe

Sir John Constable knighte an Annuyte of xx li during his lif of the Revenues of Pountfreit

Humfrey Swynerton an Annuyte of xl s during his lif of the Revenues of Dynbieghe

Sir William Ingilby an Annuytie of xx li during his lif of the Revenues of Knaresburghe

Thomas Garne Thoffice of Raglership of Bromefeld & Yale during the kinges pleasure with fees & wages accustumed

224

Nicholas Batenlan the keping of the parke of Morley in Derby shire with fees & wages due and accustumed / and an Annuyte of iiij li xj s iij d of the Revenues of Tutbury during his lif

[f81] *Octobre Anno ij* Sir Gervaux Clifton hathe the lordship of Bawtre with thappurtenaunces to ferme for xij yeres for xiij li vj s viij d ut patet in billa

Sir Humfrey Talbot a licence for an hundrethe towne of wyne to be shipped in his shippe called the Elizabeth at oon tyme or diverse tymes within a yere

Janne Colyns an Annuyte of ten markes for terme of her lyf of the Revenues of Wakefeld

John Wilson / the forstershippe of Fulwithe and Harlow within the Forest of Knaresburgh during his lif / with the fee of iij d by the day of the Revenues of the lordship of Knaresburghe

Doctor Roby an Annuyte of xl li unto the tyme he be otherwise prefered / to be taken of the fee ferme of the Citee of Coventre

Morice ap Rees / thoffice called portReveshippe of Prescheunde in the marche of Wales for terme of his lif with the fee of xl s of the Revenues of his said office

Humfrey Wynnyngton an Annuite of xl s during his lif of the Revenues of the lordship of (Dynbighe) Norwiche within the Countie of Chestre

Therle of Notingham & Jahanne his wif / an Annuyte of Cxxxiiij li during the lif of the said Johanne his wif to be perceived in forme folowing l li of feeferme of Bristowe xxx li of the feeferme of Cambrigge xx li of the feeferme of (Northt) Suthampton xx li of the feeferme of Notingham & xiiij residue of Ippeswiche

Mair & Citizens of York hath a prive seale directed to the Tresourer and barons of theschequier for their discharge of the paiement of Clx li the fee ferme of their Towne unto suche tyme as they otherwise in commaundement

David ap Jenkyns Thoffices of keper of the warderobe ledes & Chambres within the Castelle of Pountfreit & porter of the same during his lif / perceiving for the said office of keper iiij d by day & for thoffice of porter ij d of the Revenues of the honnor of Pountfret

Thabbot and Convent of Fourneys hathe licence to absent them out of Irland for xx yeres / and x yeres to Receive the profites of (the s) their lyvelode there / and every yere to bring C quarters whete from thens to forneys

Richard Redeman an Annuyte of xx marc during his lif of the Revenues of the lordshippe of Carnonton in Cornewaille

John (Twislyngton) Twyselton hath confirmed the keping of the parke of Cradeling in the Countie of York for terme of his lif with the wages & fees accustumed / and also an Annuyte of vj li of the Revenues of the Wapentake of Osgattecrosse within the honnor of Pountfreit

Laurence Werham thoffice of baillief of Drakelow & Rudhethe in the Countie of Chestre for terme of his lif with the wages & fees accustumed

John Wake squier an Annuyte (an Annuy) of x marc for terme of his lif of the Revenues of the Counties of Cambrigge & Huntyngdone

a prive seale directed to thauditors of the Comote of Horvayn in the lordship of llanymthemery to allow the bedelle there x marc toward the bulding of oure lady Churche there

[f81b] Nicholas Agard hathe confermed unto him the keping of the warde called Tutbury warde within the Chace of Nydewood parcelle of the duchie of Lancastre during his lif with the fees (etc) accustumed of thissues of the same etc And also an Annuytie of xx s of thissues of a pasture called Laurence Hayes during his said lif per confirmacionem

Robert Jenkyne yoman huissher of the kinges Chambre Thoffice of Cowner of youre lordships of Uske Tirleke & Nedyrwent parcelle of Therldom of the Marche during his lif with the wages of x markes of the Revenues of the said lordshippe

Thomas Lynom Thoffice of the kinges Solicitor during the kinges pleasure . perceyving for the same from the xxvj day of Juyne Anno primo x li of the fee ferme of the Towne of Bristowe with the suburbis & (p) appurtenaunces by the handes of the maire Comonaltie or Shirieffes . and for his expenses in the said office xx li during the kinges pleasire of the said ferme etc

John Jervays thoffice of Chief Juner within the Toure of Londone during his lif with xij d by the day of Havering Wrottylle etc

226

William Harrys yoman of the Crowne vj d by the day for the fee of the same during his lif of the fee ferme of Lystarde in Cornewalle

Sir Charles Pylkingtone hathe a prive seale to the Tresourer and barons to acquyte and discharge (him and) Sir Thomas Wortelcy & (Sir) dame Jane his wif for the payment of xl li yerely to him payed for thexhibicion of Edward son and heire of Sir John Pylkingtone decessed during his nonnage

The pryor and Convent of Worsop Sir Gervais Cliftone late Shirief of Notingham and Derby and Sir Charles Pilkingtone have a prive seale to the Tresourere and barons to discharge theim of an Annuyte (paied yerely to) of vj li xvij s ij d payed yerely to the said pryoure of Wyrksoppe during the nonnage of George Erle of Salop

Nicholas Clyveley yomane of the Crowne vj d by day during his lif of the fee ferme of Lystard

Sir Charles Pylkington (a prive) shirief of Notingham and Derby hathe a prive seale to the Tresourer and barons to make his accompt in theschequiere by Attorney

Sir William Houghton knighte shirief of Worcestreshire hathe a like prive seale

John Wake Shirief of Huntingdone and Cambrigge hathe a like prive(s) seale

[f82] Piers Courteys hathe confermed unto him his graunt (f) of a horse mylne and ij messuages with thappurtenaunces in Leicestre in Swynesmarket strete & xij d of Rent going out of a pecce of lande late William Braunstone of the value of ix li ij s vj d for terme of his lif in Recompense of the fee of the Crowne without any thing yelding etc Also his graunt of derefalwode pale and toppe-wode within Leicestre Frithe without any thing etc Also his graunt of the manoire of Rye in Gloucestershire and Eltowe in the forest of dene to the yerely value of xij li during his lif Also of the Bailliship of Leicestre for terme of his lif with fees accustumed etc Also the keeping of the warde in Leicestre frithe with fees accustumed during his lif etc Also his graunt of the feodaryship of Leicestre during his lif withe wages accustumed

Edward Gower hathe a (Commission) licence to goo into Scotland with oon vessaille or divers vessailles to fetche fisshe there by him boughte of the portage of lx tonnes paying custumes etc

Master Edmond Chadertone hathe the warde and mariage of William Bothe during his nonnage etc son and heire of George Bothe

Sir John Savage thelder hathe a warrant to the Auditors of the Countie palantyne of Chestre to discharge him of xvj li whiche the king hathe pardonned him

Thomas lord Stanley hathe the manoirs of Shotewyk & Frodesham in the Countie of Chestre in ferme for xij yeres paying therefore like as he hathe paied heretofore

Mathewe Andrewe hathe a licence for his ship(es) called the James of the portage of vij^{xx} tonnes and his ship called the Margrete of the portage of Cx tonnes to goo to Bourdeux as oft etc during a hool yere charged etc and recharge with wynes etc

William Wilcokes Comptroller of the (Cust) Subsides in the poort of London hathe a prive seale to the Tresourer and Chambreleyns of theschequier . (and) to strike out and levie in due forme oon taille or diverse tailles (cut) conteignyng the summe of vij^{xx}iiij li ij s ij d of the said subsides to be perceived by the Colectors of the same / and the same taille or tailles to deliver to the said William for his contentacion for certen salt petir clothes & velwettes by him delivered to the kinges use

Thomas Bradley hathe a prive seale to William Wycam Mair of Bristow for the deliveraunce of a Breton shippe called the Michelle late of Crowdon of the kinges gift

Richard Lilley Thoffice of baillieff of the lordshippe of Hoton Panelle within the Countie of York with the wages of ij d by the day of the said lordship during his lif

Richard Hogges of Fulbrok in the hundreth of Chadlington in Oxfordshire hathe a prive seale to John Baratyne Shiref of the said Countie to deliver him xl s by the said Shiref from him wrongfully taken / or elles to appere Crastino Assisarum

Thomas Leghe of Northwood in the Countie of Chestre hathe a generalle pardone

[f82b] Roger Whitington / the pencione of Seint Friswyde within Oxonford

William Aston / An Annuyte of v marc during his lif of thissues etc of the lordshippe of Bussheley within the Countie of Worcestre

Robert Langtre hathe an Annuyte of iiij li during his lif of thissues etc of the ferme of the water of Rybille in the Countie of Lancastre

Walter Graunt / An Annuyte of viij li during (his) the nonne Age of Therle of Warrewyk of thissues etc of the lordship of Haddesoure within the Countie of Worcestre

John Jakes hath aswele a licence forto bring into this Royalme v^C tonnes of Gascoigne wyne enduring unto the fest of the purificacion of oure lady next commyng / as lettres of Saveconduyt by him self or his factors to come two tymes during the said saufconduyt into this Royalme with a ship called the Marie of seint Paule de Lyon of the portage of CCl tonnes charged at every tyme with C tonnes of gascoigne wyne & othere merchandises whereof John Pykyard is Master / or with a nother ship of the said Countre of the same portage / the same John Pikard being Master thereof with master mariners pages harneys etc / And the same to freghte ayen with alle maner marchandises to oure stapule of Calais not apperteignyng / the said saufconduyt to endure unto the fest of Cristynmesse come twelmonethe Yeven etc at Notingham the xixth day of octobre Anno ij^{do}

The same John Jakes (have) hath lettres to Sir John Savile Captaigne of thisle of Wighte to deliver xj personnes (out) their lieng prisoners / (out of Captivitie) and raunsomed to M^{1}M^1 scutes / out of Captivitie without payment of any fynaunce

[a line erased and illegible]

Thomas Banke / the kepyng of the New parke of Tatersale / and of the Cunes aswele within the same as without for terme of his liff with the wages & fees accustumed / and also xij lodes of hey yerely for terme of his said lif / to be taken by the handes of the keper of the medows there for the sustentacion of the dere

A prive seale directed to the Tresourer & Barons of Theschequier forto discharge aswele Sir Gervaux Clifton late shireff of Notingham & Derby as Sir Charles Pilkington / of lxvj s viij d for the Master of the game of Worshop parke graunted to the said Sir Charles during the nonne Age of Therle of Shrewesbury

William Acham hath confirmed unto him vj d by the day for the fee of the Corowne to be perceived of the Revenues of the Countie of Suthampton for terme of lif

A prive seale to the Tresourer & Barons aswele to discharge William Say knight late Shiref of the Counties of Essex & Hertford of xvj li xiij s iiij d of thissues & proffuytes of the hundreth of Barstaple as John Sturgeone now Shiref

John Duc of Norffolk & Thomas Erle of Surrey the warde & mariage of Henry Erle of Essex

A prive seale to Piers Curteys to deliver alle suche lyverey clothing furres & lynynges / as is behinde & awning to Rauff Wolseley late Baron of theschequier aswele in king Edwardes dayes as in oures

[f83] John Agard hath confirmed unto him Thoffice of supervisor of the Chace & parkes of Nedewode in the Countie of Stafford for terme of his lif / And also the keping of the parke of Castelle hay for terme of his lif with the wages & fees accustumed

The lord Lovelle an Annuite of x li from the fest of seint Michelle Anno primo / unto the ende & terme of viij yeres of thussues etc of the maners of Cokeham & bray / and also an Annuite of xl li from the said fest of seint Michelle during (his said lif) the lif of Margarete Harecourte vidue late wif of Sir Robert Harecourt of the Revenues of the said lordships And also an Annuite of xxiiij li from the said fest during the lif of Anne sumtyme wif of John Stoner of the Revenues of the said lordshippes

John Bradbourne the keping of the parke of Maunsille in the Countie of Derby with the wages of j d by the day of the Revenues of Tutbury for terme of his lif

Nicholas Kneveton Thoffice of parker of Rennesdale in Duffeldfrith in the Countie of Derby for terme of his lif with the wages & fees accustumed of the Revenues of Tutbury

John Woderove & Richard Woderove his sonne the Receivorship of the lordshippes of Connesburghe Hatefeld and Wakefeld with thappurtenaunces in the Countie of York for terme of theire lyfes & aither of them lenger lyvyng with the fees & wages accustumed

Henry Hikkes Thoffice of keping of the Gaole within the Castelle of York during the kinges pleasure with the wages & fees accustumed

William Ferror hathe confirmed unto him Thoffice of Marshalle of the Stude

230

and yong horsses / aswele within the parkes of Tonneworthe Fernhille Budbroke / as in any other place within the Countie of Warrwik during the nonne Age of Therle of Warrwik with the wages of j d by day by the handes of the Reve or Baillif of Tomworthe etc Also the same (John) William hathe a tenement with a forge lying upon the hie payment within oure burghe of Warrewik during the said nonnage (he to) without any thing but oonly to doo Reparacions

Novembre James Blount lieutenaunt of the castele of Hammes hathe a generalle pardone with a specialle graunt of alle his offices graunted by king Edward the iiijth xxx die novembris

The said James hathe a like pardone Datum xvj die novembris

Richard Alibone Rauf Cursone George Pole Adam Clerc Thomas Bulcle William Rigmeydone Robert Mountgomery William Stevons Thomas Stevons Roger Halle Herry Mortene Nicholas Lee Robert Lee Piers Oldfeld William Lee Edmond Wettone Rauf Bentley Thomas Punt Hugh Whistanley Robert Bukley William Cloghe James Chaturtone John Bulde James Ellertone Richard Shottiswalle Nicholas Monyfold John Lokeley Thomas Coke Reynald Dentone John Uttersalle William Carvere Rauf Coterelle Richard Salford Richard Barbor Stephan Smythe Piers Gunner Goskyn Trip John Gilis (w) John Wylde John Calverley Symon Fakennere Thomas Parsons William Tavernere Herry Burwey William Dyksone Herry Camine Richard Gulde John Brewer John a Dower Robert Smythe John of the stable & John Patenmaker Souldiors of Hammes have a pardone of theire lyves Datum xvj die novembris

The same persones have a like pardonne Datum xxx° die novembris /

[f83b] John Kendale yomane of the Crowne hathe graunted unto him by prive seale alle the Rentes and issues commyng and growing of certain tenementes without Temple barre in the kinges handes by the forisfaiture of the Bishop of of [sic] Excester To have the same aslong as the said tenementes shal Remayn in the kinges handes without any accompt etc

Thomas Tropenelle of Chaldefeld in the Countie of Wiltshire Squier hathe a generalle pardonne

Sir Charles Pylkingtone (hathe) Constable of the Castel of Notingham hathe a prive seale to Sir John Babingtone Shirief of the Counties of Notingham and Derby for the payment of xxij li vij s viij d by the said Shirief to him to be made of thissues of the lordships of Bollesover in Derbyshire and Maunsfeld in Notinghamshire of the kinges Reward etc

The said Sir John Babingtone hathe a nother prive seale for his discharge of the payment of the same / to the Tresourer and Barons

William Shirborne hathe an Annuytie of x marces from mighelmasse Anno ij^{do} (tille) during his lif of thissues etc of the lordship of Knaresburghe

John Ap Morgane hath thoffices of Bedelle of the lordship of Uske and Levenethe and Delogane & treygreke and the Constableship of Delogane and treygrek in Wales during the kinges pleasire with the wages and fees accustumed etc of thissues of the said lordships etc

John Thomsone hathe Thoffice of gaderer of the tolle at the northe ende of Boroghe brigge called Richmondshire tolle during his lif with the fees of iiij markes by yere of thissues of the said tolle etc

William Erle of Notingham & Johanne his wif have an Annuytie of Cxxxiiij li yerely during the lif of the said Johanne . that is to wit xx li thereof of the fee ferme of Bristowe etc by the handes of the Shirief lx li thereof yerely of the fee ferme of Cantebrigge . xxiiij li thereof yerely of the fee ferme of Suthampton . xvj li of the fee ferme of Notingham and xiiij li thereof residewe of the fee ferme of Yeppeswiche provyded alwayes that if the said Johanne dye (befor) the said Erle lyvyng this graunt to be voyde

Thabbot and Convent of Gloucestre have to theim and theire Successors an Annuytie of iiij li of the Revenues of Staunty Lacy in the Countie of Salop unto suche tyme as they be Recompensed for landes of like value inclused to the parke of Okeley in the said Countie by king Edward the iiijth

The maire and Burgesses of Leicestre have an Annuytie of xx li of thissues of the honor of Leicestre during the space of xx yeres

Thomas Wildecotes hathe the manoire of Westcapelone in the Countie of Somerset during his lif without any accompt

Sir Herry Wentworthe knighte hathe Thoffice of Steward of alle manoirs landes and tenements late the bisshops of Ely in the Countie of Suffolk . aslong as the said landes shal Remayne in the kinges handes with C s by yere

[f84] George Stanley knighte and Johanne his wif have a prive seale to the Tresourere and barons to surcesse of almanere processe ayenst theim aswele for doing homage and fealtie of alle Castelles manoirs etc late the lord straunges

232

etc as for accomptes and (other) delyvere of Estreytes etc

William Otter Thoffice of keper or forster of the (Forest) bailiwik of Stratford within the forest of Waltham during the kinges pleasire with the wages of ij d by the day like as Mathewe Skarden had it

George lord Grey Ruthyne hathe the manoire of Herlingdone withe thappurtenaunces in Bedfordshire annui valoris xxxix li x s And the manoire of Crendone in the Countie of Bukingham annui valoris xxvij li xij s iiij d to him and his heires masles by knightes service and the Rent of C s yerely

Olyver Warner of Londone Taillor hathe a prive seale to the Tresourere and barons of theschequiere to discharge aswele him of ij carpettes and certaine other goodes presented into theschequier to be in his keping and longing to the late duc of Bukingham as John Manyngham Marten William Rollesley and Richard Aldar his sureties . and to surcesse of al processe ayenst them

Thomas Fowleshurst hathe Thoffice of Constable of the Castel of Chestre during his lif with the wages and fees accustumed by the handes of the Chambrelain of Chestre

Thomas Canceller hathe Thoffice of Comptrollere of the werkes within the Castel of Windesore and other manoirs and lordships to the said Castel apperteynyng for terme of his lif with the wages accustumed etc of the Revenues of the said Castelle etc by the handes of the Constable

John Higford and Humfrey Beaufoo Squiers have thoffice of Constable of the Castel of Warrewik & Thoffice of Steward of Warrewik and of al other lordships in the Countie of Warrewik and thoffice of maister of game of al parkes chaces warennes in the same Countie also Thoffice of maister of al Ryvers & pondes and supervisour of Swannes & of the Stode in the same Countie during the nonnage of Edward Erle of Warrewik . perceyvyng for the said office of Constable x li of thissues of the lordship of Warrewik and for the said office of Steward x marces of thissues of the lordship of Brayles And for the said office of maister of the game and Ryvers pondes and supervisor of Swannes & of the Stode the fees and wages accustumed

Thomas Bankes Thoffice of Sergeant at Armes for terme of his lif withe the wages of xij d by the day of thissues etc of oure Citie of Londone & the Countie of Middlesex by the handes of the Shirief with lyvere etc per confirmacionem

Walter ap Thomas ap Roger hathe an Annuytle of x marces during his lif of the

Revenues of the lordship of Wynfirtone in the marches of Wales . And that he during his lif shal make the Ryve and Ryngyld (and) of glandester & Radnors landes taking therefore fees and wages accustumed

[f84b] John Jakes of Britayne merchaunt hathe a saufconduyt for a Ship called the Mary of Saint Pawle de Lyone in Britayne of the portage of CCl li or with any other Ship of the same Contrey of the same portaige whereof John Pycard is maister to come into England with gascoigne wynes and other godes and merchandises and there discharge and Recharge havyng iij^{xx} maryners and iiij pages (as) to come and go (asoft) as oft etc the said saufconduyt during xiiij monethes etc

Thomas Hunt Clerc of the Werkes hathe a prive seale to the Tresourer and barons of Theschequiere that they Respite the day of the morowe after saint Martyn last past to him Inioyned to appier and bring withe him the Appelle of his Receipt upon payne of x li / unto the xv^{ti} of Estre next comyng (and)

Thomas Grame of Scotland borne is made densyne and his heires

The same Thomas hath the manoire of Randel Lentone in Cumbreland to him and his heires masles by knightes service without accompt etc

A warrant to Richard Pole and John Abelle Receyvors of the temporalites of Ely to content to Sir Robert Gryme parsone of Saint Olaves the some of xlj li of thissues of the same temporalites . And thereupon a warrant to the Tresourere and Barons for the discharge of the said (Barons) Tresourer and Barons etc

William Brewere yomane of the Chambre hathe an Annuytie of ten marces of the Custumes of Fowey by the handes of the Custumers there . unto suche tyme as he be preferred unto office etc

A prive seale to Sir William Husy chief juge to surcesse of almaner processes made or to be made by reason of an endytement ayenst Thomas Beene late of Fustone Robert Slyngesby late of the same John Bekwith (in the same Countie of) with many other in the Countie of York of what name etc and if processe be made to commaunde Herry Herman Coroner & Attorney to make out Writtes of Supersedeas

Sir Richard Ratclyf knighte Thoffice of Steward of the lordship of Wakefeld of (th) maister of the game within the said lordship a primo die novembris Anno ij^{do} during his lif with the wages and fees accustumed etc

George Cheynewe hathe Thoffice of keping of the north parke of the leghe and le northlaundes parcel to the manoire of Penshurst a iiij^{to} die decembris Anno primo during his lif withe the wages of iiij d by the day of thissues of the manoire of Tunbrigge and Penhurst . withe almanere othre proffites commodities & advailles etc

[f85] Thomas Blount Squier for the body hath an Annuytie xx^{ti} marces to be perceyved of thissues etc of youre lordships of Clubury Mortymer Beaudeley and Stauntonelacy in youre Countie of Salop quousque etc

John Mortymer Squiere for the body an Annuytie of xl li of thissues of the lordships of Abbotley and Shrawley in the Countie of Worcester during the nonneage of Edward Erle of Warrwik

David Vaghan Walshemane is made denzin

John Punche yomane of the Crowne hathe vj d by the day for the fee of the same of the custumes of Pole during his lif Also thoffice of Constable of the Castel of Shrewesbury during his lif with the wages and fees accustumed etc

Nicholas Cleveley yomane of the Crowne hathe ij prive seales oon to the Bailliefes of Northamptone and a nother to the Tresourer and Barons of Theschequier for there discharge upone payment made by the said Baillieffes to the said Nicholas of the somme of xiij li xiij s ix d due unto him of his fee of the Crowne

John Cledon hathe confermed unto him an Annuel poort of Cs for terme of his lif of the prior & Convent of Wenlok

Maymfray Gogiers hathe an Annuytie of vj marces for terme of his lif of the Revenues of the lordship of Barkeswelle

Herry Michel hathe an Annuytie of x marces during his lif of the lordship of Moreyende in the Countie of Northamptone

Thomas Sayvile Thoffices of keping of the manoire of Epworthe and Surveyor of the said manoire with the membres for terme of his lif with the wages accustumed

Edward Hardgille hathe a prive seale to the Shirief of Suthampton for hey and other thinges for fremantel parke

Waltier Hanard an Annuytie of x mark during his lif of the Revenues of Brekenok in Southwales

Thomas Hanard an Annuytie of (x) fyve li during his lif of the same lordship

William Bracher hathe a prive seal to the Tresourere and barons of theschequier for somme of vj li. xj d. due unto him (of) for the keping of the (keping) estbaillifwik of the forest of Purbek to discharge Thomas Bradley and John Kyme Custumers pole for the said somme

Sir Thomas Markenfeld an Annuytie of C marc during his lif of the Revenues of Myddelham

[f85b] Sir Thomas Markenfeld Shirief of Yorkshire hathe a prive seale to the Tresourere and Chambrelains of theschequier for to make unto him assignement of the somme of CCCxl li by taille or tailles upon the Receipt of his baillifwik

Thomas Meres Squier Shirief of Lincolneshire hathe a prive seale to the Tresourere and barons of theschequier that in his accompt they demaund noo thing of him by extent by approwment

Herry Johnesone of Flaundres borne is made denzin during his lif

Halnath Malyverere hathe the manoire of Bokennek in Cornewail annui valoris xxxviij li vj s & the manoire of Elyne in the same Countie annui valoris xv li viij s viij d & the manoire of Brodok annui valoris xiij li iij s to him and his heires masles by knighte service & the Rent of C s

John Bunting yomane of the vestiary hathe the Corrody of Monnemouthe

Robert Pembertone huissher of Chambre hathe ix li ij s vj d yerely during his lif of thissues etc of the fee ferme of Northamptone by the handes of the Baillif per confirmacionem

The merchauntes of Italy have theire privileges graunted upon custumed to theim confermed

Sir John Done knighte hathe a prive seale to the Tresourere and Chambrelains of theschequier for assigement to be made to him of lxx li by taylle or tailles upon his Shiriefwik of Bedford & Bukingham

The merchauntes of Hanse have theire privileges of the guyld hal in Londone confermed

Robert Appulby hathe the keping of the kinges prive palois in Westminster & keping of the beddes clothes there with the wages (of) of vj d by the day for the keping of palais and xiij s iiij d for a gowne yerely . and viij d by the day for himself & for a grome undre him for the said office of keping of the beddes of thissues of the fee ferme of Suthampton

Edward Redmayne hath the manoire of Illubruare in Somersetshire late Thomas Arundelles & al landes & tenementes in the Townes of Middeltone Cowlestone Eilestok Wortone Poterne Wyke Nustede Southbrome Stret Cotes Ryndewey Cannynges Estone Ore Aubury Roucley Ricardestone Stokley Whetham Bromeham Sanderghil Toderingtone Kayleweys Chippenham Stanley Buddestone Uphaven Altone Milstone Duringtone & Sherebetone in Wiltshire late Roger Tocotes to him and his heires masles forever by knightes service and the Rent of vj li yerely

[f86] Richard Boughtone Squier Shiref of Warrwik & Leicestre hathe a prive seale to the Tresourere and Chambrelains of theschequier to make unto him assignement of Clx li by tail or tailles of thissues of his bailliefwyk to (be) be leveyed etc

Sir Thomas Fraunceys oon of the Chapellains of the kinges Chapelle hathe the pension of Sarum whiche the Bisshop there geveth

A warrant to the Shiriff of the Countie of Wilteshire to doo paye yerely from the tyme of Michelmasse the first yere of the Reigne of king Richard the iij^d unto viij kepers of the Forestes and park of Claryngdone Bukholt Mulchet and Groveleghe and to ij palicers of the said park of Claryngdone (of thissues of) to every of (theym) the said kepers ij d by the day and to every of the said palicers j d ob by the day for theire wages / And also that the said Shiriff doo bye or to be broughte yerely in somer season for the feddyng of the dere there asmoche heye as shalle amounte unto the some of x li or within and the same do to be kept in the barne within the said parc with due alowaunce of the same at his accomptes

John Wroughtone John Newburgh John Mordaunt and John Newburghe the manoirs or lordshippes of Divelishe & Duntishe in the countie of Dorset and al landes & tenementes Rentes services etc in Divelish and Duntish Loxtone

Estpullyan Whitchurch Stoket Okford & Eltone & elleswhere in the countie of Dorset which were Sir (Wi) Nicholas Latymer knight / to thaym thair heires & assignes without any thing payeng

A warrant to the Receyvours of therldom of Warwik within the countie of Warwik to paye to John Hugford maister of the Stode fyfty Nene poundes fyve shelinges & xj d for contentacion of provisions made by William Bramerey yeoman of the stode for thexpenses of the yong horses and for wages and bourdewages of divers gromes kepers of the same after ij d by the day wages & x pens bourde wages and soo to paye yerely after the nombre of the personnes after the said rate with payment of like provisions yerely etc

A warrant for Griffith Floide otherwise called Lloide yeoman of the crowne for (to surcesse) for the pardonne of xl li / by hym forfaited to the king in theschequier & to surceise of al processes in that part to (the) the tresourer and barons of theschequier etc

Henry Brathwayte thoffice of oone of the Custumers of Suthamptone during pleasure

Decembre Henry Gray knighte / An Annuyte of x li during his lif of the fee ferme of the Citee of Norwiche

[f86b] The Clerkes and ministres of the Receipt have a prive seale for contentacion of theire fees and wages . whiche is directed to the Tresourere and Chambrelains

A prive seale for Herry Gray knighte to the Tresourer and barons to allowe Robert Roos (of) and William Ferror late Shiriefes of Norwiche upon theire accompt in anno primo xij li viij s (xij) xj d and in likewise John Ebbes and William Curteys (p) Shirieffes Anno ij^{do} of the said Citie in theire accompt the somme of iiij li xiij s ij d ob whiche was due and paied by theim to the said Harry for thexercising of thoffice of keping of the Armor within the Toure of Londone

Sir Thomas Broughtone Steward of the lordships of Dertingtone & Bovytracy in Devone and maister Forster of the Chaces and parkes there hathe a prive seale to discharge John Hayes upon the payment to him made of Ciiij li for thexercising of the said office in Anno primo

John lord Dynham hathe a like prive seale to the Tresourere and barons for the payment of C li (for thexercising of thoffice) to him graunted by king

Edward the iiijth of thissues of the lordships of Sampford Courteney Chalne-
leighe Torbryane & Slaptone in Devonshire

Richard Pole Shirief of Norffolk and Suffolk hathe a prive seale to the
Tresourere and barons for assigmentes to be made to him Clx li by taille or
tailles of thissues of his baillifwik

Rauf Serle hathe thoffice of keping of the parke of Hungerford in Berkshire
during his lif withe the wages and fees accustumed of thissues of the Towne and
lordship of Hungerford

Robert Cresset Shirief of Salop hathe a prive seal for assignementes of C li of
his baillifwik

William Taptone hathe an Annuytie of v li during his lif of thissues of the
lordship of Maunsfeld by the handes of the Receyvor

Thomas Gargrave hathe an Annuytie of x markes of thissues of the manoire of
Wakefeld during his lif

John Penyngtone Clerk hathe the Free Chapel of Saint John Baptist besides
Hungerford during his lif with al rightes

John Beerdisley an Annuytie of vj markes from mighelmasse Anno ij^{do} during
his lif of the lordships of Cokeham & Bray

Sir Marmaduc Constable Sheref of Stafford a discharge for C li.

Margarete

[f87] Margaret Blasy an Annuytie of x markes during the nonneage of Edward
Erle of Warrwik of the lordship of Hawnehope [sic] in Herefordshire

The president and felowes of (Cante) the quenes Colleigue of Cantebrigge
have a (pres) prive seale to the Chauncellere of England and to the Maister
(Clerc) of the rolles for ta amend there patentes of there landes graunted to the
said place that is to wite to take out thise wordes in Comitatu Bukinghamie and
put in thise wordes in Comitatu Northampton and also take out thise wordes
ville de Ramesey and put in thise wordes ferie sive nundinarum ville Sancti
yvonis etc

Herry Cley hathe landes and tenementes in Cheversham called Dengayns whiche late appertaigned to John Bale . & by reason of his rebellion forffaicted to the kinges handes / during the lif of the said Herry without accomt etc

Elizabeth Tyringham widowe hathe the keping of alle landes manoirs and lordships whiche late were John Tyringhams Squier

Item the same Elizabeth hathe the warde and mariage of John Son and heire of John Tyringham

Richard Burtone Shirief of Northamptone hathe a prive seale for assignement of a C li of his Shiriefwik

Sir Robert Rither hathe an Annuytie of xx li during his lif of thissues of the lordship of Pountfreit in the Countie of Yorke in recompense of thoffice of Constable of the Castel of Yorke

Robert Brakenbury Shirief of Kent hath a prive seale for assignement of C li of his Shiriefwik

William Erle of Notingham hathe a pardone of al trespasses and adiugementes of fynes amerciamentes

Sir Richard Huddlestone hathe xxiiij souldiours in Beamares over the persones in thordinary charges there during half yere withe the wages of iiij d by the day for every Souldior

John Baptist Gentille and his heires ben made denzins

A prive seale to the Tresourere and Barons of theschequier to discharge Edward Hardgille late Shirief of Wilteshire for the payment of vj li (xiij) xiij s vj d by him made to Thomas (ha) Stafford for the keping of the parke of Ludgarsale

Item a prive seale to the said Edward for to paye the said somme to the same Thomas

William Blake hathe thoffice of (Smythe of) keping of the forge within the Castelle of Windesore with the wages accustumed during his lif per confirmacionem

[f87b] Maister William Villers hathe the iij^de prebend in the Churche of Leicestre voide by the Resignacion of Sir William Raulyns

Harry Huddlestone hathe Thoffices of Raglowe and Raglowe advowrie with the stewardship of Menna and Rosfawe in Caernervanshire and in thisle of Anglesey in Northwales during the kinges pleasire with wages and fees accustumed

John Musgrave hathe the keping of the Castel in Sarum during his lif withe wages and fees accustumed

Raclyn Werbertone hathe an Annuytie of iiij marces during his lif of the Revenues of the lordship of Dynbighe

John Musgrave is launderere of the parke of Claringdone in Wiltshire during his lif with iij d by the day and yerely xiij s iiij d at Cristemasse for a wynter gowne & x s yerely at Ester for somer clothing to be perceived aswele of thissues of the Shiriefwik of Wiltshire as of the ferme of the conyes in the said parke with al other proffites etc

The same John hathe Thoffice of Ranger of the Forest of Grovele in Wiltshire during his lif with like wages as John Knottingley somtyme had of thissues of the said Countie

Domynyk Lynche of Galeway hathe licence to make a mille upon the water of Galeway within the walle of the Towne and to have the same to him and his heires forever paying iiij d by yere and noo thing elles

Thomas Hardegrove & Thomas Dormer have Thoffice of Otter huntes during theire lifes and either of theim lenger lyving with iij d ob by day for either of there wages and iiij d ob by the day for the mete of six dogges for the said office and j d ob by the day for the wages of a grome undre theim and ix d by the day for xij dogges for every of them ob qr of the Custumes of Chichestre poort

Thomas Stanes hathe Thoffice of berer of lyvereys of the grete warderobe with the wages accustumed & al other proffittes etc

Thabbot and Convent of Saint Mary besides York have to theim and there Successours a pardon of xx li of the fee ferme of Cxx marc by theim paied of the manoire of Whitgyft Rednesse Hule etc

Sir Herry brokas Chapellain within the manoire of Eltham hathe x markes yere for his Salary of thissues of the said manoire

[f88] William Husy chief Juge William Beverley dean of the Chapelle William Catesby Squier & maister Edmond Chadertone have the Manoire of Stafford Barnyngham in Norffolk fro Mighelmasse Anno primo during the terme of vij yeres without accompt etc and the said terme expired the said Manoire to remayne to the maister of the Colleige of the Trynitie of Plesshey & to his Successors

William Olyver hathe an Annuytie of x li during his lif of the Revenues of the manoire of Doweltone in Devone

William Smythe of Stratford in Suffolk hathe a licence to passe to Island with a ship called the Kateryn of Orwelle of the portage of iiij^{xx} tonne as oft etc during a yere

Robert Waring is presented to the parsonage of Bestone in the diocise of Norwiche

Sir John Bromeley knighte hathe an Annuytie of x li of the lordship of Dynbighe in Wales

William Shore merchant of Londone and Robert Chapmane of Kyngestone upon Hulle merchauntes have a licence to pass to Island with ij shippes of the portage of iiij^{C} tonnes . the licence during a yere

A prive seale to the Tresourer and barons to allowe John Hayes the somme of DCCxxvj li xviij s iiij d in his accompt etc

John Musgrave hathe a prive seale to the Tresourere and Barons for to allowe Edward Hardgille of the somme of vij li x s whiche he paied to the said John for Thoffice of kepar of the Castelle of Sarum of thissues of the Shiriefwik of Wiltshire when he was Shirief of the same

Item the same John hathe a like prive seale for the payment of xiij li iiij s to him made by the said Edward late Shirief for thoffice of Ranger of the forest of Grovele

Item a like prive seale for the payment of vj li xiiij s. vj d for the keping of the launde within the parke of Claringdone and xxiij s iiij d for gownes etc

Item iij severelle privy seales to the said Edward for the payment of the said sommes

Item the lord Matravers hath a prive seale to the Tresourer and barons for the discharging of the Custumers of Suthampton for the payment of certaine sommes of money to the said lord by vertue of certaine lettres patentes

[f88b] The same lord Matravers hathe a like discharge for the Custumers and Collectors of Londone of the payment of lviij li vj s viij d & a nother prive seale to the Custumers for the payment therof

The lord Grey hathe Thoffice of Constable of the Castelle of Pevesey in the Countie of Sussex with thoffice of Steward of the lordship of Pevensey & of the honor of Thegle in the said Countie and the maister Forster of the forest and chace of Asshedowne and al forestes and chaces within the said lordship honor and Forest during his lif withe the wages and fees accustumed

John Uptone thoffice of baillif of the Franchise within the Rape of Pevensey & thonor of Egill in Sussex during his lif with wages and fees accustumed etc

Sir William Stanley knighte hathe the Castel towne and lordship of Denasbrayne the Castel towne & lordship of Lyons lordship landes & tenementes called Hewlingtone Bromfeld Yale Wrixham Almore Burtone Hosseley Rydley (Isto) Iscoyde Hem Cobham Almore Cobham Iscoyd Estlusham Eglosfeile Ruyabone Abunbury Dymulle Mortone Redwalle Pykhille Sessewik Sonford & Osselestone in the Marches of Wales in (Sh) Shropshire and al Castelles lordships Townes & manoirs of Merford & Hosseley & other Ragles late John duc of Norffolk and George Nevilles to the said Sir William & his heires masles by the service of oon knightes fee

A licence to Master Robert Bothe dean of Yorke Thome Portingtone Tresourer William Pottemane & John Hert chanons of Yorke to kepe Courtes letes etc & make officers for the leveying of almanere Rentes and duties apperteignyng to the C prestes at Yorke

Laurence Mountford hath the free Chapelle in the parisshe Churche of Flamstede

A prive seale to the Tresourer and barons to discharge Herry Roos knighte of the somme of viij li ix s and of the somme of xviij s by him due of thissues of the Shiriefwik of Surrey and Sussex whiche the king hathe pardonned him

Robert Vyse hathe a prive seale to the Tresourer etc aswele for his owne discharge as the Shirief of Suthampton for the somme of ix li. ij s. vj d. for thoffice of Ryding forster in the Newe forest pro Anno primo

Anne Bapthorp hathe an Annuytie of x marc of thonor of Tutbury during hir lif

[f89] Herry Smythe hathe a prive seale to the Tresourere and Barons for the discharging of (th) John Rogiers late Shirief of Suthampton upon his payment of ix li ij s vj d to the said Herry made for thexercising of Thoffice of Baillif of Burley in the newe forest

The maire etc of the Citie of Lincolne hathe Wasshingburghe & Highingtone with other hamelettes graunted to the body of theire Citie with many other privileges

The baillif Burgesses and Comonalties of Galwey have al theire privileges of theire Towne confermed

John Bisshop of Ely hathe a general pardonne

The lady Dynham hathe iiij tonnes of wyne yerely during hir lif of the prynse wynes of Dertmouthe Plymmouthe and fowey

George Byrde hathe a prive seale to the Collectors and Custumers of Newcastel upon Tyne for to pay him liij li v d due to him by the king for wyne Glasse yron lede etc

Item a nother prive seale to the Tresourere and Barons for the discharging of the said Collectors and Custumers

Sir Richard Croft Shirief of Hereford hathe assigment for fyfty li of his Shiriefwik

The maire and Burgesses of Lincolne have pardonne of theire fyftenes and alle other taxes and tallages for the terme of lx yeres

John Andree Cyny borne in the parties of Ytaly is made denzine

John Piltone Shirief of Roteland (for) hath assignement of xiij li vj s viij d of his baillifwyk

Sir Thomas Burgchier of Ledes hathe confermed unto him Thoffices of Constable and parker of the Castel and parke of Ledes for terme of his lif withe wages and fees accustumed and also the keping of the parke of Langley and jayler of the Castel of Ledes etc

Halnath Malyverere hathe a prive seale to the Tresourer & Barons for to allowe him C marces of the Shiriefwyk of Devone for anno primo like as Charles Dynham and other Shirieffes there had

William Husey hathe Thoffice of Steward of al landes and tenementes late George duc of Clarences in Rutland during his lif withe wages and fees accustomed and after his decesse Thomas Sapcotes to have the said office during his lif

Rouland Symondes hathe confirmed unto him to be oon of the kinges ser- ieauntes at Armes with the fees & wages accustumed / of xij d by the day to be perceived of the lordship of Fekenham by the handes of the bail[l]ief for terme of his lif

Yvonem Michelle Yvonem Bouther & Henry Ligadet britans hathe a sauf- conduyt for them self & a ship of Britayne of Ciij° tonnes or under / during the space of xiij monethes

[f89b] William Baker John Courvant & Richard Butteler hath a licence for a ship of the portage of xl Tonne or under in Englisshe ship to passe to be yonde the see / to endure by an hool yere

Morgan Kydwelly hathe the keping of that parte of the Chace of Cranborne called Chitret with thappurtenaunces in the Countie of Dorset as long as he berethe him wele in the same with wages and fees accustumed

Maister John Hubert is presented to the Churche of Boxwelle in the diocise of Norwiche

John Hayes hathe a prive seale to the Tresourere and Barons for the payment of CCCC li to the lord Scrope of the kinges Rewarde

The Vicars of the Cathedralle Churche of Yorke have have the parisshe Church of Cotingham in Yorkshire to theim appropred

John Jaques Ivon Michelle Ivon Bocher Herry Lagadie Tanquyn Ligildie Rouland Souchard & John de Bose of Britayne merchantes have a saufconduyt for a Ship of CC(x)l^{ti} tonne to come into England the said saufconduit during xiiij monethis

Nicholas Mountgomery Shirief of Notingham and Derby hathe a prive sele for assignement of C li of his Shiriefwik etc

John Burnard yomane of Chambre hathe an Annuytie of C s of thissues of Salesbury landes unto suche tyme as he be promoted etc

Nicholas Taillor hathe a like annuytie in like forme of the same landes

John Cole hathe an Annuytie of x li of the Custumes of Sandewiche during his lif

Herry lord Grey hath a licence for a ship called the George of Winchelsey of the portage of xl tonne to goo into other landes withe almanere merchandises not apperteynyng to the Staple of Calais the said licence tendure a yere

The same lord Grey hathe a like licence for the Ship called the Nicholas of Winchelsey late of Bylboo

Halnath Malyverer hathe Thoffice of Constable of the Castel of Launcestone in Cornewail during his lif with the wages and fees accustumed etc

William Cranewel of Cranewel in the Countie of Lincolne hathe a generalle pardonne

James Auber & John Fabry hathe a Saufconduyt of Normandy have a Saufconduyt for xiiij monethes for ship (f) or Shippes of CC tonne

[f90] John Belbury of Listard and John Toser of Excester have a generalle pardonne

246

John Joy hathe the keping of (the houses) the houses inward within the Castel of Windesore with wages of iiij d by the day of thissues of the said Castelle per confirmacionem

Robert Russelle hathe an Annuytie of C s during the nonneage of Edward Erle of Warrwik of the Revenues (Revenues) of Elmeley Castelle

To the Custumers and Collectors of Hulle is directed a prive seale for to suffre Jaques Aubier to Reteigne in his owne handes xl li of suche custumes as he aughte to pay to the king of his merchandises there discharge

A prive seal to the Tresourere and barons for the discharge of the said Custumers and Collectors upon the same

(Jal) Jaques Auber hathe a licence to ship within a yere iij^{xx} fodres of lede & xv pakkes of wollenclothes grayned or not grayned etc and the same convey to outward parties

William Waren hathe thoos vj markes yerely whiche the prior of Folkestone is bounde to pay to the king in tyme of werre betwix Fraunce & England . during his lif etc

Richard Massy is appointed oon of the Sergeantes at lawe within the Countie of Chestre and Flynt with the wages and fees accustumed

Rouland Chouchart Tanguy le Glindic John Flouriet Philip Martyne Yvon de Valle Peter le Bloussart merchantes of Bretaigne have a saufconduyt for a Ship called the Frauncoys of Bretaigne of the portage of ij^{C} tonne of wyne or within . etc during a hole yere

Richard Williams gentilmane huissher of the Chambre hathe the Castelle and manoire of Manerbere and Pennalee with the membris and appurtenaunces in the Countie of Pembroche annui valoris C li / to him and his heires masles by knightes service

Christofir Welfeld hathe Thoffice of Baillif of Ryngwode in the Countie of Suthampton during the kinges plaisire with ij d by the day of the said Towne of Ryngwood

Rauf Endsone hathe Thoffice of keping of the forest or chace of Stervile beside Cristeschurche in oure Countie of Suthamptone for terme of his lif withe ij d by the day of thissues of Cristeschurche

Robert Michelsone hathe an Annuytie of x li from the fest of Saint Mighelle tharchangelle Anno primo during his lif of the Custumes of Hulle

[f90b] A prive seale to the Tresourere and Chambrelains of theschequier to make out severelle tailles of the somme Dlxij li xviij d upon the Subsidie and pety custome of Londone . and the same delyver to Anthony Kele of Ande-warp in Braband

John Grenehille hathe Thoffice of Baillif of Hasfeld with the keping of the parke there in Gloucestreshire during his lif with ij d by the day (of) for every office of thissues of the said lordship

George Erle of Shrewesbury hathe an Annuytie of viij li sterlinges of the lordship of Alburbury during his nonneage

Thomas Greyson hathe a prive seale to the Tresourer and Chambrelains of Theschequiere (upon the) to make unto him assignement of the somme of Clvj li xiij s iiij d by taille or tailles in due forme to be leveyed upon the said Thomas and Robert Code Collectors of the poortes of Excestre and Dertmouthe

Richard Scopeham hathe the keping of the Toure nye theschequier within the palois of Westminster with ij d by the day of the fee ferme of Yeppeswiche and an Annuytie of ij d by the day of the said fee ferme during his lif

John Treviliane the yonger of Netilcombe in the Countie of Somerset hathe a generalle pardonne

William Hotone hathe a prive seale to the maister of the kinges halle within Cantebrigge to be a felawe there when suche Rome shal voide

Alice the wif of John Shipward of Bristowe merchaunt hath an Annuytie of xl li during hir lif of the fee ferme of the hundred or lordship of Bartone in Gloucestreshire and also oon tonne of wyne yerely of the prise wynes of Bristowe etc

A prive seale to the Clerc of the hanaper for to delyver alle suche lettres patentes as apperteigne to the (va) C prestes of Yorke unto Master John

Harringtone without fyne or fee

John Bardefeld hathe Thoffice of Receyvor of al Castelles lordships etc parcelle of the duchie of Lancastre within the Counties of Essex Hertford Middlesex Surrey and Londone during the kinges pleasire with wages and fees accustumed etc

John Kendale Secretary & George Dale have thoffice of keping of the manoir of Havering at Boure alias thoffice of Baillif there . with the keping of the warenne there and the yate of the parke called Southgate during theire lyves & either of theim lenger lyving perceyving for the keping of the manoir iiij d by the day . the keping of the warrenne ij d by day & the keping of the said yate ij d by the day . and the said George xx li of Reward for thexercising of the said office heretofore of thissues of the said manoire

[f91] Thomas Tawke of Hamptonet and William his son have a general pardon

John Peke hathe Thoffice of Rangier within the forest of Dene during his lif with wages and fees accustumed per confirmacionem

Thomas Rogers Clerk of the Shippes hathe a prive seale to the Tresourer and Chambrelains of Theschequier for to make unto him by way of assignement by taille or tailles upon the Custumers and Collectors in the portes of Excester and Dertmouthe aswele of the somme of xliiij li xviij s iij d for thexercising of the said office as of the somme of xx li of the kinges Rewarde

John Frisley and John Perot mercer have a prive seale to the maire and othre officers of the Towne and poort of Kingestone upon Hulle to see that a ship laden with wynes apperteynyng unto theim be delyvered in whoos handes soever they be whiche late was taken upon the see by men of the said Towne because the wynes were shipped in a Shipp of Middelburghe

Giles Brigge hathe a prive seale to John Harrecourt Receyvor of the Spensers landes Warrewik landes and Sarum landes in the Counties of Warrwik Gloucestre Hereford and Oxonford . to content unto him of thissues of the same xviij li sterling of the kinges Reward

Hugh Lawtone hathe a prive seale to the Tresourere and Chambrelains to doo strike out a taille (of) conteynyng the somme of C s to be leveyed upon the Custumers of the pety Custume in Londone . and the same delyver unto him as of the kinges Reward

Robert Conyers Scoler of Cantebrigge hath a prive seale to the maister of the kinges halle to be a felowe there

The Burgesses of Scardeburghe have graunted unto the [sic] a maire a Shirief and xij Aldermene and the same Towne to be a poort with many other privileges

Januer Johanne the late wif of Warrewik herauld hathe a prive seale to the Receyvors and Auditors of the lordship of Elmeley in the Countie of Worcestre to content unto hir yerely during the nonnage of Edward Erle of Warrwik an Annuytie of xl s of thissues of the said lordship etc

Thomas Gibbes is made oon of the Almoux knightes of Saint George of Windesore with proffites Rightes etc

Richard Suttone (ser) thoffice of Sergeant at lawe in the Countie palantyne of Chestre during his lif with wages and fees accustumed

[f91b] George Grey Clerk convyct hathe a pardone for thabbot of Westminster upon his escape

Richard Beestone hathe Thoffices of Constable & Jayler of the Castel of Sandehalle in the Countie of York during his lif with the wages of C s yerely of thissues of the said lordship. and also C s in Reward for thexercising of the said Offices of the said (offices) issues An [sic] also an Annuytie of (C s) xv li during his lif of the same issues

Sir John Savage the yonger hathe an Annuytie of xl^{ti} marces during his lif of thissues of the Forest of Macclesfeld in the Countie palantyne of Chestre

Sir Richard Surland hathe the free Chapel within the Castelle of Plasshe with almanere rightes & duties during his lif

Frydeswide the wif of Edward Norys Squier Suster to the lord Lovelle hathe an Annuytie of C marc during hir lif of thonor of Walingford in the Countie of Berkshire

Maistre Peter Wybbe doctor (of div) in theologie hath an Annuytie of x markes of the Revenues of Elmeley Lovet in Worcestreshire quousque etc

Gilbert Cowper Clerc hathe the parsonage of litel Fransham in the diocise of Norwich by the Resignacion of Sir Richard Cutteler

A prive seale to the Tresourere and Barons to allowe acquyte and discharge Sir Thomas Wortley and Jane his wif of the payment of iiij^{xx} li yerely to my lady of Warrwik of thissues of the landes of the landes longing to Edward son and heire of Sir John Pilkingtone during his nonneage and also to discharge suche Shirief or Shirieffes of suche shire or shires as the said landes lyen in / and (the) my said lady of Warrwik for the Receipt thereof

John Bulle thoffice of Baillif of the lordship of Warblyngtone with the keping of the parke there during his lif . with the wages and fees accustumed etc

Robert Brakenbury hathe Thoffice of Constable of the Castel of Tunbrigge in Kent from saint Bartholomewe last past during his lif with x markes fee of the Revenues of the lordship there

The same Robert hathe the Stewardship of the lordship of Ware for terme of his lif with the fee of C s of the Revenues of the same

Humfrey Stanley hathe alle landes and tenementes Rentes & services late Sir William Norreys knighte in the Townes of Campden in the old and aston undre Egge in the Countie of Gloucestre . for terme of his lif without any accompt etc

[f92] Anne Harecourt widowe hathe an Annuytie of xx^{ti} marces of Warrwik landes in Oxonfordshire during the nonnage of Edward etc

William Mistelbroke hathe the manoire or lordship of Hortone with the appurtenaunces in the parisshe of Hortone and a certaine tenement lying to the same in the Countie of Kent & certaine Rentes to the said manoire perteynyng late Sir William Stoner annui valoris xx li the manoire of the feld C acre lande & C acre pasture with thappurtenaunces in Comptone nighe Gildeford late Sir Thomas Saintleger knighte annui valoris iiij li vj s viij d the manoire of Donne place under Gyldoune late the said Thomas annui valoris iiij mark . the manoire (of) or chief messuage called Wheteham at Wheteham hille in the Countie of Suthampton late the said Thomas annui valoris iiij mark to him and his heires masles by knightes service and the Rent of xxx s

Richard Llouyd yoman of the Corowne vj d by the day for his fee of the same from Estre last past during his lif of thissues of the manoire of Walden parcel of the duchie of Lancastre in the Countie of Essex

Michael Skilling late of Caundel Chidiok in Dorset shire hathe a pardonne for his lif

John Pole and Richard Pole Squiers have the manoir of Northhoughtone in the Countie of Suthampton & al landes tenementes medewes woodes pastures in Northhoughtone forsaid Swamptone in the parisshe of Saint Maryborne Est tyderley & Winchestre in the said Countie late Michaell Skilling & al landes and tenementes in Blokkesworthe Milborne stileham & Brodewey in the Countie of Dorset late Michael Skillinges as in the right of his wif to theim and theire heires forever without any accompt etc

Fraunceys lord Lovel hathe Thoffice of Steward of the lordships of Cokeham and Bray in the Countie of Berkshire (during his) from Mighelmasse Anno primo during his lif with wages and fees accustumed and power to make the make the Baillif there

John Bonyngtone hath Thoffice of Constable of youre Castel of Guysnes for terme of his lif with suche nombre of Souldiors and wages as Herry Yong late had

A licence geven to Thabbottes of Tewkesbury and Morgan to make eschaunge of certain landes of the Quenes fundacion

John Kendale Secretary and William Joseph Squier have thoffice of keper (of) or governor of the parke of Hethenden in the Countie of Kent during theire lives and eithre of theim lenger lyving with wages and fees accustumed and the said John Kendale thoffice of maister of the game there

Sir Robert Percy knighte Shirief of Essex and Hertford hathe a prive seale for assignement to be made by the Tresourer and Chambrelains of the somme of Ciiij^{xx}xviij li of thissues of his Sheriefwik etc

The warden and his brethren of Frere mynors of Saint Fraunceys ordre in youre Citie of Worcestre of youre Fundacion have vj li of the moyte of the manoire of Pyry of the kinges gift in almoux

[f92b] James Fryse phisiciane hathe a prive seale to the Tresourere and barons of theschequier to surceasse forever of almanere processe to be made ayemst him for that he did not his homage upon that he was made denzine before the king nowe but oonly afore king Edward etc

Thomas ap John gentilman hathe an Annuytie of xx^{ti} markes from Mighelmasse last past during his lif of the Revenues of the lordship of Bergavenny in Wales etc

(Thabbotes and Conventes of Morgan and Tewkesbury have a warrant to the Clerc of the hanaper to delyver the kinges lettres patentes)

William Skele of the Towne of Calais Brasyer borne in luke is denzin

Lewes Bragadyne (and) Anthony Baveryne Stephan Cateryne and Pancras Justynyane merchantes of Venyce have a prive seale to the Tresourere and Chambrelains of theschequier for to make out severel tailles to theim that is to say to the said Lewes a taille of lxv li xij s viij d to be leveyed upon the Custumers & Collectors of Suthampton of the goodes of Peter Couteryne for the said Lewes . A nother taille conteynyng xlvj li xiij s iiij d upon the said Custumers and Collectors of the goodes of Anthony Bavaryne . An othre taille conteynyng xiiij li upon the said Collectors of the goodes of Stephan Kateryne and the fourthe taille conteynyng xiiij li upon the (goodes) said Collectors of the goodes of the said Pancras Justynyane whiche the king owethe to theim severelly for bowe staves

William Uvedale of Wykeham in the Countie of Suthampton hathe a pardone for his lif

Frideswide wif unto Edward Norres Squiere hathe a prive seale to the Receyvor general of Walingford to content unto hir . l . markes of the kinges Reward

John Stapletone yoman of the Corowne hathe a prive seale to Edward Hardegille late Shirief of Wiltshire to content unto him of thissues of his Shiriefwik ix li ij s vj d (for thex) of the kinges reward for thexercising of Thoffice of Ranger of Mylchuyt

The same John hath a nother prive seale to the Tresourere and barons for to discharge the said Edward of the said some in his accompt

Robert ap Howelle hath thoffice of Constable of the Castel of Skenfrithe in the marches of Wales parcel of the duchie of Lancastre with thoffice of maister Sargeant of the lordships of Monmouthe Whitecastel Skenfrithe & Grosmond for terme of his lif with wages & fees accustumed etc

Richard Rugge Squier hathe an Annuytie of xx (marcs) li that is to say x marces of thissues of the lordship of Salwarp and xx markes thereof of the lordship of Elmeley from mighelmas last past during the nonnage of Edward Erle of Warrwik

The Freres of the house of Saint Augustyne within the universitie of Oxonford have a prive seale to Sir Edmond Rede keper of the Forest of Shotover & al others kepers there to suffre them to take Frestone in any quarry there not laten to ferme for the buylding of theire house of the kinges gift

[f93] John Frye late of Plymmouthe hathe a pardonne for his lif

A prive seale directed to Thomas Thwaytes Tresourer of Calais to delyvere to Richard Warmyngtone Tresourere of the werres there CC li sterling

Robert Elwald huissher of the Chambre hathe an Annuytie of xx li of thissues of the lordship of Kermerden in Southwales quousque terre etc

John Belle yomane of the Chambre hathe an Annuytie of (viij markes) x markes from mighelmasse last past during his lif of thissues of thonour of Tutbury in the Countie of Stafford

Robert Roo hath Thoffice of Baillif of the hundred of Somborne and the haywardship of the lordship of Somborne with the keping of the waters betwene Tittecombrigge and youre mede called kingsmede beside Stokbrigge during his lif with wages & fees accustumed etc

Thomas Skarisbrik Clerc of theschequiere of Caernarvon hath Thoffice of Supervisor of youre werkes within youre Castel and Townes of Caernarvon Beaumares Conway and Hardlaghe in Northwales during the kinges pleasire with the wages of iiij d by the day by the handes of the Chambrelain of North-wales for the tyme being with al other proffites etc

Sebastian de Giglis is made denzin

Sir John Conyers knighte hathe an Annuytie of CC marces from michelmasse last past during his lif of thissues etc of the lordships landes & tenementes of Skalepark Rande Swaldale Bowes with the tolle of Sleghtholme the newe Forest Thornetone Steward & Erle Orchard in the Countie of Yorke by the handes of the Receyvor etc

Sir Thomas Beverley hathe the pension in the monasterie of Mertone

Petre Hoke hathe a licence for a C oxen to have to Calais without paying of any custume etc

William Bury hathe thoffice of pety Custumere in the poort of Pole during the kinges pleasire with fees & wages accustumed answering the Custume as apperteignethe

William Browne of Staumford hathe a licence to founde an Almoux house there forever

William Bensted gentilmane hathe a general pardone

William Goaez hathe a licence to ship asmoche clothe in grayne or out of grayne & as many peces of tynne as the Custume thereof wille amount to the somme of CCxiij li in the hole . without paying any custume . making endentures with the Custumers as it is shipped

The same William Goaez Peter le Gadec John le Goaez John Loz & Yvon Michel (h) merchantes of britayne have a saufconduyt for a ship called the Mary of britaigne of the portage of Cl tonne . the saufconduyt during xv moneth

John Lucymane hath thoos x markes whiche the bailliffes of the Towne of Wiche besides Worcestre be bounde to pay to the king during the nonnage of Edward Erle of Warrewik

William Pouche hath al suche landes and tenementes to ferme within the lordship of Hammes as Alybone had . paying as he did etc

[f93b] William Capelle of Londone draper and Thomas Pays of the same Skynner have a prive seale to the Tresourer and Chambrelains to (make unto theim assignementes by) doo stryke out twoo severel taylles to be leveyed upon the Collectors of the pety Custume in the poort of London oon of theim conteynyng xxxiij li ix s iiij d for the said William Capelle and a nother conteynyng xvj li xvj s for the said Thomas Payes whiche the king oweth to theim for silkes & furres

Geffray Whitford hathe an Annuytie of liiij s v d ob during his lif of thissues etc of suche annuytie as he yerely payethe to the king for certaine landes and tenementes that he holdethe as in the righte of his wif within the lordship of Wynnesse in Lancasshire

The maire and burgesses of Oxford have a prive seale to the Tresoror and barons of theschequier to discharge theim of x marc which they oughte to pay to the king at Estre anno primo for theire Fe ferme

Richard Leptone hathe thoffice of Baillif of the Westgate of Excestre othrewise called Exiland . of Topsham / of Colompjon & of the hundred of Harigge during the kinges pleasire withe wages & fees accustumed . And also the ferme of the Crane and Sellers in Topsham paying as Richard Cruse did

Wiliam Porter an Annuytie of x marc during his lif of thissues of the lordship of Ware

Sir Edmond banke hath the Chauntery in the Castel of Sandalle

A prive seal to the Custumers and Collectors of Suthampton to suffre Jerom Salvaige patron of a Carrak to discharge suche merchandise as (w) is in the said Carrak there and to recharge the same ayen in other vesselles without paying any Custume because the king hathe taken the said Carrak to doo him service

John Snowdon yomane of the Quenes Chambre hath the keping of the manoire and wareyne of Writtylle in Essex for terme of his lif with iiij d by the day of thissues of the same lordship

Sir James Tyrelle is made Supervisor of the Castel of Guysnes in Picardie & of the Towne of Guysnes during the kinges pleasire in thabsence of the lord Mountjoy gevyng saufconduytes etc

Thomas Craford hathe an Annuytie of xx marces during his lif of the Revenues of oure lordships of Penpon & Tentone in the Countie of Cornewaille

John Wayte oon of the squiers of youre household hathe thoffice of Raunger of the Forest of Bere in the Countie of Suthampton during his lif withe wages and fees accustumed

John Fynaunce hathe a saufconduyt for a ship of vij^{xx} tonne to be charged with wynes & al othre merchandises to the staple of Calais not apperteynyng as oft etc during oon hole yere

[f94] Thomas Knighte and Robert Dymmok (have) late Shirieffes of the Countie of Lincolne have a prive seale to the Tresourer and barons of Theschequier to discharge them of x li whiche by theim shuld have ben payed yerely of landes apperteynyng to the lord Roos

Robert Poyntz hathe a pardonne upon fynes & amerciamentes

John Agard hathe a prive seale to the Tresourere and barons of theschequiere to admytte suche Attorney or Attourneys as the said John shal assigne to make his accompt upon thescheytorship of Stafford shire and to surcesse of al processes to be made ayemst for lak of apperaunce

Benedict Spynelle of Januey is made denzine for terme of his lif

William Dobynsone hathe alle (lyueds) landes & tenementes within Londone that late apperteyned to John Assheford for terme of his lif without any accompt etc

the Burgesses & inhabitantes of Llanymthenery in Wales have theire Towne made corporat with a baillif & Burgesses & other privileges etc

Maister Thomas Forster phisician hathe an Annuytie of xl li during his lif of thissues of Kingestone lacy in the Countie of Dorset

John Bonyngtone Squier hathe an Annuytie of xx^{ti} markes during his lif of thissues of the Countie of Guysnes by the handes of the Tresourere of the Towne of Calais

Christofre Colyns hathe the Ship called the Barbara of Fowey whiche was taken with Staple ware & forfaicted geven to him of the kinges Rewarde

Sir Thomas Cornewaille knighte Shirief of Herefordshire hathe a prive seale to the Tresourer and Chambrelains for assignementes to be made unto him of the somme of xxvj li vj s ij d of thissues of his Shiriefwik

John Coket hathe Thoffice of parker of Sodbury within the Countie of Gloucestre during the nonnage of Edward Erle of Warrwik and also an Annuytie of ij d by the day of thissues of the same from the furst day of octobre anno primo during the said nonnage

Sir Hugh Levered of the Chapelle hathe the parsonage of Northrippes in the diocise of Norwiche by the dethe of maister Robert Aspatry

Thomas Delahay yomane of the Crowne hathe vj d by the day for the fee of the same during his lif of the fee ferme of Norwiche by the handes of the Shirieffes there for the tyme being

John Belle Coferer hathe a prive seale to the Tresourer and Barons of the-eschequier to discharge him and his meynpenors of the ferme of xx li yere for the ferme of the manoire of Worplesdone from mighelmasse Anno primo unto the day of cancellacion of (y)oure lettres patentes to him made of the said ferme

[f94b] John Bell Coferer hathe (an Annuytie) hathe a prive seale to the Chaunceler of England to take of him lettres patentes to him made of the manoir of Worplesdone in the Countie of Surrey in ferme for vij yeres paying xx li yerely . and the same lettres patentes dampne and cancelle for that Sir Christofre maister of the herthoundes hathe Receyved thissues of the said lordship

Maistre John Taillor hathe the prebend of Husburne & Burbage in the Churche of Sarum by the Resignacion of maister Edward Pole

John Baptist of Grymalde in Jaunay borne is made denzin for terme of his lif

Sir William Heryot hathe a prive seale to the Tresourere and Chambrelains for a taille to be levied upon the Collectors of the subsidie of the port of Suthampton of the merchandises of the said (som) Sir William conteynyng the somme of iiij^{xx}xvij li iij s j d. whiche king Edward the iiij th owed him

Sir Alexandre Baynham knighte hathe an Annuytie of xl li during his lif from mighelmasse Anno primo of thissues of al manoirs lordships etc late Erle of Warrwik in the Counties of Oxonford Worcestre Gloucestre & Hereford

David Goughe hathe a pardonne for thescape of Sir Lewes Dakkyne prest out of the Castel of Radnor whereof he is Constable

Richard Hansard hathe the manoirs or lordships of Chedhamwiche Segille Gremstede Alwerbury Abbetston & More in the Countie of Wiltshire of the yerely value of xxxviij li and also landes & tenementes in Farneham in Surrey late William Clyffordes of the yerely value of xxxiij s iiij d to him and his heires masles by knightes service and the Rent of iij li yerely

258

Thomas Rogers hathe a pardone upon accomptes trespasses etc

Sir John Huddlestone knighte hathe a prive seale to the Tresourer and Chambrelains of Theschequiere to make assignement of the somme of C marc unto him upon thissues of the Shiriefwik of Huntingdon & Cantebrige whereof he is Shirief in Recompense of suche losses as he shal susteigne there

John Rither marshal of the halle hathe an Annuytie of x li from michelmasse last past during his lif of thissues of thonor of Pountfreit

John Middeltone Squier & Helene his wif have an Annuytie of x marc from mighelmasse last past during theire lifes & eithre of theim etc of the Revenues of the lordship of Kyrkeby Mallesorthe

Thomas Babham and William Margery vergeor of Windesore have the corrodie or sustentacion in the prioury of Herley in the Countie of Berkshire during theire lifes and eithre of theim etc

Christofre Colyns hathe a prive seale to Sir Thomas Thwaytes Tresourer of Calais to content him xx li which he delyvered William Boltone to content certaine Souldiors in Guysnes

John due close of the Citie of Rouen merchant hath a prive seale to Sir Thomas Thwaytes Tresourer of Calais to delyver him his ship & merchandises there late arrested because parcelle thereof was staple ware the said forfaicture not-withstanding

[f95] Richard White of Bostone hathe ij Saufconduytes for ij Shippes of Fraunce that oon of lx tonne and that othre of xl tonne to be laden with wynes etc during oon hole yere

John Walle yoman of the Corowne (for) hath vj d by the day for his fee of the said Crowne from mighelmasse last past during his lif of thissues etc of the lordships of Preston and Uppingham

John Ford yomane of the Crowne hathe the moytie (p) of alle Rentes perquisite of Courtes & other proffites of the Towne (of) and hundred of Shaftesbury extending to the yerely value of Cvj s viij d late Sir William Berkeleys without accompt etc

Maister Edmond Chadertone hathe the ferme of a place called the temple besides Marleborowe whiche William Colingborne late had of the pryor of Saint Johns in ferme for certaine yeres not yet expired etc

John Kighley hathe thoffices of Constable of the Castelle of Okehamptone in the Countie of Devone & maister of the game in the parke and Chace there perceyvyng for the said offices C s yerely from the furst day of Aprille last past during his . And also from the same tyme an Annuytie of xv li of thissues of the lordship of Okehamptone

Thomas Grey Squier hathe an Annuytie of xl li for terme of his lif of thissues of the ferme of the Towne of Cantebrigge by the handes of the baillif or othre occupiors there for the tyme being per confirmacionem

Edward Blount Squier for the body hathe an Annuytie of ten poundes of the Revenues of the Revenues of the lordship of Fawnehope during the nonnage of Therle of Warrwik

Richard Shermane and John Dale executors of the testament of John Hosier late of Ludlowe have licence to founde a Chauntery in the paroche churche of Saint Laurence of Ludlowe at the aulter of the trynitie with a prest the same to be called the Chauntery of John Hosyer forever

John Kendale Secretary thoffice of maister Forster or of the game of Haveryng at bowre and Supervisor and Steward of the lordship of Havering at boure during his lif with the fees and wages accustumed etc

Petit John maryner hathe an Annuytie of xx li of the Custumes in the port of Pole during his lif from mighelmas last past by the handes of the Custumers there for the tyme being

Rauf Astry and William Boske have a prive scale to the Tresourer (of) & Chambrelains of theschequier to levye a taille for theim upon the Custumers & Collectors of Suthampton of the somme C li of the goodes of the said Rauf Astry and Thomas Graftone . Also the said Rauf Guy Wolstone Thomas Graftone and John Baxster to have a nother taille of CCC li upon the said Custumes

Walter Hungerforde Squier hathe al the messuages landes & tenementes Rentes and services in litelle Cheverelle in Wiltshire annui valoris xxv li also landes and tenementes Rentes & services called Hunnebrige nighe Westbury in the same Countie annui valoris iiij marces a messuage called Hankessoke of xl acre land [f95b] acre mede xx^{ti} acre pasture with thappurtenaunces in litelle Somerford annui valoris xl s . Also the manoire of Stanwelle in the Countie of Middlesex annui valoris viij marces / the manoire of Pynkenesse with thappurtenaunces in the Countie of Berkshire annui valoris iiij li Also iij mesuages lying at Dowgate in the parisshe of Alhalowen & ij mesuages lying in the Ryalle in the Citie of Londone whiche v mesuages be of the yerely value of v li to him and his heires forever

John William of Exmouthe hathe an Annuytie of xl s for terme of his lif yerely of the Custumes of Excestre by the handes of the Custumers

Richard Hardsang and William Barker late Shireffes of Yorke have a prive seale to the Tresourere and Chambrelains to entre in theire bokes the some of lx li ix s x d and to make thereupon a taille of Solle of the same some of thissues of the baillifwik which the king hathe geven to theim

Richard lord Beauchamp hathe thoffice of Steward of the lordships & hundredes of Tewkesbury and Whitingtone in the Countie of Gloucestre of the lordships of Hanley Uptone Bussheley & Rydmereley in the Countie of Wigorn Also maistre and keper of the game in the Chaces of Malverne & Cors & of the parkes of Tewkesbury Hanley Blakemore Bussheley and Ridmerley during the nonneage of Edward Erle of Warrwik with wages & fees accustumed Also the (same John) said lord beauchamp hathe ij tonne of wyne during his lif of the prisewynes in the port of bristolle by the handes of the Chief butiller per confirmacionem

Thomas Graftone merchant hathe a prive seale to the Tresourer and Chambrelains of theschequier to levie (of) a taille of C mark upon the subsidie in the port of Londone and the same delyver him for a ship whiche the king hathe boughte of him called the Nicholas of Londone

John Smythe and Thomas Smythe have the keping of the parc of Kypax in Yorkshire for terme of theire lyves and eithre of theim lenger lyving with the fees of ij d by the day of thissues of the honor of Pountfreit

Thomas Bruyne Squier hathe out commissions to enquere upon certaine lyvelood

Fevriere John Poleyne Squier Sergant of the Seler hathe an Annuytie of xl (li) markes of thissues of the lordship of Knaresburghe parcelle of the duchie of Lancastre quousque etc

John Swale Squier hathe an Annuytie of x li of the said lordship for terme of his lif by the handes of the Receyvor etc

[f96] John Langtone hathe Thoffice of Baillif of the lordship of Lughburghe during his lif with wages and fees accustumed

Robert Merbury of Tunbrigge Thomas Colyn Thomas Durbarre and other have a prive seale to the juges & Coroner (to) not to awarde any processe ayemst theim upon an indytement had ayemst theim for weryng of lyverees

Laurence Towneley hathe an Annuytie of xx markes during his lif of thissues of the Countie of Lancastre

John Browne of Cottone and John Byritone have a prive seale to the Tresourer and barons to allowe and discharge Hugh Rowles and Thomas Westone baillieffes of the Towne of bruges upon the payment of lx s x d made to the said John and John for thexercising of Thoffices of Steward or Ryder of the Forest of Morff

Robert Thorne and Edward Wottone merchauntes of Bristowe have a prive seale open to al Custumers Comptrollers within the poort of Bristowe & al other portes in this Royaulme not to take any Custume of theim for alle suche merchandises as shalbe charged in theire shippe called the Mary of grace for the furst voiage that she shal make inward & outward

William Wadnowe thoffice of keping of the parke of Marsfeld in Sussex from the furst day of marche during his lif with wages accustumed

John Uptone hathe Thoffice of Baillif of the Franchise within the Rape of Pevensey & of the honor of the Egle in like wise

William Myrfeld hathe a prive seale to the Tresourer & Barons to discharge aswele him as the Shirieffes of Suthampton for the payment of his wages made by the said Shirieffes for his offices at Portesmouthe & Porchestre

Sir Gervays Clyfton and maister Edmond Chadertone have the warde and mariage of Robert son and heire of Christofir Cressy late of Frithlek to them & eithre of them lenger lyving during the nonnage of the said Robert

Richard Walter late of Lyd in Kent and Alice his wif have a general pardone

Thomas Graftone hathe a licence for his Ship called the Peter of Londone of Cxx^{ti} tonne to goo to Island the statute notwithstanding staple ware oonly except

Richard Owen is made Receyvor of the lordship of Kydwelly in Southwales during the kinges pleasire with wages & fees accustumed

Hamond Claxtone hath a (wa) like licence as Thomas Graftone hath for a ship called the Powle of Blakney of like portage to go to Island

John Paynter serieaunt at Armes hathe an Annuytie of v li of thissues of the lordship of Barkeswelle during the nonnage of Edward Erle of Warwik

Richard Hilles trumpeter hathe an Annuytie of x markes during his lif of the ferme of al wastes purprestes of the forestes within the Forestes betwene the brigges of Stanford and Oxonford during his lif etc

[f96b] William Penny hathe an Annuytie of v markes of the Revenues of Uptone upon Severne in Worcestershire during the nonnage of Edward etc

Sir Thomas Ormond knighte hathe a prive seale to the kinges Attorney to confess for the king in the Chauncery alle thinges to be true by the said Sir Thomas allegged concernyng the manoire of Racheford

John Wake Squier a pardone upon accomptes & other offenses doon by him as Shirief of Huntingdon

Sir Christofre Talbot hath the parsonage of Whitchurche by the Resignacion of Sir Thomas Suttone

Thomas Harringtone Squier is made maister Forster of the Forest of Enerdale in the Countie of Cumberland & Steward of al lordships manoirs etc in Cumbreland & Lancastreshire late marques Dorsettes with thoffice of Baillif of Copeland with wages and fees accustumed to the same of thissues of the said lordships And over xx li of Annuytie of the same lordships aslong as they shal happen to Remayne in the kinges handes

Richard Hatfeld hathe an Annuytie of xx markes from mighelmasse last passed during his lif of thissues of Cramborne

John Molle hathe the keping of the parke of Potenalle within the Forest of Windesore during his lif with iiij d by the day of thissues of the Castelle of Windesore with x marces of Reward

William Peter hathe ij frensshe botes of the kinges gyft lying at Weymouthe and a prive seale to the Bailliffes there for delyveraunce of theim

Sir Robert Waryng hathe the parsonage of beestone in Norwiche diocese by the permutacion of Sir Robert Warde parsone of Saint Mary Magdalene of Bermondsey

Thomas Ormonde alias Botiller lord ormonde hathe a licence during a hole yere to absent him out of Irland and enioy his possessions there etc

John duc of Norffolk hathe thoffice of Constable of the Castel of Norwiche from marche last past during his lif (of thissues) withe xx li fee of thissues of Norffolk and Suffolk

Morice Berkeley an Annuytie of x markes of thissues of Northwythom during the kinges pleasire

the president and felawes of the Quenes Collaige of Cantebrigge have a (president) pardon of xx li due by theim to the king for licence to accorde with the Quene in a plee of covenant of iiij M^l acres land

William Langford (Richard) late Escheator of Kent Richard Wrotesley & John Hulcote of Berycote in the Countie of Oxonford have a pardon of alle fynes trespasses

John Abelle yomene of the Corowne hathe thoffice of Jayler of the Castelle of Hertford parcelle of the duchie of Lancastre during his lif with wages & fees accustumed to be perceyved of Hertfordingbury

[f97] Doctor Penkithe an Annuytie of x li of the fee ferme of Dorcestre unto the tyme he be provyded for / . for terme of his lif of like value

A prive seale to the chief Juge and othre Juges to surcesse processe made ayemst Thomas Been late of Fustone in Yorkshire yoman Robert Slyngesby & other upon any indytementes

Rauf Willugheby late Shirieffes of oure Counties of Norffolk & Suffolk hathe a prive seale to the Tresourere and barons to surcesse of al processes made ayemst him by reason of any duties by him owing to king of the Fraunchise of Ely within the said Counties or otherwise

William Tavernere hathe alle landes & tenementes Rentes & services late John Trenchardes in Southtawtone during his lif without accompt or other thing

Thomas Otter hathe the manoire of Westone in Warrwikshire annui valoris xv li late William Brandons knighte / to him and his heires masles by knightes service and the Rent of xx s yerely

William Tyrwhit the manoire or lordship of Swalowfield with thappurtenaunces in Berkshire during the kinges pleasire without accompt etc

Master Thomas Baret Bisshop of Enachdune hathe the moyte of the lordship of Bren in in Brentmarshe aslong as he shal stand parsone there . Soo that he with the Revenues fortefie the See walles & bankes for the salvacion of the said lordship

Jenkyn Havard of the lordship of Brekenok hathe a warrant to the Auditors of the same lordship to discharge him and his suerties of CC markes forfaicted by a Recognoissaunce Soo that he pay xx^ti markes thereof at midsomer next commyng

William Taverner hathe thoffice of keping of the parke of Okehamptone in the Countie of Devone during his lif with wages & fees accustumed

John Strangways Squier hathe a warrant to (the) Nicholas Leventhorp Receyvor of the duchie of Lancastre to content unto him of his Receipt xx li due of an Annuytie to him graunted by Edward the iiij^th

Sir Robert Fenys knighte an Annuytie of xl li from mighelmasse last past during his lif of thissues of the manoire of Elmeset Somersham & Offetone

Edmond Verney Squier Thoffice of Baillif of Suttone in Colfeld during the nonnage of Therle of Warrwik with the wages of iiij d by the day with an Annuytie of x li of the Revenues of the said lordship

The maire Comonaltie & Burgesses of Bristowe have theire privileges confermed &

A warrant to the Receyvor and baillif of the lordship of Brekenok in Wales to content xxvij li x s iiij d unto Richard Baker Roger Baker & other of Brekenok for brede & ale by theim delyvered to the late duc of Bukingham household

[f97b] Maister John Topclif hathe the parsonage of Helmeswelle by the resignacion of Sir Clement Argent

Sir Robert Chambrelain hathe the keping of the manoire of Bavsey with the warde & mariage of Thomas Conyers

Richard Draper Clerc of the Werkes within the Towne and Castel of Berwik during the kinges pleasire with xij d by the day of the ferme of the Towne & Chambre there

Thomas Fowleshurst an Annuytie of xx^{ti} markes of thissues of the lordship of Warmyncham during the nonnage of Edward Trusselle

The lord Dynham hathe a prive seale to the Tresourer of Calais to content unto him vj hundrethe poundes of the Revenues of his office of the kinges reward

A prive seale to the Tresourer and Barons to discharge the Tresourer thereupon

Andre James borne in geldreland is made denzyn during his lif

John Hugford hathe thadvouson of the prebend of Saint James within the Churche collegiat of Warrewik

Martyn Lonore & vij othre merchantes of Bretaigne and (othre merchantes of) Bretaigne and Fraunce have ij saufconduytes for ij shippes eche of theim of C tonne of the parties of Spayne or britaigne to come into England etc during a yere

Edward Franke Squier Shirief of Oxonford and Berkshire hathe a prive seale to the Tresourere and Chambrelains for assignement to be made unto him iiij^{xx}x li of thissues of his Shiriefwik

Maister Robert Moine the iiij^th prebende in the collegiat Churche of Leicestre by the dethe of Master John Billesdone

Thabbot of Leicestre hathe licence tappropre the Churche of Stoke to there Churche forever

The same Abbot hathe thereupon thadvouson of the said churche graunted

Thomas Meryng hathe the manoire of Rammardewik in Hertfordshire annui valoris vj li xiij s viij d the manoire of Ikilford in the same Countie annui valoris lj s ix d the manoire of Pyritone of the same annui valoris iiij li xiiij s iiij d vij mesuages CC acre of land xxviij acres of mede xl acre of pasture xx acre of wode and the Rent of a Capone & a Rason of gynger with thappertenaunces in Holwelle in the Countie of Bedford annui valoris Cxij s viij d a mesuage a Curtilage & ij yerdes of lande in Arkesey in the same Countie annui valoris xl s iij mesuages iij^xx acre of land x acre of mede xij acre wode in Eyone in the same Countie annui valoris xxvij s ij d lat Roger Tocotes to him & his heires masles by knightes service and the Rent of xl s yerely forever

John duc of Norffolk hathe the manoirs & lordships of Middeltone Hillingtone Tylney Iselingtone Clenchwartone Scaleshowe Reynham Scales Hekeling Hokkewold Wiltone Bertone Bendisshe Wygenhale with Fisshinges there & the tolle in Bisshoppis Lyne the hundred of Febrigge with membres in Norffolk the manoirs of Lavenham & Wirdelingtone in Suffolk the manoirs of Canfeld Stanstede Monfichet Bentley & Wodehamferrers in Essex the manoirs of Berkewey Rokehey & Newsolles in the Countie of Hertford the manoire of Haselingfeld in Cantebriggeshire the manoire of Langham alias Langnam in the Countie of Dorset the manoire of Kyrres & Retire in Cornewaille . the manoirs of Extone Southbrent Chillingtone Strattone [f98] Yeviltone and Spekingtone in the Countie of Somerset the manoire of Berlorty in Dorset the manoire of Foxhunt in Sussex the manoire of Fryd in Bederesden in Kent to him and his heires masles forever by knightes service and the Rent of of tyme passed therefore payed And over this the said duc hathe the Reversion of the manoirs of Petersfeld Upclatford Knouoke Bedwyne & Orchestone etc

Therle Douglas an Annuytie of iiij^xxij li during his lif that is to say iij^xx li thereof of the fee ferme of Cantebrige & xxij li residue of the fee ferme of Suthampton

John Bereve hathe a licence to goo to Island etc during a yere etc with a Ship of the portaige of vij^xx tonne

Sir Richard Widevile knighte a pardone for his lif

John Swale the keping of the parke of Postron & Cage in Kent during his lif with iiij d by the day and an Annuytie of vj li xiijs iiij d of thissues of Tunbrigge in Kent

John duc of Norffolk an Annuytie of xlv li ij s v d during the terme of vj yeres & di' that is to say xij li yerely of the ferme of Kyngtone in Warrwikshire xviij li ij s v d of the fee ferme of Yeppiswiche xv li thereof of the ferme of Radwelle in Essex

Margret Percy alias Dowglas nece to therle Douglas hathe a licence to dwel in England during hir lif

George Porter thoffice of chief Carpenter of the Towne and Castel of Berwik during the kinges pleasire with the wages of xij d by the day that is to say xiiij li v s of thissues of the Citie of Norwiche & iiij li thereof of thissues of the Towne of (G) Yeppeswiche

Randolf Cholmeley yoman of the Crowne vj d by the day for the fee of the same during his lif of thissues etc of the lordships of Norbury & Althurst in Chesshire

The pryor and Convent of the holy Trinitie in Londone have a licence to graunt forever unto thabbesse of Berking an Annuytie of xx li of al there landes in Londone

Maister Robert Bothe dean of Yorke maister Portingtone and other have a prive seale to the Chaunceller of the duchie of Lancastre to suffre theim to levey gadre and Receyve alle suche Rentes of lyvelood as the king hathe graunted of his said duchie for the prestes of Yorke

Sir John Fogge knighte a pardone for his lif and a graunt of certaine maners

Charles Dynham hathe the warde and mariage of Johanne Durneford with a pardone of viij^{xx} li by yere whiche he payed for the same yerely

Sir Thomas Bryane chief Juge of the benche an Annuite of xxviij li xvj s viij d of the lordships of Eppeworthe & Haxey with thisle of Axholme in Lincolnshire for the terme of vij yeres

(George Williams hathe the warde and mariage of John Asshe son and heire of James Asshe decessed late of Monmouthe)

268

Yvon Michael merchant of Britaigne hathe a licence for ix^ti quarters of whete to goo to Portingale etc paying the Custumes

Marche Sir John Donne knighte thoffice of Sergeant or maister of the armery within the Toure of Londone during his lif with wages (and fees accustumed) of xij d for himself vj d for a yoman & iij d for a grome by the handes of the Sherieffes of Londone and Middlesex of thissues etc per confirmacionem

[f98b] The bisshop of Saint Assaphe hathe a prive seale to John Hayes Receyvor in the west parties to content unto him during the kinges pleasire v^C markes yerely of thissues of his Receipt . before al other de primis denariis

Martyn Lonore of Bretaigne merchant hathe a prive seale to the Tresourer and Chambrelains to strike out a taille of xij li x s upon the Collectors in the poort of Dertmouthe whiche the said Martyn oughte to pay for custome of certain goodes apperteynyng to the Bisshop of Leon

John Dawson late of Assheby folville in the Countie of Leicestre yoman John Suttone of Hilridwere and many other have prive seale to the kinges Juges and Coroner to surcesse al processe made ayemst theim upon Indictementes

James Molyneux Clerc hathe the parsonage of Beere Ferres of Excestre diocese by the dethe of thincumbent thereof

Raignold Pympe a pardone for his lif

John Whitledale thoffice of Baillif of the towne & lordship of Mesen during the kinges pleasire with the keping of the woodes there and the swannes in the water of Idelle & north Idelle with the membres of the same during his lif withe wages fees & proffites used and of olde tyme accustumed

Waltier Walker (of) late baillif of the lordship of Nortone in youre marches of Wales hathe a pardone of iij li of arrerages of the said Baillifship

John Kendale Secretary hathe the keping of the place called the princes warderoble during the kinges pleasire with ij d by the day of the Revenues of the duchie of Cornewaille

The same John hathe the keping of Badowe parke in Essex for terme of his lif with fees and wages accustumed of thissues of the lordship of Badowe

A prive seale to the Tresourer and Chambrelains Reciting that the Tresourer and Undretresourer of England to pay from hensforth al suche sommes of money as shalbe necessary for thexpenses of his household and the Towne of Calais and also alle other Offers in theschequiers Calais & other places theire wages with paper ynke etc

Nicholas Knevetone an Annuytie of iiij markes xij s & ij d during his lif of thissues of a parcelle of lande called Underwode close stanaige and Parkclose within the Countie of Derby

Robert Ratclif an Annuytie of xl li during his lif of the Revenues of thonor of Pountfreit per confirmacionem

Sir William Berkeley of Weley knighte hathe the Castel or lordship of Bever- stone with thappurtenaunces in Gloucestreshire annui valoris lx li late William Berkeleys of Beverstone during the nonnage of therle of Warrwik

A prive seale to the Custumers Comptrollers & Sercheors of the port of Londone to suffre the Bisshop of Saint Paule de Lyon in Britaigne to ship vj^C lb of pewter vessel and thre Carpettes for his household in a ship called the Fraunceys of Morleys·without paying of any Custume

[f99] William Erle of Huntingdon and Katheryn his wif have iontly an Annuytie of Clij li x s x d of the Revenues of al Castelles lordships etc in the Counties of Caermerden & Cardigane & of the lordship of Haverfordwest in Southwales . by the handes of the Receyvor or Receyvor Chambrelain (of) or Chambrelains quousque maneria (ill) providentur ille & heredis masculis tanti valoris etc

The maire Baillieffes & Burgesses of Dertmouthe have a prive seale to the Clerk of the hanaper for to delyver theim the kinges lettres patentes of confirmacion upon theire privileges & fredoms without fyne or fee

(A commission to alle officers Ministres Fermors tenauntes and inhabitauntes of the lordship of Setone)

The pryor of Dover hathe a prive seale to John Hayes Receyvor of the temporalties of the Bisshopriche of Excestre & of other lyvelood in the west parties to content unto him C li of his Receipt (the towardes) that is to say l li at Mighelmasse next commyng & l li at pasche than next ensuyng to be taken of the kinges gift towardes theire buyldinges of theire places

Charles Dynham Squier hathe alle lordships landes & tenementes late John Halwelles Squier in (We the) Halwelle Westpralle Colatonpralle Combe in parochia de Biggebury Langestone Sterte Westlake Holbetone Were in Estingmouthe Lydestone Halwelle in parochia de Halwelle Southpole Faldepite Torre in Cornewode in the Countie of Devone Annui valoris . l . li to him and his heires masles forever by knightes service and the Rent of iij li xv s yerely

Thomas Hethenesse hathe certaine landes & tenementes lying in the Towne of Dorchestre late John Trenchardes a mese lying in Wacchingwelle in Suthamptonshire & a Fulling mille in Cassebroke annui valoris Cvj s viij d for terme of his lif without any accompt etc

Rouland chauchard of Morelais in Bretaigne hathe a saufconduyt for himself & iij other merchauntes of Fraunce & Breitaigne for a Ship of Spayne or Britaigne of C tonne to come into England etc during a hole yere

John Jaques Ivon Michel and othre have a saufconduyt for a Ship called the Mary Griffone of Saint Powle of Britayne of the portaige of iij^C tonne etc during a yere

Maister Edmond Chadertone hathe the manoire of Bradfeld Luydeyard Milcent Mantone & Westbedwynde in Wiltshire & al landes & tenementes lying there & in Quydhamptone Shawe Puritone Preshute Elcote Marleburghe Colyngburne Westbedwynde Hullcinyngtone & Wotton Basset in the said Countie with a burgage in Newe Sarum . & alle other possessions in England late William Colingbornes to him and his heires forever by the service accustumed heretofore

Sir William Houghtone thoffice of Steward of the lordship of Chadsey in the Countie of Somerset & maister of the Forest of Hay ac kepar of the park of Pedertone . perceivyng for the Stewardship xxvj s viij d by yere for thoffices of maister Forester & parker x li yerely during his lif of thissues of Chadsey with annuitie of lv li vj s viij d during his life of the same

[f99b] Robert Tylney of Witlesford in the Countie of Cantebrige Squier hathe a pardone of his lif and almaner escapes

James Bolle & Cornelius Johnsone of Barowe in Brabante have a saufgard to come into England with almaner merchandises etc during six monethes

Charles le Dannoys Jacob le Dannoys & John Broquet of Fraunce have a saufconduyt for for a Ship of Cxx tonne etc during a yere

John de Pountfreit Bastard thoffice of Capteyne & lieutenaunt of Calais & the marches there and of the towre of Risebank of Guysnes & Hammes during his lif with almanere Wages fees & rightes & honors etc

John Fitzherbert Thoffice of Remembrancer in the kinges Eschequiere during his lif with almaner fees & wages as William Essex had it per confirmacionem

Sir Richard Haute a pardone for his lif

The prior & Convent of Saint Mary of York have theire (Ab) temporalties in keping during there vacacion by the Resignacion of dompne Thomas Bothe without any accompt

The maire Baillieffes Citezins inhabitantes & Comonaltie of Waterford in Irland have a prive seale to Sir Thomas Thwaytes knighte Tresourere of Calais and to alle other the kinges officers to see a ship of Irland there arrested to be discharged according to suche privileges as they have of the kinges progenitors and by him confermed whiche ship apperteigneth to William Lumbard John Comyne & Thomas Seffe merchantes of Waterford

Nicholas Palmer & John Lokysden his depute have a prive seale to the maire Shirieffes Custumers Comptroller & Sercheors of Hulle to delyvre there lx tonnes of wyne there seised in a ship of Britaigne called the Faucone of Brest and forfaicted to the king

Sir John Pykering knighte an Annuytie of x li during his lif of thissues of Shiriefhotone in Yorkshire

Petro Salamanca Sancheo de Valmazeda John Pardo Diego di Cadagua Fernand de Carrione Martyn de Cordoigna Diego de Castro Peter de Valdoyt & Martin de Malvenda have licence to percieve iiij^C markes of the Custumes & subsidie commyng of almanere wollen clothes grayned or not (un)graynced of lede tynne Alum wyne yron to be shipped in the portes of London and Suthampton

Sir John Pykering knighte & Hugh his Son the Manoire of Parkehale in Essex late the Duchesse of Somerset annui valoris xxvj li xiij s iiij d to theim and to the heires masles of the said Hugh by knightes service and the Rent of xl s

James Roos Squier thoffice of baillif of Thriske and Hovingham in Yorkshire during his lif withe wages accustumed or Annuelle Rent of x li of the same

Robert Estone keper of the gaole of Meltone hathe a pardone for thescape of Richard Fleccher

Sir Christofir Warde a pardone offenses dettes acomptes & Arrerages

Sir Robert Brakenbury hathe a prive seale to the Tresourer & Chambrelains to content unto him CCxv li vij s v d in redy money orelles by suffisaunt assignement whiche he hathe employed to the kinges use

[f100] Anthony Spynelle hathe a saufconduyt (of) for a hulke called the George of the portage of CCCl tonne during a yere

Randolf Franke the keping of the warderobe within the Castel of Notingham & the parke there with the logge & the gaole in the Towne during his lif

James Stanley Clerc the Chauntership in the Churche of Sarum by the Resignacion of Edward Pole

David Vaughan yomane of the Cler the ferme of al the Towne of Carewys within Flyntshire for terme of xl^{ti} yeres paying yerely vj li xij d at theschequier of Chestre

Thomas Rogers & Thomas Gale have thoffice of Clerc of the Shippes with xij d for (h) themself & vj d for a Clerc during theire lifes & eithre of theim etc with iij s by the day whan they Ryde about the (sam) besynesses

Maister Alexander Lye thoffice of Chambrelain & Custumer of the Towne (of) & poort of Berwik upon Twyde & supervisor of there werkes there with like wages as Robert Roos knighte and Herry Roos had during the kinges pleasire

Richard Lloyd yomen of the Crowne hathe the Baillifship of Estbudley and Westbudley in Devone with almanere commodities without any accompt

Adryan Whetehille Comptroller of Calais an Annuytie of C markes during his lif aswele of the surplusage money as of the seale of saufconduytes

Richard Lovelas a like Annuite there for terme of lif

Thomas Talbot an Annuite of x li there during his lif

Richard Whetehille an Annuite of xx^{ti} markes there

Herry Salman yomane of the Crowne vj d by the day for the fee of the same during his lif of thissues of Havering in Essex & Middelton & Merden in Kent

John Atkynsone an Annuelle Rent of x markes of the same lordships pro termino vite

Rouland Nicholson yomane of the Crowne vj d by the day for his fee of the same

Mathewe Brigges Thomas Hakley Richard Dalamere and William Honylane have to every of theim an Annuytie of v li during theire lifes of thissues of Londone & Middlesex

Sir Edward Bramptone knighte (an Annuite of) hathe a prive seale to the Tresourere & Chambrelains to paie unto C markes by tailles to be leveyed in the port of Londone of the subsidies of the goodes of Anisram Spynelle & Cosine Spynelle

Thomas Bawdrip thoffice of Gayler of the Castelle of Newport & keper of the wareyne of conys there during his lif with iiij d by the day

The Tresourer of Calais & William Rosse vitailler there have a prive seale to the Tresourere & Barons to allowe & discharge of theim of C li vij s vj d paied to the said William Rosse etc

John Dyke thoffice of chief Smyth in Calais during his lif withe wages & fees accustumed per confirmacionem

Thomas Feryere thoffice of chief masone there during his lif with wages accustumed

William Rosse vitailler of Calais hathe a prive seale to the Tresourere of the same to content him his wages of ij s by the day for himself xij d by the day for his Clerc and for iij yomen for every of theim vj d by the day from the vj day of August anno primo forthward

274

Sir Edward Stanley knighte hathe al suche sommes of money as Llewellyn ap Tudor ap Guilt of Anglesey hathe forfaicted for nonapperaunce in theschequier there

[f100b] Rouland Chouchart hathe a prive seale to the Tresourere & Chambrelains to levye a taille of xv li upon the Collectors of the Subsidies of Excestre

Richard Copeland hathe a pardonne of xv li (d) being in Arrerage for the Baillifship of Estgarstone

The Towne of Pembroke have there (priviel) privileges confermed with diverse newe grauntes

Laurence Strozzi president of Englisshe merchauntes in the port of Pisana etc

the lord Mountioy hathe a prive seale to the Tresourer of Calais for the payment of his fee for the lieutenantship of guysnes and for his Retynue due from the vj day of Octobre unto the xxij^{ti} day of Fevriere

The Towne of Scardeburghe have there new grauntes of maire & xij Aldermen (and) etc

Aprille John Laverok thoffice of (Gayler) porter of the Castelle of Yorke with the keping of the gaole there during the kinges pleasire with the wages of ij d by the day for the portersship of thissues of Shiriefhotone & for the said keping the fee & Reward accustumed

Peter Shaffer of Spire in Almayne borne is made denzyn pro termino vite sue

John Sanches Darys procurator of Biscaie hathe endented with the king for the payment of M^l vj^C li to be paied in eight yere in the port of Londone

William Hungate hath the Corodye of Thetford in Norffolk by the Surrendre of William Newerk for terme of his lif

Thomas Ormond knighte hathe a pardone of alle errores (had) by reason of a peticion made concernyng the manoire of Racheford

John Sanches Darys (hathe) & other persones have a graunt to perceive viij M^l Corones of gold of the Custumes commyng of theire goodes in Londone

Robert Ratclyf an Annuytie of lx li of thissues of the duchie of Cornewaille for terme of his lif

William Worseley Soldior of Calais hathe thoffice of Collector or Receyvor of Custumes at newenhambrigge during his lif with the wages of xx^{ti} marc

Philip Constable an Annuytie of xx li of the manoire of South Carletone during his lif

William Tyrwhit hathe a prive seale to the Tresourere & Barons to discharge him of x li of the Revenues of Frestone

Gilbert Leghe hath licence to have a Free wareyne

William Herbert Squier an Annuite of xl^{ti} markes from Mighelmas last during his lif of thissues of the Towne & Burghe of Pountefrect

Roger Laurence Citezin and taillor of Londone is (own) oon of the yomane taillors of the warderobe with vj d by the day of the Citie of Norwiche

Christofre Colyns hathe a prive seale to the Tresourer & Chambrelains to content unto him Cxxviij li iiij s ij d in redy money orelles make unto him assignement of the same by the said Christofre paied for the wages of CC men

[f101] Sir Guy Fairefax & other Justices have a warrant direct to them to surcesse of making of processe ayemst William Stringer and other upon an enditement

The Towne of Tutbury have licence for ij faires that is to wite oon on thinvencion of the Crosse & that other in the fest of Saint Katheryn

Rauf (Clerk) Elcok John Oxclif & Rauf Grenebanke have licence to founde a Chauntery in the Churche of Lancastre

John Kendale Secretary & Thomas Otter have thadvouson of the deanry of

Saint Birians in Cornewaille for oon tyme oonly

John Dawney Squier an Annuite of xl li of thissues of Pountfreit pro termino vite

Giles Briges hathe a prive seale to John Cut to content him xviij li of his Receipt of the kinges Reward

William Newerk an Annuite of xx li of the manoire of Blecchinglye pro termino vite

Maister William Beverley the pension of Thabbey of Yorke

Robert Nortone doctor a pardon of his lif

Sir Edmond Shaa & William Dunthorne have advouson to geve a prebende in Saint Saint Stephans in Westminster for oon tyme next voide

The maire Bailliffes & Comonaltie in Prestone of Amoudernes have the somme of iij li during iij yeres and have also a pardonne of xlv li due at by theim at Mighelmasse last passed

Amyse Pawlet a pardonne (a pardonne) for his lif

John Fabry Jacob auber & other have a sauf conduyt for a Ship of Cxx li during a yere

Sir Thomas Malyvere knighte the chief messuage within the Castel of Plymtone & the Bughe & hundred of Plymtone in Devone to him & his heires by knightes service paying for the warde of the Castelle of Excestre fyfty markes

Christofre Baynbrigge Clerc the parsonage of Pembrigge by the Resignacion of the Bisshop of Sarum

Thabbot of Barmondsey hathe a prive seale to John Hayes Receyvor of the temporalties of Excestre the somme of CC markes

The merchantes of the Staple have a prive seale to the Tresourer & Chambrelains to entre a (mit) mutuum in the boke called the Appele and to make plaine issue of lxiij li viij s iiij d

Robert Clyfford Squier a generalle pardonne

Maister Hugh Pavy the keping of alle temporalties of Saint David with knightes fees advousons of Churches etc

John Pykering hathe a prive seale to the Receyvor generalle of Cornewaille to pay unto him ix^{C}lxxij li xvij s ij d of his Receipt quarterly

Maister William Talbot hathe the parsonage of Alhalwyne of Berking of Londone

[f101b] Sir Thomas Thwaytes hathe a prive seale to the Tresourer & Barons to discharge him (of) in his accompt of diverse paymentes made at Calais amounting to the Somme of M^{l}M^l CCCCix li viij s ix d q^r

Herry Vernone Squier Nicholas Mountgomery & other have licence to founde a Chauntery in the parisshe Churche of Assheburne the same to be called the Chauntery of John Bradburne forever

John Hardewik hathe the warde of William Dyngley son & heire of William Dyngley of Reptone in Derby

Thomas Abbot of the monasterie of Saint James of Wigmore in the Countie of Hereford have an acquytaunce of the gadering of alle dismes & taxes without any wrytte of allowaunce

May Anno secundo John Vernay Squier hathe the manoire of Huysshe Chaumfloure with thappurtenaunces in the Countie of Somerset annui valoris vj li late Edward Courteney & certaine landes & tenementes in Nybury in the same Countie annui valoris xxx s late Sir Giles Daubeney to him and his heires masles by knightes service & the Rent of x s

Thomas Davy hath the parsonage of Suttone in Bedfordshire by the Resignacion of Master John Elmytte

John Ley of Bristowe merchaunt hathe xl li of Reward towardes his losses of the Custumes of Bristowe

Richard lord Welles hathe thoffice of Supervisor of the lordship of Tateshale in the Countie of Lincolne the Castel & the scite of the same only except & thoffice of maister of the game there during his lif with fees & wages accustumed

Maurice Barowe hathe a generalle pardone aswele of trespasses & offenses as of alienacions & perquisicions

Othes Gilbert hathe a licence to founde a Chauntery in the parisshe Churche of Saint John Baptist of Marledone in Devone to be called his Chauntery forever etc

Richard Woodhouse gentilmane hathe a generalle pardonne

John Willemere hathe the Custody of Thomas Wollecombe son & heire of Thomas Wollecombe with his mariage & alle landes

Thomas Franke late Eschetor of Yorkshire hathe a pardone for the said office

Fawcone herauld hathe an Annuytie of xl li of the manoire of Cheddesey in Somersetshire & Yelhamptone in Devone during his lif

Grymonde Desture an Annuite of xx li during his lif at the Receipt of theschequier

[f102] Thinhabitauntes of Dudley in Worcestershire have threscore Okes towardes the buylding of theire Chauncelle out of the Forest of Kynvare in the Countie of Stafford Anno ij^{do}

The Burgesses and Comonaltie of Yoghulle in Irland have certaine privileges to theim graunted

Sir William Parker knighte hathe the Manoire of Tenbury alias Temedisbury in Worcestreshire withe alle advousons of Churches to him & his heires

The Maire & Comonaltie of Plymouthe have C markes towardes the building of theire walles (whiche) during the terme of xx yeres next ensuying to be employed by thoversighte of the pryor there and by him yerely to be certefied into theschequier howe the same is disposed

Richard Heven thoffice of keping of the parke of Clybury during his lif withe wages accustumed per confirmacionem

The Burgesses of Huntingdone have a prive seale to thauditors of the duchie of Lancastre for the discharging of xxj markes parcelle of xlj li of theire fee ferme

Elizabethe Abbesse of Berking hathe an Annuytie of xv li graunted by Doctor Talbot parson of Berking in Londone and the same graunt to hir & hir Successours is confermed by the king

The maire & felisship of the Staple(s) have a prive seale to the Tresourer (merchauntes of the Chaple for the payment) Chambrelains of theschequier for assignementes (of) to be made for the payment CCCiiij^{xx}xvij li xj s viij d & of the somme of (CClx) CClj li v s whiche they have delyvered to the kinges use

A licence (made) geven to Maister Chadertone dean of Berkyng & to the Chanons there to graunt to Elizabeth Abbesse of Berking that if an Annuytie of xv li to theim graunted by the parson there be unpaide it shal be lefulle for theim to distrayne etc

Rauf Willughby late Shiref of Norffolk & Suffolk hathe a prive seale to the Tresourer & Barons for thallowaunce of xl li for his creacion of duc of Suffolk & xx li for creacion of Erle of Suffolk

Thomas Stokes of Maydenhethe a generalle pardonne

Rauf Willughby Steward of alle landes of the honor of Richemond in Norffolk & Suffolk & Receyvor of the same during his lif with x markes etc

A Fundacion made of (the kinges) a dean and Chanons of Berking

A licence to the parson of Berking to graunt an Annuytie of xv li to thabbesse there

Katery (Pere) Pressure a pardone for hir lif

[f102b] Maister Thomas Huttone hathe the prebende of the Collegiate Churche of Saint George in Windesore by the decesse of Maister William Towres

Maister Richard Brakynburghe hath the denry of the Collegiate Churche of Warrwik by the Resignacion of Maister Albone

Sir John Savage knight the yonger hathe the warde & mariage of Thomas Culpeper son & heire of Richard Culpeper

Therle of Arundelle hathe a prive seale to the Tresourer and barons for thallowaunce of a Cxiij s to Sir Herry Roos (for) shirief the furst yere of the kinges Reigne in Surrey & Sussex & John Dudley Shirief in the ij^de yere of a like som payed to the same Erle for an ayde of the said Shiriefwik to him & his predecessors graunted by the kinges progenitors

Thomas Vaghan yoman of the Corowne hath vj d by the day for the fee of the same during his lif of thissues of Nerbert in Southwales

Thomas Browne Clerc under Tilles late (Clerk) Comptroller of the kinges werkes hathe a prive seale to the Tresourere & Chambrelains for the contentacion of xiiij li xij s vj d of the kinges yeft

A prive seale to the Maire of Londone to se that the paker in the port there pak noo clothes nor other merchandises but if it be sealed by the pakers seale

A nother priviseale to the Custumers Collectors etc there for the same matere

A Saufconduyt graunted at thinstaunce of Elyot Ugane for a Ship or Shippes of the portaige of M^l tonne during a hole yere

John Slyngesby an Annuytie of x li during his lif of the Revenues of the Castel of Skyptone in Craven

Avery Corneburghe hathe a prive seale to the Tresourere & Chambrelains to content to (Av) him quarterly xxxiij li vj s viij d for occupying of thoffice of undretresourer aslong as he shalle be in the said office

Sir John Henyngham knighte hathe the manoire of South Wokingtone & other by Inquisicion late Sir William Brandons

A nother (gau) graunt made to the dean & Chanons of Berking of certain landes

William Abbot of Saint Mary of Yorke hathe a pardone of alle mesprisions forisfaictures issues & amerciamentes etc

An Inquisicion of Thomas Bruyne of certaine landes

Tharchbisshop of Canterbury hathe a prive seale to the Tresourer and Chambrelains for to stryke out & levye ij tailles of CCCCxlvij li xiij s iiij d

Elizabethe Reyner an Annuite of v markes of the Revenues of thonor of Pountfreit quousque etc

Elizabeth Bapthorp an Annuite of xx li of the same honor quousque etc

[f103] John Ambrose de Nigrono hathe a prive seale to the Tresourere & Barons to discharge him & the Collectors of Londone & Suthampton aswele of the somme of lj li x s iij d as of xiiij li xv s iiij d

Maister William Daubeney hathe a prive seale to the Tresourere & Chambrelains to levye iij tailles for him oon of CCs a nother of x markes & the third xx^{ti} markes etc

John Ulvestone and Thomas Bramptone late Escheators of Norffolk & Suffolk have a prive seale to the Tresourere & Barons of theschequier for thallowaunce of certaine sommes of money by them due for the manoire of Cropping that is to saye the said John Ulvestone vj li xviij s & the said Bramptone of viij li

John Wrothe Squier an Annuytie of x markes of the lordship of Enfeld parcelle of the duchie for terme of his lif

Philip Bytterly hathe the manoire of Agmondesham Wodderewe in the Countie of Bukingham to ferme during his lif for l s yerely knightes fees wardes etc oonly except

Maister Edmond Chadertone hathe the Manoire of Knesale in the Countie of Notingham late the duc of Bukingham for terme of his lif paying yerely xx^{ti} markes

John Wode Squier wardeyne of the mynte hathe a prive seale to the Tresourere & Chambrelains for ij tailles to be leveyed upon him oon of C markes and a nother of xx^{ti} markes whiche the said wardein to Sir Thomas Saintleger & Sir Robert Brakenbury etc

John Dudley Squier late Shirief of Surrey & Sussex hathe a prive seale to the Tresourer & Barons to allowe unto him x li paide of thissues of his Shiriefwik to Sir Richard Ratclyf for paling of the parc of guyldeford

Sir Richard Radclyf thoffice of keping and palastre of the parc of Guyldeford in Surrey during his lif withe wages & fees accustumed of thissues of the Castelle of Windesore

Fraunces lord Lovel hathe the keping of the manoire of Langley withe thappurtenaunces during the nonnage of therle of Warrwik with the maister-forstership of Wichewood and Stewardship of Burford Shiptone Spellesbury & the hundred of Cadlingtone with the keping of the launde of Burford & the logge within the Forest of Wichewood & keping of Chadworth woodes in the Countie of Gloucestre during his lif with wages & fees accustumed

Sir Thomas Wortley the lieutenantship of the Castel of Hampnes for the terme of vij yeres with souldiors undre him specified in an endenture

Rauf Adelyne hathe a warrant to the Constable of the Castelle of Windesore to content unto him ij d by the day (of) for keping of the vynes during his lif

Thomas Kydale thoffice of Feodor of thonor of Leicestre parcelle of the duchie of Lancastre during the kinges pleasire

Richard Heven the Rentes of alle tenementes in the Citie of Worcestre longing to Therle of Warrwik during his nonnage

Herry Michel an Annuytie of vij markes during his lif of the lordship of Morende in the Countie of Northamptone

[f103b] John Hethe hath a generalle pardonne

Robert Graunt of Westchestre hathe a saufconduyt (of) for a ship of the parties of Britaigne Fraunce etc of the portage of ix^xx tonnes during a yere

Margret Clyfford wydowe hath licence to graunt thadvouson of the Churche of Beltone in the Ile of Axholme to the prioresse of Saint Leonard of Axholt in Ardale forever and they licence to appropre the same to theimself etc

John Mountegewe thoffice of Sergeaunt of the Faucons within England during his lif with xx li yerely for his awne wages & v li vj s viij d for ij yomen undre him & (iiij markes) viij li for iiij gromes & xxiiij li. xvj s for mete drinke & clothe of the said yomen & gromes & xxj li v s x d by yere for keping of xiij Faucons of thissues of the Castel of Windesore

George Neville the manoirs of Falledestone Shawe Bassettes Court in (Sw) Shawe Quarles Court in Hortone Overwroughtone Nether Wroughtone & Tollard in Wiltshire with thadvouson of the Churche of Tollard a M^l & iiij^xx acres of land arrabylle iij^C acres of mede M^lv^C acres of pasture iij^C acres of wode (Clij) with divse other (acres) maners etc to him & his heires masles by knightes service & the Rent of xv li

Margret Elringtone widowe hathe a generalle pardone upon alle office that Sir John Elringtone hir husband late had

Thomas Archiebisshop of Canterbury hath the keping of alle manoirs Castelles lordshippes etc with advousons of Churches etc late Herry Erle of Essex . & of alle lordships Castelles etc late Isabelles Countesse of Essex . except the manoirs landes & tenementes called Stansted Halsted Claverynges Lucas Pichardes Prioures Eystone Fordham parva Messyng Bourchiers in Rewenhale Halyngbury Knypsoo Totham Ovesay Legates Maldon magna & parva Assheldham Raminyngsmarsshe & Mottes Staunford Ultyng Swaynes Brox-hede in Essex except also the Castelle lordship or manoire of Tyndale & xx li granted by Edward the iiij^th to the said Erle for mayntenyng of his estate . to (the) have the said keping during the nonneage of Herry now Erle of Essex

George Neville thoffice of maister & keper of the Chace of Cramborne & of alle Forestes parkes chaces and warennes in the Countie of Dorset & of al game (w) there except a parcelle called Chiterelle within the said Chace for terme of lif & like fees and wages as the lord Audeley late had Also maister & keper of the Chaces parkes & warennes of Canford & of the Isle of Purbek & of the game there And constable of the Castel of Corff during his lif with wages & fees accustumed of thissues of the manoire of Cramborne

[f104] (Richard Warmyngton) Sir Thomas (Twh) Thwaytes knighte Tresourere

of (the werres) of Calais hath hath [sic] a prive seale to the Tresourer & Barons to discharge him of the somme of M^{l}M^{l}CCxliij li x s vij d ob flemmysshe (to) payed to Souldiors of Calais

William Harreyse yomane of the Corowne vj d by the day for the fee of the same of (thissues) the ferme or fee ferme of (leste) Lystarde in Cornewaille for terme of his lif

(Richard Laurence)

John Kendale yomane of the Corowne a Rent called Grandeson Rent in the hamelettes & parisshes of Dertford Stone Wilmyngtone Suttone Gravesende & Milton & ellewhere in Kent & a parcelle of lande called Chaynecourt in the parisshe of Suttone during his lif

William Slyfeld hathe a prive seale to the maire Shirieffes & Baillieffes of Suthamptone to (suffre) see al goodes there longing to John de Sare to be Sureley kept the said William be contented of suche duties as is owing him

Ambrose de Nigrono Gabrielle of Furnarys and Anthony Sawly merchauntes of Jene have a prive seale to the Tresourer & Chambrelains of theschequier for leveying of a taille conteynyng lxv li xiij s x d ob upon the Collectours of Londone

John Ambrose de Nigrono hathe a licence to perceyve Clix li xviij s iiij d of the Custumes commyng of almaner merchandises in the portes of Londone Sandewiche & Suthamptone of his owne goodes or other mennys goodes

John Ocley hathe a prive seale to the Chambrelain of Northwales to paye him during his lif the wages accustumed yerely for keping of the Towne gate of Caernarvan in Northwales forsaid

Juyne The lord Lovelle hathe a warrant to the Receyvor of Walingford to paye unto him xx li whiche he payed for the king by his commaundement

Anne Downeham an Annuite of xx li of the Revenues of Walingford in Berkshire during hir lif in Recompense of certaine landes of like value geven to hir by Sir Thomas Saintleger

Agnes Wylde of Kingesnortone a pardone for hir lif

in oon bille

Margrete Ronkehorne a like pardone

John Yerdeley Abbot of Kenelworth and his Successors have forever a Close or a parcelle of land called Cowcastelcroft in Kenelworthe

Richard Vaghan an Annuite of x li during his lif of Dovercourt in Essex

William Erle of Notingham hathe a prive seale to the Tresourere and Chambrelains to levye a taille for him of CC markes upon the dismes

Frauncise lord Lovelle & William Catesby have the Constableship of the Castelle of Rokingham in the Countie of Northampton & overseers of the hunting within the said Forest & Steward of al lordships & manoirs of Rokingham Brykstok & Clyf & parkers of Brykstok & overseers of therbage & pannage of the same and of the Foreyne wodes called Brykstok bailly Rokingham Bailly & Clyf bailly during the lif of the said William

[f104b] The maire Baillieffes & Comonaltie of Dublyne have certaine privileges

Thomas Patryk of the Chapelle hathe the Corrody of Circestre by the dethe of   Forster

Paule Godfrey berebruer of the duchie of Holand is densyne during his lif

Thomas Danyelle yoman of the Corowne vj d a day for the fee of the same of the ulnage of clothe in the Countie of Gloucestre per confirmacionem

Roger Whitingtone the Fre Chapelle of Saint John without Stafford

Maister John Tesedale thospitalle of saint John Baptist without the northe yate of Chestre

The pryoure & Convent of Leutone have x li (have) of the fee ferme of Arnolle during the lif of Leonard Say

Garard Terlee of Gelderland borne is made denzin during his lif

John Hache trumpeter x markes yerely during his lif of the Revenues of the Countie of Devone per confirmacionem

Sir James Tyrelle thoffice of Constable of the Castel of Dundagelle within the duchie of Cornewaille during his lif with wages & fees accustumed

The dean & Chapitre of Sarum have a pardonne of al debtes & accomptes etc

Piers Unton hathe a licence fo l^{ti} Sakkes of wolle to passe the straytes of Marrok of his owne goodes or othre

The same Piers a nother for twenty sakkes of wolle

Richard Laurence thoffice of Forester of oure Forestes of Kery & Kedewen with Thoffice of lirwite or Amobreith in the lordships of Kery & Kedewen within therldom of the marche during his lif per confirmacionem

Richard Goughe thoffice of Clerc & keper of the Dee mylnes within the Citie of Chestre during his lif

Maister Edmond Chadertone the deanry of the free Chapel of Berking

Maister Thomas Cowtone a Chanon there

Maister Richard Baldry a nothre Chanon there

Maister   Jane a nothre Chanon there

Maister James Molyneux a nothre

Maister Richard Celsie a nothre

Maister Maculm Cosin a nothre

William Langley and Richard Porter thoffice of Jailer in the Castelle of Northamptone with therbage within the said Castel & the Bascourt (alle) otherwise
called Castel orchard with the proffites of the dyke of the said Castelle called
Castel medowe with the Fisshing of the waters there . during theire lifes &
eithre of them lenger lyving

[f105] John Wilcok thoffice of (Gayler) porter of the Castelle of Tykhille in
Yorkshire during his lif withe wages and fees accustumed . and thoffice of Reve
of the Towne of Tykhille in like manere . yelding yerely accompt of the kinges
Revenues

John Smethurst yoman of the Corowne the Baillifship of Knesalle with the
keping of the parke there during his lif with wages & fees accustumed

Edward Pilkingtone hathe a prive seale to the Shirief of Notingham & Derby to
content unto him fees and wages for half a yere due unto Sir Charles
Pilkingtone for the Constableship of the Castelle of Notingham & other offices
and also an Annuite of ix li due for ix Forsters for a hole yere

Waltier Evers gentilman the kinges Solicitor in Irland with x li fee during his lif
of thissues of the lordships of Newcastelle & Cromlyne

John Robertes an Annuite of v li of the Revenues of landes and tenementes late
Peter Curteys in the Towne of Leycestre during his lif

Richard Knaresburghe thoffice of Baillif of the Towne of Leicestre during his
lif with wages & fees accustumed and an Annuite of C s (la) of thissues of the
landes late Piers Curteys in the said Towne

The pryor & Convent of the Frere precheors in the Towne of Rutland have a
prive seale to the Constable of the Castelle there to suffre theim fisshe with oon
nette in the water of Clowde from Rutland to the See and to be fre and quyte of
paying of multure for almanere graynes for theim to be grownde in the mylnes
of Rutland etc

Robert Ratclyf the Constableship of the Castelle of Notingham & portership of
the Castel there . Also Steward & maister Forster of Shirwode Beskewode &
Clypstone & of the wodes of Billowe Birkland (Ro) Rumwode Custland &
Fulwode with thappurtenaunces in the Countie of Notingham during his lif
with xl markes fee of the manoire of Bollesover & ix li for ix Forsters aswele of
thissues of Maunsfeld as of the fee ferme of Retford in le Clay

The same Robert the Baillifship of Hatfeld with the keping of the manoire there & the chace & herde there with the ferme of the water called Brathmere during his lif with wages fees proffites & commodities accustumed etc

Piers Stanley & Margery his wif have a warrant to thauditors of the Countie palantyne of Chestre and Flynt to allowe lettres patentes of confirmacion made by Edward the iiij^{th} of certaine landes & tenementes in the same Countie

John Woderof Squier a tonne of wyne yerely during his lif of the pryuse wynes of Hulle

Sir John Hynyngham knighte hathe a licence to entre in the manoire of Bekyngham & (tha) to have thadvouson of the Churche there etc

John Warde hathe xl li yerely during his lif of the fee ferme of quenehithe in Londone whiche Sir John Grey Wiltone late had

Rauf Bygod maistership of thordenaunce during his lif with C markes fee for himself and the wages of vj d by the day for a clerk & vj d for a yoman . of thissues of the manoire of Kyrtone in Lyndesay in Lincolneshire with knightes lyvery of household

[f105b] Humfrey Spice hathe a warrant to Morgan Kydwelly the kinges attorney to confesse for the king al thinges to be true (of) in a peticion of righte late made by the said Humfrey concernyng certaine landes

John Goulson oon of the kepers of the Chace of Suttone in Warrewikshire of that parte called Lynreth during the nonneage of therle of Warrewik with wages & fees accustumed

Sir Robert Spicer parsone of Ilfardecombe a pardone for his lif

William Wilcokkes hathe a prive seale to the Tresorer & Chambrelains to levye a taille of xx li upon the Collectors of Londone & the same delyvere unto him for xx li by him lent to Vincent Tutelere the kinges Armourere to by harneys at Andewarp

The tenauntes of Guyldeford have a prive seale to the Tresourer & barons to descharge theim of Cs & Richard Rayman & Richard Hulle of xiij li xiiij s viij d & the Shirief of certaine several sommes & Sir Christofre Warde of the same sommes etc

Herry Mylwrighte borne in Brabance is made denzin pro termino vite

John Rogers & (Roger) Robert Dupliche have thoffice of Baillif of the Towne & port of Sandewiche during theire lifes & eithre of them with wages & fees accustumed etc